AN INSIGHT STUDIOS PRODUCTION

HAMMER of the GODS

MORTAL ENEMY

by MICHAEL AVON OEMING & MARK OBIE WHEATLEY

CREATED, CO-PLOTTED & DRAWN BY
MICHAEL AVON OEMING
CO-PLOTTED, WRITTEN, LETTERED, COLORED & BOOK DESIGNED BY
MARK OBIE WHEATLEY
SCANS & COLOR BY JOHN HARRIS STATON
LETTERING ASSISTED BY TIMOTHY WALLACE
CHAPTER FIVE ART ASSISTED BY KELSEY SHANNON

COMICMIX LLC
BRIAN ALVEY
CHAIRMAN

MIKE GOLD
EDITOR-IN-CHIEF
& PRESIDENT

GLENN HAUMAN
PRODUCTION DIRECTOR
& VICE PRESIDENT

MIKE GOLD — EDITOR

GLENN HAUMAN
PRODUCTION DIRECTOR &
ASSISTANT EDITOR

ADRIANE NASH
ASSISTANT EDITOR —
PRINT

IDW PUBLISHING

OPERATIONS:
TED ADAMS, CHIEF EXECUTIVE OFFICER
GREG GOLDSTEIN, CHIEF OPERATING OFFICER
MATTHEW RUZICKA, CPA, CHIEF FINANCIAL OFFICER
ALAN PAYNE, VP OF SALES • LORELEI BUNJES, DIR. OF DIGITAL SERVICES
ANNAMARIA WHITE, MARKETING & PR MANAGER
MARCI HUBBARD, EXECUTIVE ASSISTANT • ALONZO SIMON, SHIPPING MANAGER
ANGELA LOGGINS, STAFF ACCOUNTANT

EDITORIAL:
CHRIS RYALL, PUBLISHER/EDITOR-IN-CHIEF • SCOTT DUNBIER, EDITOR, SPECIAL PROJECTS
ANDY SCHMIDT, SENIOR EDITOR • JUSTIN EISINGER, EDITOR • KRIS OPRISKO, EDITOR/FOREIGN LIC.
DENTON J. TIPTON, EDITOR • TOM WALTZ, EDITOR • MARIAH HUEHNER, ASSOCIATE EDITOR
CARLOS GUZMAN, EDITORIAL ASSISTANT

DESIGN:
ROBBIE ROBBINS, EVP/SR. GRAPHIC ARTIST • NEIL UYETAKE, ART DIRECTOR • CHRIS MOWRY, GRAPHIC ARTIST
AMAURI OSORIO, GRAPHIC ARTIST • GILBERTO LAZCANO, PRODUCTION ASSISTANT

ISBN: 978-1-60010-631-6
12 11 10 09 1 2 3 4

**HAMMER OF THE GODS, VOL. 1:
MORTAL ENEMY TPB.** SEPTEMBER 2009.
FIRST PRINTING. HAMMER OF THE GODS
is ™ Michael Avon Oeming and © 2009 Michael
Avon Oeming & Mark Obie Wheatley. "Modi's
Quest" © Peter David. Afterword © Raven. All
Rights Reserved. IDW Publishing, a division of
Idea and Design Works, LLC. Editorial offices:
5080 Santa Fe St., San Diego, CA 92109. The
IDW logo is registered in the U.S. Patent and
Trademark Office. All Rights Reserved. ComicMix
logo is a trademark of ComicMix LLC. Insight
Studios logo is a trademark of Insight Studios. Any
similarities to persons living or dead are purely
coincidental. With the exception of artwork used for
review purposes, none of the contents of this publi-
cation may be reprinted without the permission of
Idea and Design Works, LLC. Printed in Korea.

IDW Publishing does not read or accept unsolicited
submissions of ideas, stories, or artwork.

Originally published as HAMMER OF THE GODS
Issues #1-5.

www.IDWPUBLISHING.com
www.ComicMix.com
www.InsightStudiosGroup.com

Modi's Quest

Growing up, I just absolutely loved ancient myths. I had a paperback copy of **BULLFINCH'S MYTHOLOGY** that I wore out, and the "Mythology" category on *Jeopardy* was the first one I was ever able to ace.

And of all the myths of various cultures, my personal favorite was the Norse. The others had their charm, but the Norse were just so... so pleasingly bleak. Particularly into my teen years, the Norse mythos spoke to me in a way that Greek, Roman, Egyptian and others didn't.

The thing is, all myths seem to have at their core a desire to find explanations for that which we can't understand. Why the heck does the sun go across the sky? Well, it's because Apollo is pulling it. Why are there earthquakes? Because Loki is chained up underground, and whenever he writhes from

snake venom dripping on his forehead, that causes the ground to shake. Where do you go when you die? Hel. Or Valhalla. Or Hades, or the Elysian Fields, or Tartarus, or a host of other equally charming locales.

As for the gods themselves, they were no omnipotent Judeo-Christian all-knowing, all-seeing entities. We were genuinely made in their images (or vice versa) because they had as many human foibles as any of us had. Worse: They routinely slaughtered their sires, married their siblings and then cheated on them with mortals. We existed primarily, it seemed, to be their playthings, their lab rats. That, and to get caught in the crossfire when the gods were bickering with each other or playing political games.

But the thing that made the Norse myths the most fascinating for me was

INTRODUCTION TO A SAGA
PETER DAVID

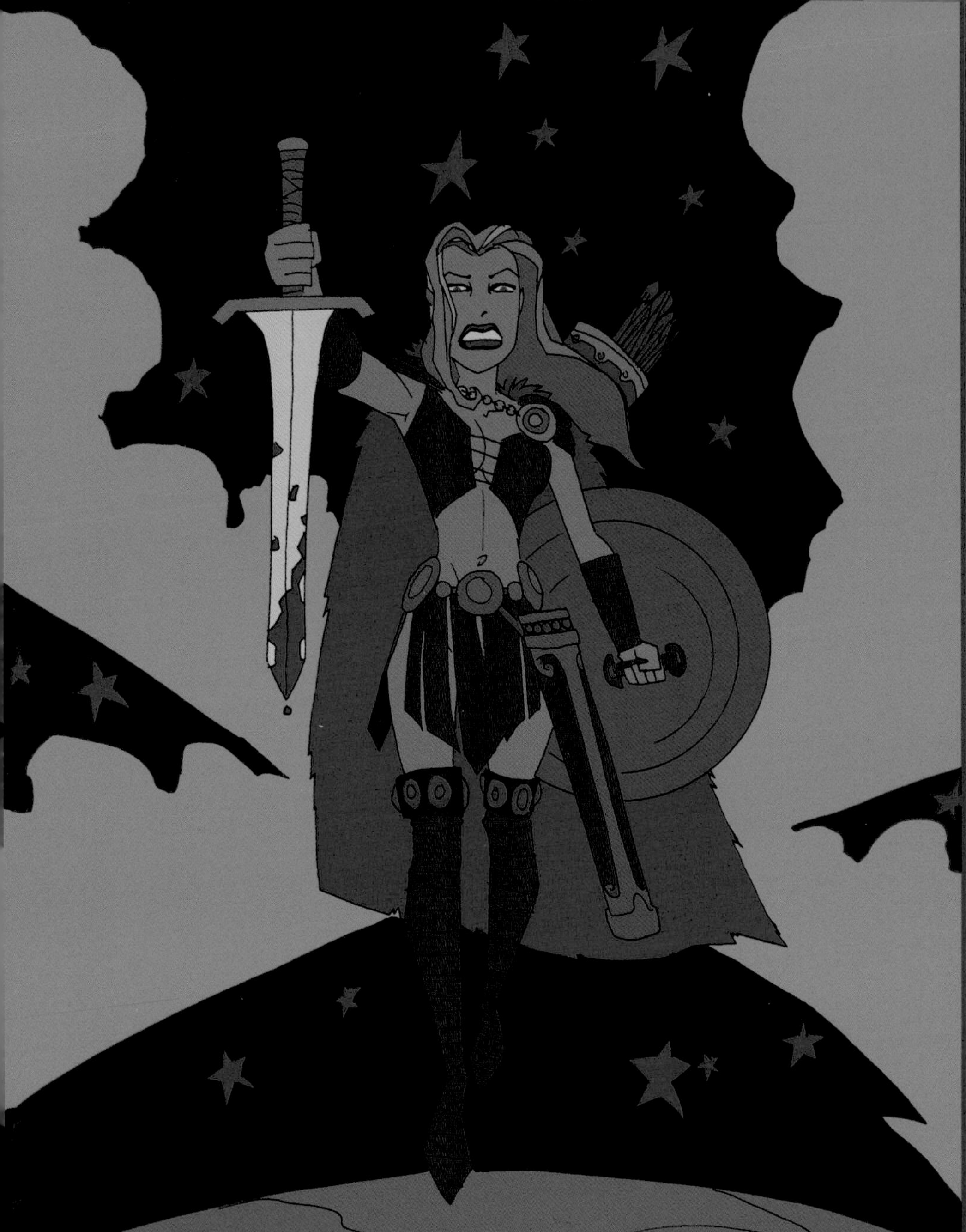

Skögul, the ugly Valkyrie. This is an early sketch by Avon. Color by Obie.

that they were the only ones I read that had a whole end-of-the-world scenario mapped out. They weren't satisfied with telling tales of the lives of the gods; they had it spelled out exactly how it was going to end. I was always a little fuzzy on that, as to whether the Norse thought that Ragnarok had already occurred and we were in some sort of second generation of man, or whether — and this is far more intriguing — the fate of the gods was completely predetermined. It didn't matter what the Aesir might have planned. Sooner or later, the Frost Giants were gonna storm Asgard, Odin was going to be devoured by the Fenris wolf, the Midgard serpent was taking down Thorr, and they were all screwed. What a fascinating concept. We, as human beings, had free will... *and the gods didn't.*

So my love of Norse tales made me a sucker for *Hammer of the Gods* from the get go, but what makes the series so special is far more than that. As noted, we look to gods for comprehension of the world around us. To explain the inexplicable, to find some sort of divine pattern in the chaos of our everyday existence. We go to churches or synagogues or shrines or clergy, and we all ask the same question: *Why?* Why do good things happen to bad people? Why are tragedies allowed to occur? Why aren't the gods, with a wave of their hands or a toss of a lightning bolt, preventing terrible events from unfolding? And it's not just questions of free will and

mankind doing horrible things to itself. There's also "acts of god," fires and floods, tornadoes and monsoons and, oh by the way, whoever's listening or not listening up there, thanks a bunch for the meteor in 2019, isn't *that* just something special to look forward to. Why is He, or why are They, doing these things to us? What the hell did we ever do to Him/Them, except offer praise and prayers and sacrifices?

And the bottom line is... we don't know. Oh, we can wrap ourselves in bland assurances that "it's God's will," but that just tells us what it is, not why it is. And that lack of information is unsettling and frustrating and pretty damned annoying, but there's not a bloody thing we can do about it.

But that's not true in Modi's case. While we resign ourselves to the capriciousness of the divine, Modi ain't taking it sitting down. *Hammer of the Gods* gives us the quest of one hero, one simple good man with one simple good question: Why? And even though it's set against a backdrop of thousands of years ago, it is a question spawned in the frustration of the human condition that has been with us since the beginning of the species and will likely continue to the end.

Modi's quest is our quest.

Come join it.

—PETER DAVID—
Long Island, NY, July 29, 2002

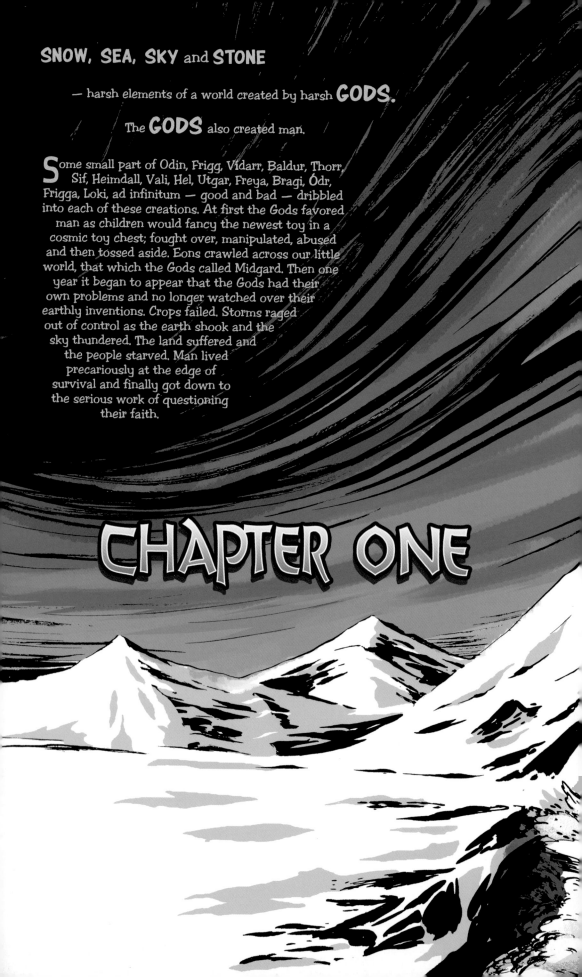

SNOW, SEA, SKY and STONE

— harsh elements of a world created by harsh GODS.

The GODS also created man.

Some small part of Odin, Frigg, Vidarr, Baldur, Thorr, Sif, Heimdall, Vali, Hel, Utgar, Freya, Bragi, Ódr, Frigga, Loki, ad infinitum — good and bad — dribbled into each of these creations. At first the Gods favored man as children would fancy the newest toy in a cosmic toy chest; fought over, manipulated, abused and then tossed aside. Eons crawled across our little world, that which the Gods called Midgard. Then one year it began to appear that the Gods had their own problems and no longer watched over their earthly inventions. Crops failed. Storms raged out of control as the earth shook and the sky thundered. The land suffered and the people starved. Man lived precariously at the edge of survival and finally got down to the serious work of questioning their faith.

CHAPTER ONE

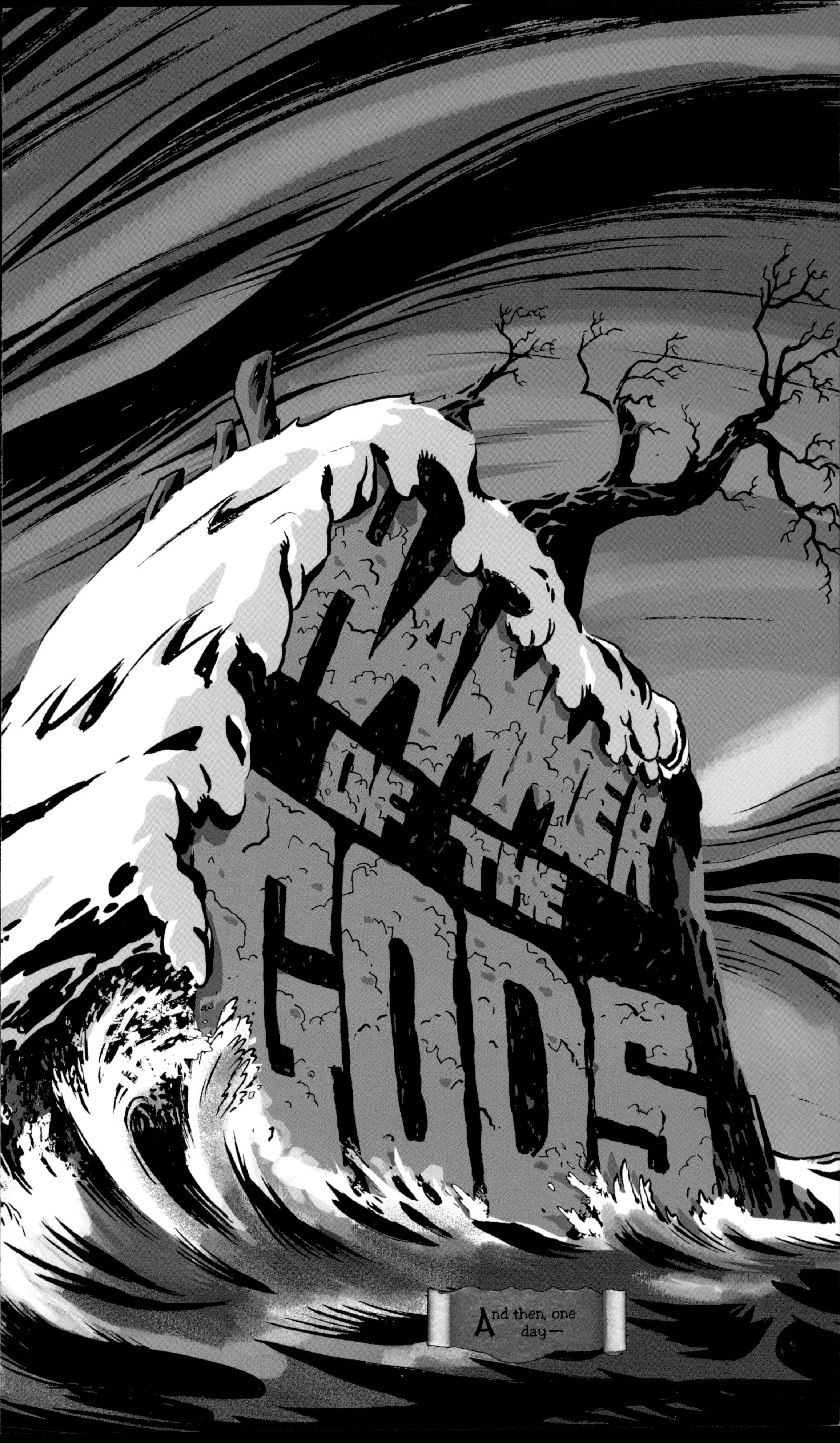
HAMMER OF THE GODS
And then, one day—

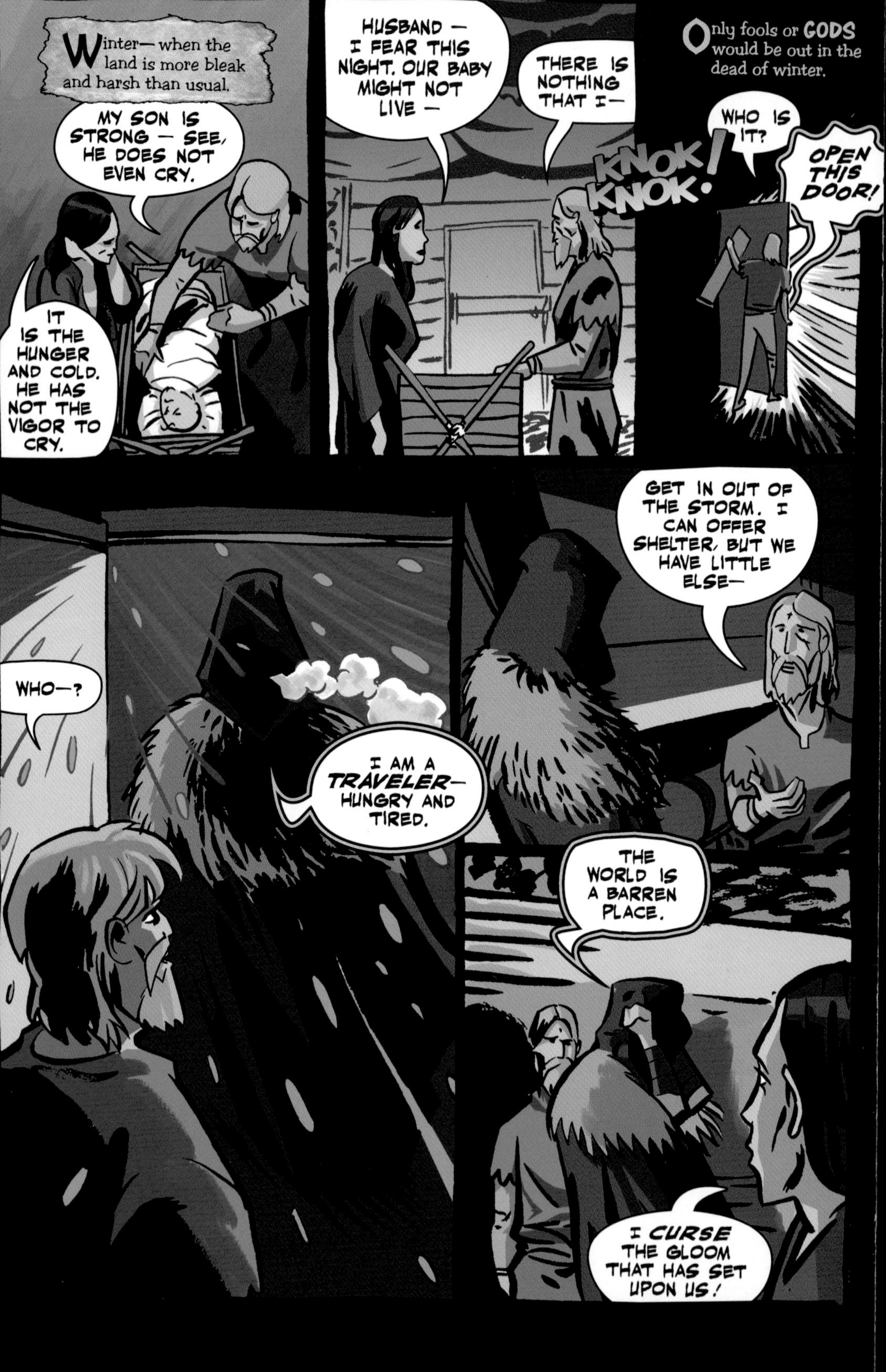
Winter— when the land is more bleak and harsh than usual.
MY SON IS STRONG — SEE, HE DOES NOT EVEN CRY.
IT IS THE HUNGER AND COLD. HE HAS NOT THE VIGOR TO CRY.
HUSBAND — I FEAR THIS NIGHT. OUR BABY MIGHT NOT LIVE —
THERE IS NOTHING THAT I—
KNOK! KNOK!
Only fools or GODS would be out in the dead of winter.
WHO IS IT?
OPEN THIS DOOR!
WHO—?
I AM A TRAVELER— HUNGRY AND TIRED.
GET IN OUT OF THE STORM. I CAN OFFER SHELTER, BUT WE HAVE LITTLE ELSE—
THE WORLD IS A BARREN PLACE.
I CURSE THE GLOOM THAT HAS SET UPON US!

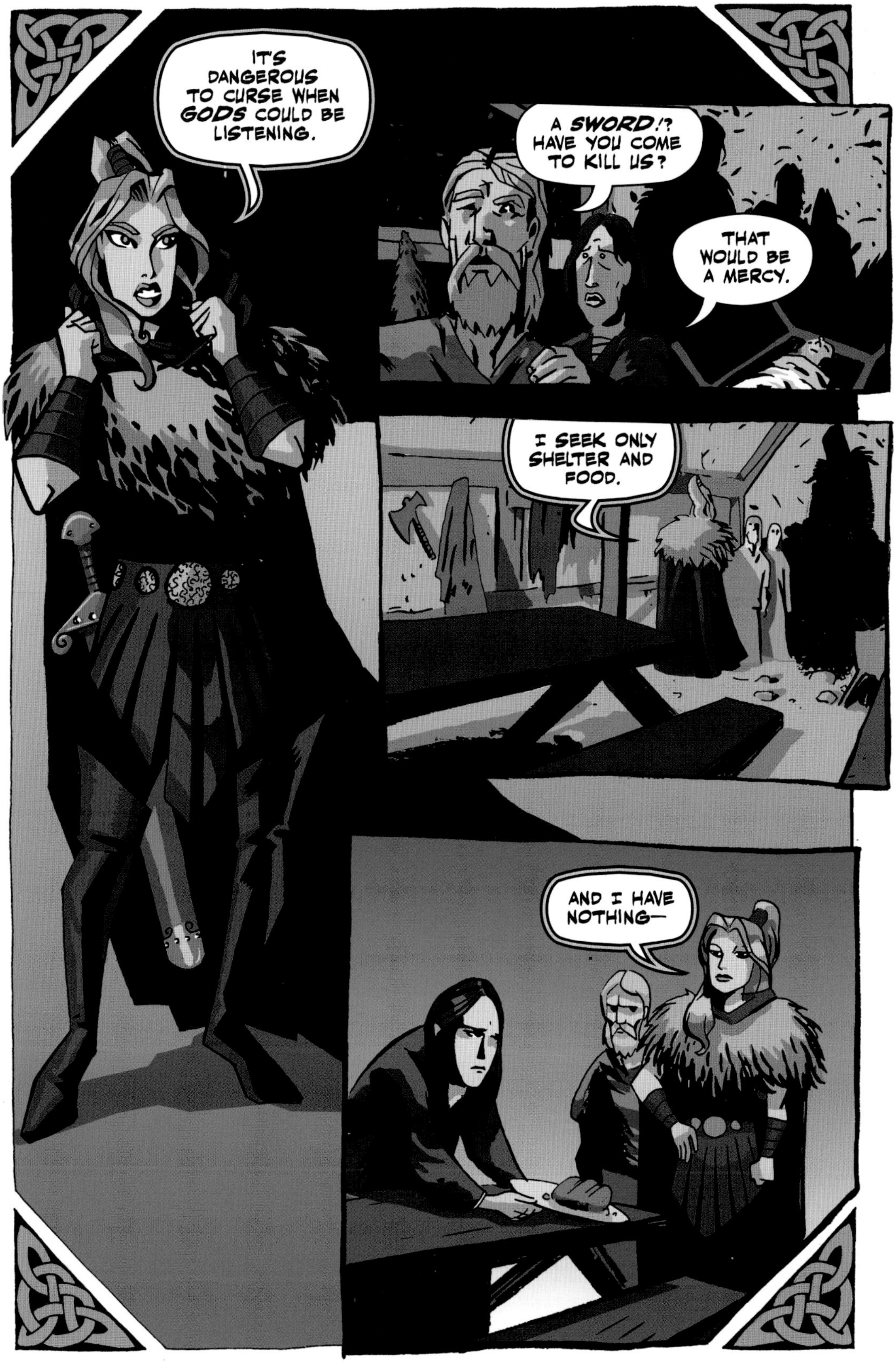
IT'S DANGEROUS TO CURSE WHEN GODS COULD BE LISTENING.
A SWORD!? HAVE YOU COME TO KILL US?
THAT WOULD BE A MERCY.
I SEEK ONLY SHELTER AND FOOD.
AND I HAVE NOTHING—

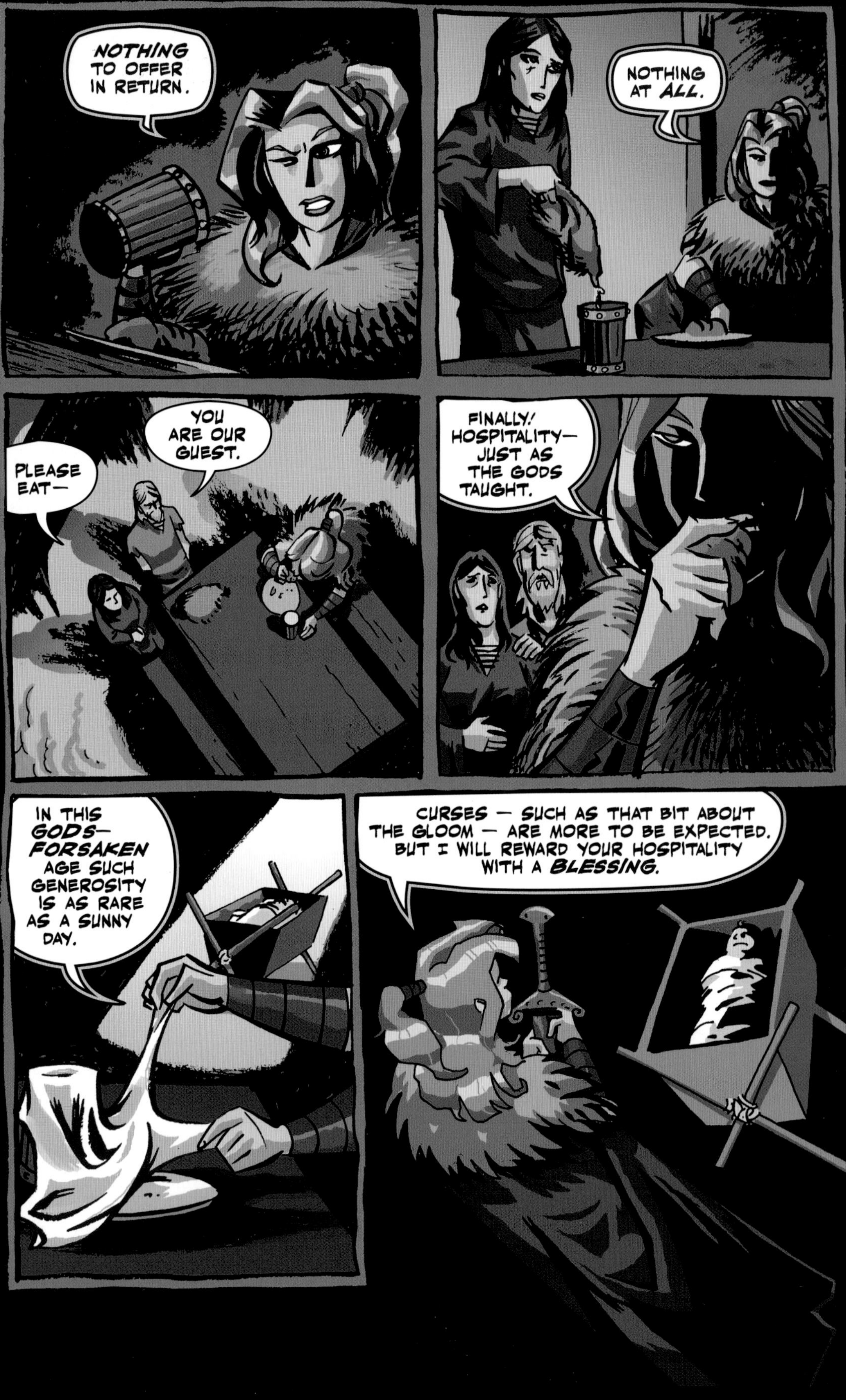
NOTHING TO OFFER IN RETURN.
NOTHING AT ALL.
PLEASE EAT—
YOU ARE OUR GUEST.
FINALLY! HOSPITALITY— JUST AS THE GODS TAUGHT.
IN THIS GODS-FORSAKEN AGE SUCH GENEROSITY IS AS RARE AS A SUNNY DAY.
CURSES — SUCH AS THAT BIT ABOUT THE GLOOM — ARE MORE TO BE EXPECTED. BUT I WILL REWARD YOUR HOSPITALITY WITH A BLESSING.

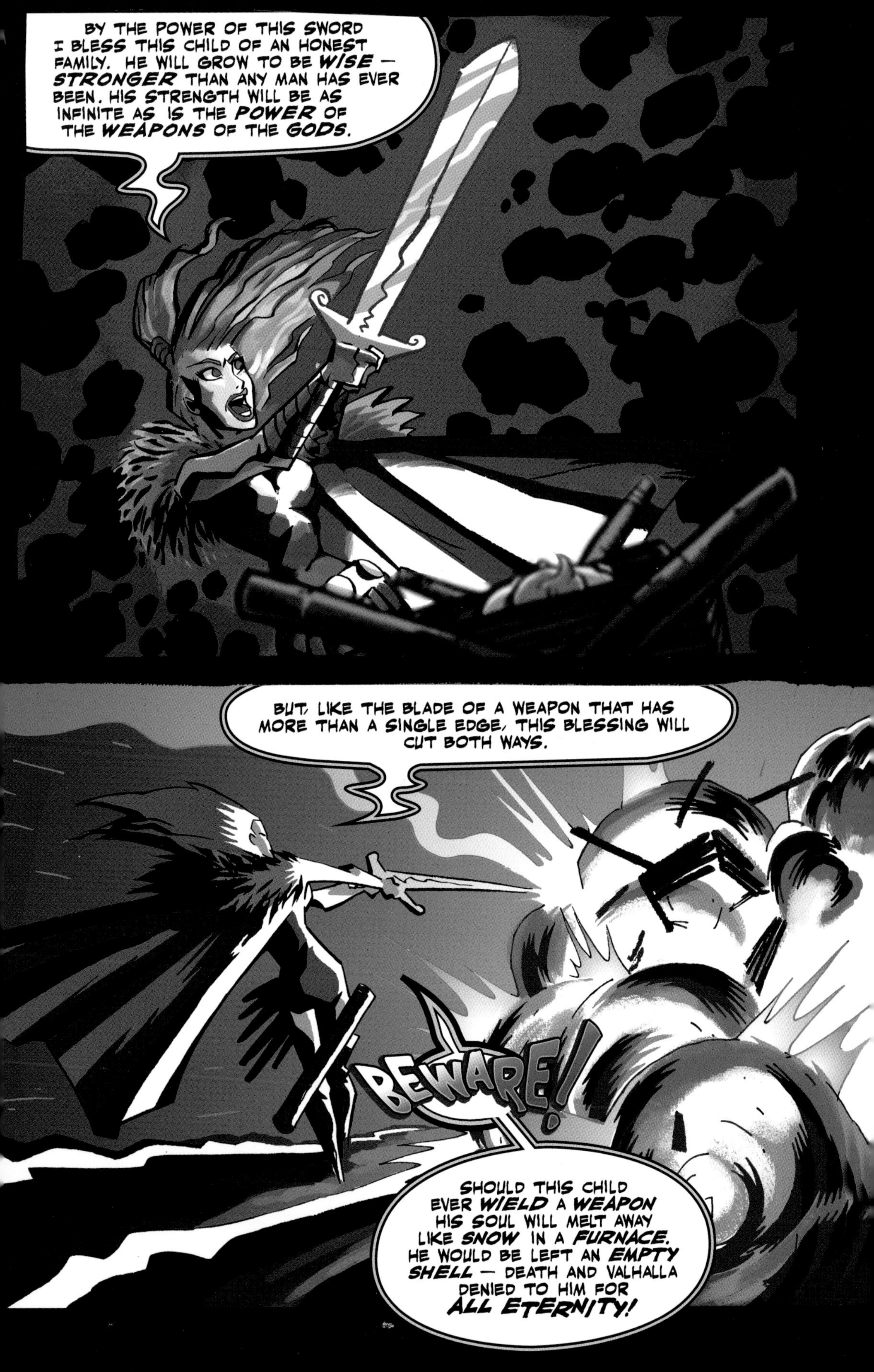
BY THE POWER OF THIS SWORD I BLESS THIS CHILD OF AN HONEST FAMILY. HE WILL GROW TO BE WISE — STRONGER THAN ANY MAN HAS EVER BEEN. HIS STRENGTH WILL BE AS INFINITE AS IS THE POWER OF THE WEAPONS OF THE GODS.
BUT, LIKE THE BLADE OF A WEAPON THAT HAS MORE THAN A SINGLE EDGE, THIS BLESSING WILL CUT BOTH WAYS.
BEWARE!!
SHOULD THIS CHILD EVER WIELD A WEAPON HIS SOUL WILL MELT AWAY LIKE SNOW IN A FURNACE. HE WOULD BE LEFT AN EMPTY SHELL — DEATH AND VALHALLA DENIED TO HIM FOR ALL ETERNITY!

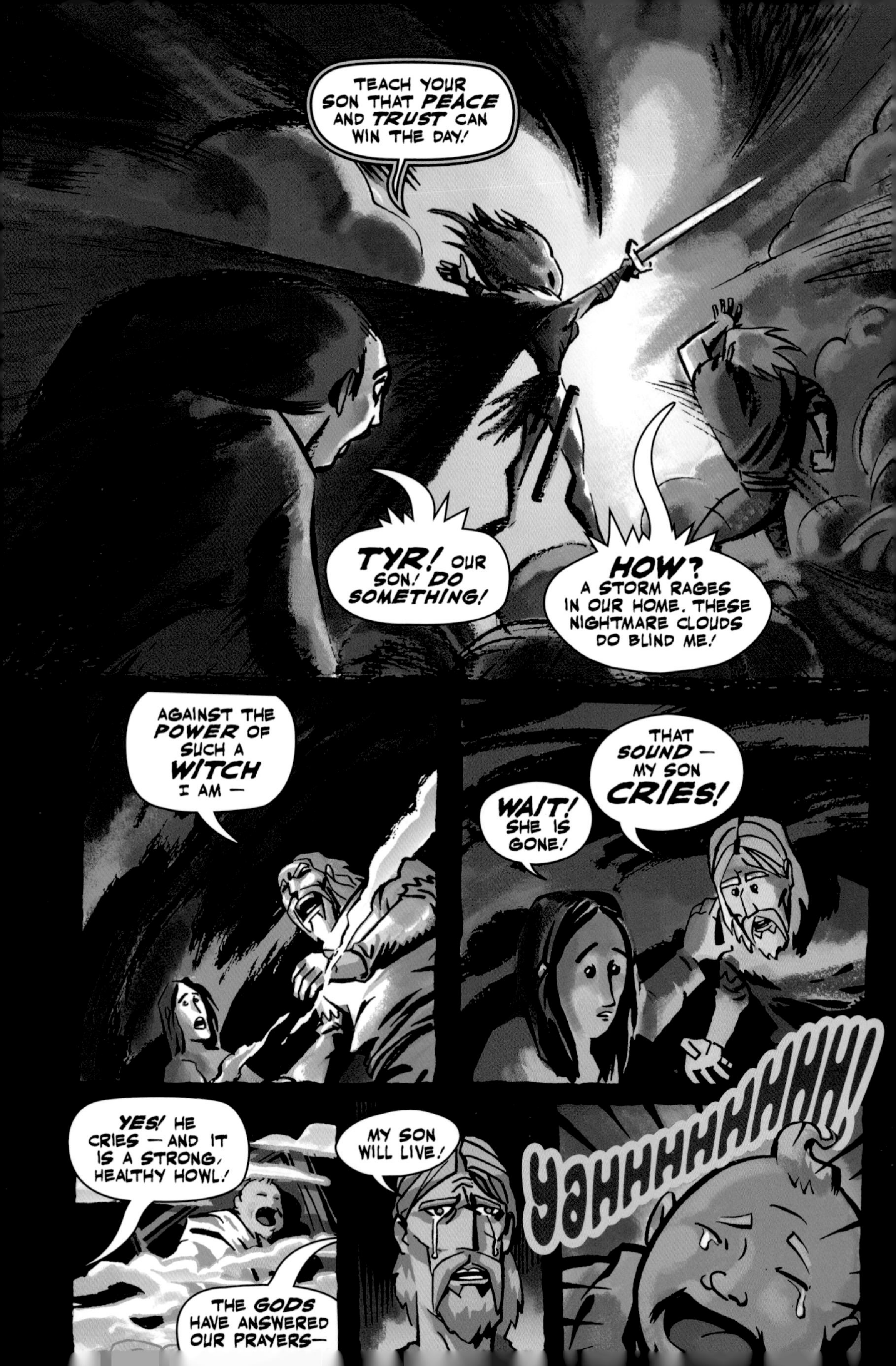
TEACH YOUR SON THAT PEACE AND TRUST CAN WIN THE DAY!
TYR! OUR SON! DO SOMETHING!
HOW? A STORM RAGES IN OUR HOME. THESE NIGHTMARE CLOUDS DO BLIND ME!
AGAINST THE POWER OF SUCH A WITCH I AM —
THAT SOUND — MY SON CRIES!
WAIT! SHE IS GONE!
YES! HE CRIES — AND IT IS A STRONG, HEALTHY HOWL!
THE GODS HAVE ANSWERED OUR PRAYERS—
MY SON WILL LIVE!
YAHHHHHHHHH!

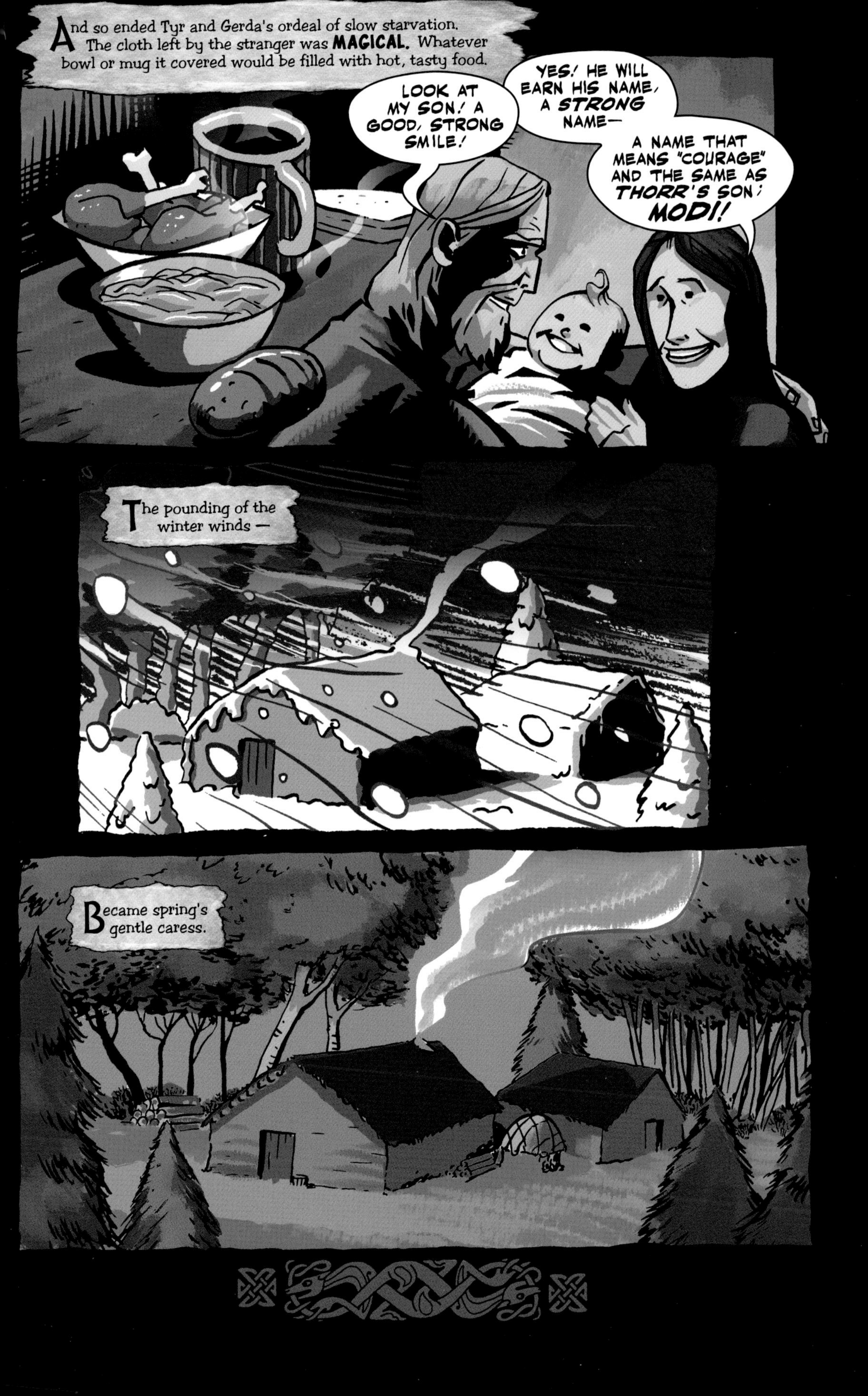
And so ended Tyr and Gerda's ordeal of slow starvation. The cloth left by the stranger was MAGICAL. Whatever bowl or mug it covered would be filled with hot, tasty food.
LOOK AT MY SON! A GOOD, STRONG SMILE!
YES! HE WILL EARN HIS NAME, A STRONG NAME—
A NAME THAT MEANS "COURAGE" AND THE SAME AS THORR'S SON: MODI!
The pounding of the winter winds —
Became spring's gentle caress.

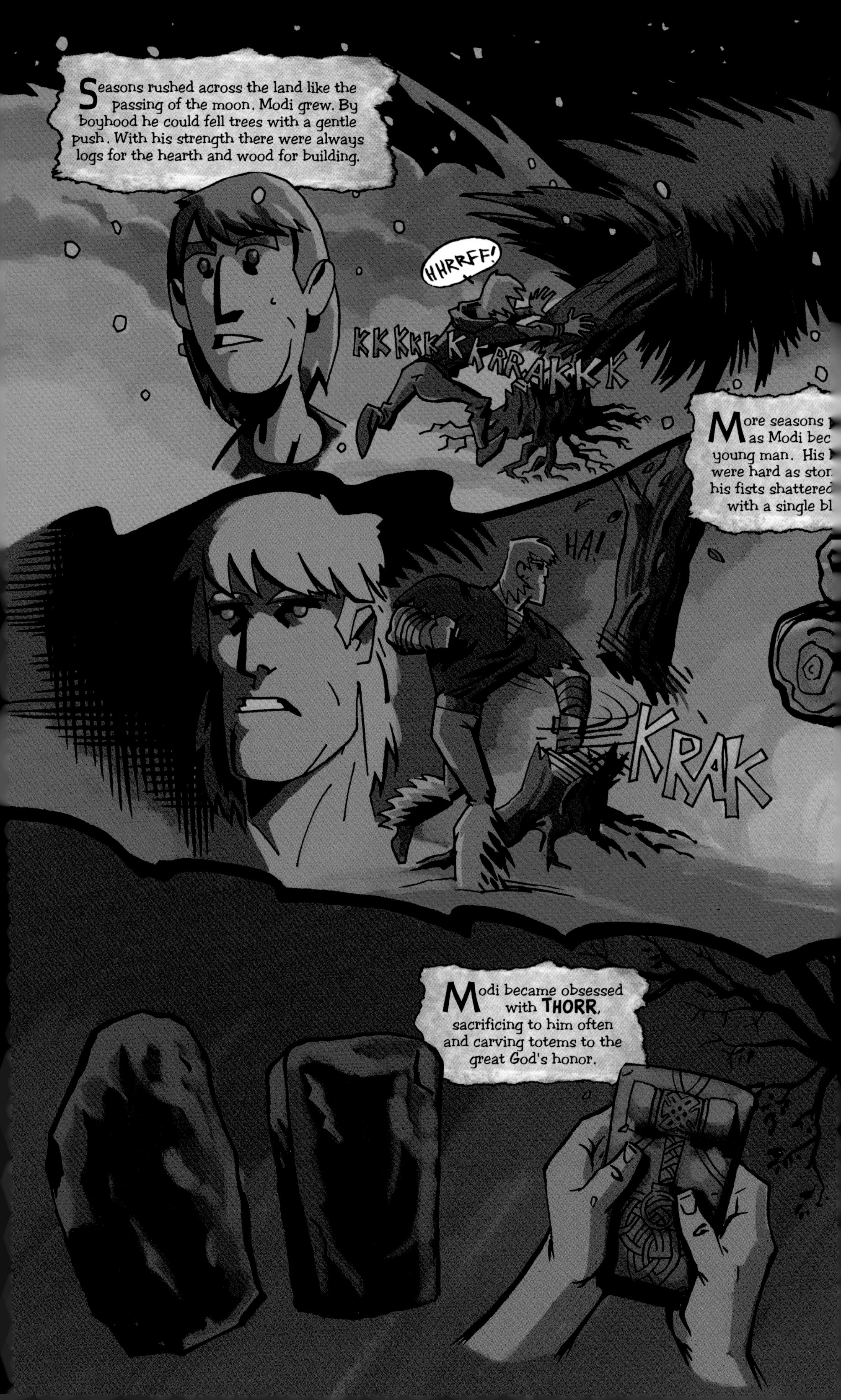

Seasons rushed across the land like the passing of the moon. Modi grew. By boyhood he could fell trees with a gentle push. With his strength there were always logs for the hearth and wood for building.
HHRRFF!
KKKKKKKRRAKKKK
More seasons
as Modi bec
young man. His
were hard as ston
his fists shattered
with a single bl
HA!
KRAK
Modi became obsessed with THORR, sacrificing to him often and carving totems to the great God's honor.

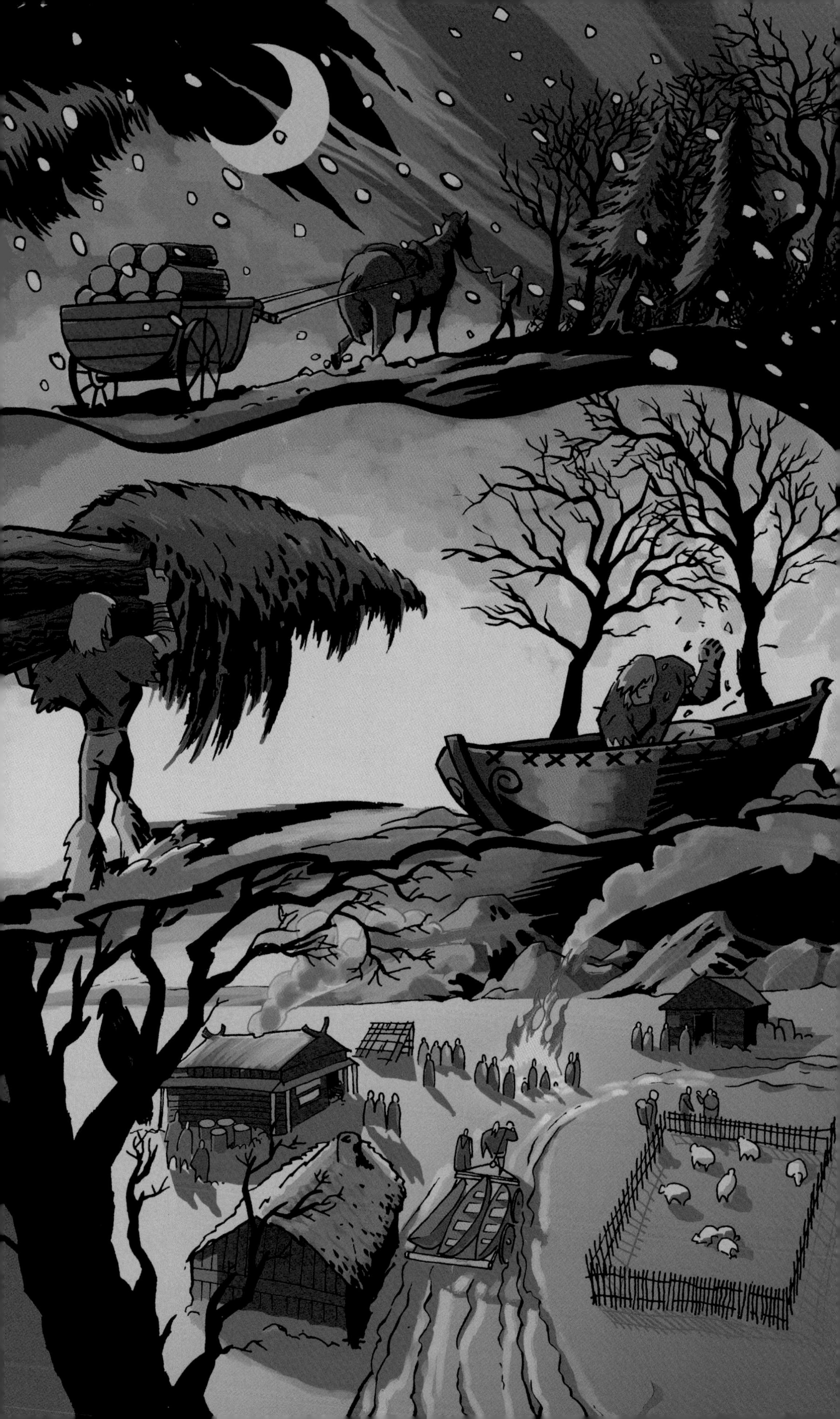

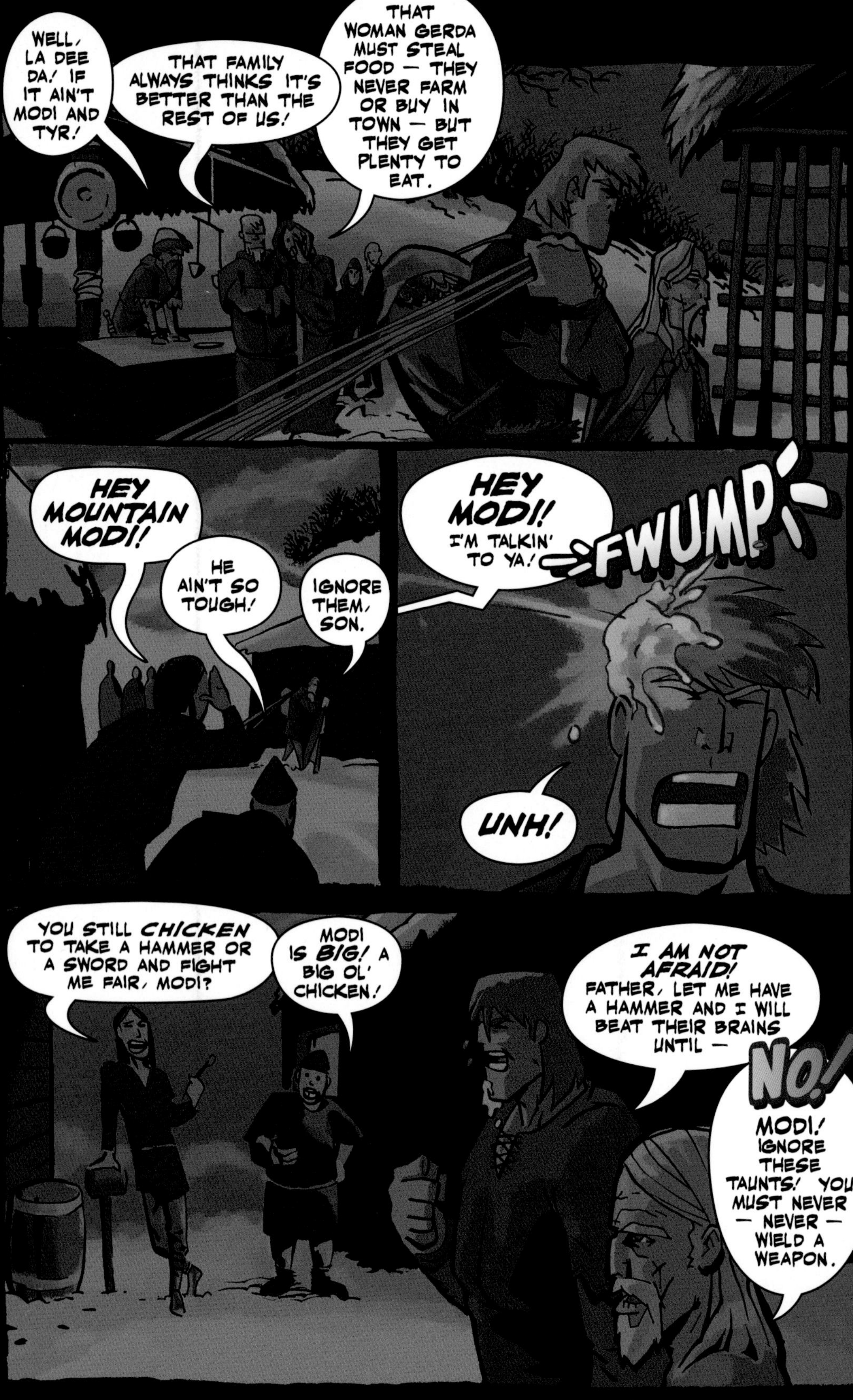
WELL, LA DEE DA! IF IT AIN'T MODI AND TYR!
THAT FAMILY ALWAYS THINKS IT'S BETTER THAN THE REST OF US!
THAT WOMAN GERDA MUST STEAL FOOD — THEY NEVER FARM OR BUY IN TOWN — BUT THEY GET PLENTY TO EAT.
HEY MOUNTAIN MODI!
HE AIN'T SO TOUGH!
IGNORE THEM, SON.
HEY MODI! I'M TALKIN' TO YA!
FWUMP
UNH!
YOU STILL CHICKEN TO TAKE A HAMMER OR A SWORD AND FIGHT ME FAIR, MODI?
MODI IS BIG! A BIG OL' CHICKEN!
I AM NOT AFRAID! FATHER, LET ME HAVE A HAMMER AND I WILL BEAT THEIR BRAINS UNTIL —
NO!
MODI! IGNORE THESE TAUNTS! YOU MUST NEVER — NEVER — WIELD A WEAPON.

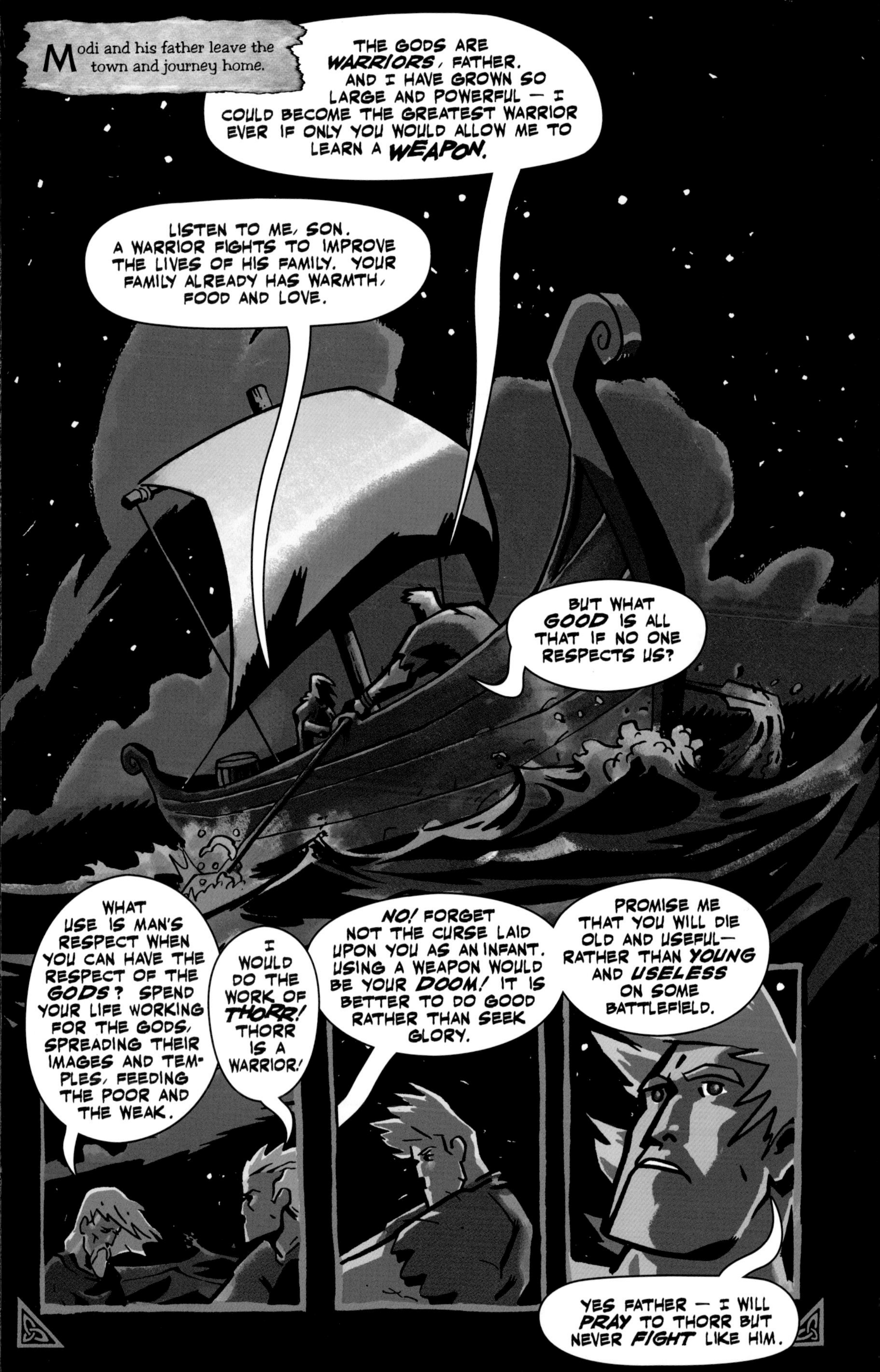
Modi and his father leave the town and journey home.
THE GODS ARE WARRIORS, FATHER. AND I HAVE GROWN SO LARGE AND POWERFUL — I COULD BECOME THE GREATEST WARRIOR EVER IF ONLY YOU WOULD ALLOW ME TO LEARN A WEAPON.
LISTEN TO ME, SON. A WARRIOR FIGHTS TO IMPROVE THE LIVES OF HIS FAMILY. YOUR FAMILY ALREADY HAS WARMTH, FOOD AND LOVE.
BUT WHAT GOOD IS ALL THAT IF NO ONE RESPECTS US?
WHAT USE IS MAN'S RESPECT WHEN YOU CAN HAVE THE RESPECT OF THE GODS? SPEND YOUR LIFE WORKING FOR THE GODS, SPREADING THEIR IMAGES AND TEMPLES, FEEDING THE POOR AND THE WEAK.
I WOULD DO THE WORK OF THORR! THORR IS A WARRIOR!
NO! FORGET NOT THE CURSE LAID UPON YOU AS AN INFANT. USING A WEAPON WOULD BE YOUR DOOM! IT IS BETTER TO DO GOOD RATHER THAN SEEK GLORY.
PROMISE ME THAT YOU WILL DIE OLD AND USEFUL— RATHER THAN YOUNG AND USELESS ON SOME BATTLEFIELD.
YES FATHER — I WILL PRAY TO THORR BUT NEVER FIGHT LIKE HIM.

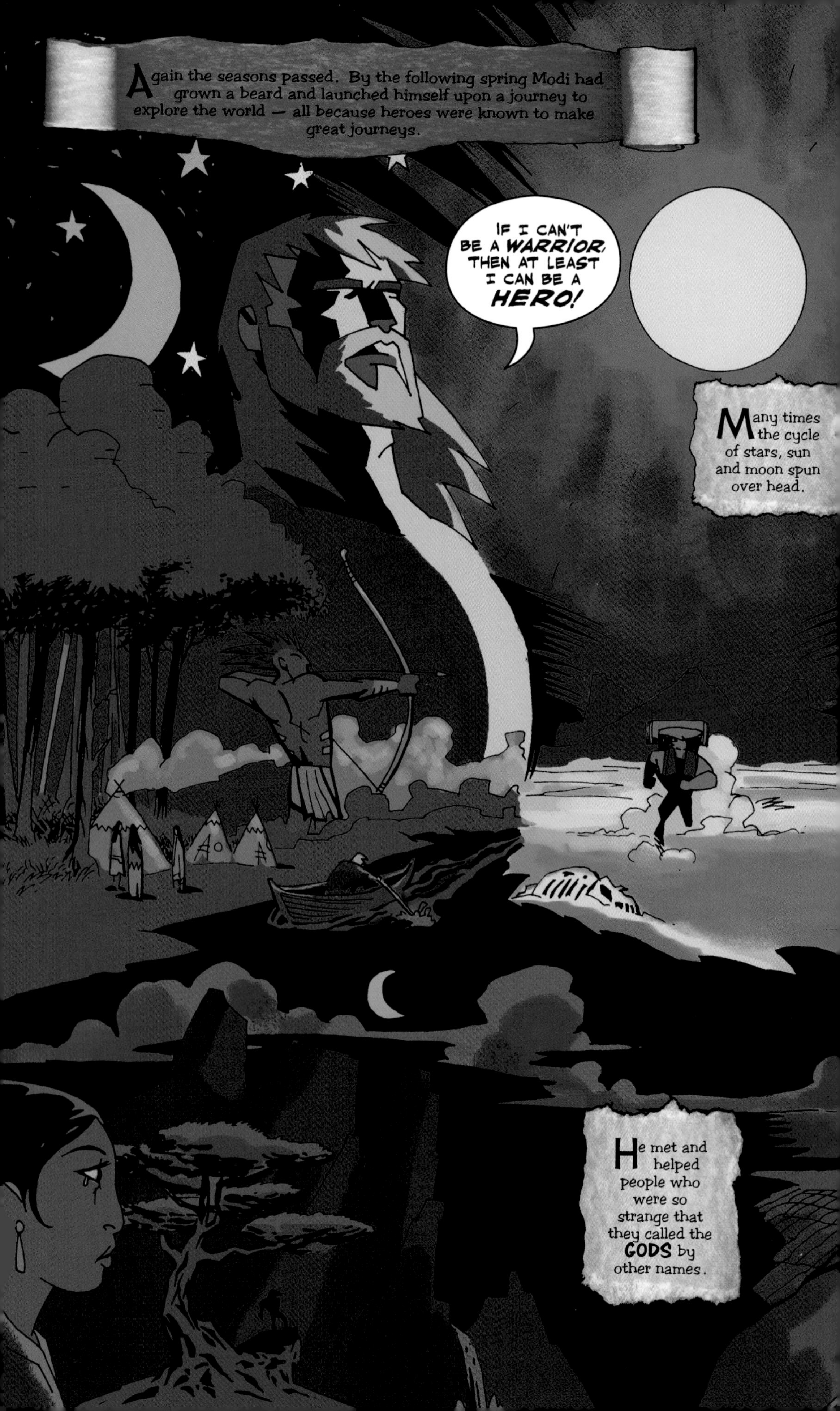
Again the seasons passed. By the following spring Modi had grown a beard and launched himself upon a journey to explore the world — all because heroes were known to make great journeys.
IF I CAN'T BE A WARRIOR, THEN AT LEAST I CAN BE A HERO!
Many times the cycle of stars, sun and moon spun over head.
He met and helped people who were so strange that they called the GODS by other names.

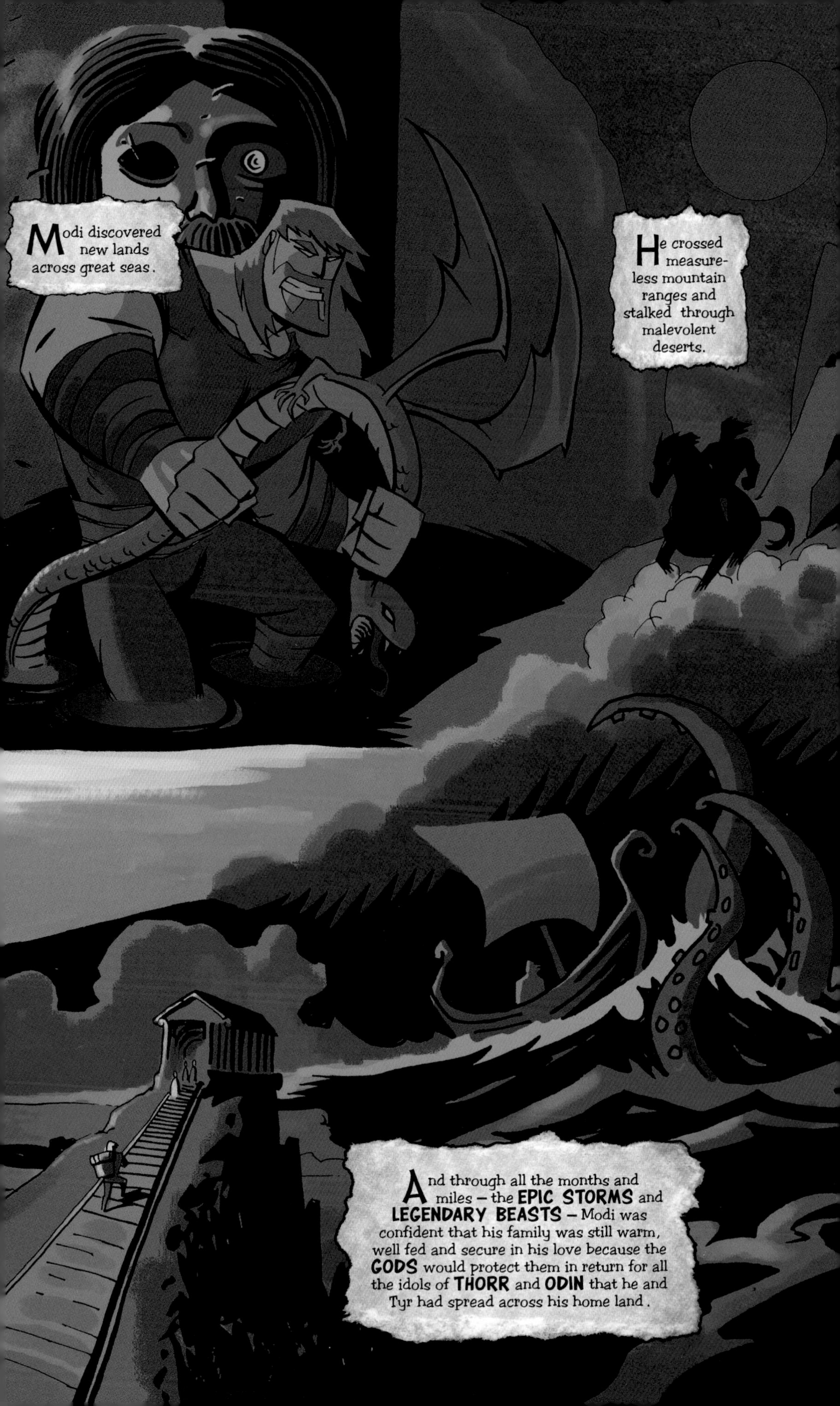
Modi discovered new lands across great seas.
He crossed measureless mountain ranges and stalked through malevolent deserts.
And through all the months and miles – the EPIC STORMS and LEGENDARY BEASTS – Modi was confident that his family was still warm, well fed and secure in his love because the GODS would protect them in return for all the idols of THORR and ODIN that he and Tyr had spread across his home land.

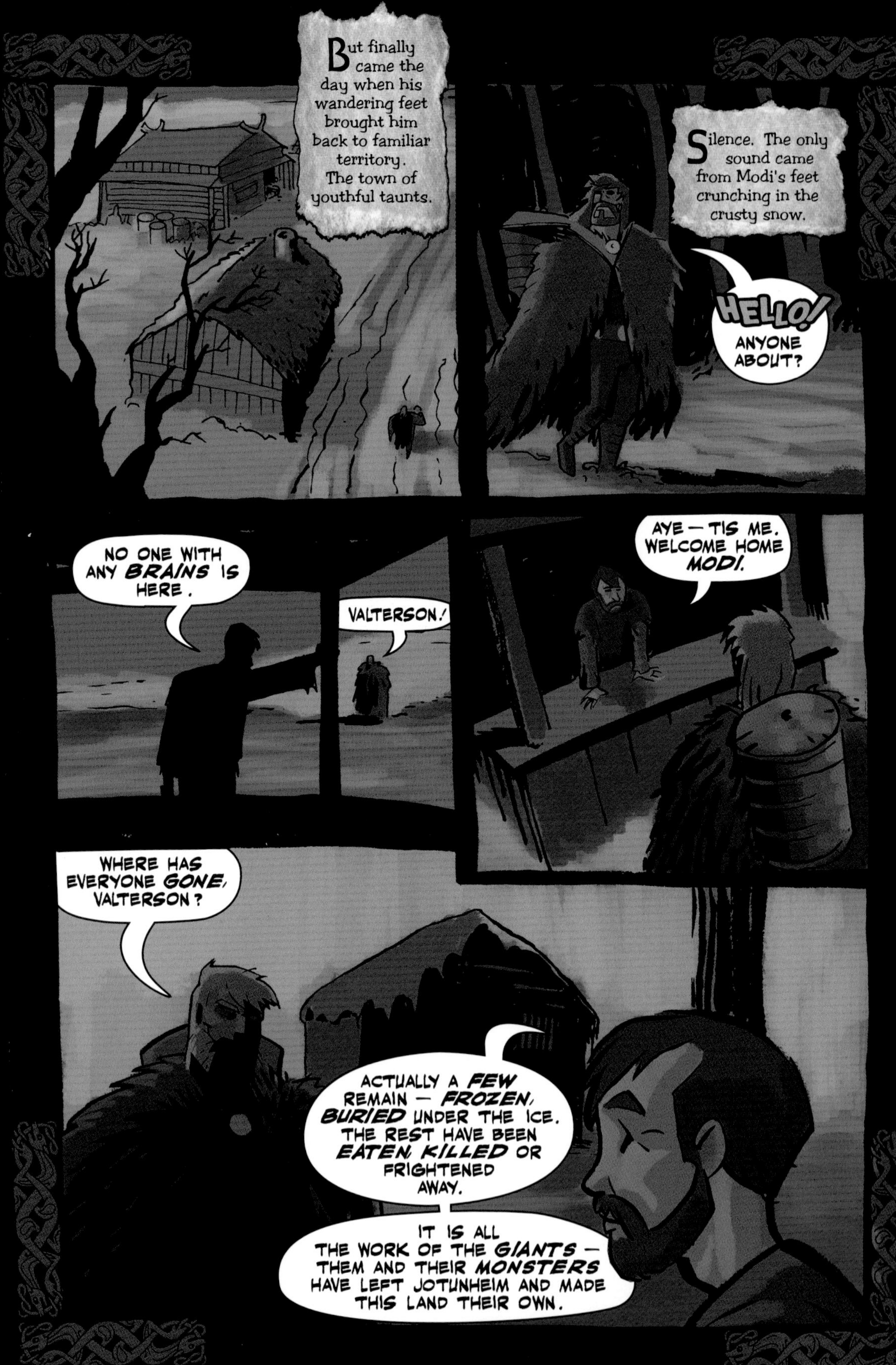
But finally came the day when his wandering feet brought him back to familiar territory. The town of youthful taunts.
Silence. The only sound came from Modi's feet crunching in the crusty snow.
HELLO! ANYONE ABOUT?
NO ONE WITH ANY BRAINS IS HERE.
VALTERSON!
AYE — TIS ME. WELCOME HOME MODI.
WHERE HAS EVERYONE GONE, VALTERSON?
ACTUALLY A FEW REMAIN — FROZEN, BURIED UNDER THE ICE. THE REST HAVE BEEN EATEN, KILLED OR FRIGHTENED AWAY.
IT IS ALL THE WORK OF THE GIANTS — THEM AND THEIR MONSTERS HAVE LEFT JOTUNHEIM AND MADE THIS LAND THEIR OWN.

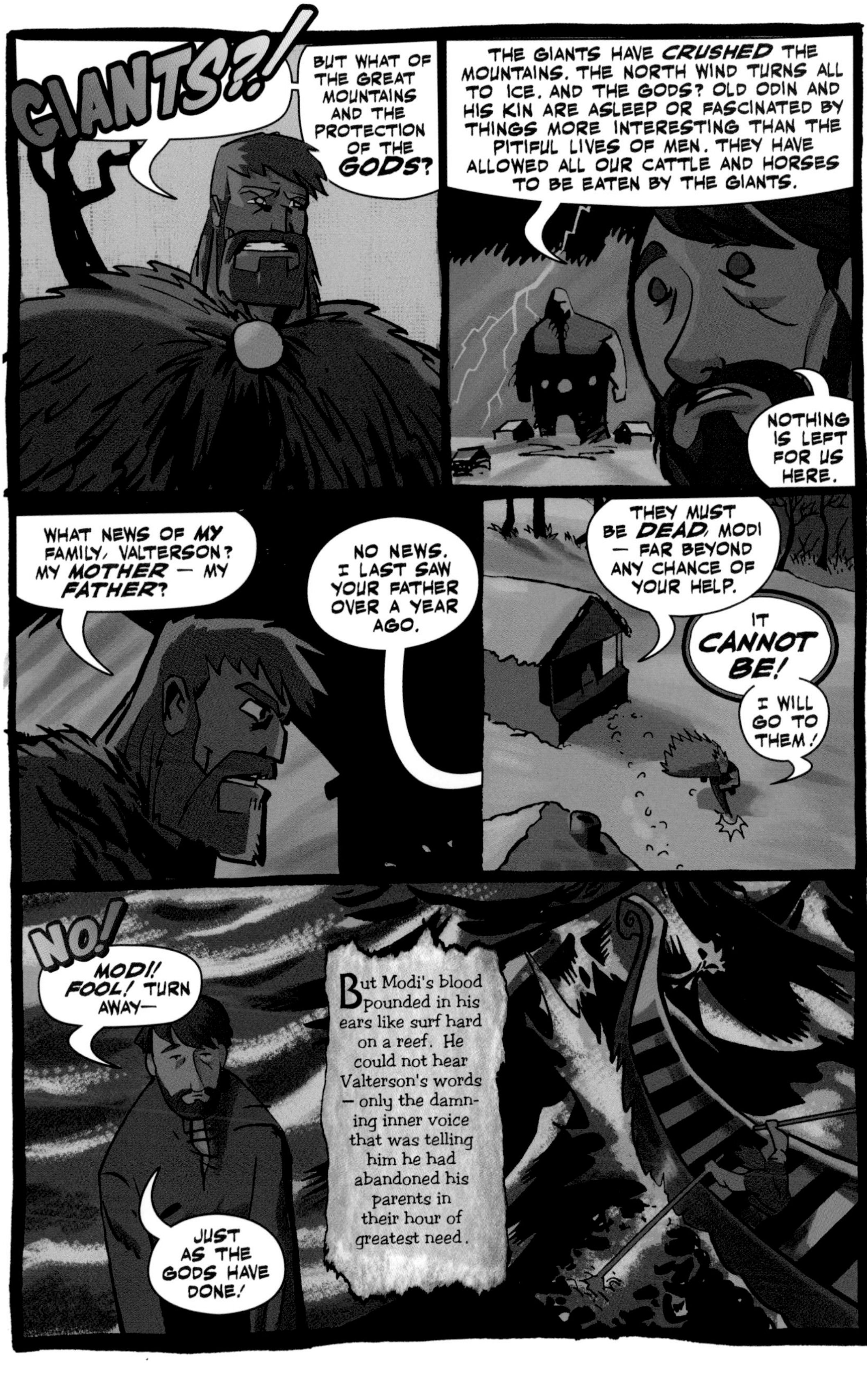
GIANTS?!
BUT WHAT OF THE GREAT MOUNTAINS AND THE PROTECTION OF THE GODS?
THE GIANTS HAVE CRUSHED THE MOUNTAINS. THE NORTH WIND TURNS ALL TO ICE. AND THE GODS? OLD ODIN AND HIS KIN ARE ASLEEP OR FASCINATED BY THINGS MORE INTERESTING THAN THE PITIFUL LIVES OF MEN. THEY HAVE ALLOWED ALL OUR CATTLE AND HORSES TO BE EATEN BY THE GIANTS.
NOTHING IS LEFT FOR US HERE.
WHAT NEWS OF MY FAMILY, VALTERSON? MY MOTHER — MY FATHER?
NO NEWS. I LAST SAW YOUR FATHER OVER A YEAR AGO.
THEY MUST BE DEAD, MODI — FAR BEYOND ANY CHANCE OF YOUR HELP.
IT CANNOT BE!
I WILL GO TO THEM!
NO!
MODI! FOOL! TURN AWAY—
But Modi's blood pounded in his ears like surf hard on a reef. He could not hear Valterson's words — only the damning inner voice that was telling him he had abandoned his parents in their hour of greatest need.
JUST AS THE GODS HAVE DONE!

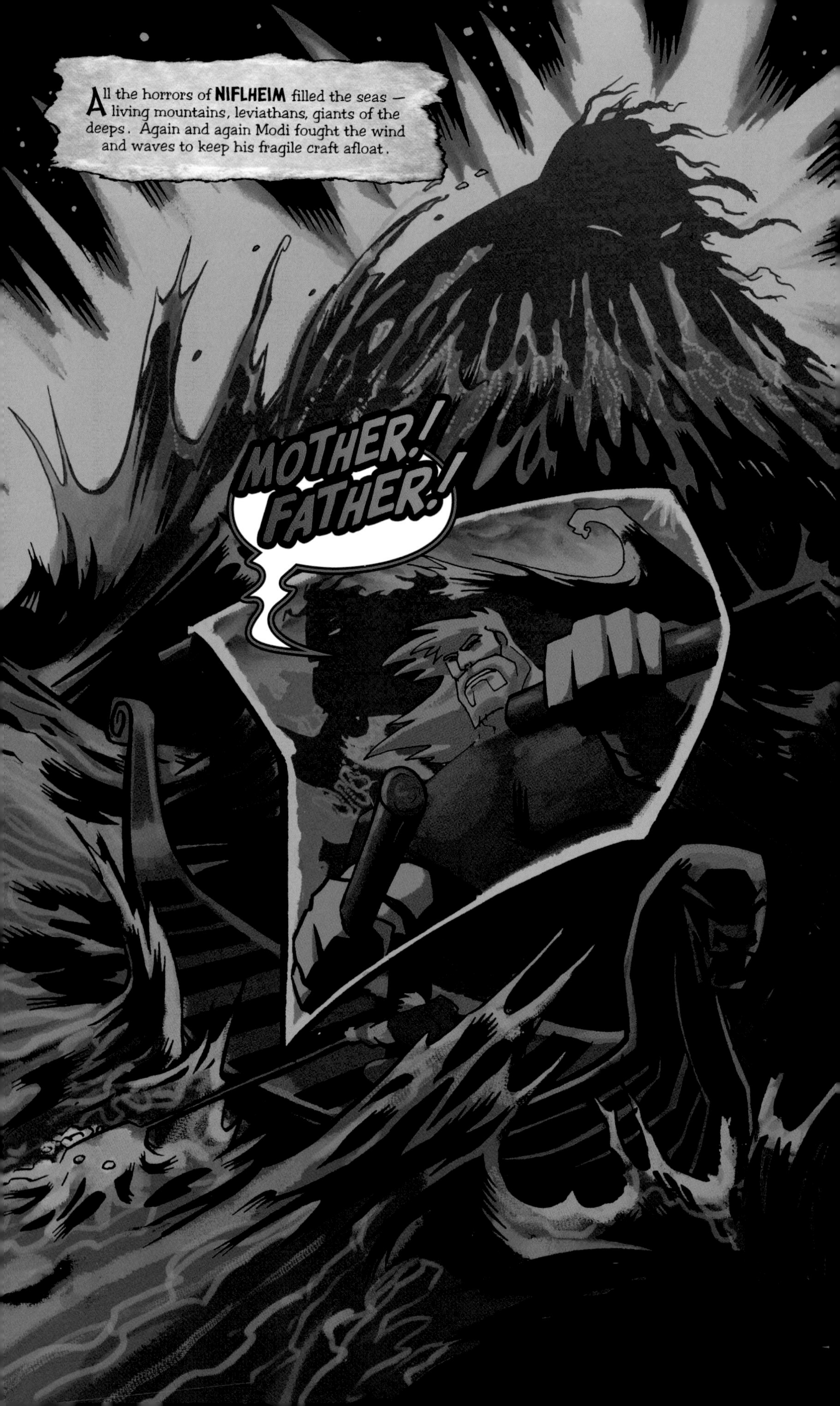
All the horrors of NIFLHEIM filled the seas — living mountains, leviathans, giants of the deeps. Again and again Modi fought the wind and waves to keep his fragile craft afloat.
MOTHER! FATHER!

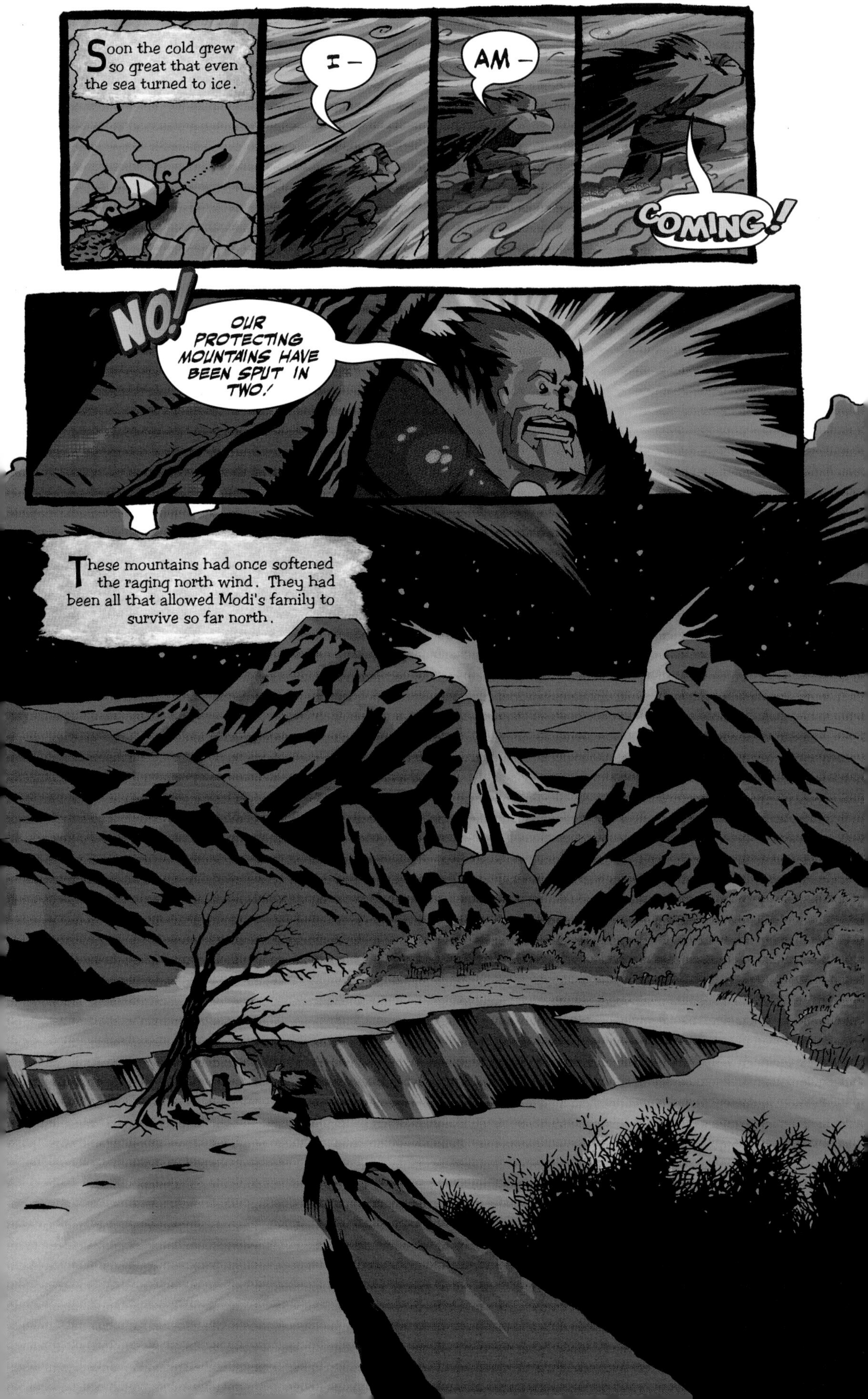
Soon the cold grew so great that even the sea turned to ice.
I —
AM —
COMING!
NO!
OUR PROTECTING MOUNTAINS HAVE BEEN SPLIT IN TWO!
These mountains had once softened the raging north wind. They had been all that allowed Modi's family to survive so far north.

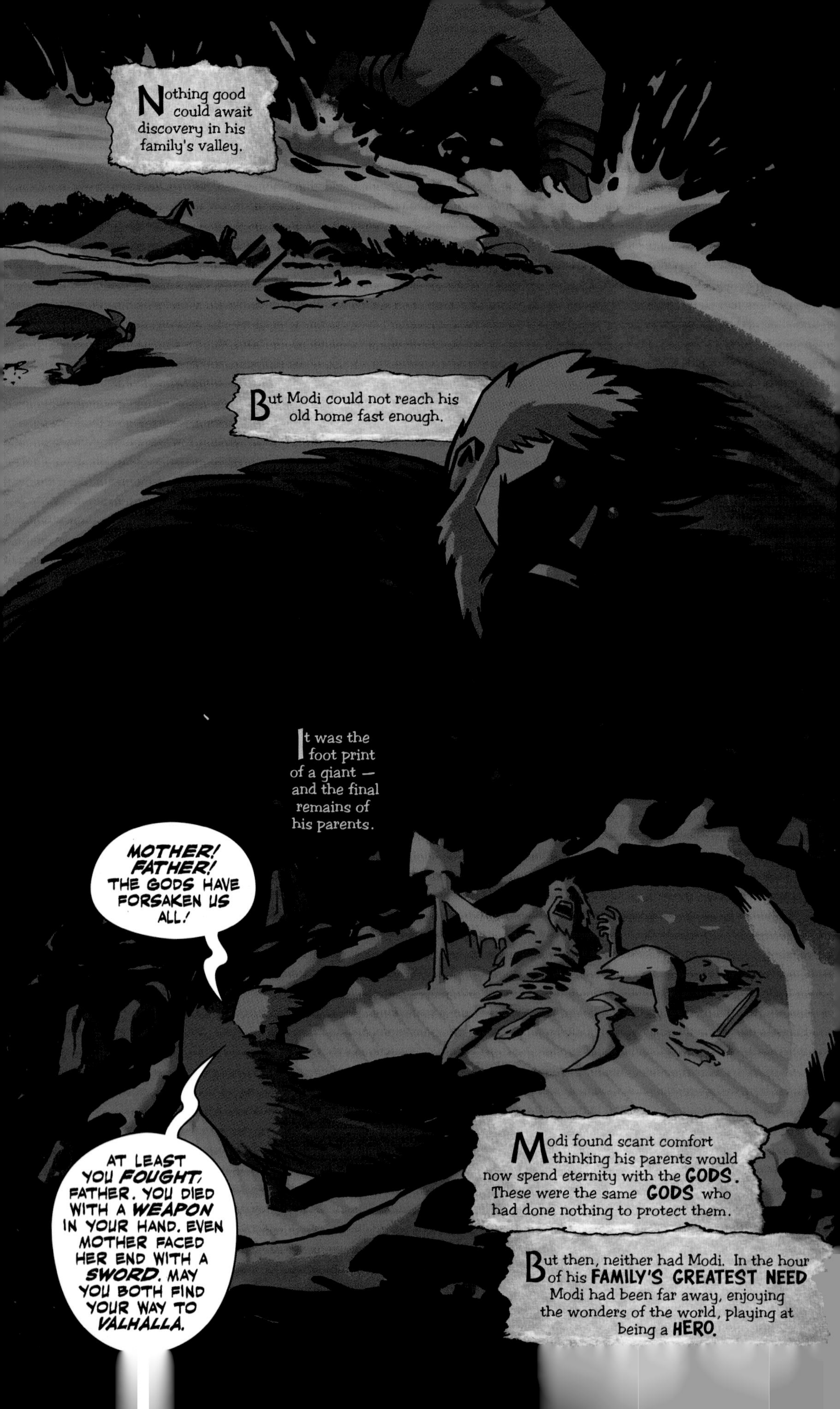
Nothing good could await discovery in his family's valley.
But Modi could not reach his old home fast enough.
It was the foot print of a giant — and the final remains of his parents.
MOTHER! FATHER! THE GODS HAVE FORSAKEN US ALL!
AT LEAST YOU FOUGHT, FATHER. YOU DIED WITH A WEAPON IN YOUR HAND. EVEN MOTHER FACED HER END WITH A SWORD. MAY YOU BOTH FIND YOUR WAY TO VALHALLA.
Modi found scant comfort thinking his parents would now spend eternity with the GODS. These were the same GODS who had done nothing to protect them.
But then, neither had Modi. In the hour of his FAMILY'S GREATEST NEED Modi had been far away, enjoying the wonders of the world, playing at being a HERO.

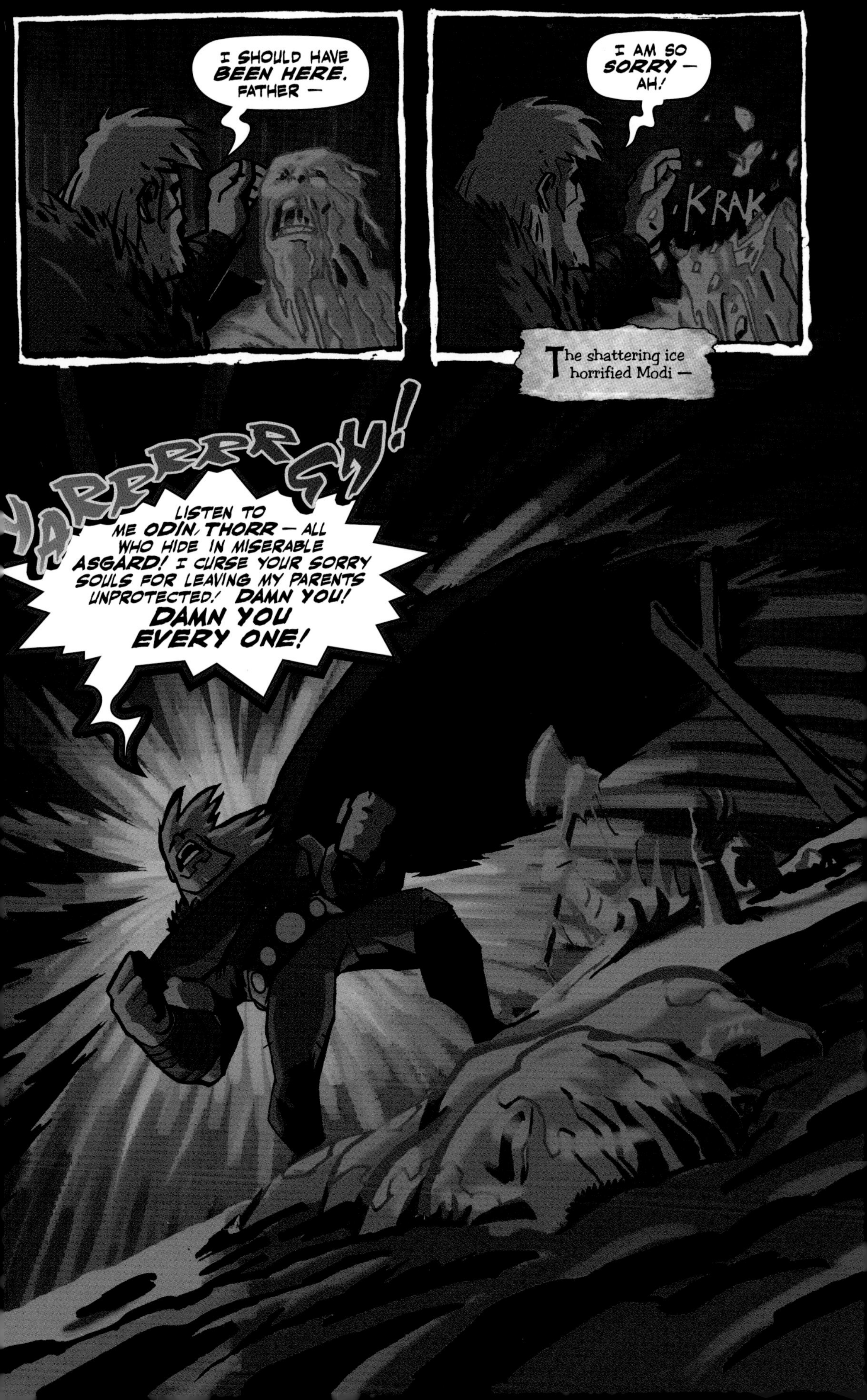
I SHOULD HAVE BEEN HERE. FATHER —
I AM SO SORRY — AH!
KRAK
The shattering ice horrified Modi —
HARRRRRGH!
LISTEN TO ME ODIN, THORR — ALL WHO HIDE IN MISERABLE ASGARD! I CURSE YOUR SORRY SOULS FOR LEAVING MY PARENTS UNPROTECTED! DAMN YOU! DAMN YOU EVERY ONE!

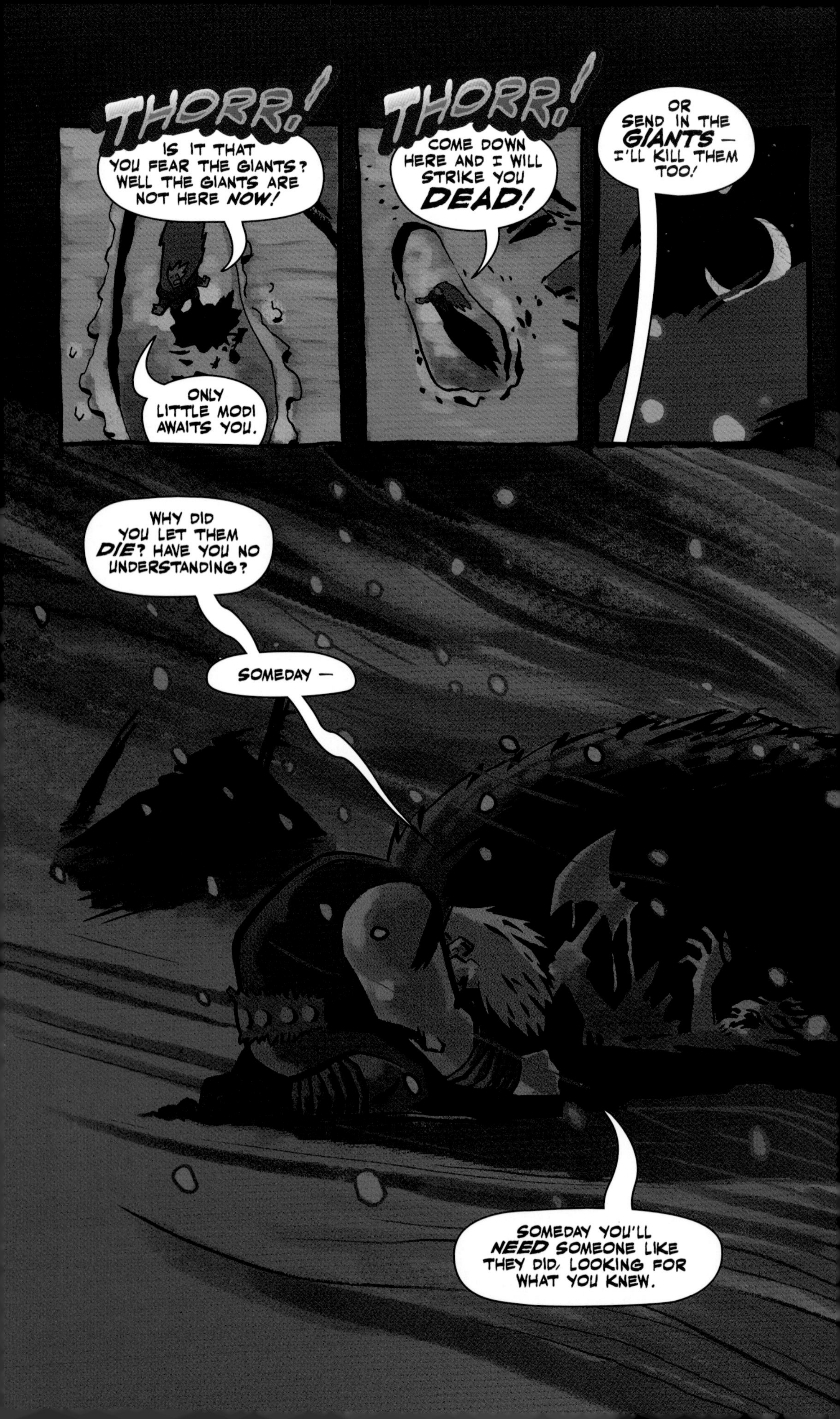
THORR!
IS IT THAT YOU FEAR THE GIANTS? WELL THE GIANTS ARE NOT HERE NOW!
ONLY LITTLE MODI AWAITS YOU.
THORR!
COME DOWN HERE AND I WILL STRIKE YOU DEAD!
OR SEND IN THE GIANTS — I'LL KILL THEM TOO!
WHY DID YOU LET THEM DIE? HAVE YOU NO UNDERSTANDING?
SOMEDAY —
SOMEDAY YOU'LL NEED SOMEONE LIKE THEY DID, LOOKING FOR WHAT YOU KNEW.

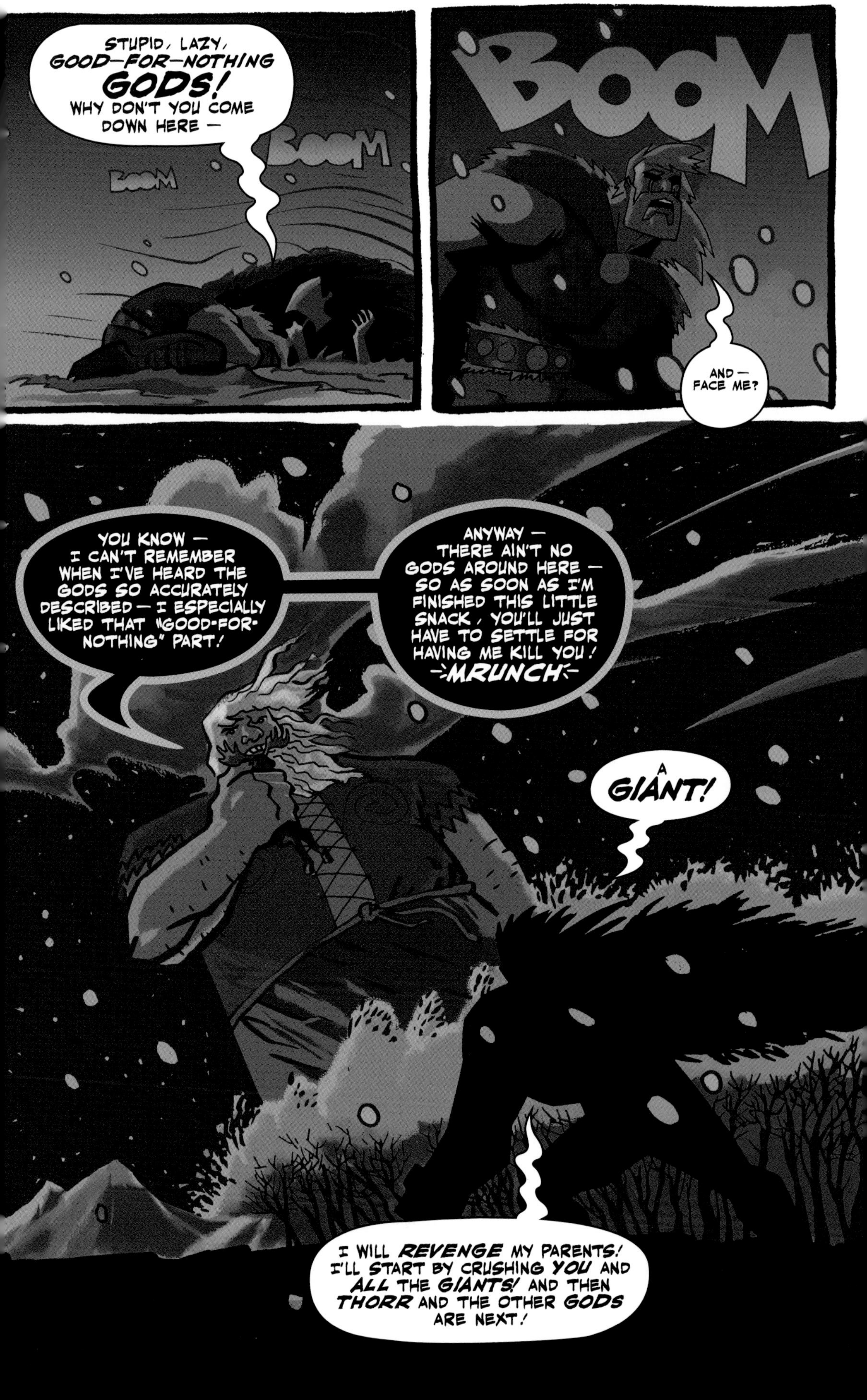
STUPID, LAZY, GOOD—FOR—NOTHING GODS! WHY DON'T YOU COME DOWN HERE —
BOOM
BOOM
BOOM
AND — FACE ME?
YOU KNOW — I CAN'T REMEMBER WHEN I'VE HEARD THE GODS SO ACCURATELY DESCRIBED — I ESPECIALLY LIKED THAT "GOOD-FOR-NOTHING" PART!
ANYWAY — THERE AIN'T NO GODS AROUND HERE — SO AS SOON AS I'M FINISHED THIS LITTLE SNACK, YOU'LL JUST HAVE TO SETTLE FOR HAVING ME KILL YOU!
MRUNCH
A GIANT!
I WILL REVENGE MY PARENTS! I'LL START BY CRUSHING YOU AND ALL THE GIANTS! AND THEN THORR AND THE OTHER GODS ARE NEXT!

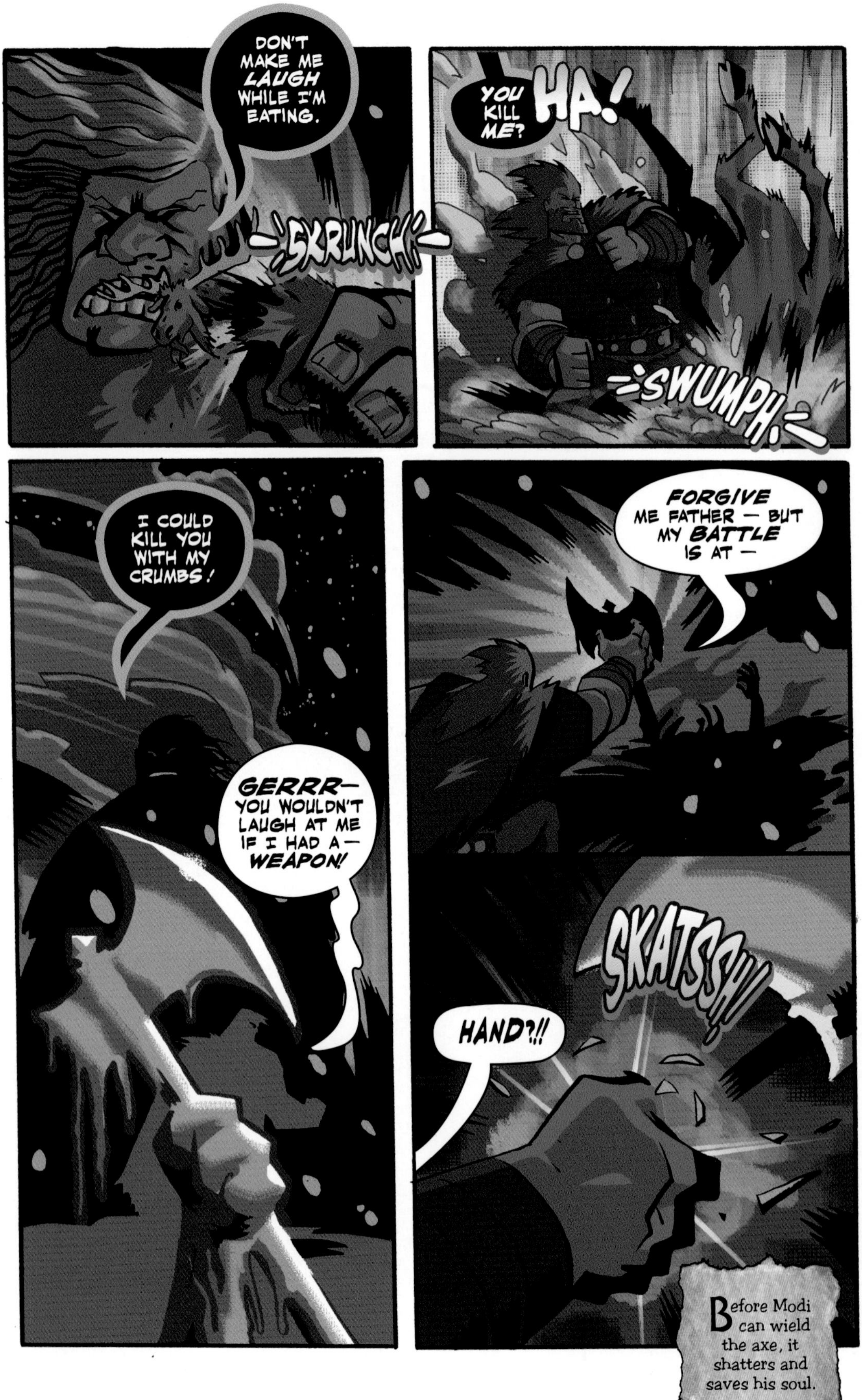
DON'T MAKE ME LAUGH WHILE I'M EATING.
SKRUNCH
YOU KILL ME?
HA!
SWUMPH
I COULD KILL YOU WITH MY CRUMBS!
GERRR— YOU WOULDN'T LAUGH AT ME IF I HAD A— WEAPON!
FORGIVE ME FATHER — BUT MY BATTLE IS AT —
SKATSSH!!
HAND?!!
Before Modi can wield the axe, it shatters and saves his soul.

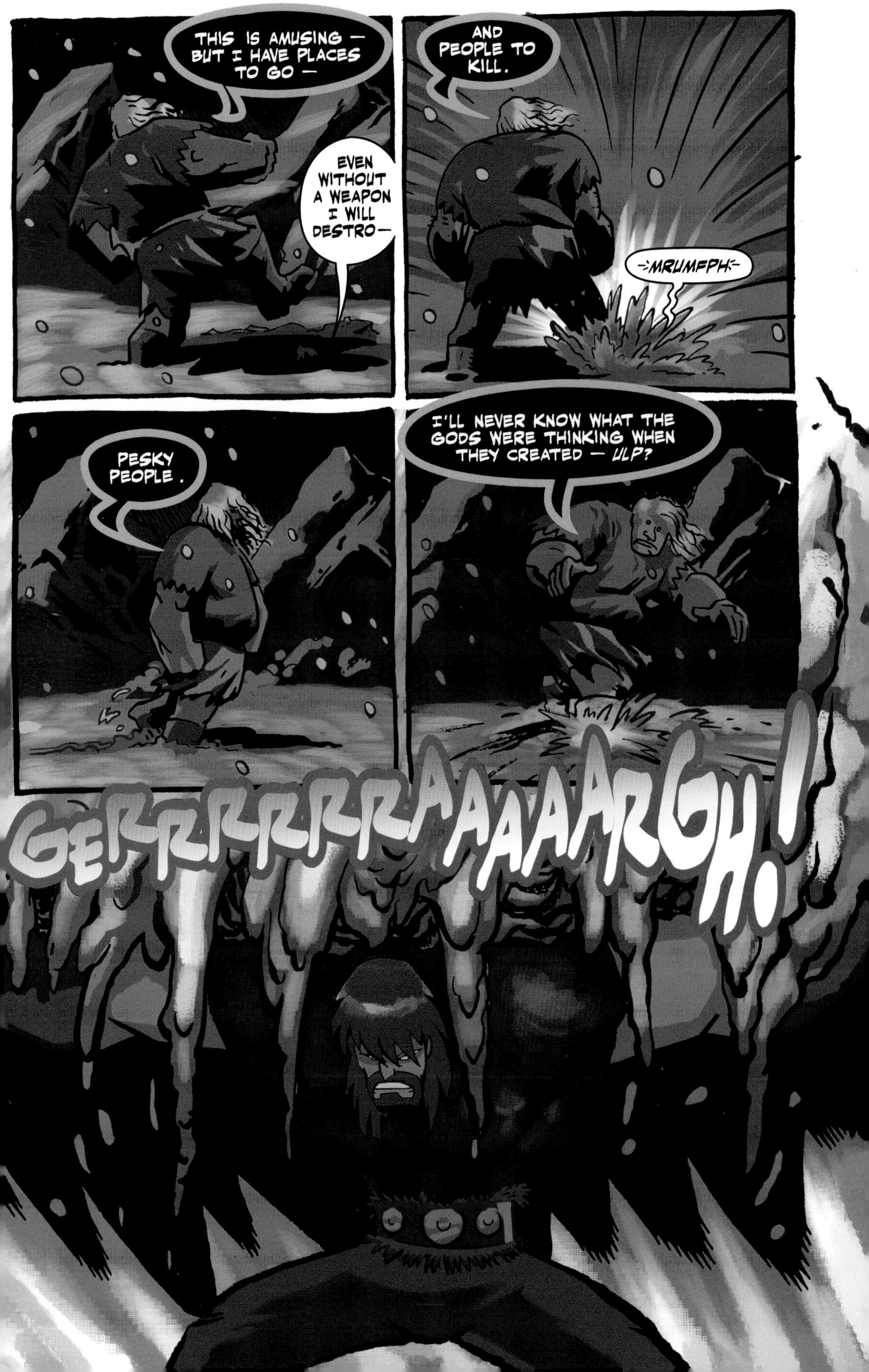
THIS IS AMUSING — BUT I HAVE PLACES TO GO —
EVEN WITHOUT A WEAPON I WILL DESTRO—
AND PEOPLE TO KILL.
-MRUMFPH-
PESKY PEOPLE.
I'LL NEVER KNOW WHAT THE GODS WERE THINKING WHEN THEY CREATED — ULP?
GERRRRRRAAAAARGH!

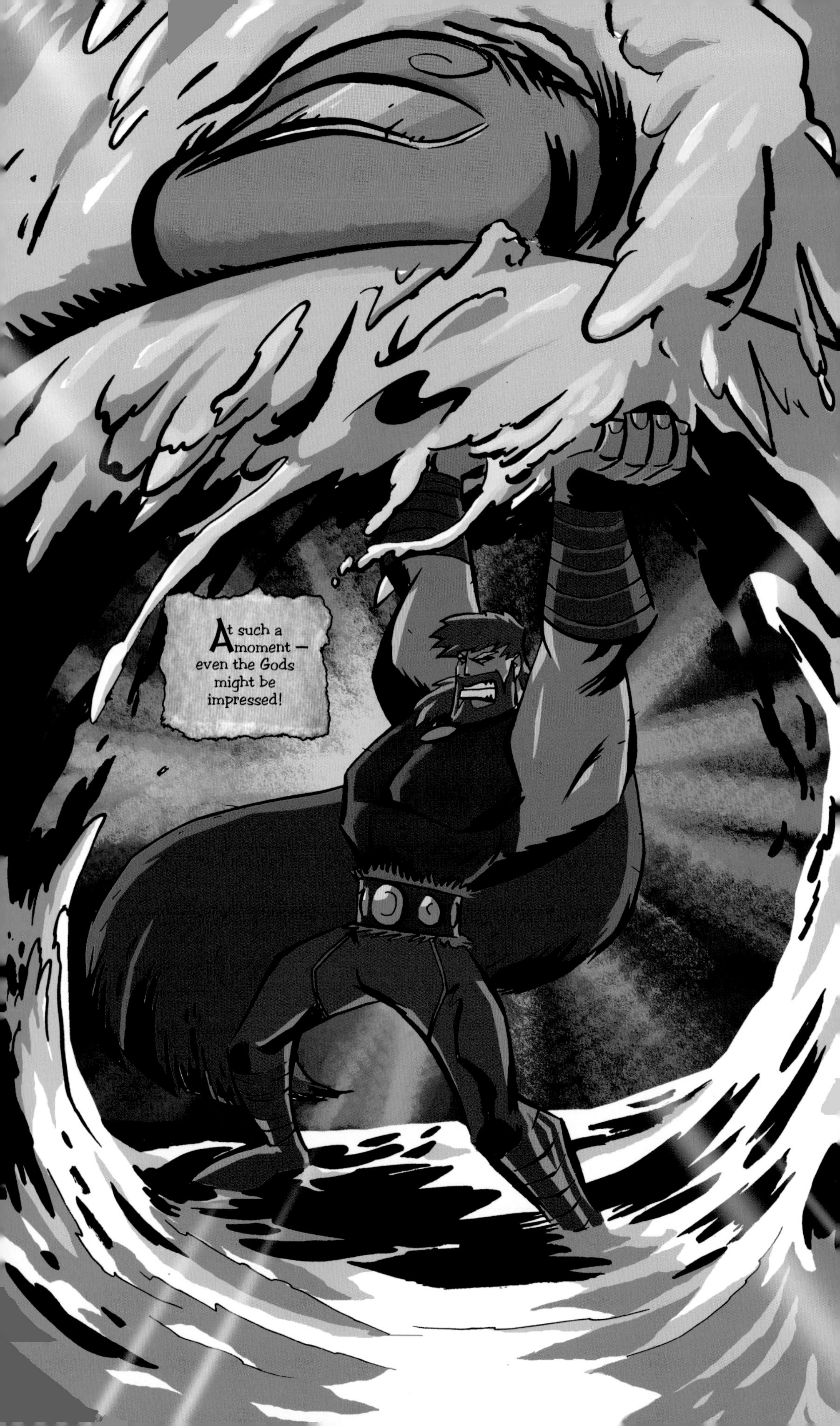
At such a moment — even the Gods might be impressed!

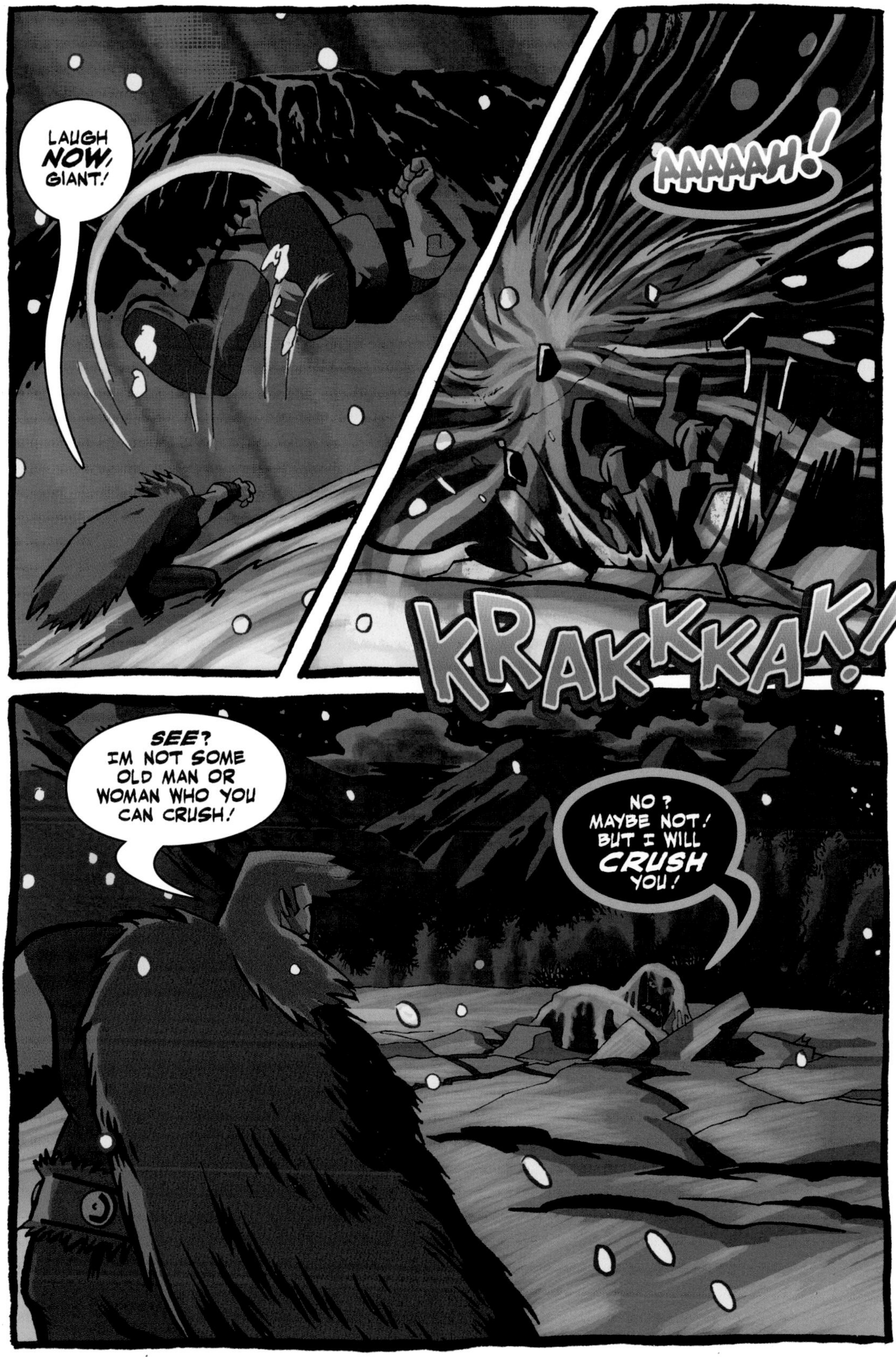
LAUGH NOW, GIANT!
AAAAAH!
KRAKKKAK!
SEE? IM NOT SOME OLD MAN OR WOMAN WHO YOU CAN CRUSH!
NO? MAYBE NOT! BUT I WILL CRUSH YOU!

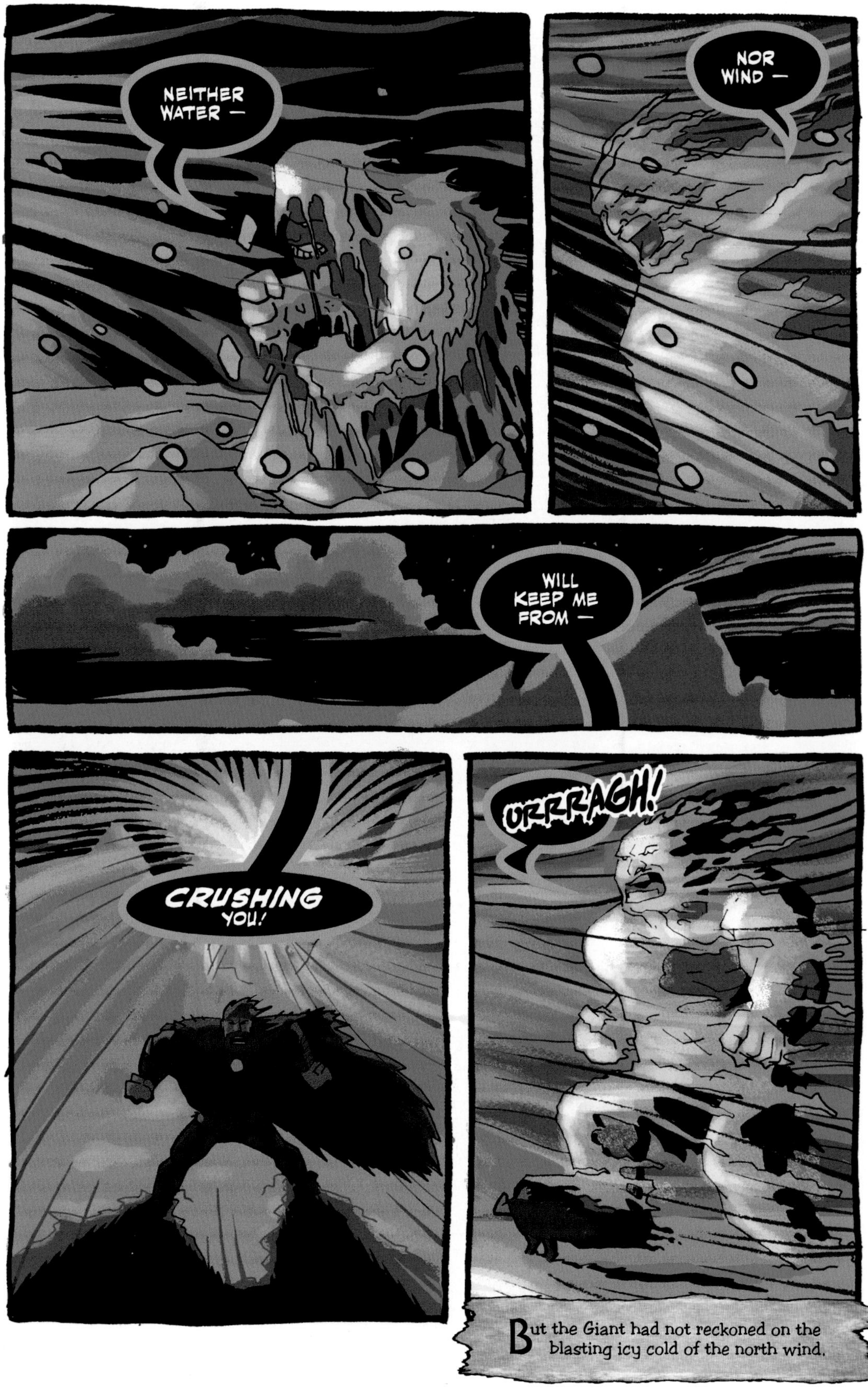
NEITHER WATER —
NOR WIND —
WILL KEEP ME FROM —
CRUSHING YOU!
URRRAGH!
But the Giant had not reckoned on the blasting icy cold of the north wind.

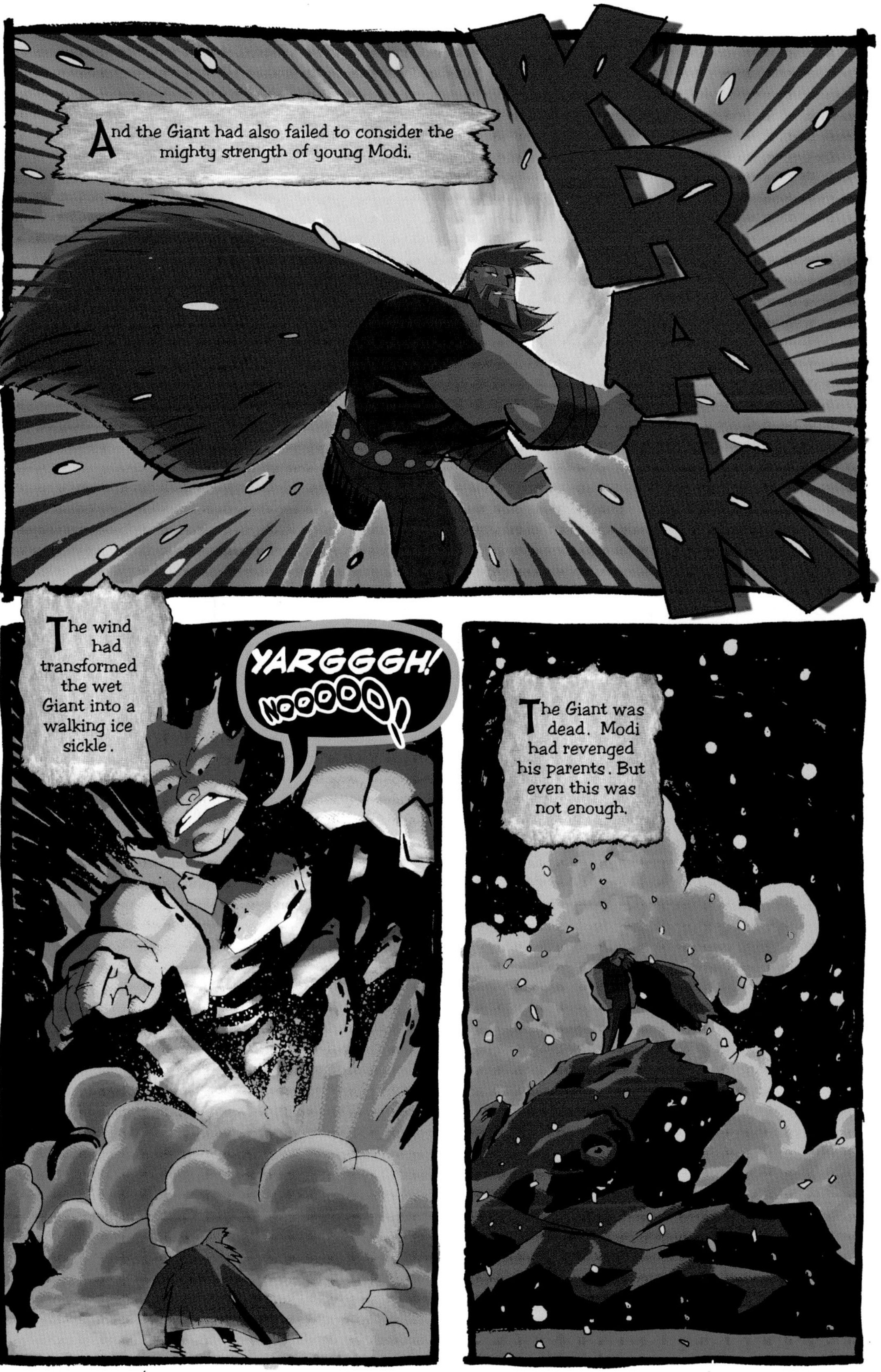
And the Giant had also failed to consider the mighty strength of young Modi.
KRAK
The wind had transformed the wet Giant into a walking ice sickle.
YARGGGH! NOOOOO!
The Giant was dead. Modi had revenged his parents. But even this was not enough.

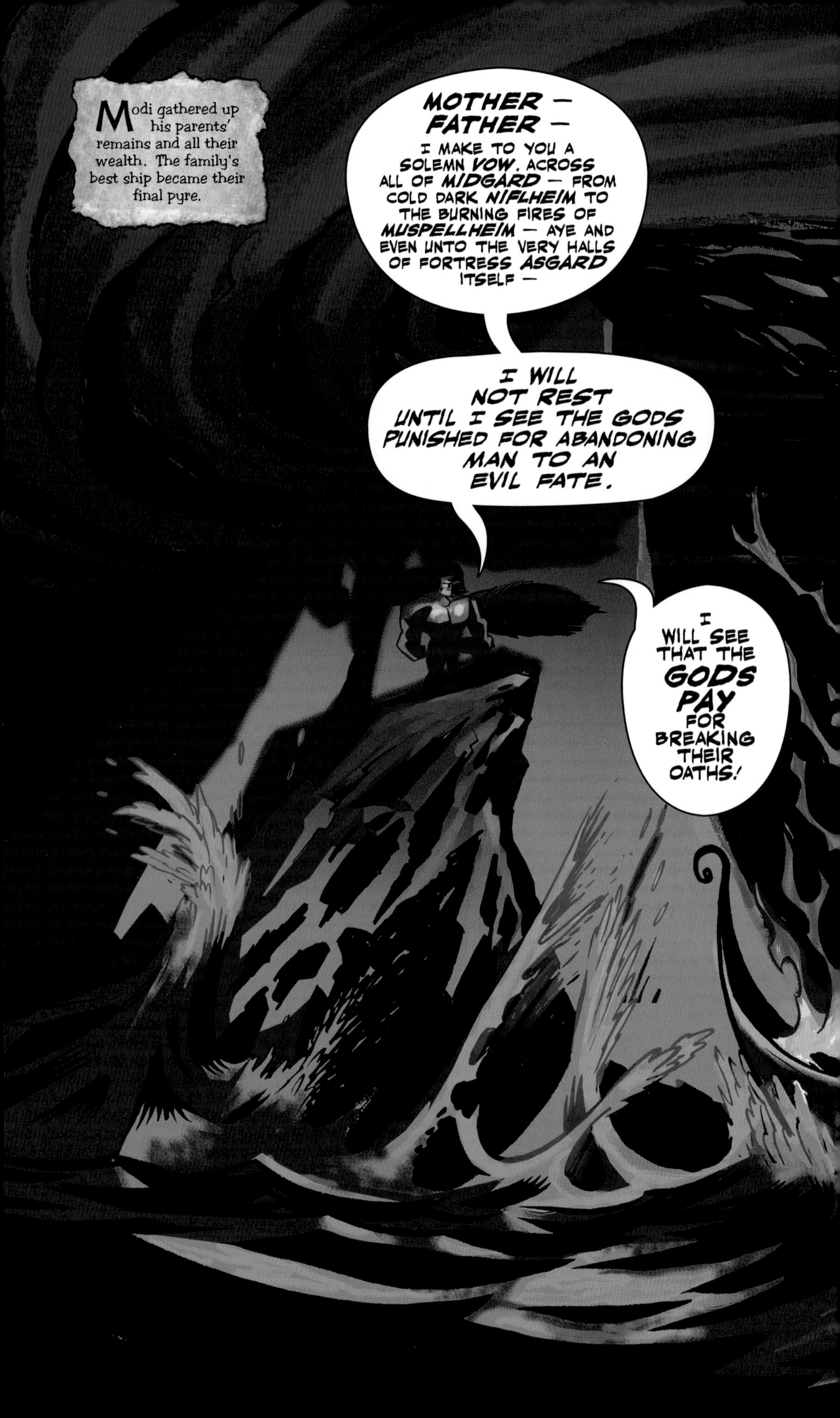

Modi gathered up his parents' remains and all their wealth. The family's best ship became their final pyre.
MOTHER — FATHER — I MAKE TO YOU A SOLEMN VOW. ACROSS ALL OF MIDGARD — FROM COLD DARK NIFLHEIM TO THE BURNING FIRES OF MUSPELLHEIM — AYE AND EVEN UNTO THE VERY HALLS OF FORTRESS ASGARD ITSELF —
I WILL NOT REST UNTIL I SEE THE GODS PUNISHED FOR ABANDONING MAN TO AN EVIL FATE.
I WILL SEE THAT THE GODS PAY FOR BREAKING THEIR OATHS!

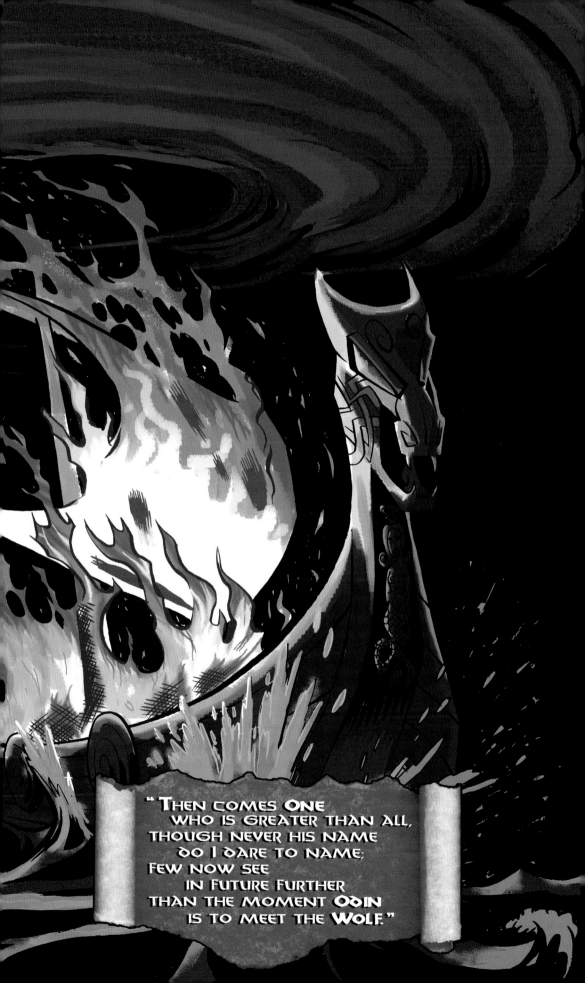

"THEN COMES **ONE**
       WHO IS GREATER THAN ALL,
THOUGH NEVER HIS NAME
       DO I DARE TO NAME;
FEW NOW SEE
       IN FUTURE FURTHER
THAN THE MOMENT **ODIN**
       IS TO MEET THE **WOLF**."

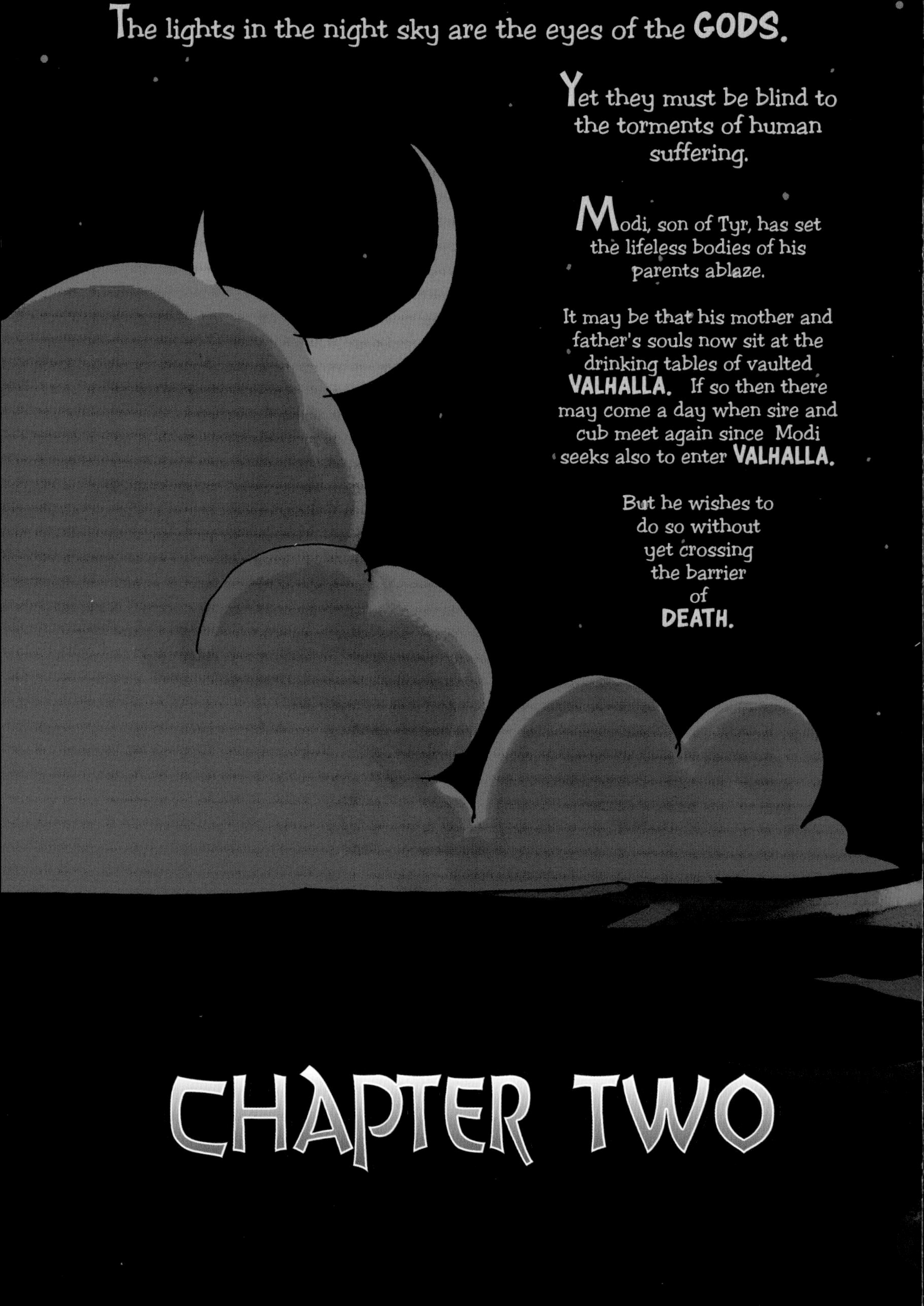
The lights in the night sky are the eyes of the GODS.
Yet they must be blind to the torments of human suffering.
Modi, son of Tyr, has set the lifeless bodies of his parents ablaze.
It may be that his mother and father's souls now sit at the drinking tables of vaulted VALHALLA. If so then there may come a day when sire and cub meet again since Modi seeks also to enter VALHALLA.
But he wishes to do so without yet crossing the barrier of DEATH.

CHAPTER TWO

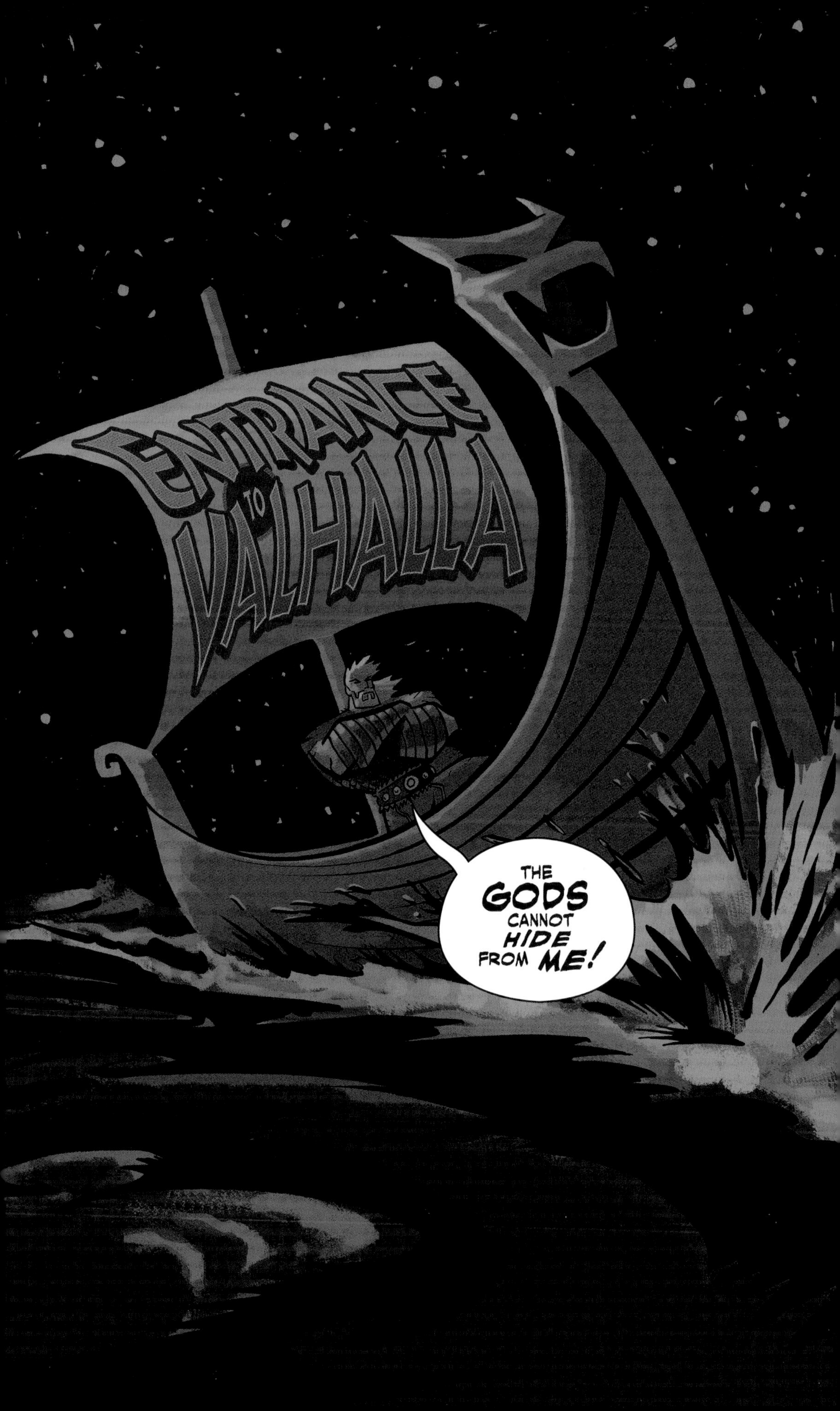
ENTRANCE TO VALHALLA
THE GODS CANNOT HIDE FROM ME!

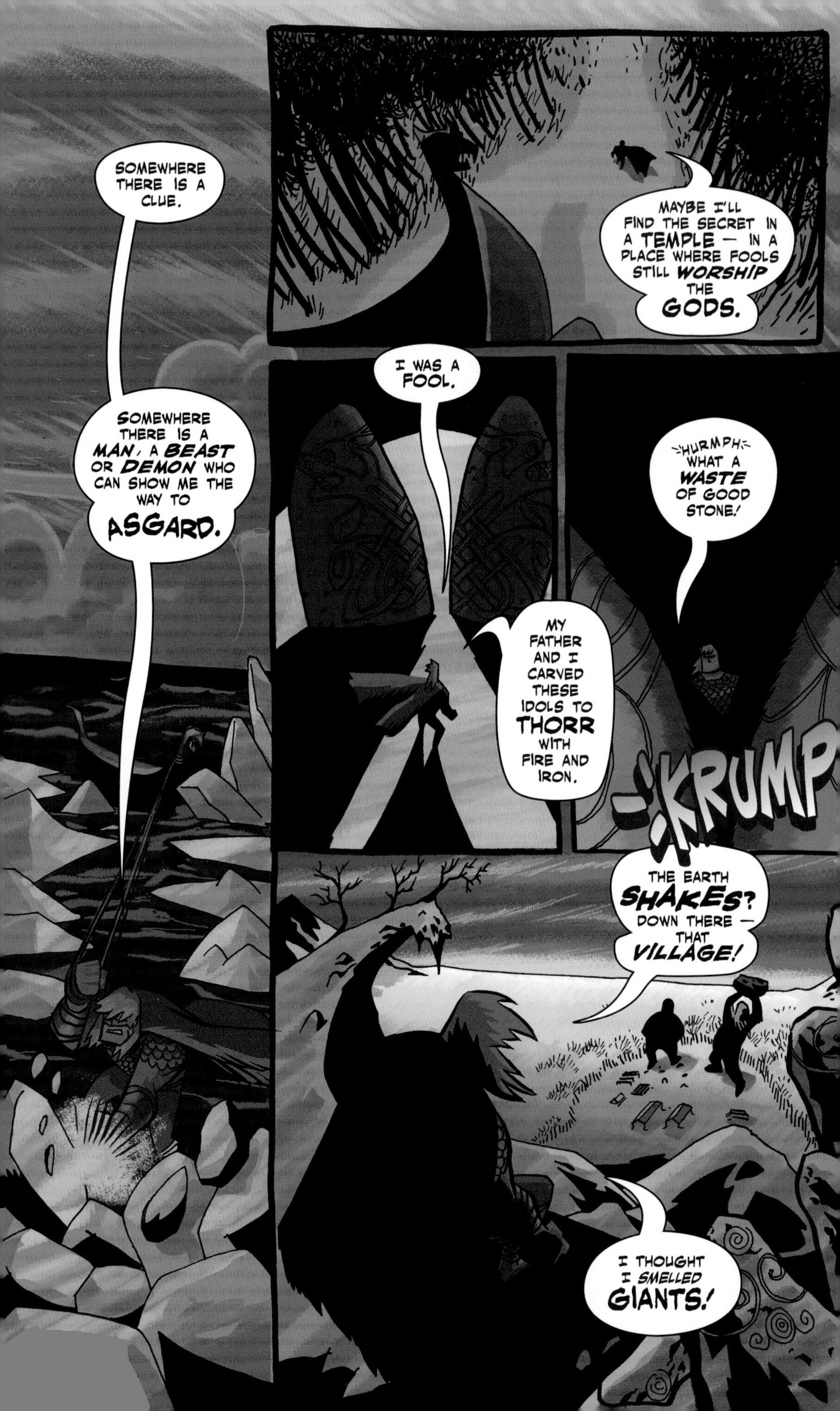

SOMEWHERE THERE IS A CLUE.
SOMEWHERE THERE IS A MAN, A BEAST OR DEMON WHO CAN SHOW ME THE WAY TO ASGARD.
MAYBE I'LL FIND THE SECRET IN A TEMPLE — IN A PLACE WHERE FOOLS STILL WORSHIP THE GODS.
I WAS A FOOL.
MY FATHER AND I CARVED THESE IDOLS TO THORR WITH FIRE AND IRON.
HURMPH WHAT A WASTE OF GOOD STONE!
KRUMP
THE EARTH SHAKES? DOWN THERE — THAT VILLAGE!
I THOUGHT I SMELLED GIANTS!

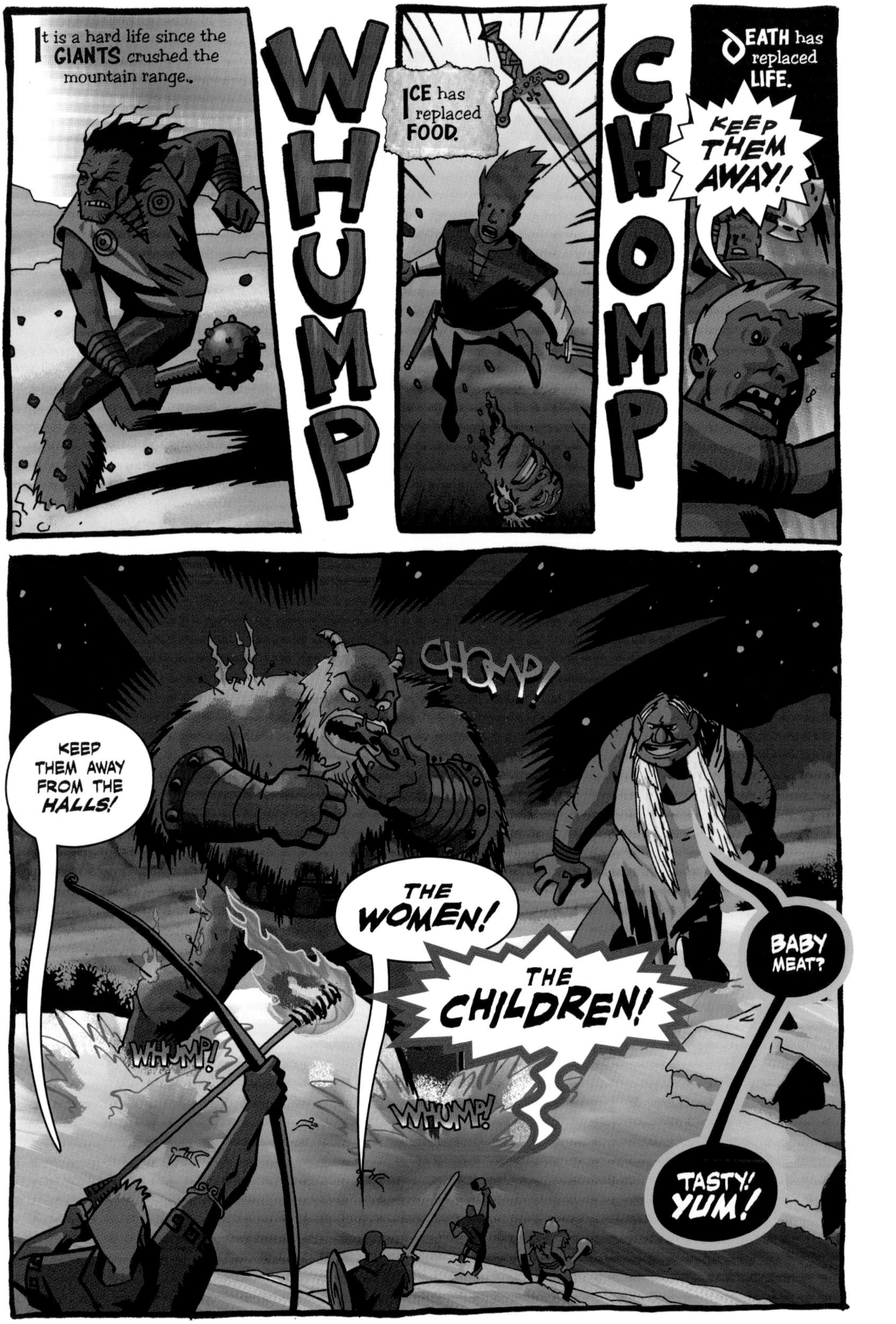

It is a hard life since the GIANTS crushed the mountain range..
WHUMP
ICE has replaced FOOD.
CHOMP
DEATH has replaced LIFE.
KEEP THEM AWAY!
CHOMP!
KEEP THEM AWAY FROM THE HALLS!
THE WOMEN!
THE CHILDREN!
BABY MEAT?
TASTY! YUM!
WHUMP!
WHUMP!

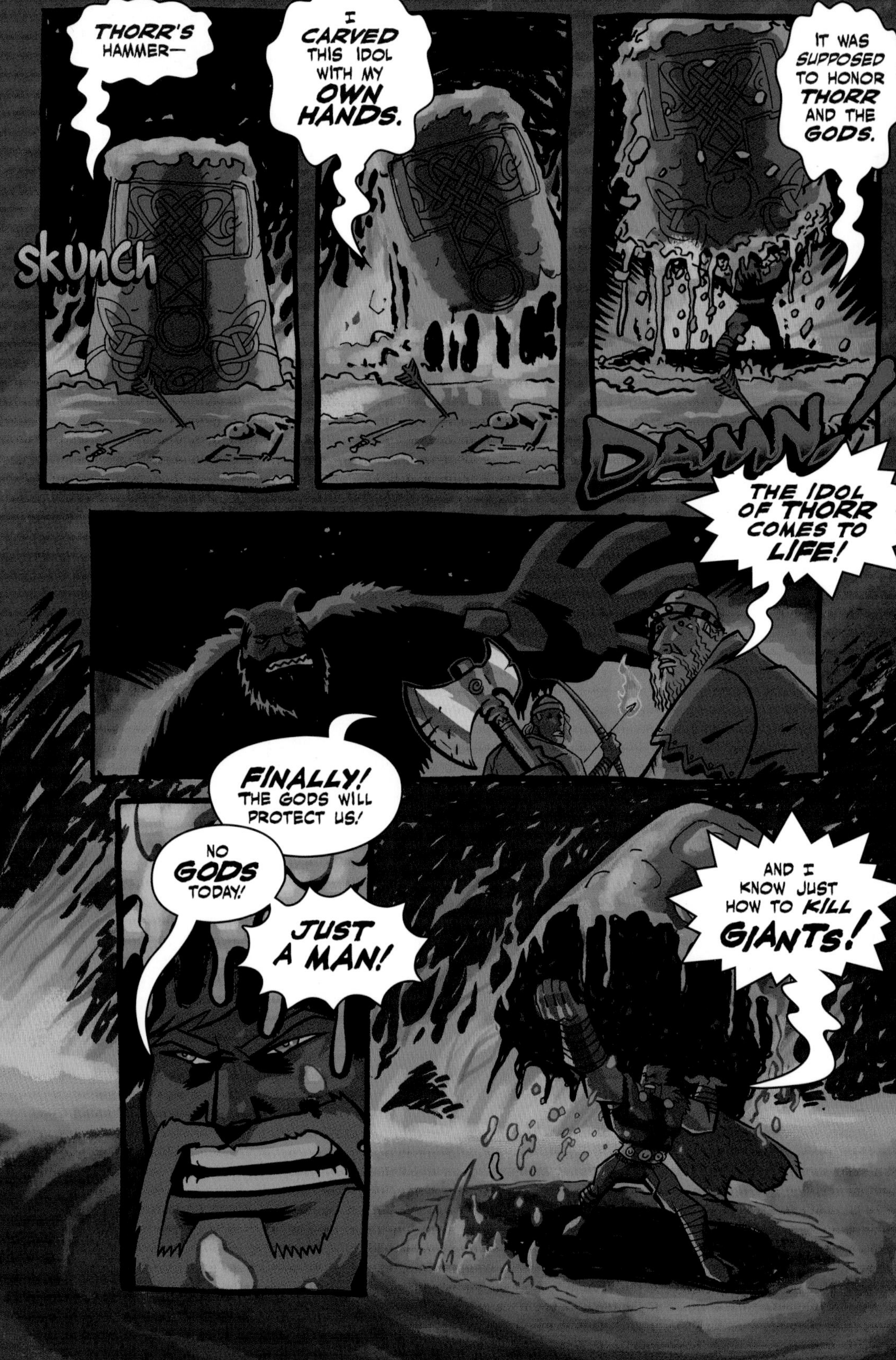
THORR'S HAMMER—
SKUNCH
I CARVED THIS IDOL WITH MY OWN HANDS.
IT WAS SUPPOSED TO HONOR THORR AND THE GODS.
DAMN!
THE IDOL OF THORR COMES TO LIFE!
FINALLY! THE GODS WILL PROTECT US!
NO GODS TODAY!
JUST A MAN!
AND I KNOW JUST HOW TO KILL GIANTS!

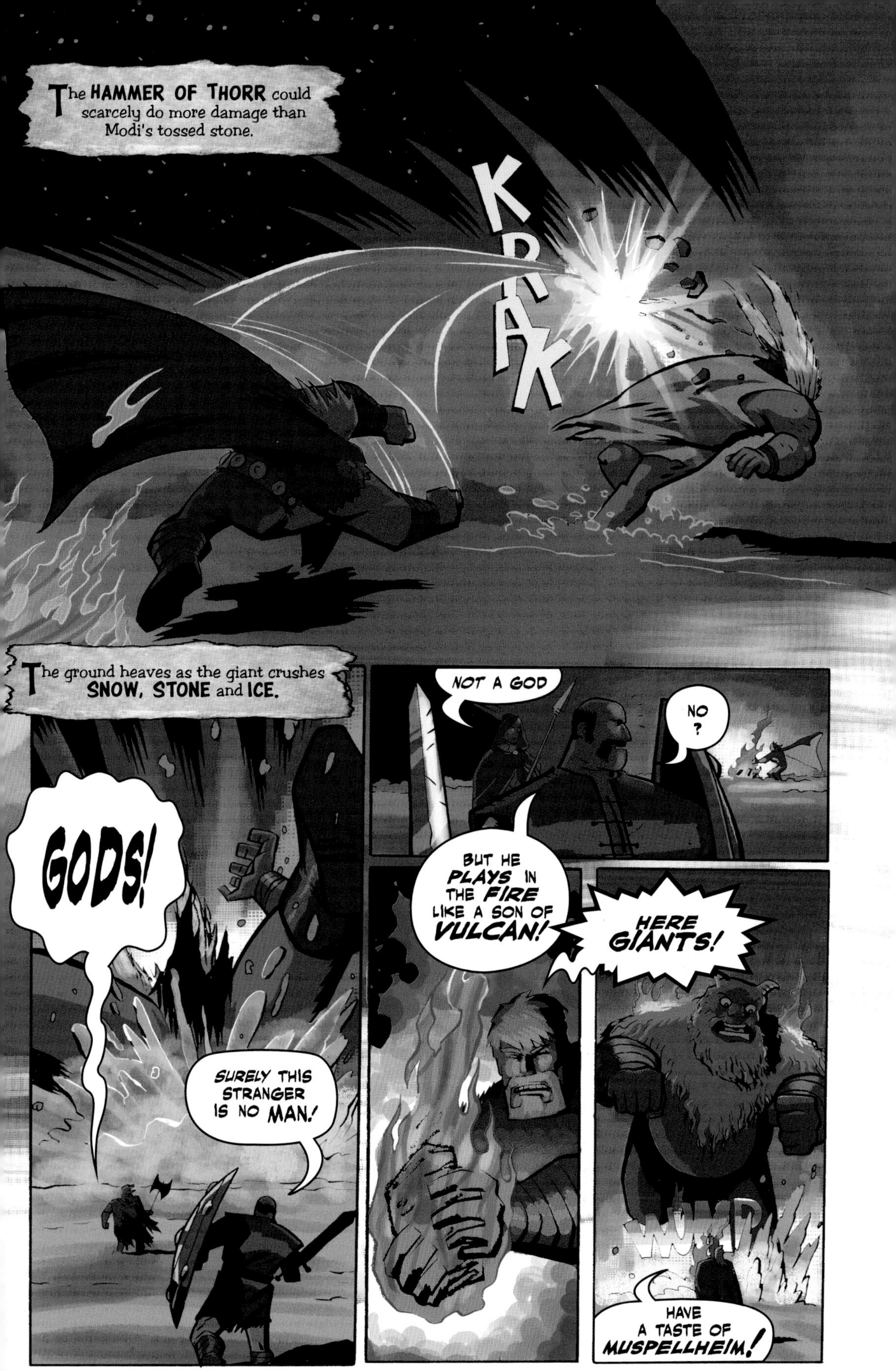
The HAMMER OF THORR could scarcely do more damage than Modi's tossed stone.
KRAK
The ground heaves as the giant crushes SNOW, STONE and ICE.
GODS!
SURELY THIS STRANGER IS NO MAN!
NOT A GOD
NO?
BUT HE PLAYS IN THE FIRE LIKE A SON OF VULCAN!
HERE GIANTS!
HAVE A TASTE OF MUSPELLHEIM!

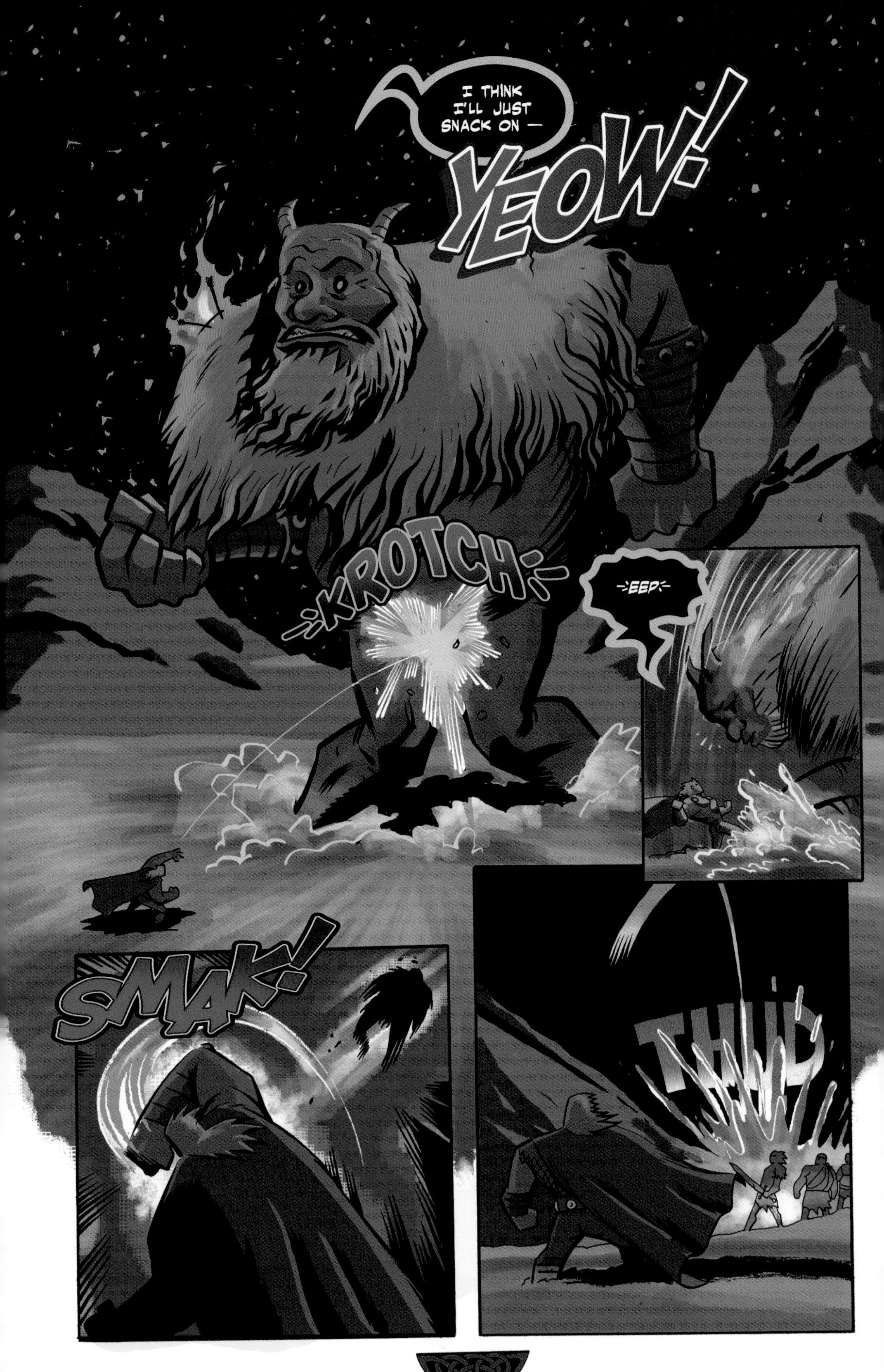

I THINK I'LL JUST SNACK ON —
YEOW!
KROTCH
EEP
SMAK!
THUD

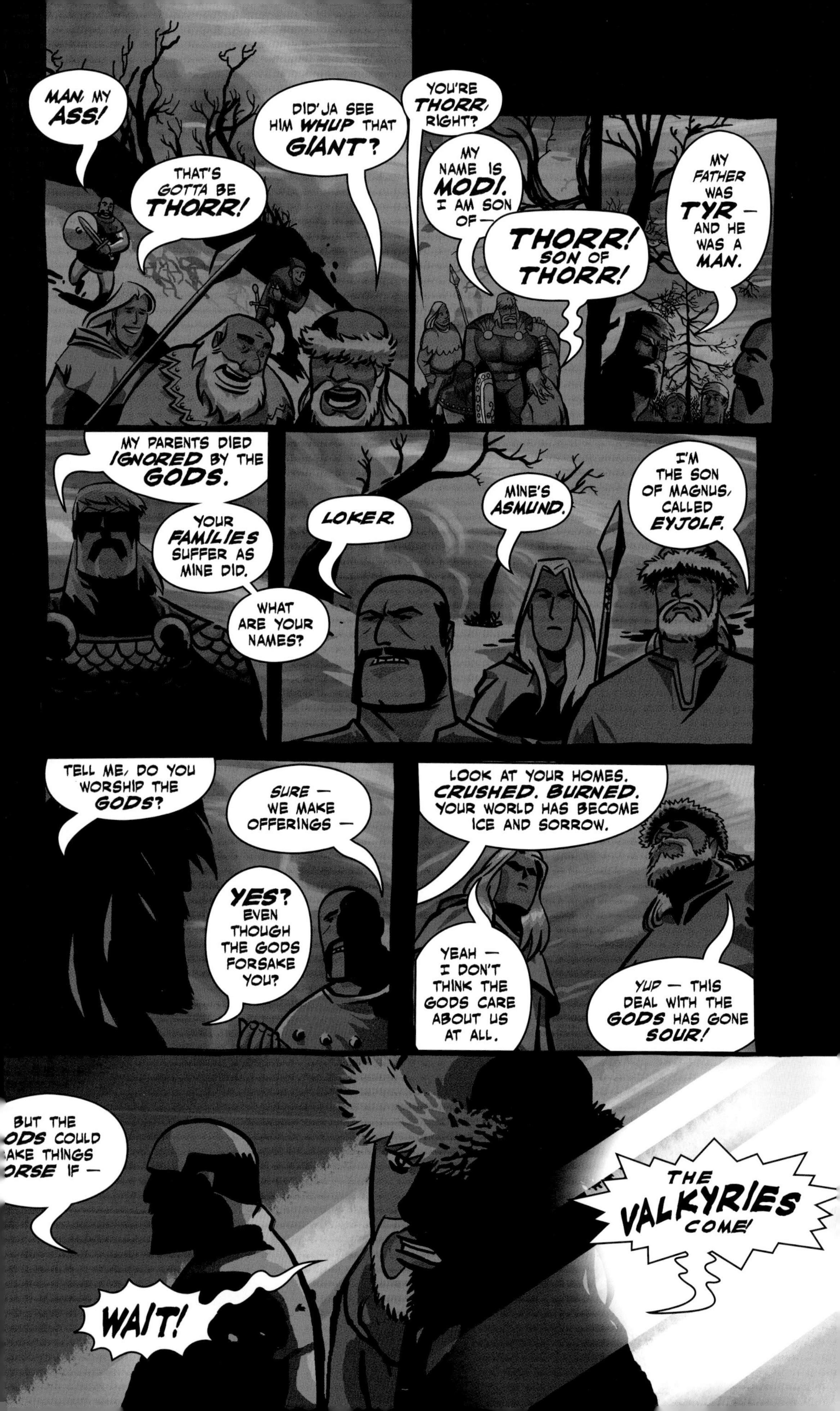
MAN, MY ASS!
THAT'S GOTTA BE THORR!
DID'JA SEE HIM WHUP THAT GIANT?
YOU'RE THORR, RIGHT?
MY NAME IS MODI. I AM SON OF—
THORR! SON OF THORR!
MY FATHER WAS TYR— AND HE WAS A MAN.
MY PARENTS DIED IGNORED BY THE GODS.
YOUR FAMILIES SUFFER AS MINE DID.
WHAT ARE YOUR NAMES?
LOKER.
MINE'S ASMUND.
I'M THE SON OF MAGNUS, CALLED EYJOLF.
TELL ME, DO YOU WORSHIP THE GODS?
SURE — WE MAKE OFFERINGS —
YES? EVEN THOUGH THE GODS FORSAKE YOU?
LOOK AT YOUR HOMES. CRUSHED. BURNED. YOUR WORLD HAS BECOME ICE AND SORROW.
YEAH — I DON'T THINK THE GODS CARE ABOUT US AT ALL.
YUP — THIS DEAL WITH THE GODS HAS GONE SOUR!
BUT THE ODS COULD AKE THINGS ORSE IF —
WAIT!
THE VALKYRIES COME!

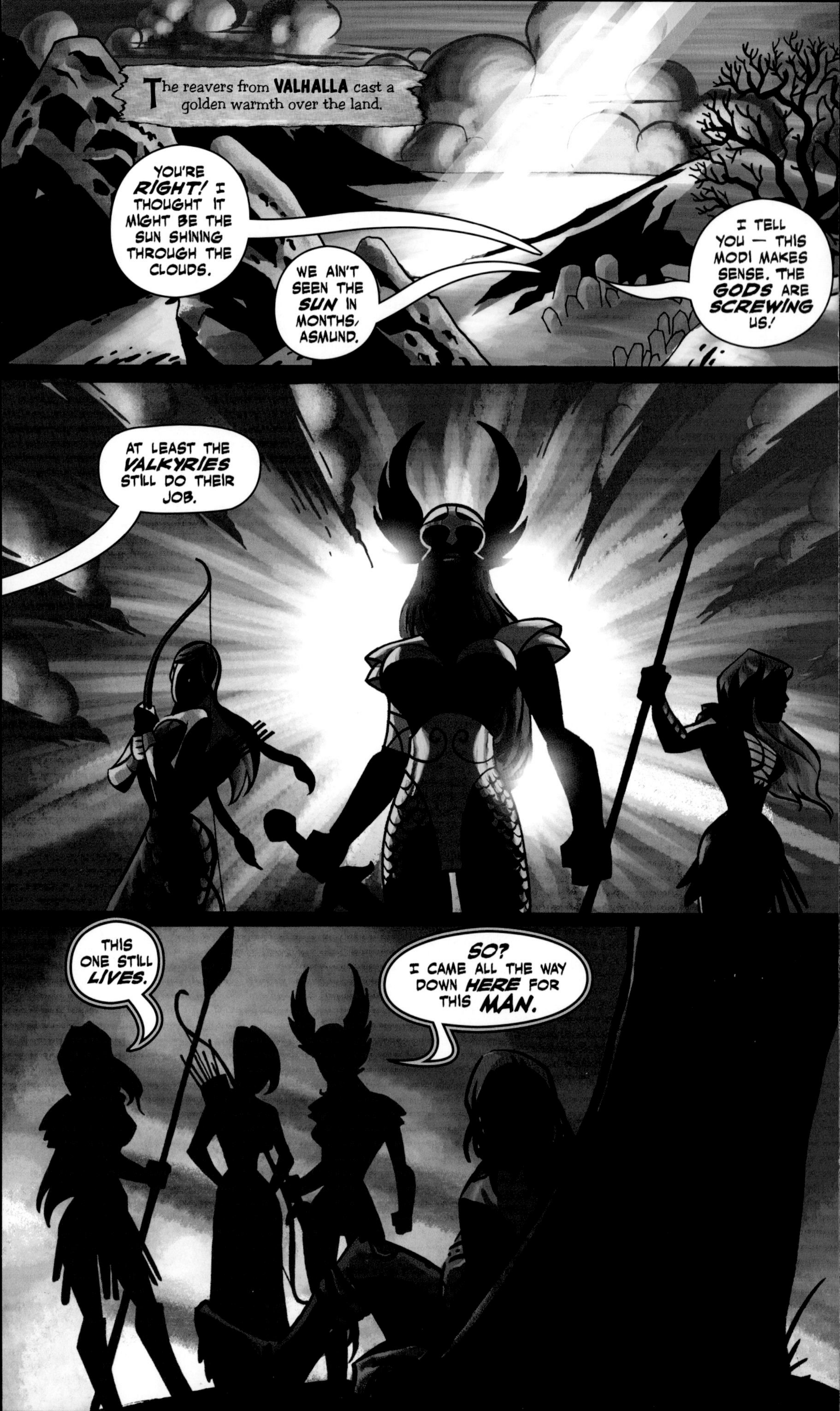
The reavers from VALHALLA cast a golden warmth over the land.
YOU'RE RIGHT! I THOUGHT IT MIGHT BE THE SUN SHINING THROUGH THE CLOUDS.
WE AIN'T SEEN THE SUN IN MONTHS, ASMUND.
I TELL YOU — THIS MODI MAKES SENSE. THE GODS ARE SCREWING US!
AT LEAST THE VALKYRIES STILL DO THEIR JOB.
THIS ONE STILL LIVES.
SO? I CAME ALL THE WAY DOWN HERE FOR THIS MAN.

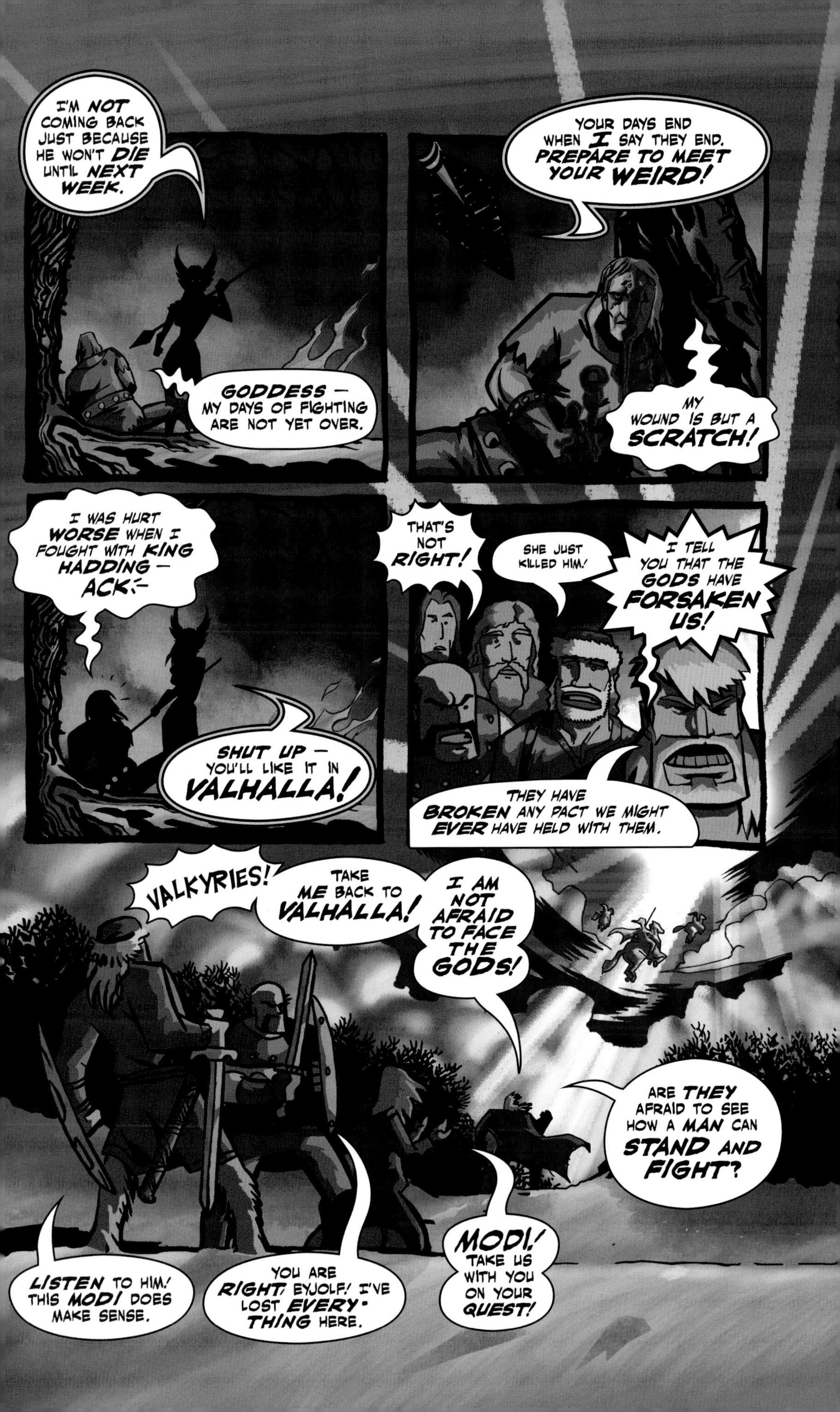
I'M NOT COMING BACK JUST BECAUSE HE WON'T DIE UNTIL NEXT WEEK.
GODDESS — MY DAYS OF FIGHTING ARE NOT YET OVER.
YOUR DAYS END WHEN I SAY THEY END. PREPARE TO MEET YOUR WEIRD!
MY WOUND IS BUT A SCRATCH!
I WAS HURT WORSE WHEN I FOUGHT WITH KING HADDING — ACK!—
SHUT UP — YOU'LL LIKE IT IN VALHALLA!
THAT'S NOT RIGHT!
SHE JUST KILLED HIM!
I TELL YOU THAT THE GODS HAVE FORSAKEN US!
THEY HAVE BROKEN ANY PACT WE MIGHT EVER HAVE HELD WITH THEM.
VALKYRIES!
TAKE ME BACK TO VALHALLA!
I AM NOT AFRAID TO FACE THE GODS!
ARE THEY AFRAID TO SEE HOW A MAN CAN STAND AND FIGHT?
LISTEN TO HIM! THIS MODI DOES MAKE SENSE.
YOU ARE RIGHT, EYJOLF! I'VE LOST EVERY-THING HERE.
MODI! TAKE US WITH YOU ON YOUR QUEST!

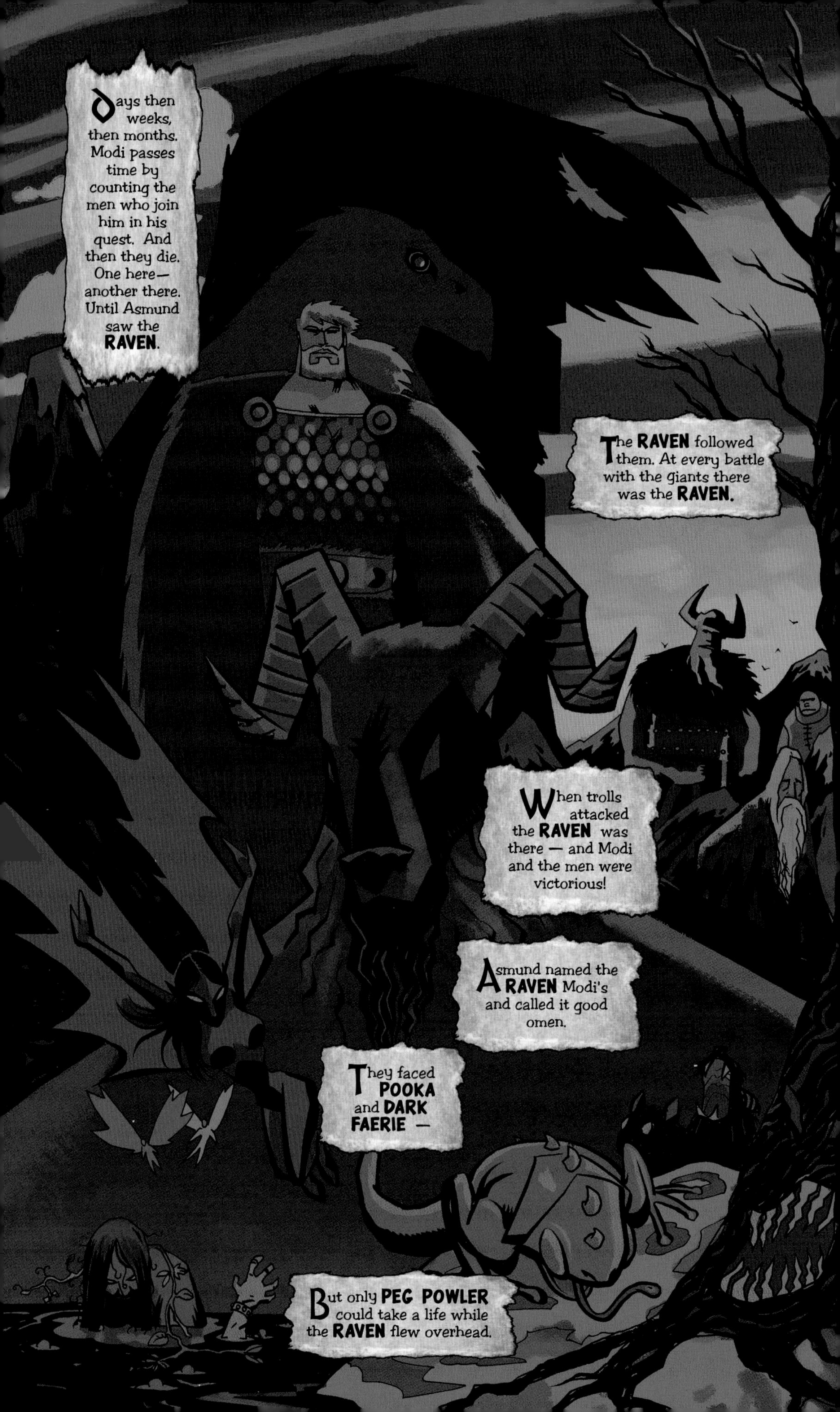

Days then weeks, then months. Modi passes time by counting the men who join him in his quest. And then they die. One here— another there. Until Asmund saw the RAVEN.
The RAVEN followed them. At every battle with the giants there was the RAVEN.
When trolls attacked the RAVEN was there — and Modi and the men were victorious!
Asmund named the RAVEN Modi's and called it good omen.
They faced POOKA and DARK FAERIE —
But only PEG POWLER could take a life while the RAVEN flew overhead.

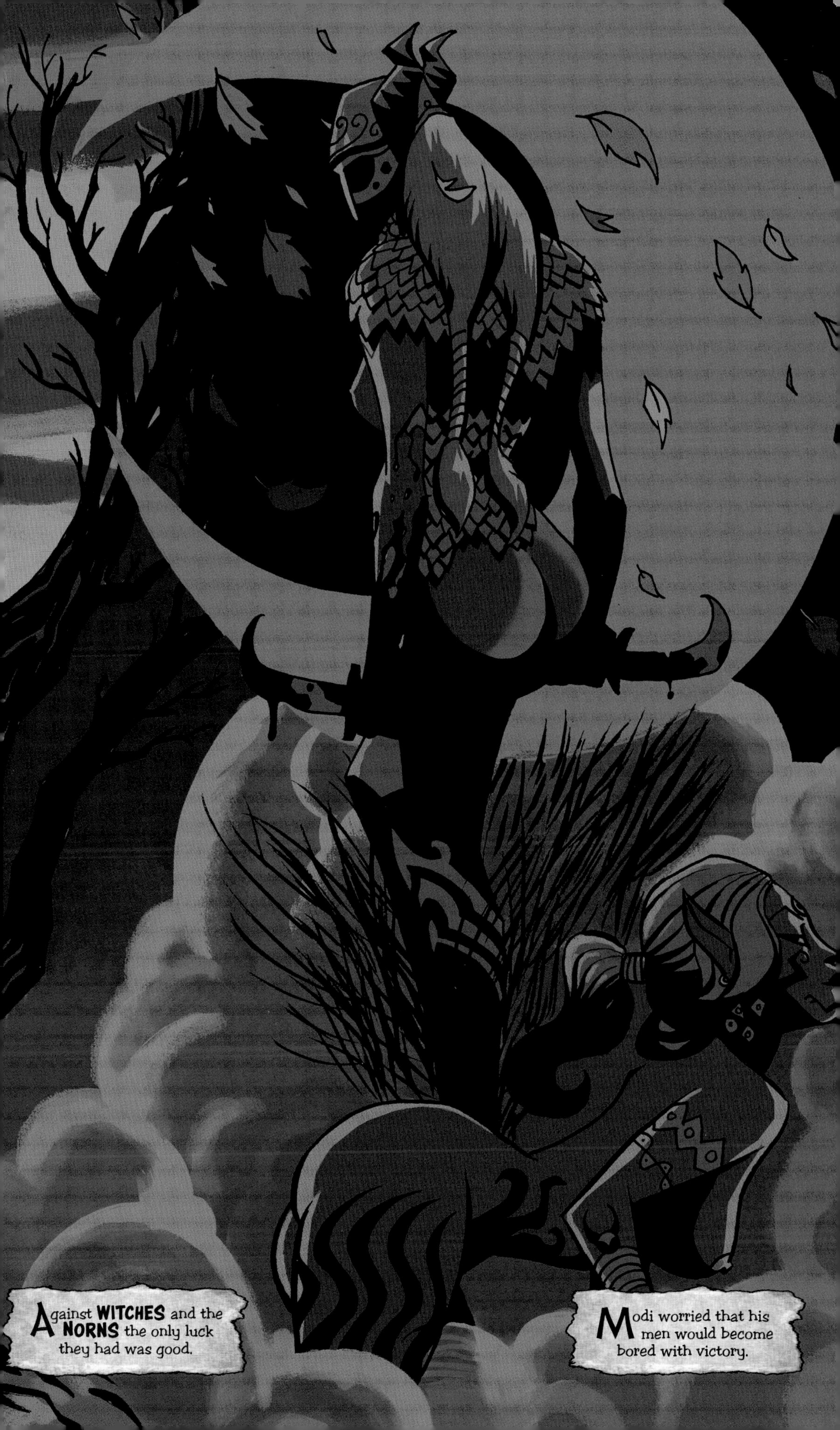
Against **WITCHES** and the **NORNS** the only luck they had was good.
Modi worried that his men would become bored with victory.

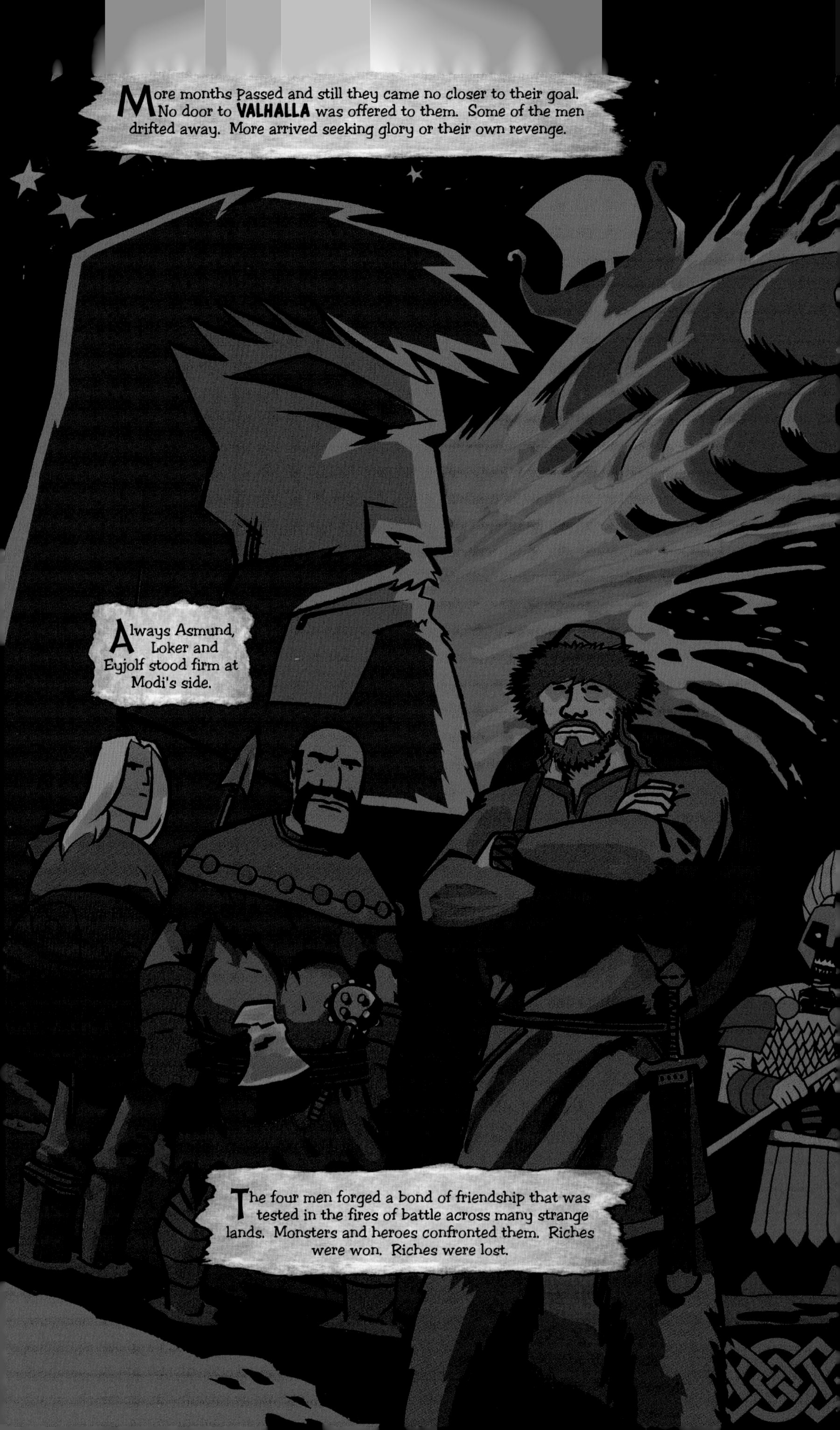
More months passed and still they came no closer to their goal. No door to VALHALLA was offered to them. Some of the men drifted away. More arrived seeking glory or their own revenge.
Always Asmund, Loker and Eyjolf stood firm at Modi's side.
The four men forged a bond of friendship that was tested in the fires of battle across many strange lands. Monsters and heroes confronted them. Riches were won. Riches were lost.

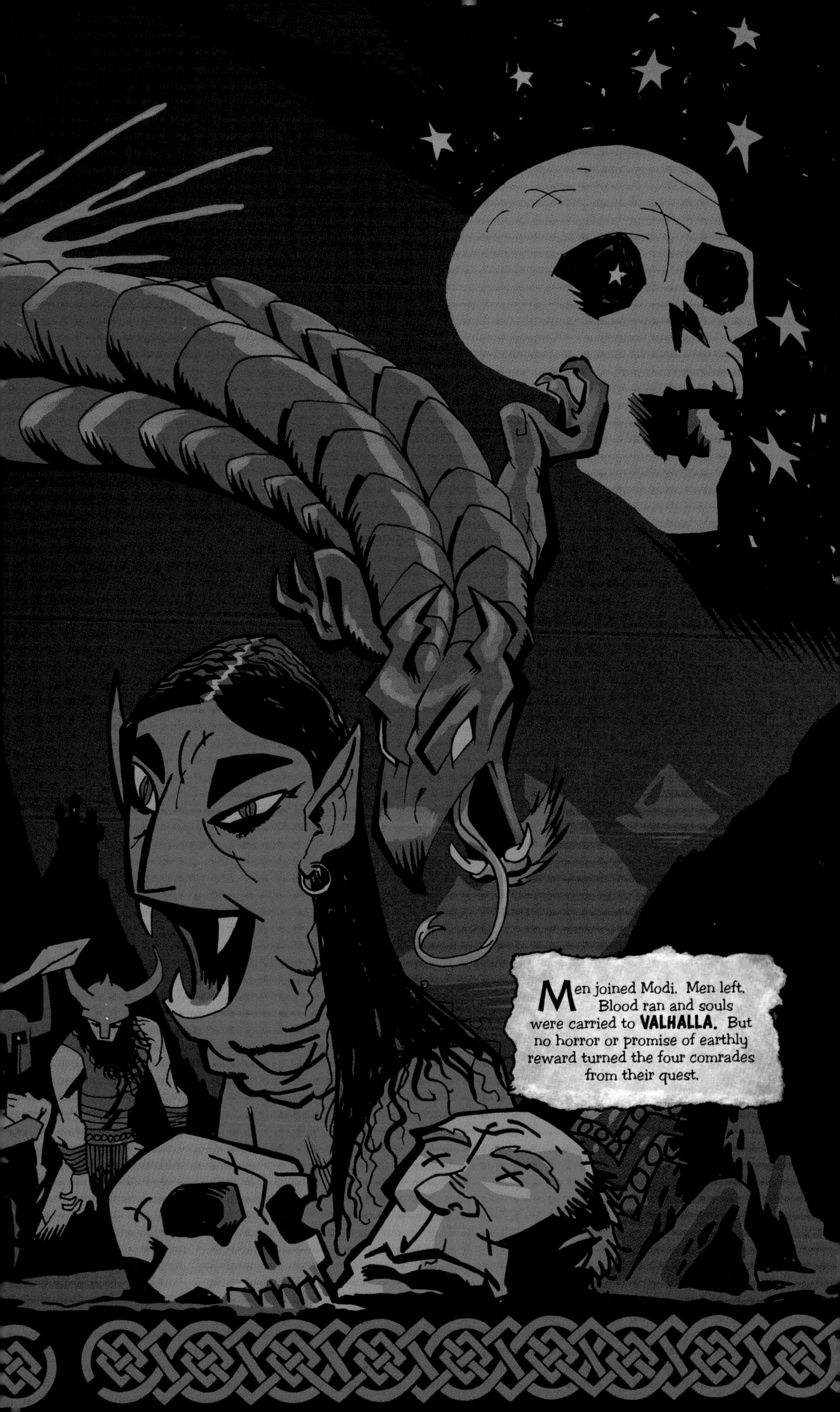
Men joined Modi. Men left. Blood ran and souls were carried to VALHALLA. But no horror or promise of earthly reward turned the four comrades from their quest.

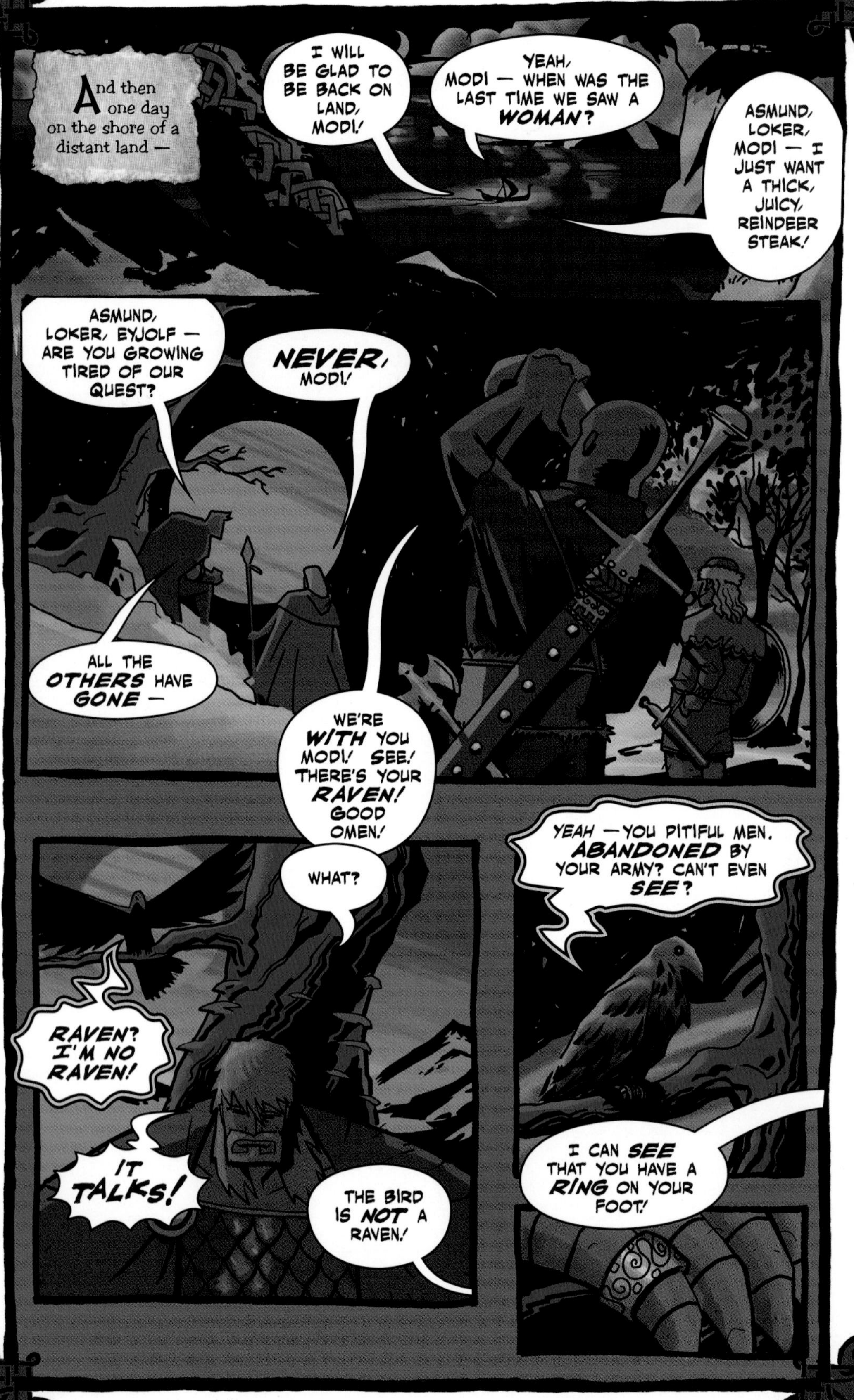
And then one day on the shore of a distant land —
I WILL BE GLAD TO BE BACK ON LAND, MODI!
YEAH, MODI — WHEN WAS THE LAST TIME WE SAW A WOMAN?
ASMUND, LOKER, MODI — I JUST WANT A THICK, JUICY, REINDEER STEAK!
ASMUND, LOKER, EYJOLF — ARE YOU GROWING TIRED OF OUR QUEST?
ALL THE OTHERS HAVE GONE —
NEVER, MODI!
WE'RE WITH YOU MODI! SEE! THERE'S YOUR RAVEN! GOOD OMEN!
RAVEN? I'M NO RAVEN!
WHAT?
IT TALKS!
THE BIRD IS NOT A RAVEN!
YEAH — YOU PITIFUL MEN. ABANDONED BY YOUR ARMY? CAN'T EVEN SEE?
I CAN SEE THAT YOU HAVE A RING ON YOUR FOOT!

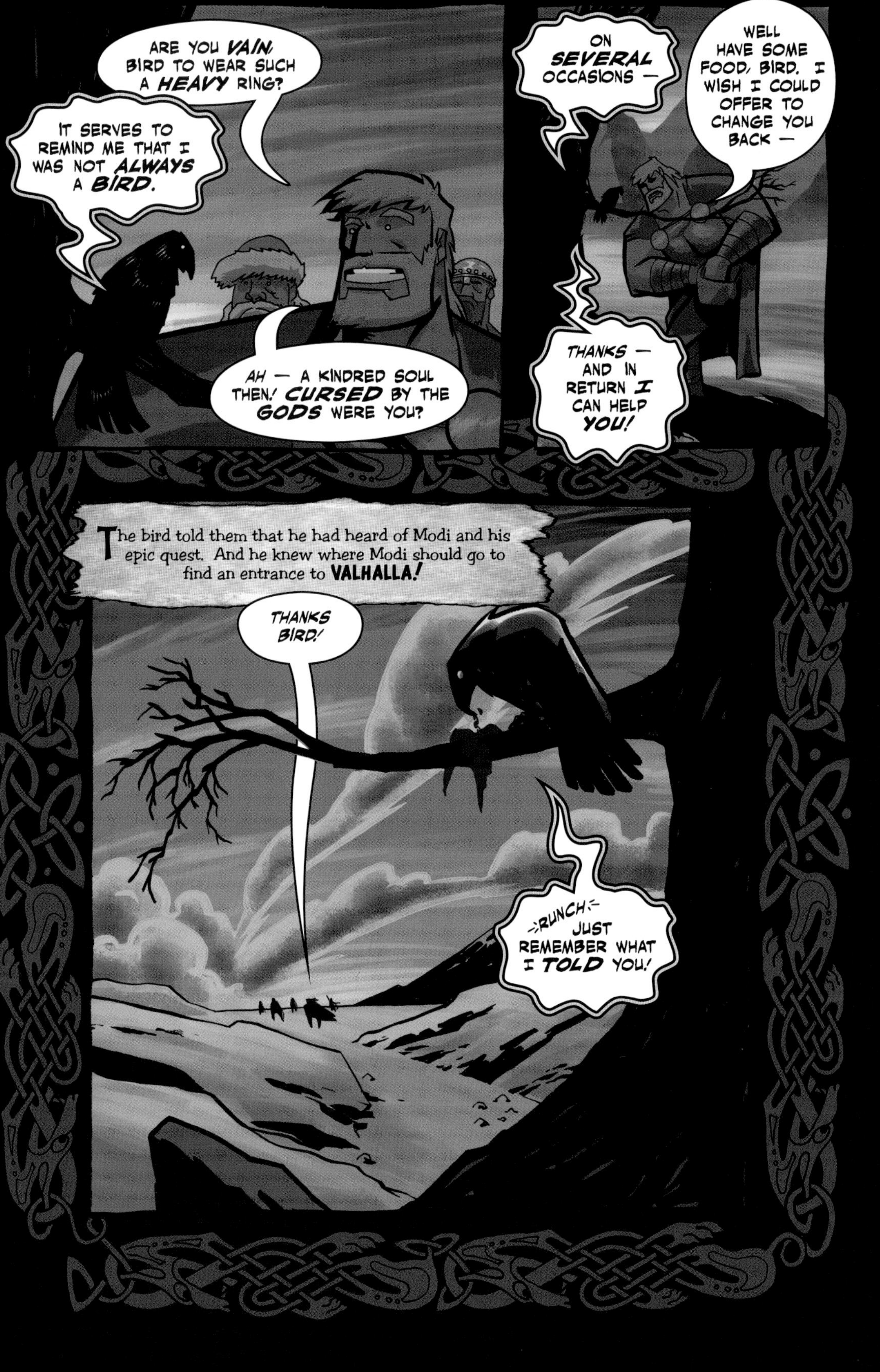
ARE YOU VAIN, BIRD TO WEAR SUCH A HEAVY RING?
IT SERVES TO REMIND ME THAT I WAS NOT ALWAYS A BIRD.
AH — A KINDRED SOUL THEN! CURSED BY THE GODS WERE YOU?
ON SEVERAL OCCASIONS —
WELL HAVE SOME FOOD, BIRD. I WISH I COULD OFFER TO CHANGE YOU BACK —
THANKS — AND IN RETURN I CAN HELP YOU!
The bird told them that he had heard of Modi and his epic quest. And he knew where Modi should go to find an entrance to VALHALLA!
THANKS BIRD!
RUNCH JUST REMEMBER WHAT I TOLD YOU!

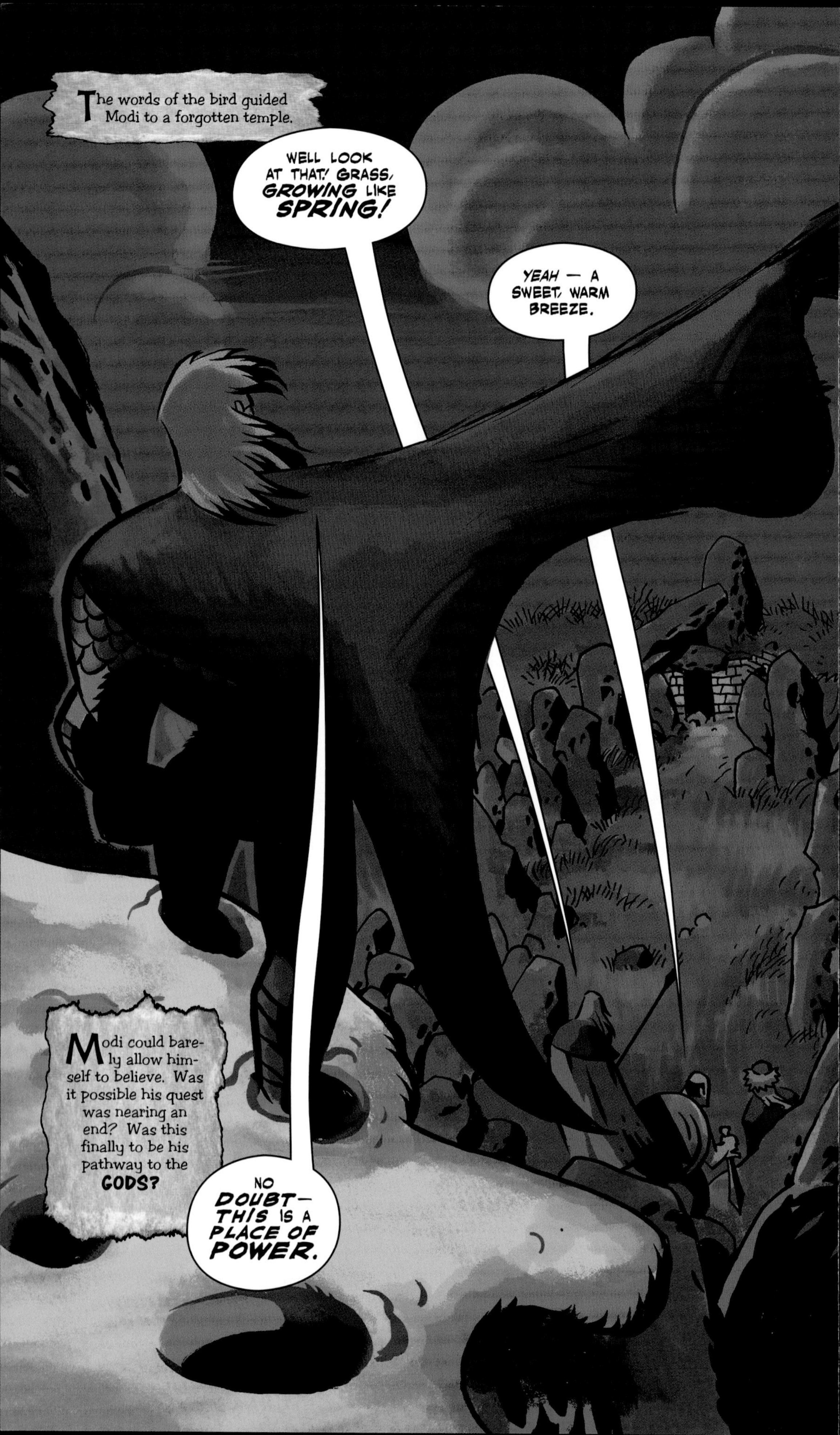
The words of the bird guided Modi to a forgotten temple.
WELL LOOK AT THAT! GRASS, GROWING LIKE SPRING!
YEAH — A SWEET, WARM BREEZE.
Modi could barely allow himself to believe. Was it possible his quest was nearing an end? Was this finally to be his pathway to the GODS?
NO DOUBT— THIS IS A PLACE OF POWER.

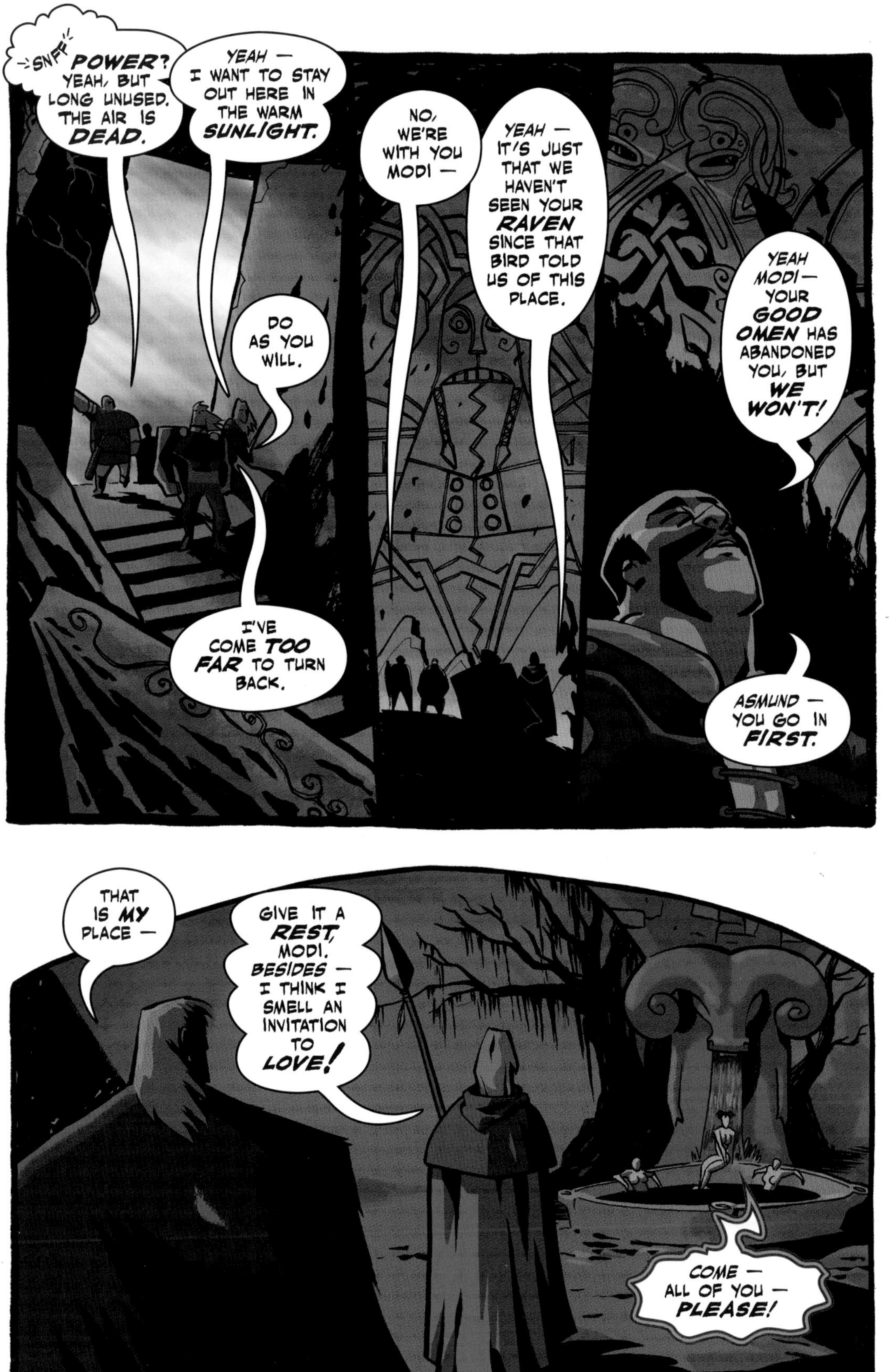

SNFF! POWER? YEAH, BUT LONG UNUSED. THE AIR IS DEAD.
YEAH — I WANT TO STAY OUT HERE IN THE WARM SUNLIGHT.
DO AS YOU WILL.
I'VE COME TOO FAR TO TURN BACK.
NO, WE'RE WITH YOU MODI —
YEAH — IT'S JUST THAT WE HAVEN'T SEEN YOUR RAVEN SINCE THAT BIRD TOLD US OF THIS PLACE.
YEAH MODI — YOUR GOOD OMEN HAS ABANDONED YOU, BUT WE WON'T!
ASMUND — YOU GO IN FIRST.
THAT IS MY PLACE —
GIVE IT A REST, MODI. BESIDES — I THINK I SMELL AN INVITATION TO LOVE!
COME — ALL OF YOU — PLEASE!

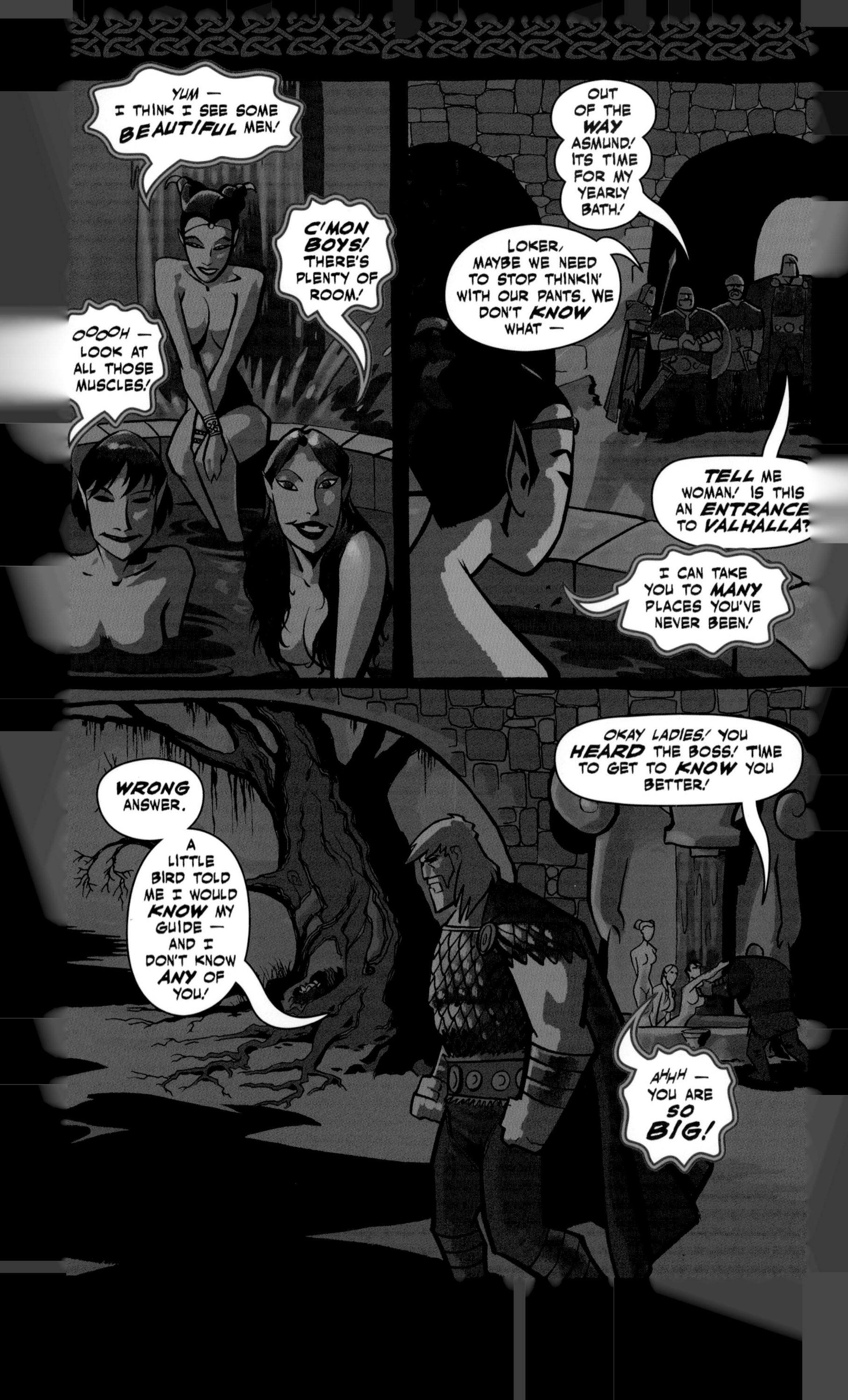
YUM — I THINK I SEE SOME BEAUTIFUL MEN!
C'MON BOYS! THERE'S PLENTY OF ROOM!
OOOOH — LOOK AT ALL THOSE MUSCLES!
OUT OF THE WAY ASMUND! ITS TIME FOR MY YEARLY BATH!
LOKER, MAYBE WE NEED TO STOP THINKIN' WITH OUR PANTS. WE DON'T KNOW WHAT —
TELL ME WOMAN! IS THIS AN ENTRANCE TO VALHALLA?
I CAN TAKE YOU TO MANY PLACES YOU'VE NEVER BEEN!
WRONG ANSWER.
A LITTLE BIRD TOLD ME I WOULD KNOW MY GUIDE — AND I DON'T KNOW ANY OF YOU!
OKAY LADIES! YOU HEARD THE BOSS! TIME TO GET TO KNOW YOU BETTER!
AHHH — YOU ARE SO BIG!

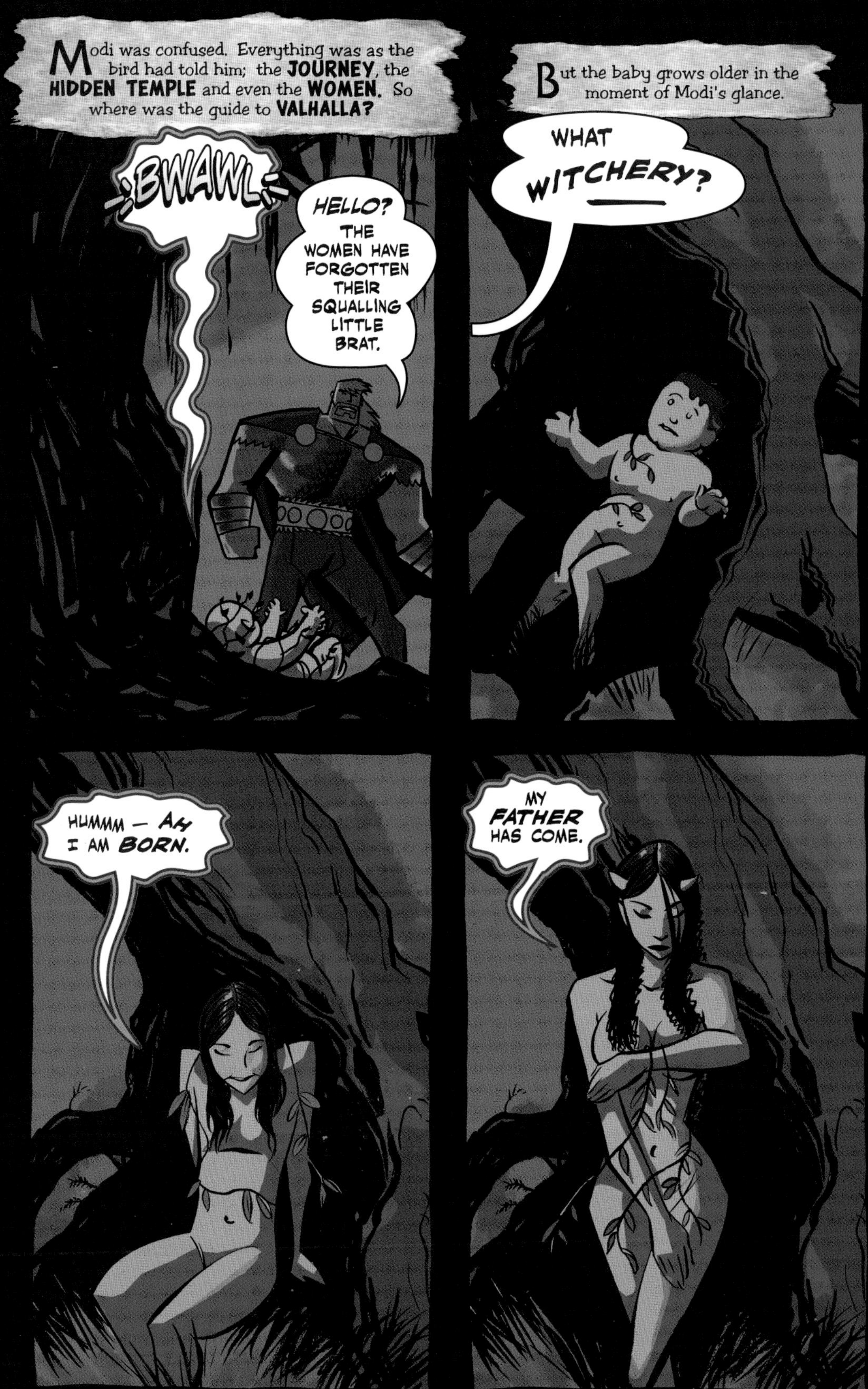

Modi was confused. Everything was as the bird had told him; the **JOURNEY**, the **HIDDEN TEMPLE** and even the **WOMEN.** So where was the guide to **VALHALLA?**
BWAWL
HELLO? THE WOMEN HAVE FORGOTTEN THEIR SQUALLING LITTLE BRAT.
But the baby grows older in the moment of Modi's glance.
WHAT WITCHERY?
HUMMM — AH I AM BORN.
MY FATHER HAS COME.

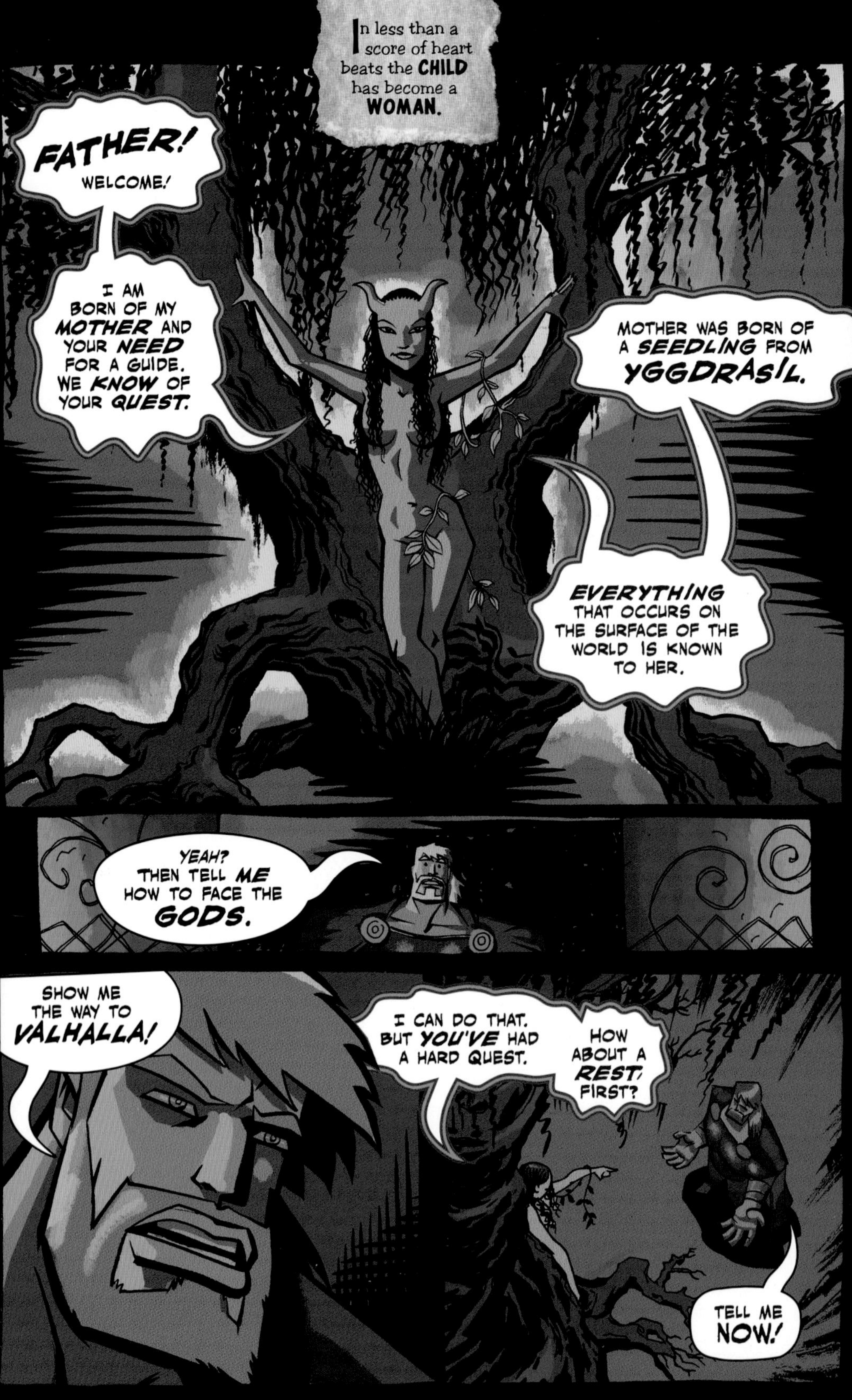In less than a score of heart beats the CHILD has become a WOMAN.
FATHER! WELCOME!
I AM BORN OF MY MOTHER AND YOUR NEED FOR A GUIDE. WE KNOW OF YOUR QUEST.
MOTHER WAS BORN OF A SEEDLING FROM YGGDRASIL.
EVERYTHING THAT OCCURS ON THE SURFACE OF THE WORLD IS KNOWN TO HER.
YEAH? THEN TELL ME HOW TO FACE THE GODS.
SHOW ME THE WAY TO VALHALLA!
I CAN DO THAT. BUT YOU'VE HAD A HARD QUEST.
HOW ABOUT A REST, FIRST?
TELL ME NOW!

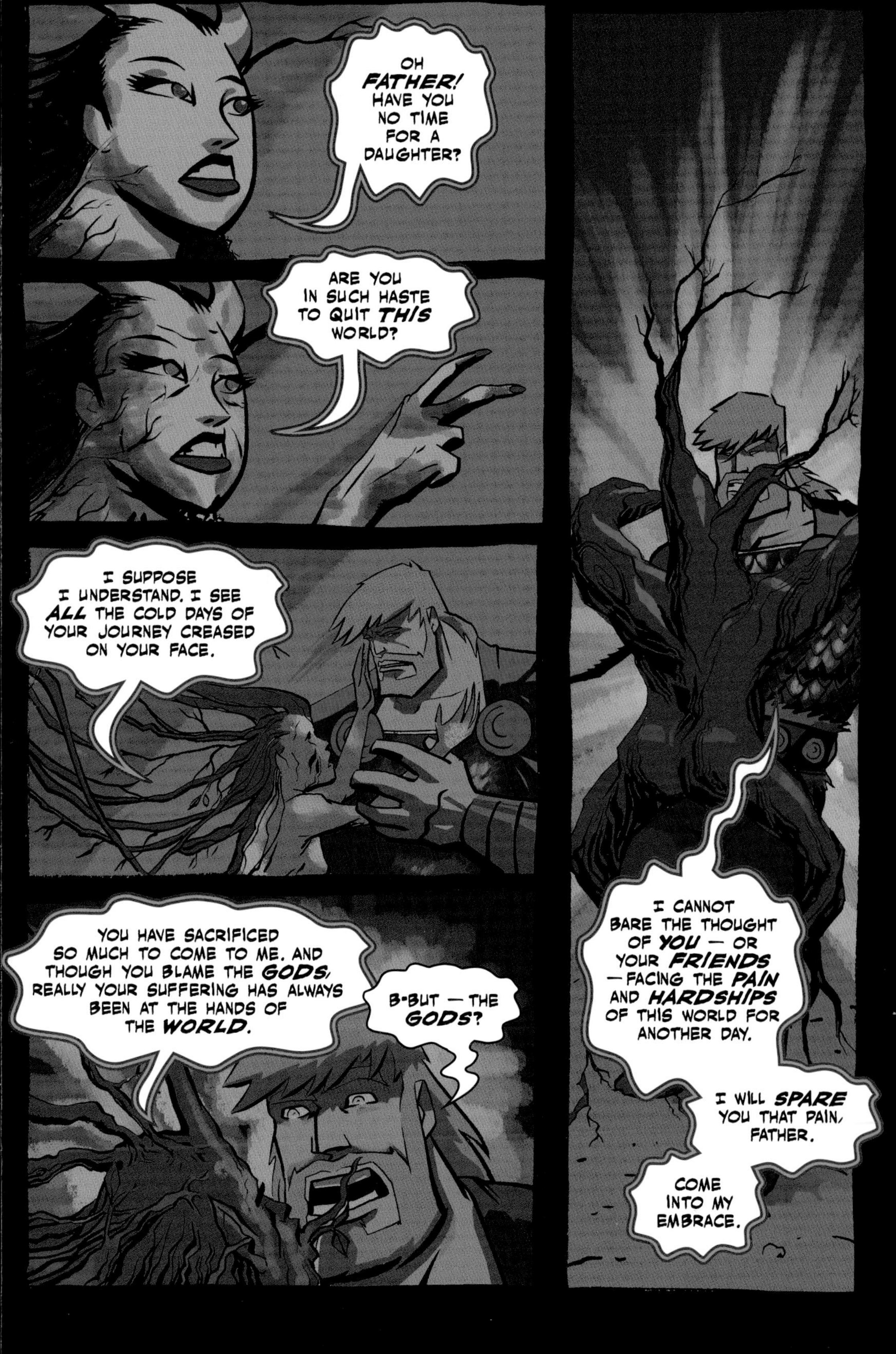
OH *FATHER!* HAVE YOU NO TIME FOR A DAUGHTER?
ARE YOU IN SUCH HASTE TO QUIT *THIS* WORLD?
I SUPPOSE I UNDERSTAND. I SEE *ALL* THE COLD DAYS OF YOUR JOURNEY CREASED ON YOUR FACE.
YOU HAVE SACRIFICED SO MUCH TO COME TO ME. AND THOUGH YOU BLAME THE *GODS*, REALLY YOUR SUFFERING HAS ALWAYS BEEN AT THE HANDS OF THE *WORLD*.
B-BUT — THE *GODS*?
I CANNOT BARE THE THOUGHT OF *YOU* — OR YOUR *FRIENDS* — FACING THE *PAIN* AND *HARDSHIPS* OF THIS WORLD FOR ANOTHER DAY.
I WILL *SPARE* YOU THAT PAIN, FATHER.
COME INTO MY EMBRACE.

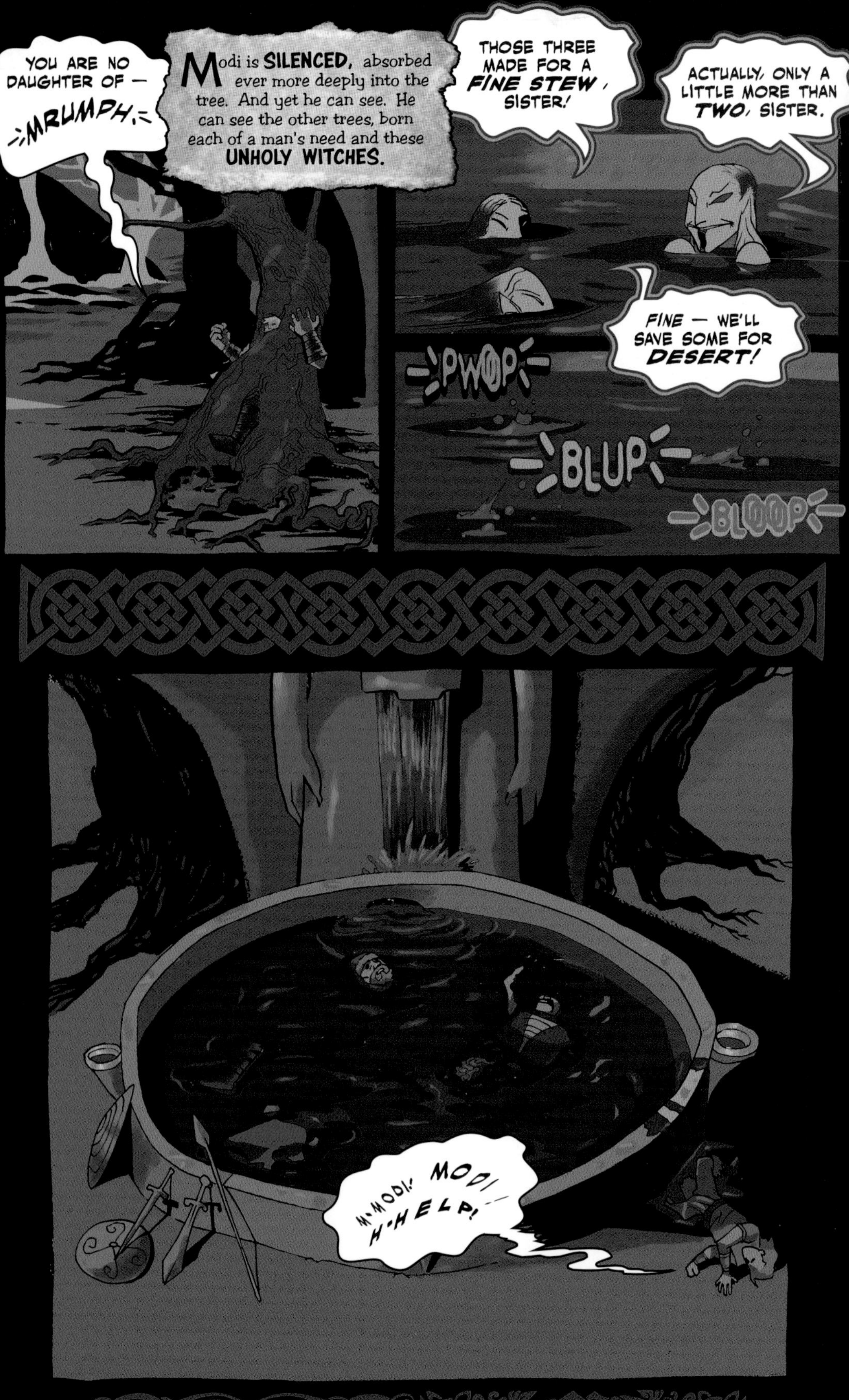
YOU ARE NO DAUGHTER OF —
MRUMPH
Modi is SILENCED, absorbed ever more deeply into the tree. And yet he can see. He can see the other trees, born each of a man's need and these UNHOLY WITCHES.
THOSE THREE MADE FOR A FINE STEW, SISTER!
ACTUALLY, ONLY A LITTLE MORE THAN TWO, SISTER.
FINE — WE'LL SAVE SOME FOR DESERT!
PWOOP
BLUP
BLOOP
M-MODI! MODI! H-HELP!

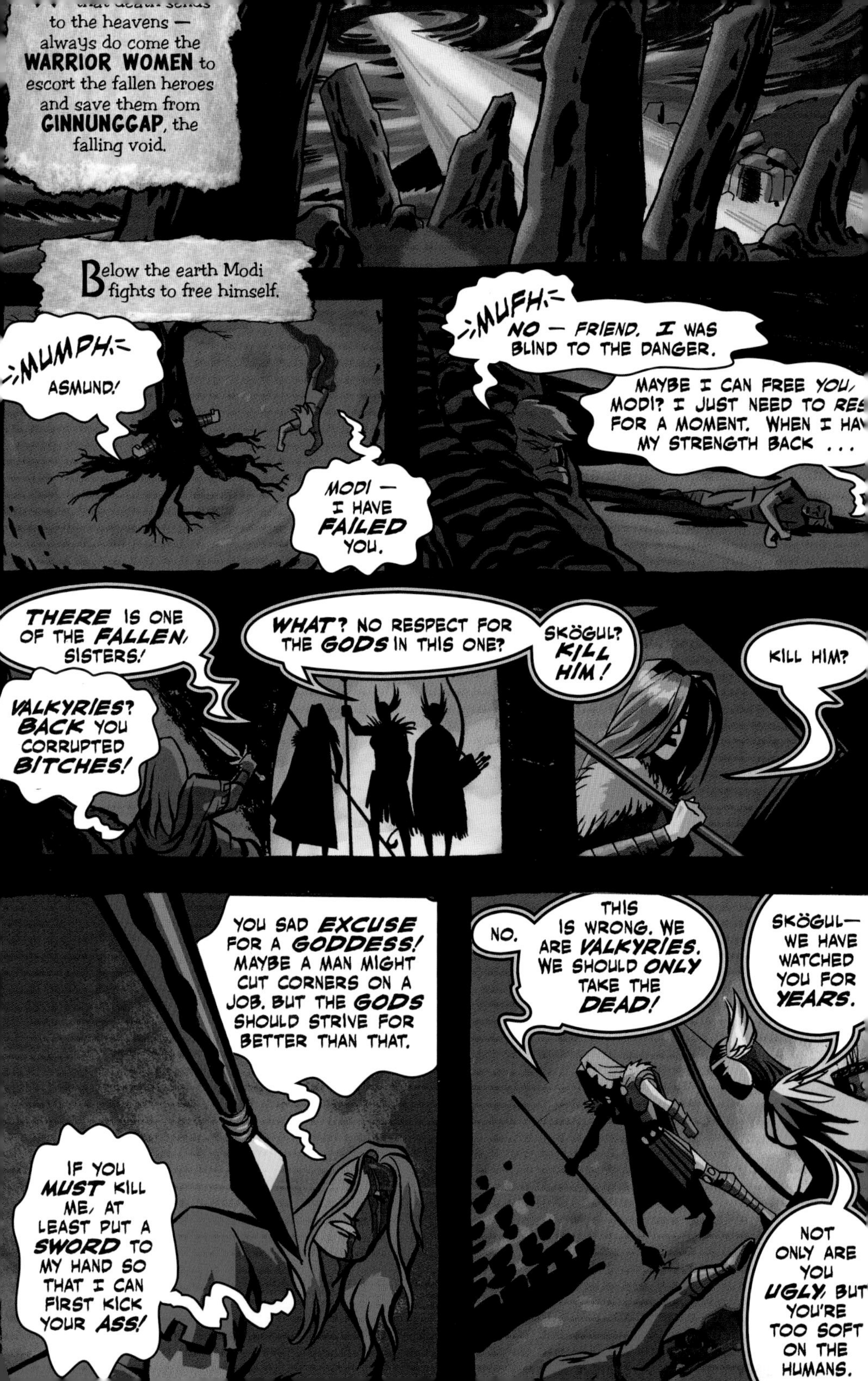
to the heavens — always do come the WARRIOR WOMEN to escort the fallen heroes and save them from GINNUNGGAP, the falling void.
Below the earth Modi fights to free himself.
MUMPH
ASMUND!
MODI — I HAVE FAILED YOU.
MUFH
NO — FRIEND. I WAS BLIND TO THE DANGER.
MAYBE I CAN FREE YOU, MODI? I JUST NEED TO RES
FOR A MOMENT. WHEN I HAV
MY STRENGTH BACK . . .
THERE IS ONE OF THE FALLEN, SISTERS!
VALKYRIES? BACK YOU CORRUPTED BITCHES!
WHAT? NO RESPECT FOR THE GODS IN THIS ONE?
SKÖGUL? KILL HIM!
KILL HIM?
YOU SAD EXCUSE FOR A GODDESS! MAYBE A MAN MIGHT CUT CORNERS ON A JOB. BUT THE GODS SHOULD STRIVE FOR BETTER THAN THAT.
IF YOU MUST KILL ME, AT LEAST PUT A SWORD TO MY HAND SO THAT I CAN FIRST KICK YOUR ASS!
NO.
THIS IS WRONG. WE ARE VALKYRIES. WE SHOULD ONLY TAKE THE DEAD!
SKÖGUL— WE HAVE WATCHED YOU FOR YEARS.
NOT ONLY ARE YOU UGLY, BUT YOU'RE TOO SOFT ON THE HUMANS.

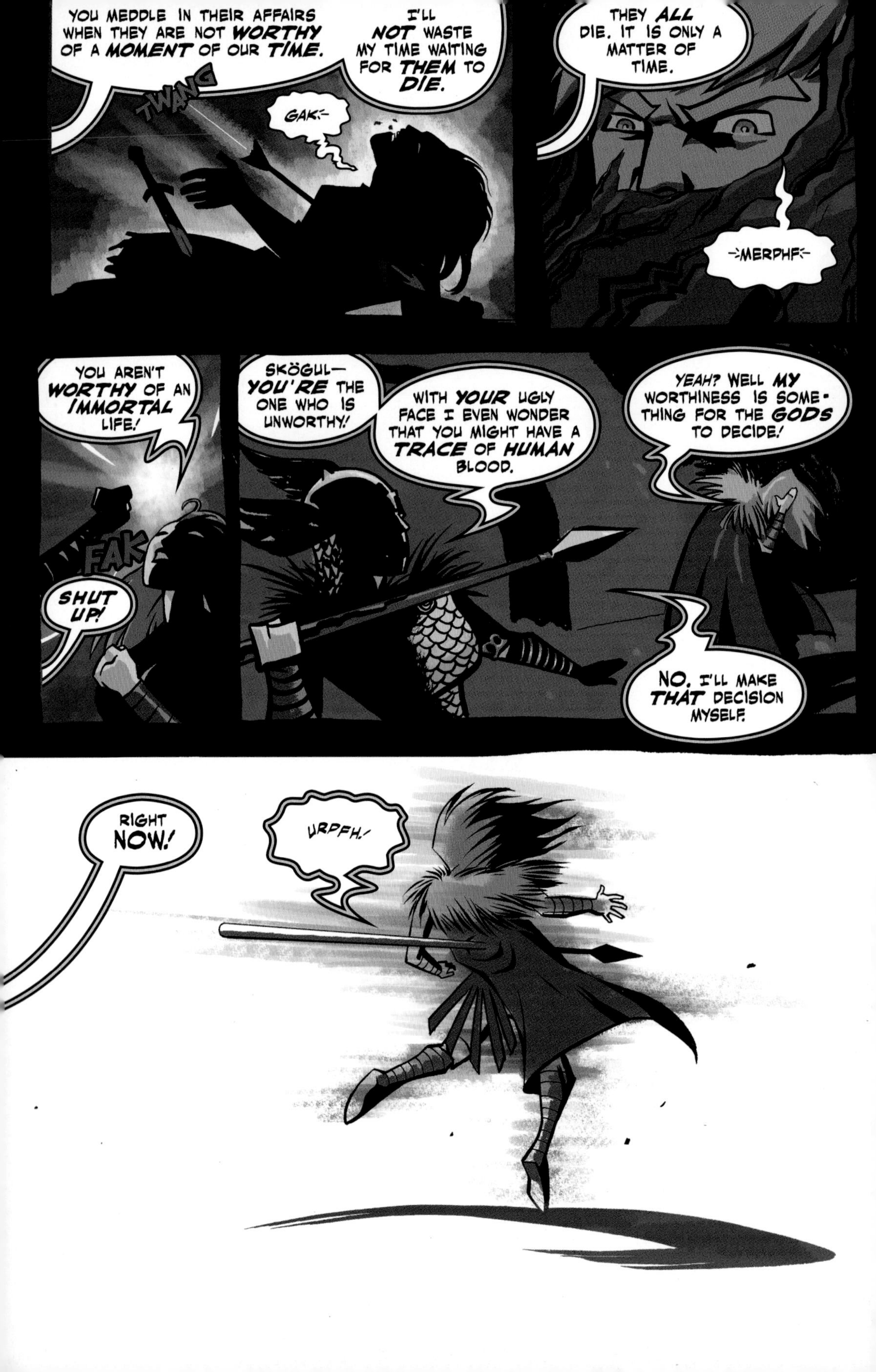
YOU MEDDLE IN THEIR AFFAIRS WHEN THEY ARE NOT WORTHY OF A MOMENT OF OUR TIME.
I'LL NOT WASTE MY TIME WAITING FOR THEM TO DIE.
TWANG
GAK-
THEY ALL DIE. IT IS ONLY A MATTER OF TIME.
-MERPHF-
YOU AREN'T WORTHY OF AN IMMORTAL LIFE!
FAK
SHUT UP!
SKÖGUL— YOU'RE THE ONE WHO IS UNWORTHY!
WITH YOUR UGLY FACE I EVEN WONDER THAT YOU MIGHT HAVE A TRACE OF HUMAN BLOOD.
YEAH? WELL MY WORTHINESS IS SOMETHING FOR THE GODS TO DECIDE!
NO. I'LL MAKE THAT DECISION MYSELF.
RIGHT NOW!
URPFH!

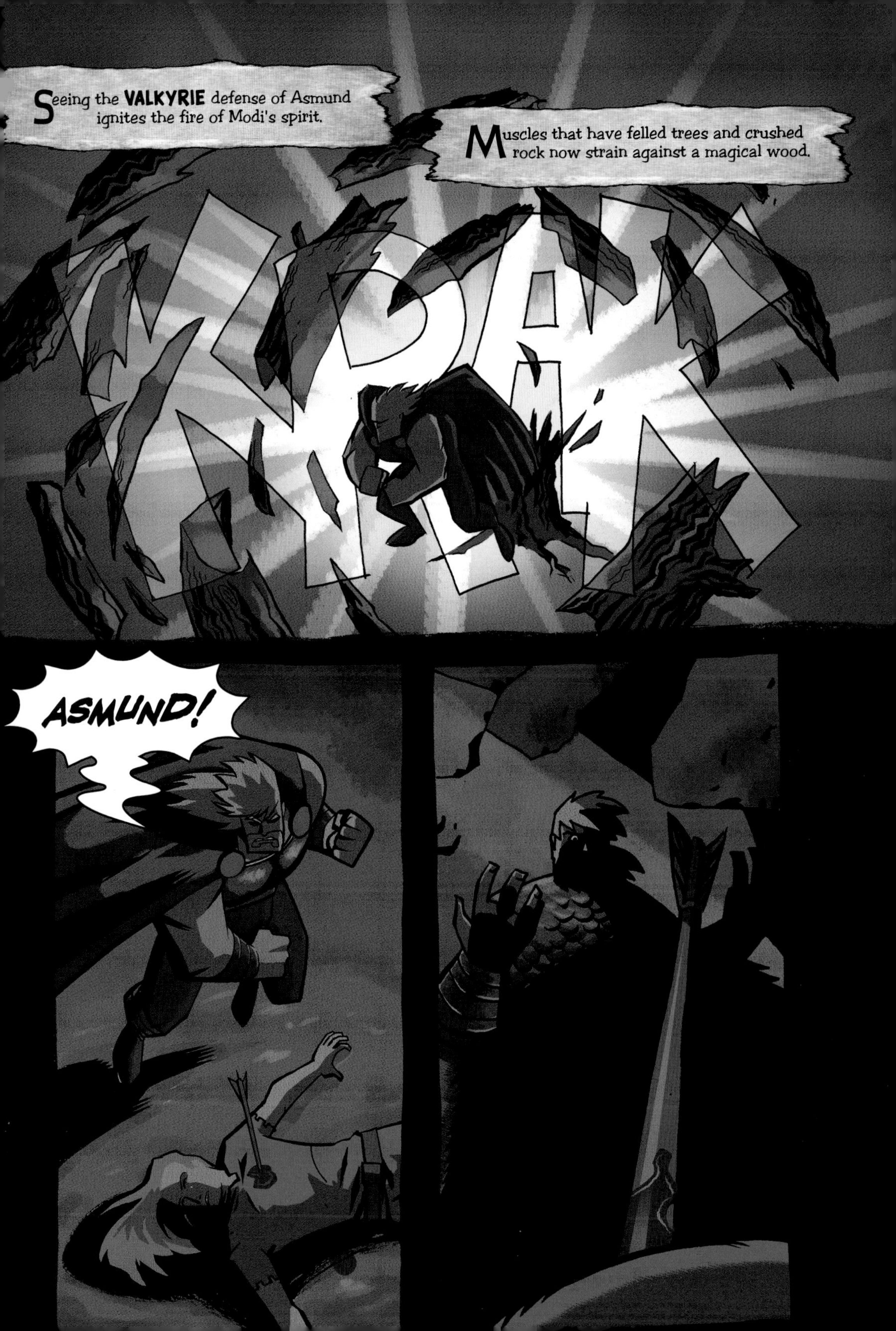
Seeing the VALKYRIE defense of Asmund ignites the fire of Modi's spirit.
Muscles that have felled trees and crushed rock now strain against a magical wood.
ASMUND!

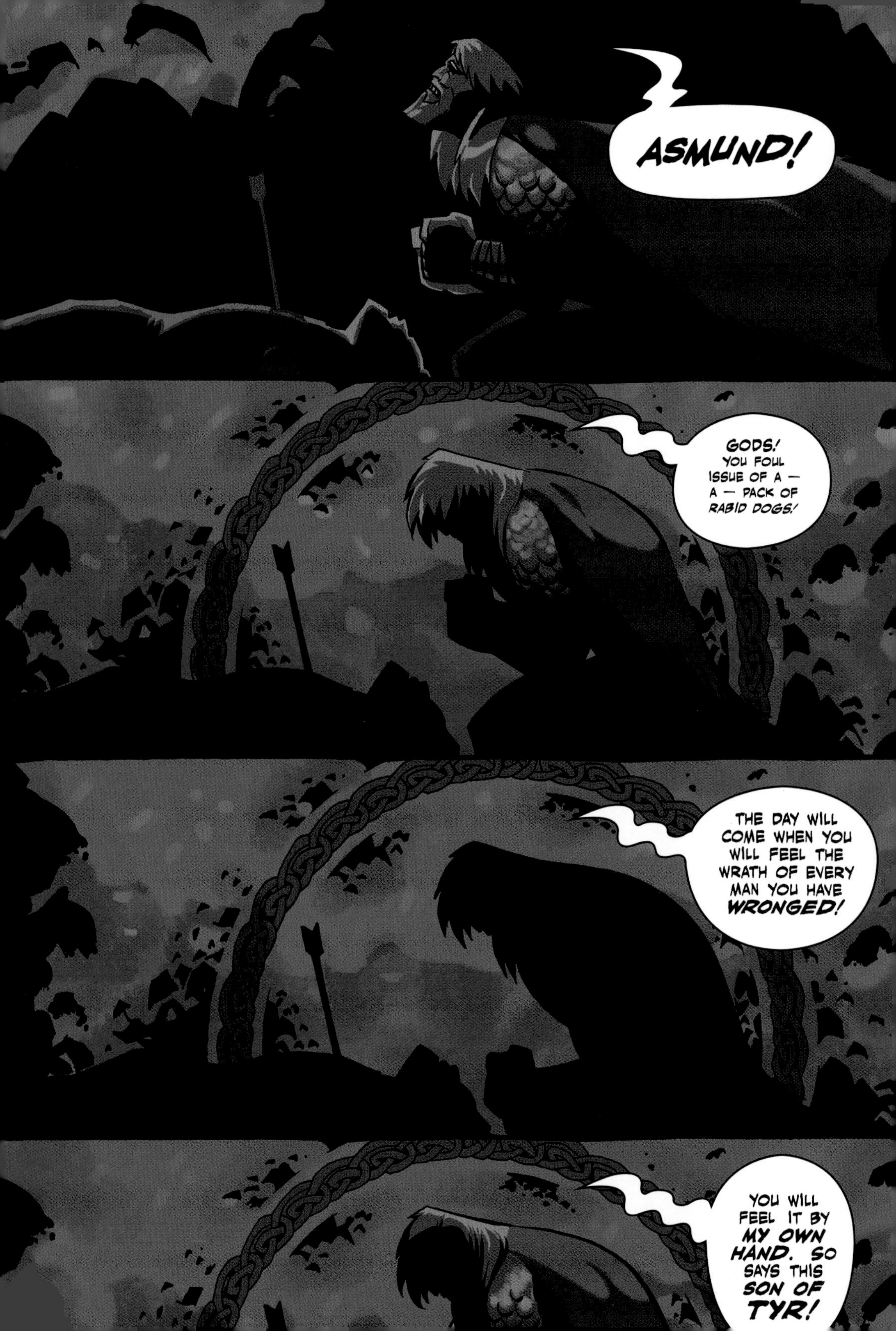
ASMUND!
GODS! YOU FOUL ISSUE OF A — A — PACK OF RABID DOGS!
THE DAY WILL COME WHEN YOU WILL FEEL THE WRATH OF EVERY MAN YOU HAVE WRONGED!
YOU WILL FEEL IT BY MY OWN HAND. SO SAYS THIS SON OF TYR!

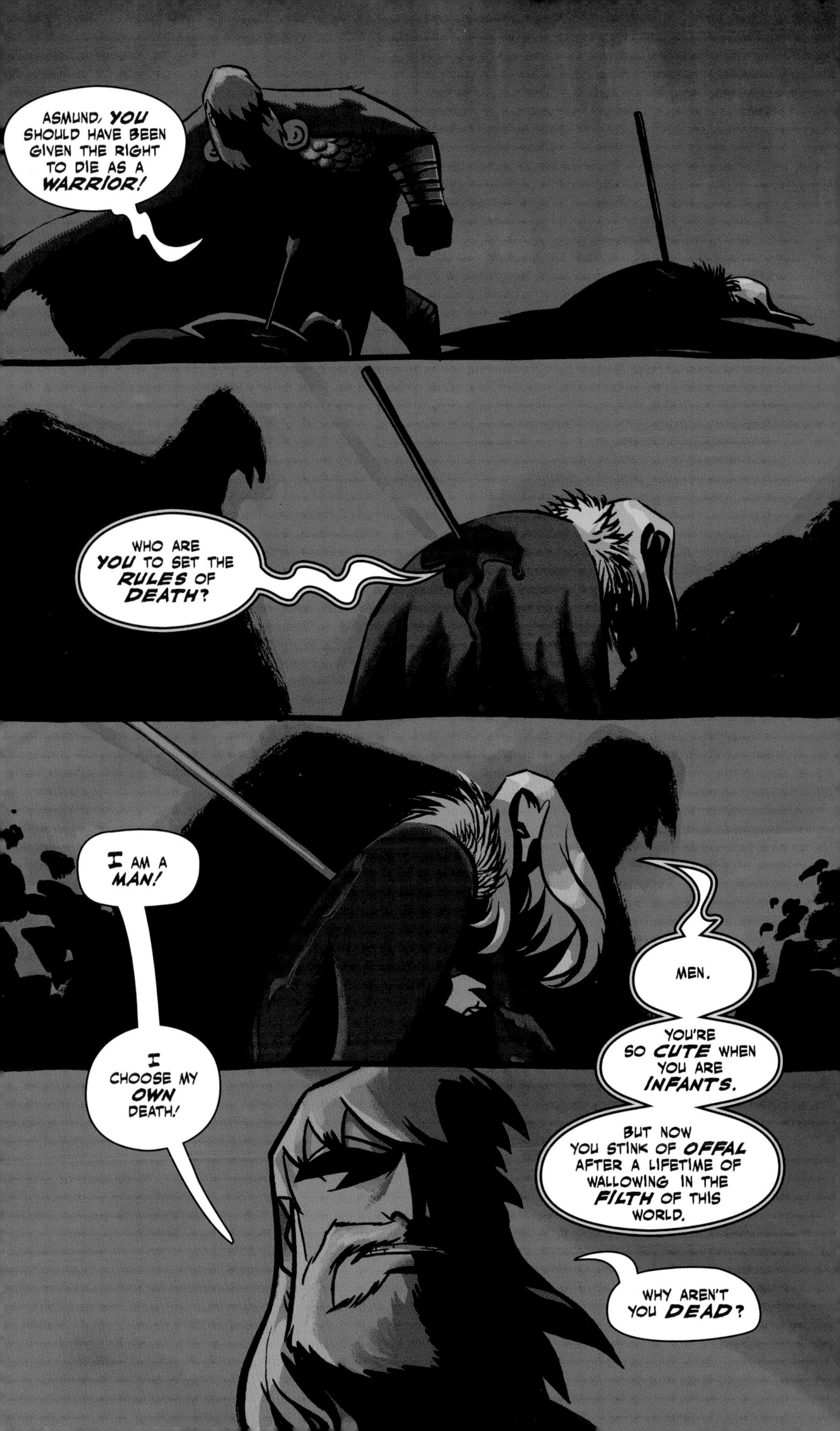
ASMUND, YOU SHOULD HAVE BEEN GIVEN THE RIGHT TO DIE AS A WARRIOR!
WHO ARE YOU TO SET THE RULES OF DEATH?
I AM A MAN!
I CHOOSE MY OWN DEATH!
MEN.
YOU'RE SO CUTE WHEN YOU ARE INFANTS.
BUT NOW YOU STINK OF OFFAL AFTER A LIFETIME OF WALLOWING IN THE FILTH OF THIS WORLD.
WHY AREN'T YOU DEAD?

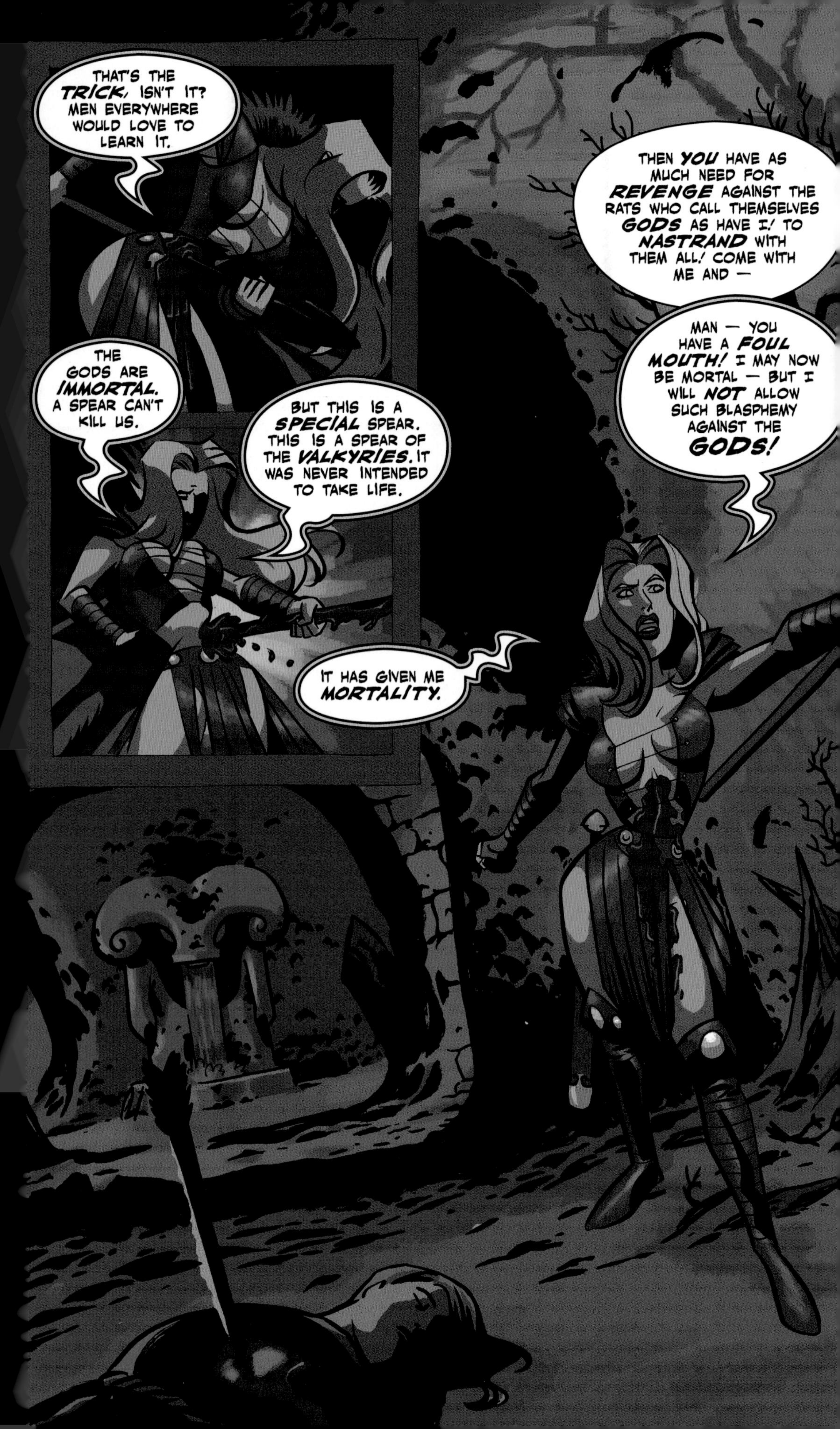
THAT'S THE TRICK, ISN'T IT? MEN EVERYWHERE WOULD LOVE TO LEARN IT.
THE GODS ARE IMMORTAL. A SPEAR CAN'T KILL US.
BUT THIS IS A SPECIAL SPEAR. THIS IS A SPEAR OF THE VALKYRIES. IT WAS NEVER INTENDED TO TAKE LIFE.
IT HAS GIVEN ME MORTALITY.
THEN YOU HAVE AS MUCH NEED FOR REVENGE AGAINST THE RATS WHO CALL THEMSELVES GODS AS HAVE I! TO NASTRAND WITH THEM ALL! COME WITH ME AND —
MAN — YOU HAVE A FOUL MOUTH! I MAY NOW BE MORTAL — BUT I WILL NOT ALLOW SUCH BLASPHEMY AGAINST THE GODS!

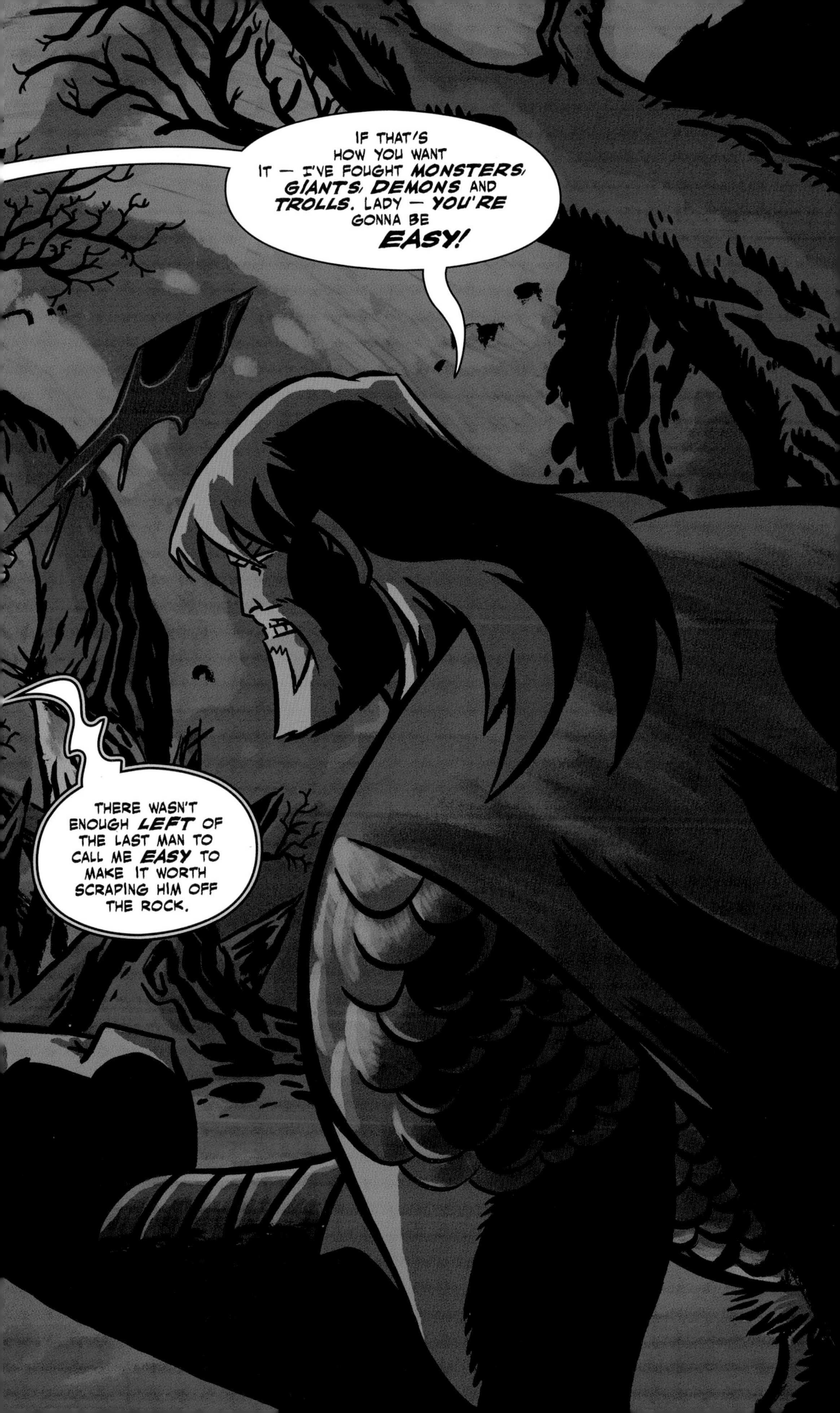
IF THAT'S HOW YOU WANT IT — I'VE FOUGHT MONSTERS, GIANTS, DEMONS AND TROLLS. LADY — YOU'RE GONNA BE EASY!
THERE WASN'T ENOUGH LEFT OF THE LAST MAN TO CALL ME EASY TO MAKE IT WORTH SCRAPING HIM OFF THE ROCK.

In the land of not quite day —
WHEN YOU KILL HIM DEAR, WOULD YOU DRAG HIM OVER HERE?
HE LOOKS GOOD ENOUGH TO EAT!
CHAPTER THREE

FALLING FOR GODS!
I LOST EVERYTHING BECAUSE OF YOU!
ME? IT WAS YOUR KIND WHO KILLED ASMUND!
DON'T YOU COMPARE ME TO THOSE VOW-BREAKING VALKYRIES!
COMPARE? YOU'RE ONE OF THEM, AREN'T YOU?
NOT ANY MORE — AND ACCORDING TO THEM I WAS NEVER GOOD ENOUGH TO BE CLAIMED BY THEIR ORDER!
THIS SPEAR CUT MY TIES TO THE VALKYRIES!

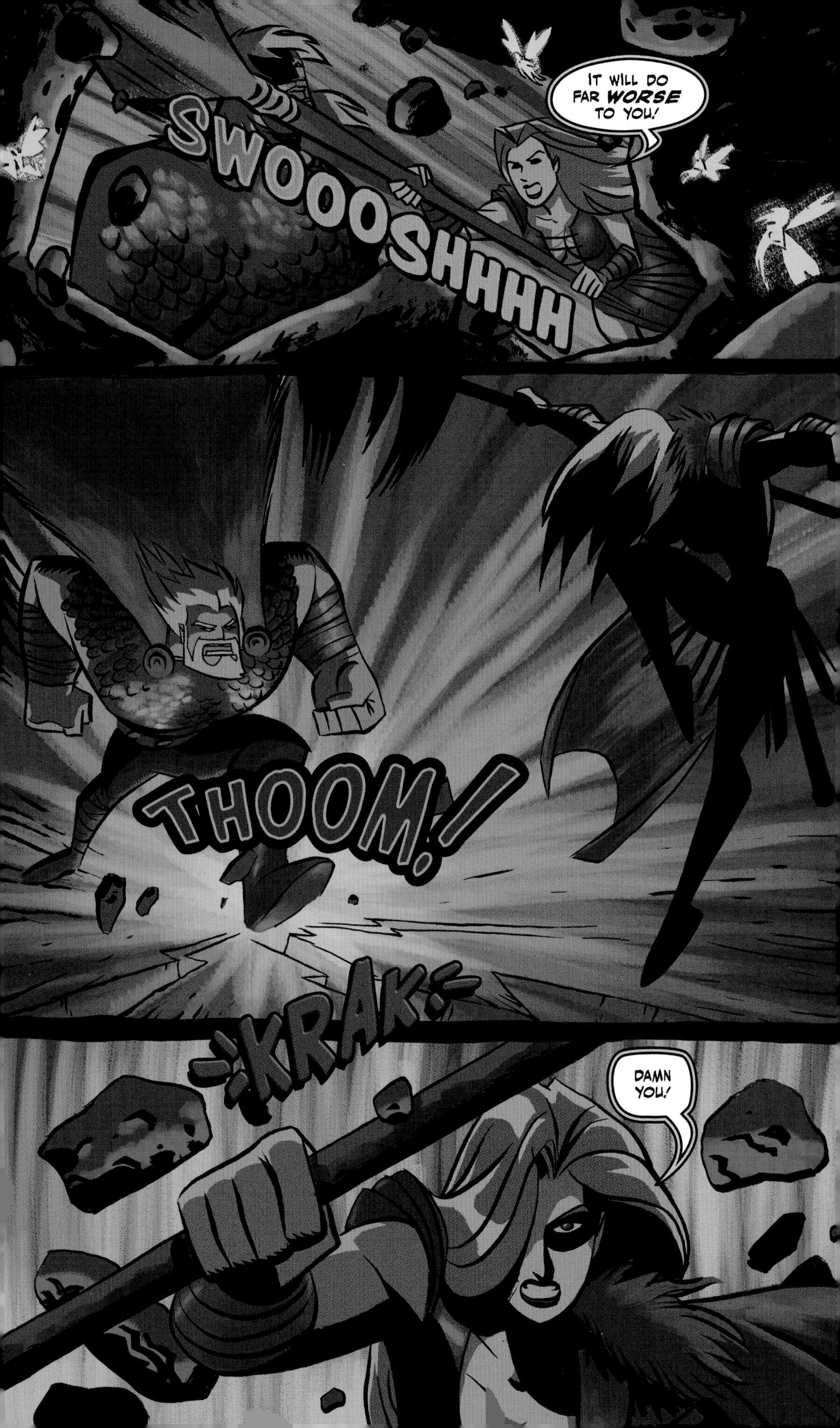
IT WILL DO FAR WORSE TO YOU!
SWOOOSHHHH
THOOM!
KRAK
DAMN YOU!

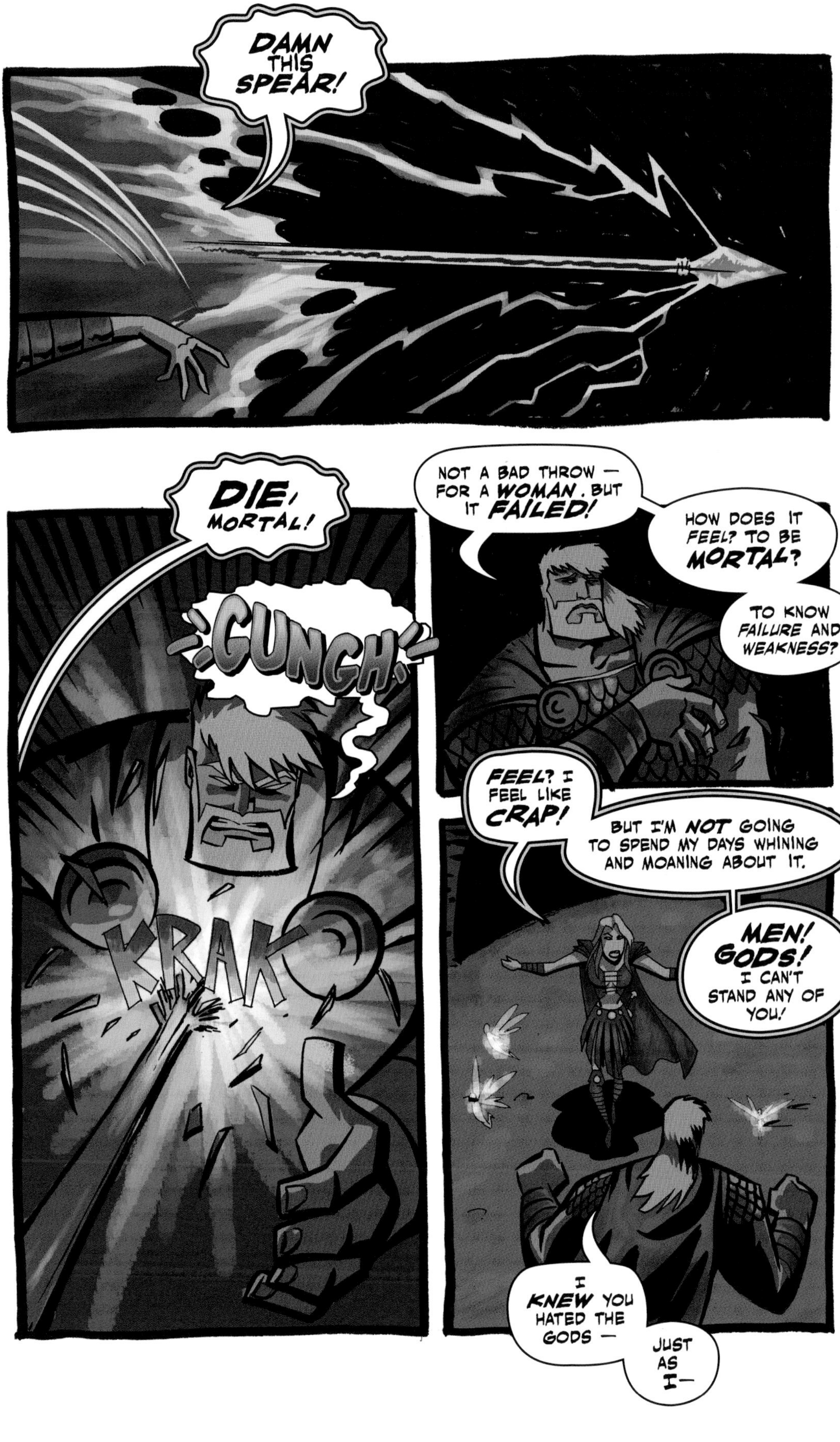
DAMN THIS SPEAR!
DIE, MORTAL!
GUNCH
KRAK
NOT A BAD THROW — FOR A WOMAN. BUT IT FAILED!
HOW DOES IT FEEL? TO BE MORTAL?
TO KNOW FAILURE AND WEAKNESS?
FEEL? I FEEL LIKE CRAP!
BUT I'M NOT GOING TO SPEND MY DAYS WHINING AND MOANING ABOUT IT.
MEN! GODS! I CAN'T STAND ANY OF YOU!
I KNEW YOU HATED THE GODS —
JUST AS I—

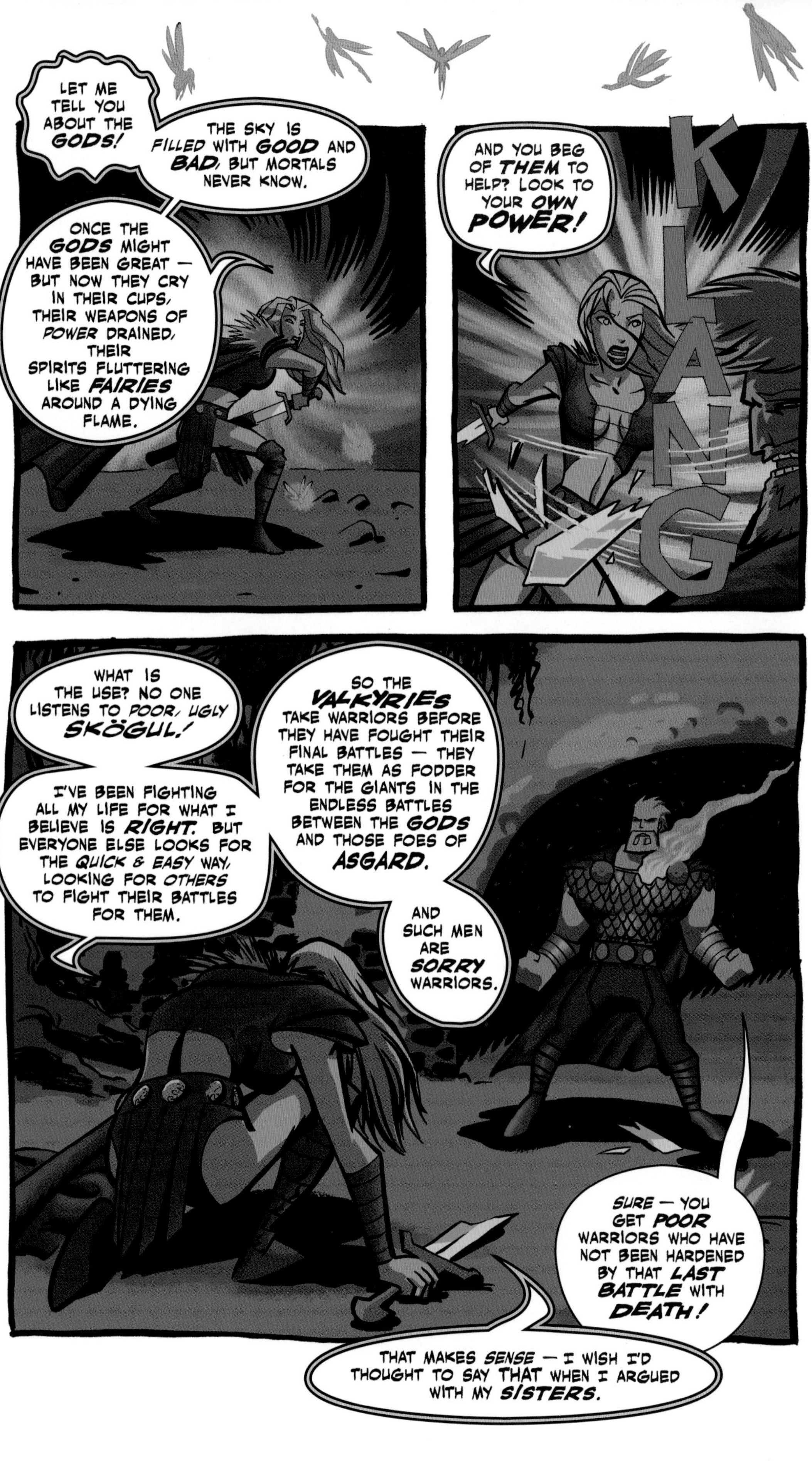
LET ME TELL YOU ABOUT THE GODS!
THE SKY IS FILLED WITH GOOD AND BAD, BUT MORTALS NEVER KNOW.
ONCE THE GODS MIGHT HAVE BEEN GREAT — BUT NOW THEY CRY IN THEIR CUPS, THEIR WEAPONS OF POWER DRAINED, THEIR SPIRITS FLUTTERING LIKE FAIRIES AROUND A DYING FLAME.
AND YOU BEG OF THEM TO HELP? LOOK TO YOUR OWN POWER!
KLANG
WHAT IS THE USE? NO ONE LISTENS TO POOR, UGLY SKÖGUL!
I'VE BEEN FIGHTING ALL MY LIFE FOR WHAT I BELIEVE IS RIGHT. BUT EVERYONE ELSE LOOKS FOR THE QUICK & EASY WAY, LOOKING FOR OTHERS TO FIGHT THEIR BATTLES FOR THEM.
SO THE VALKYRIES TAKE WARRIORS BEFORE THEY HAVE FOUGHT THEIR FINAL BATTLES — THEY TAKE THEM AS FODDER FOR THE GIANTS IN THE ENDLESS BATTLES BETWEEN THE GODS AND THOSE FOES OF ASGARD.
AND SUCH MEN ARE SORRY WARRIORS.
SURE — YOU GET POOR WARRIORS WHO HAVE NOT BEEN HARDENED BY THAT LAST BATTLE WITH DEATH!
THAT MAKES SENSE — I WISH I'D THOUGHT TO SAY THAT WHEN I ARGUED WITH MY SISTERS.

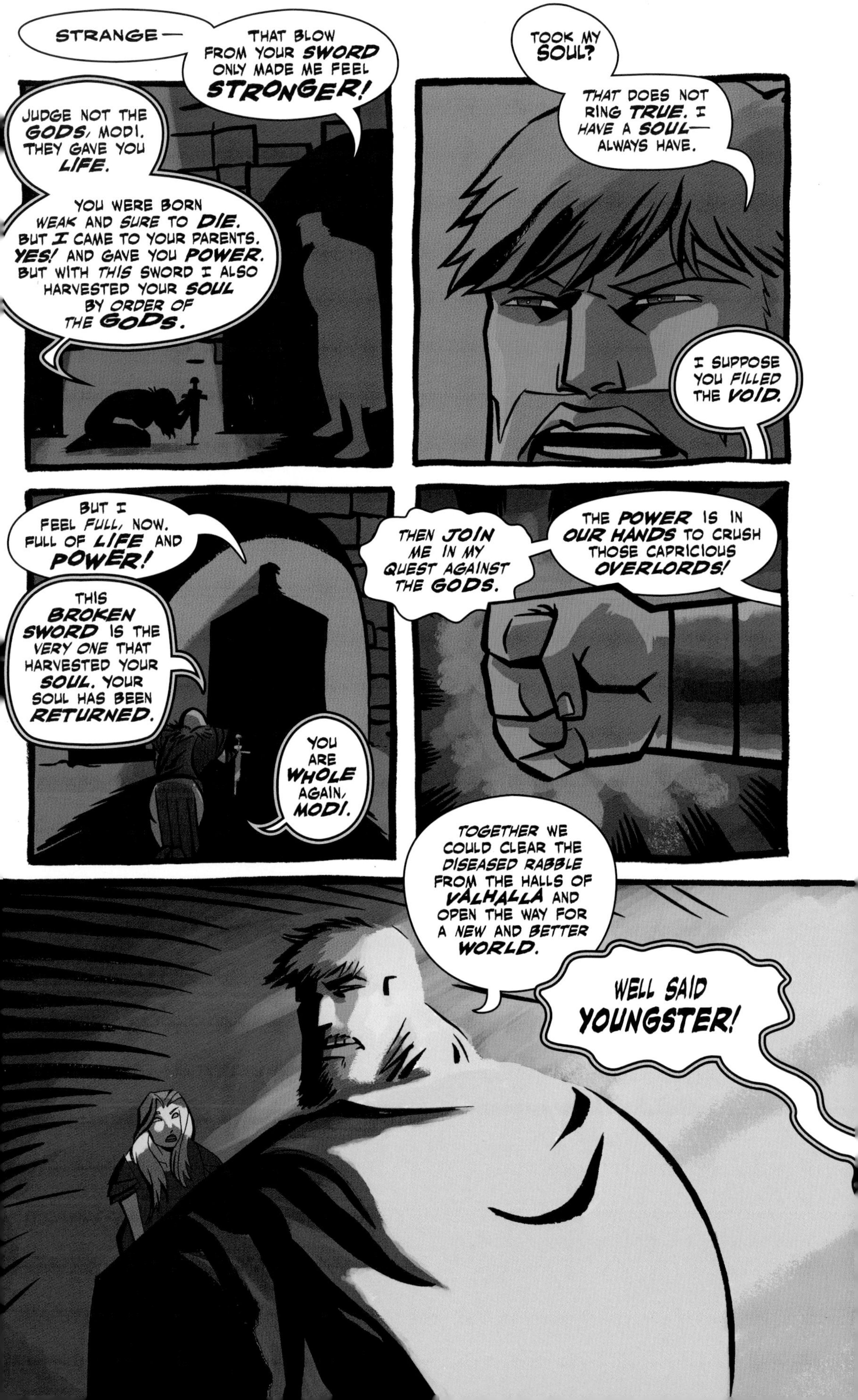
STRANGE—
THAT BLOW FROM YOUR SWORD ONLY MADE ME FEEL STRONGER!
JUDGE NOT THE GODS, MODI. THEY GAVE YOU LIFE.
YOU WERE BORN WEAK AND SURE TO DIE. BUT I CAME TO YOUR PARENTS. YES! AND GAVE YOU POWER. BUT WITH THIS SWORD I ALSO HARVESTED YOUR SOUL BY ORDER OF THE GODS.
TOOK MY SOUL?
THAT DOES NOT RING TRUE. I HAVE A SOUL— ALWAYS HAVE.
I SUPPOSE YOU FILLED THE VOID.
BUT I FEEL FULL, NOW. FULL OF LIFE AND POWER!
THIS BROKEN SWORD IS THE VERY ONE THAT HARVESTED YOUR SOUL. YOUR SOUL HAS BEEN RETURNED.
YOU ARE WHOLE AGAIN, MODI.
THEN JOIN ME IN MY QUEST AGAINST THE GODS.
THE POWER IS IN OUR HANDS TO CRUSH THOSE CAPRICIOUS OVERLORDS!
TOGETHER WE COULD CLEAR THE DISEASED RABBLE FROM THE HALLS OF VALHALLA AND OPEN THE WAY FOR A NEW AND BETTER WORLD.
WELL SAID YOUNGSTER!

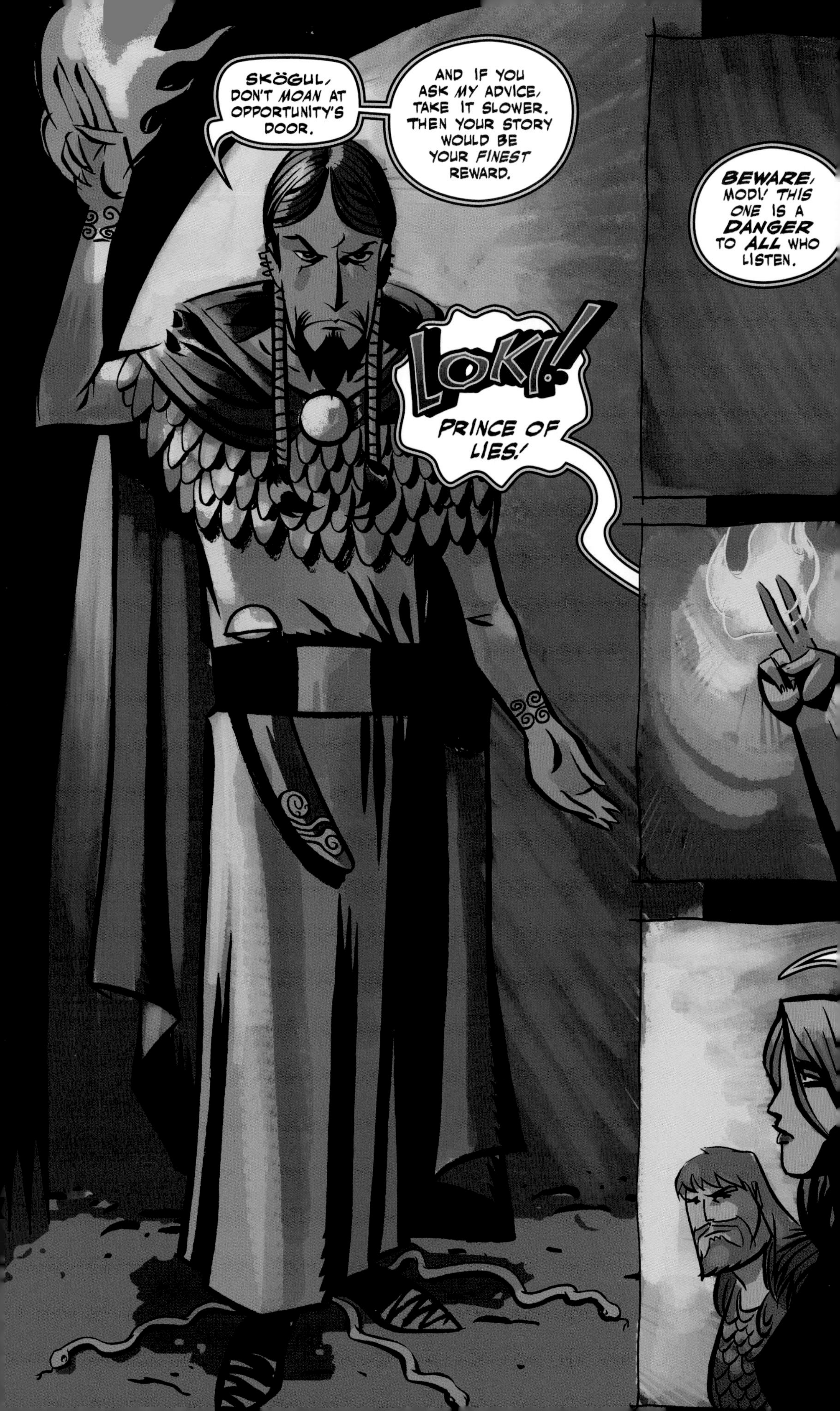
SKÖGUL, DON'T MOAN AT OPPORTUNITY'S DOOR.
AND IF YOU ASK MY ADVICE, TAKE IT SLOWER. THEN YOUR STORY WOULD BE YOUR FINEST REWARD.
BEWARE, MODI! THIS ONE IS A DANGER TO ALL WHO LISTEN.
LOKI!
PRINCE OF LIES!

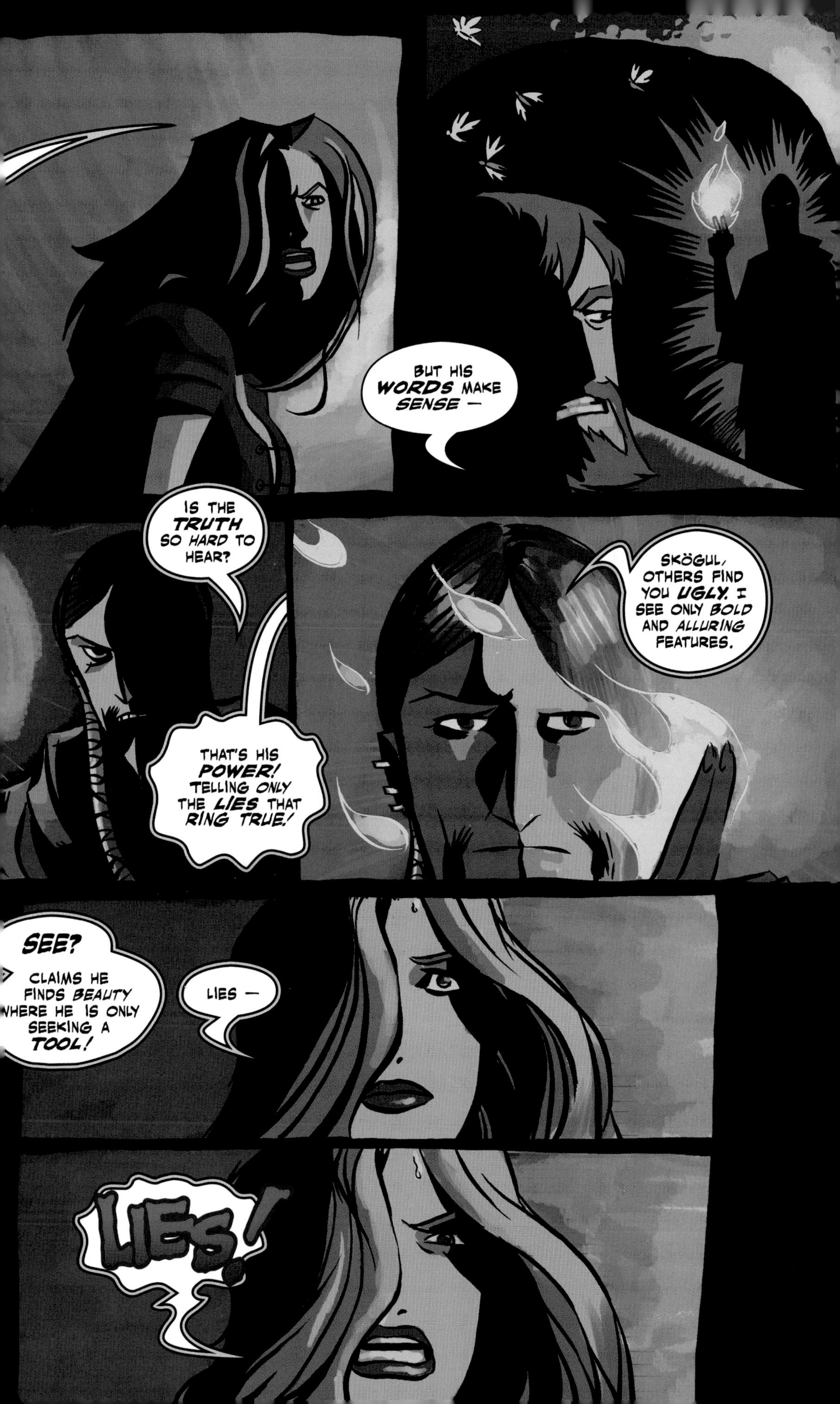
BUT HIS WORDS MAKE SENSE —
IS THE TRUTH SO HARD TO HEAR?
SKÖGUL, OTHERS FIND YOU UGLY. I SEE ONLY BOLD AND ALLURING FEATURES.
THAT'S HIS POWER! TELLING ONLY THE LIES THAT RING TRUE!
SEE?
CLAIMS HE FINDS BEAUTY WHERE HE IS ONLY SEEKING A TOOL!
LIES —
LIES!

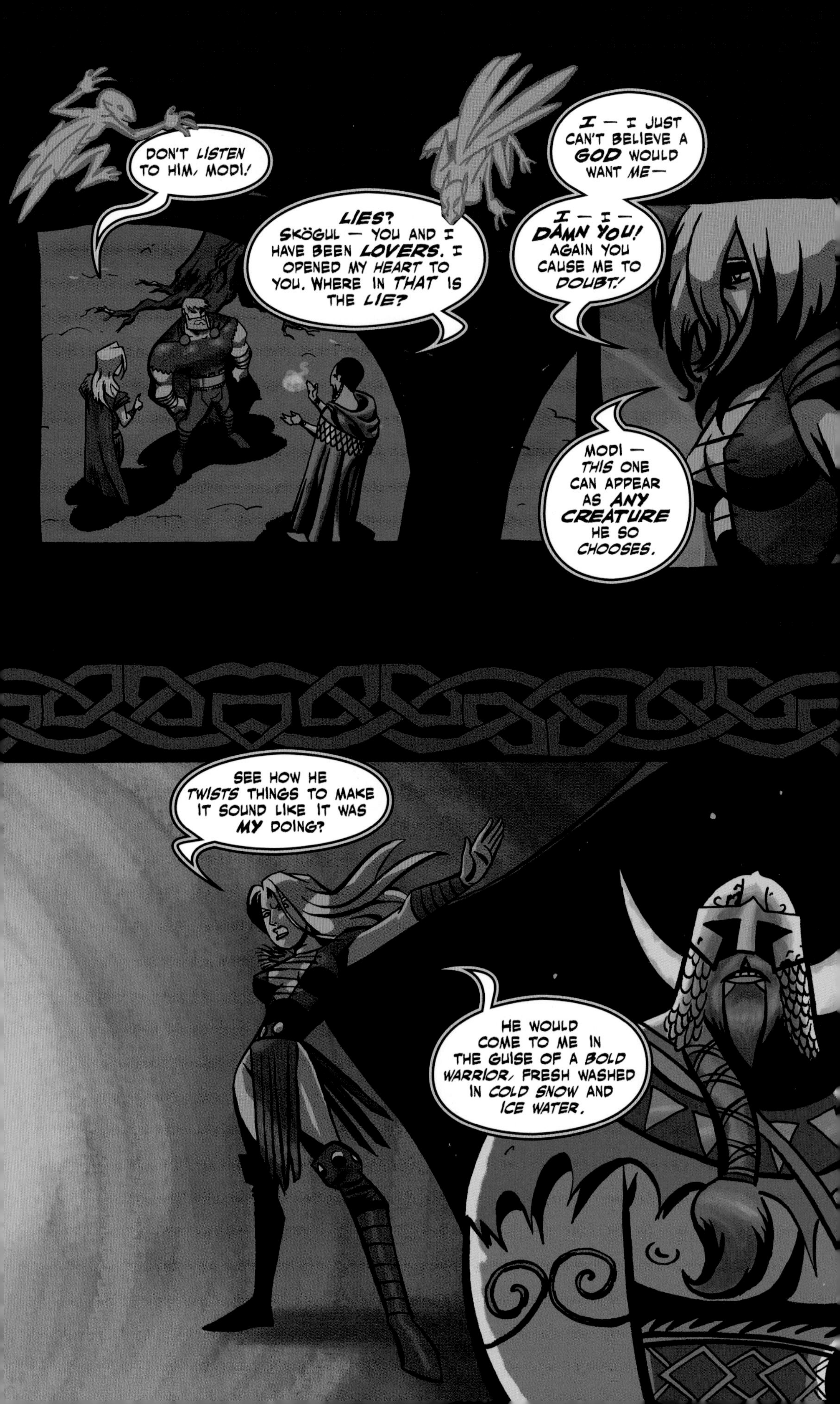

DON'T LISTEN TO HIM, MODI!
LIES? SKÖGUL — YOU AND I HAVE BEEN LOVERS. I OPENED MY HEART TO YOU. WHERE IN THAT IS THE LIE?
I — I JUST CAN'T BELIEVE A GOD WOULD WANT ME—
I — I — DAMN YOU! AGAIN YOU CAUSE ME TO DOUBT!
MODI — THIS ONE CAN APPEAR AS ANY CREATURE HE SO CHOOSES.
SEE HOW HE TWISTS THINGS TO MAKE IT SOUND LIKE IT WAS MY DOING?
HE WOULD COME TO ME IN THE GUISE OF A BOLD WARRIOR, FRESH WASHED IN COLD SNOW AND ICE WATER.

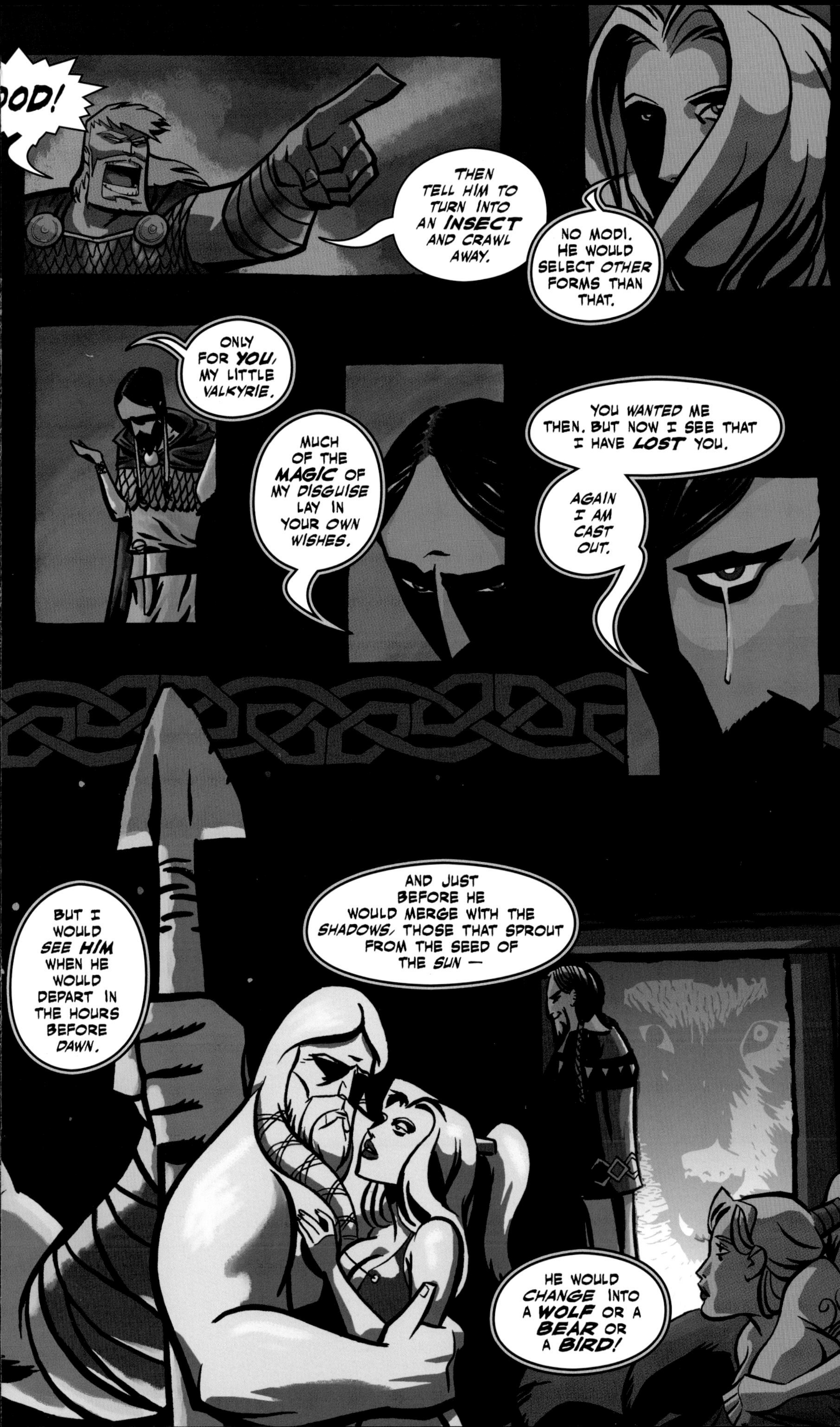

OOD!
THEN TELL HIM TO TURN INTO AN INSECT AND CRAWL AWAY.
NO MODI. HE WOULD SELECT OTHER FORMS THAN THAT.
ONLY FOR YOU, MY LITTLE VALKYRIE.
MUCH OF THE MAGIC OF MY DISGUISE LAY IN YOUR OWN WISHES.
YOU WANTED ME THEN. BUT NOW I SEE THAT I HAVE LOST YOU.
AGAIN I AM CAST OUT.
BUT I WOULD SEE HIM WHEN HE WOULD DEPART IN THE HOURS BEFORE DAWN.
AND JUST BEFORE HE WOULD MERGE WITH THE SHADOWS, THOSE THAT SPROUT FROM THE SEED OF THE SUN —
HE WOULD CHANGE INTO A WOLF OR A BEAR OR A BIRD!

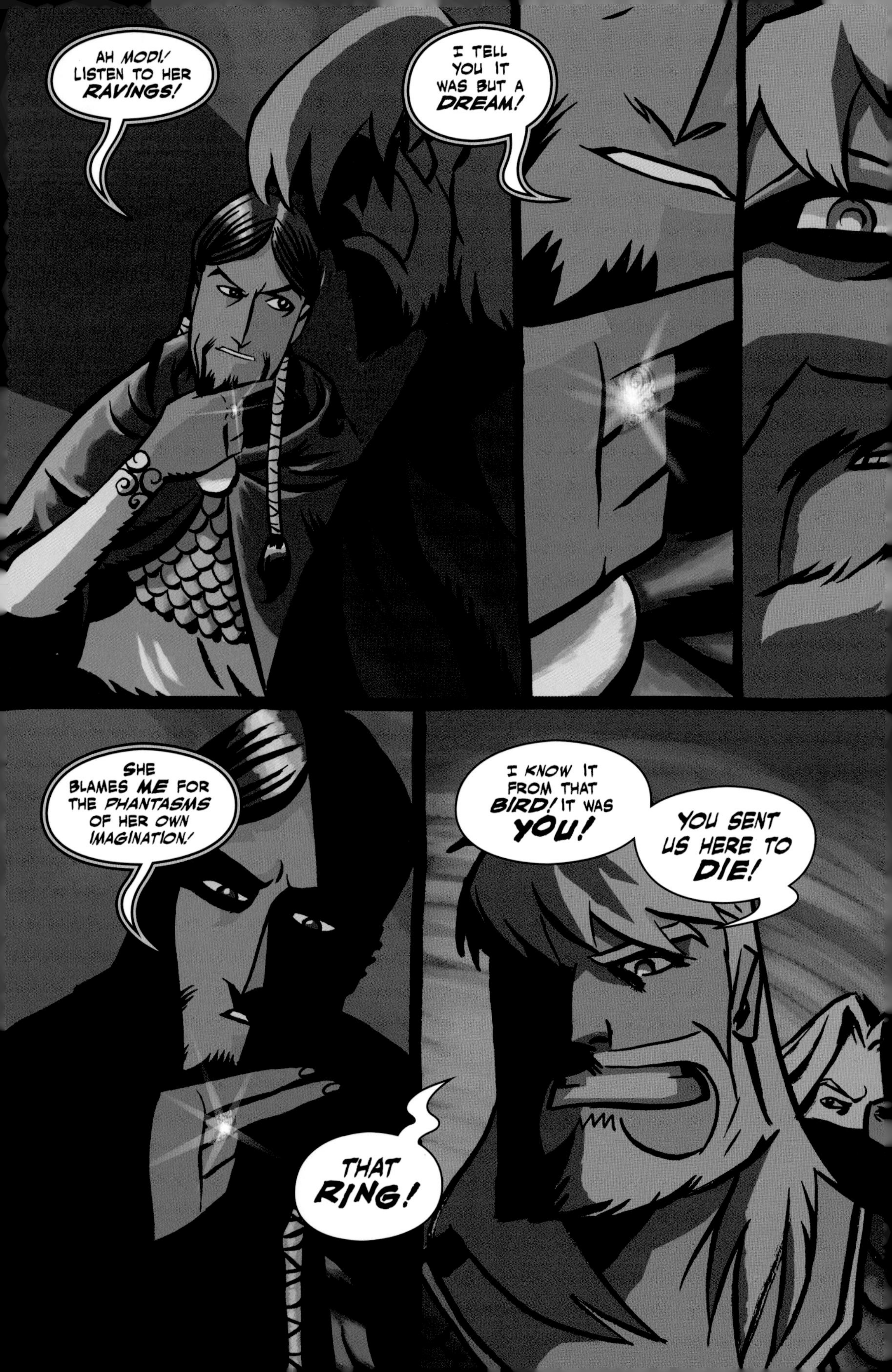
AH MODI! LISTEN TO HER RAVINGS!
I TELL YOU IT WAS BUT A DREAM!
SHE BLAMES ME FOR THE PHANTASMS OF HER OWN IMAGINATION!
I KNOW IT FROM THAT BIRD! IT WAS YOU!
YOU SENT US HERE TO DIE!
THAT RING!

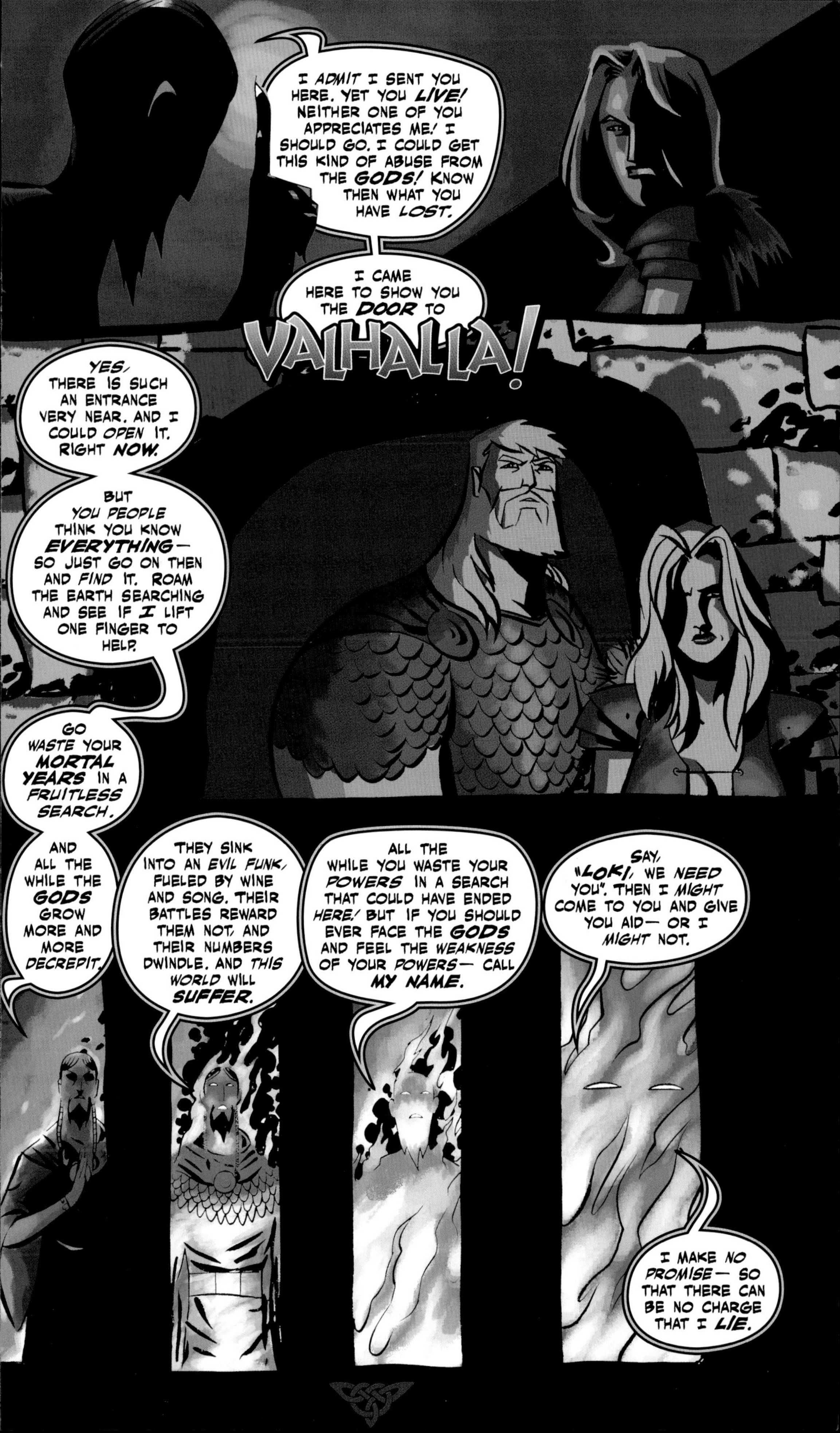
I ADMIT I SENT YOU HERE. YET YOU LIVE! NEITHER ONE OF YOU APPRECIATES ME! I SHOULD GO. I COULD GET THIS KIND OF ABUSE FROM THE GODS! KNOW THEN WHAT YOU HAVE LOST.
I CAME HERE TO SHOW YOU THE DOOR TO
VALHALLA!
YES, THERE IS SUCH AN ENTRANCE VERY NEAR. AND I COULD OPEN IT. RIGHT NOW.
BUT YOU PEOPLE THINK YOU KNOW EVERYTHING— SO JUST GO ON THEN AND FIND IT. ROAM THE EARTH SEARCHING AND SEE IF I LIFT ONE FINGER TO HELP.
GO WASTE YOUR MORTAL YEARS IN A FRUITLESS SEARCH.
AND ALL THE WHILE THE GODS GROW MORE AND MORE DECREPIT.
THEY SINK INTO AN EVIL FUNK, FUELED BY WINE AND SONG. THEIR BATTLES REWARD THEM NOT, AND THEIR NUMBERS DWINDLE. AND THIS WORLD WILL SUFFER.
ALL THE WHILE YOU WASTE YOUR POWERS IN A SEARCH THAT COULD HAVE ENDED HERE! BUT IF YOU SHOULD EVER FACE THE GODS AND FEEL THE WEAKNESS OF YOUR POWERS— CALL MY NAME.
SAY, "LOKI, WE NEED YOU". THEN I MIGHT COME TO YOU AND GIVE YOU AID— OR I MIGHT NOT.
I MAKE NO PROMISE— SO THAT THERE CAN BE NO CHARGE THAT I LIE.

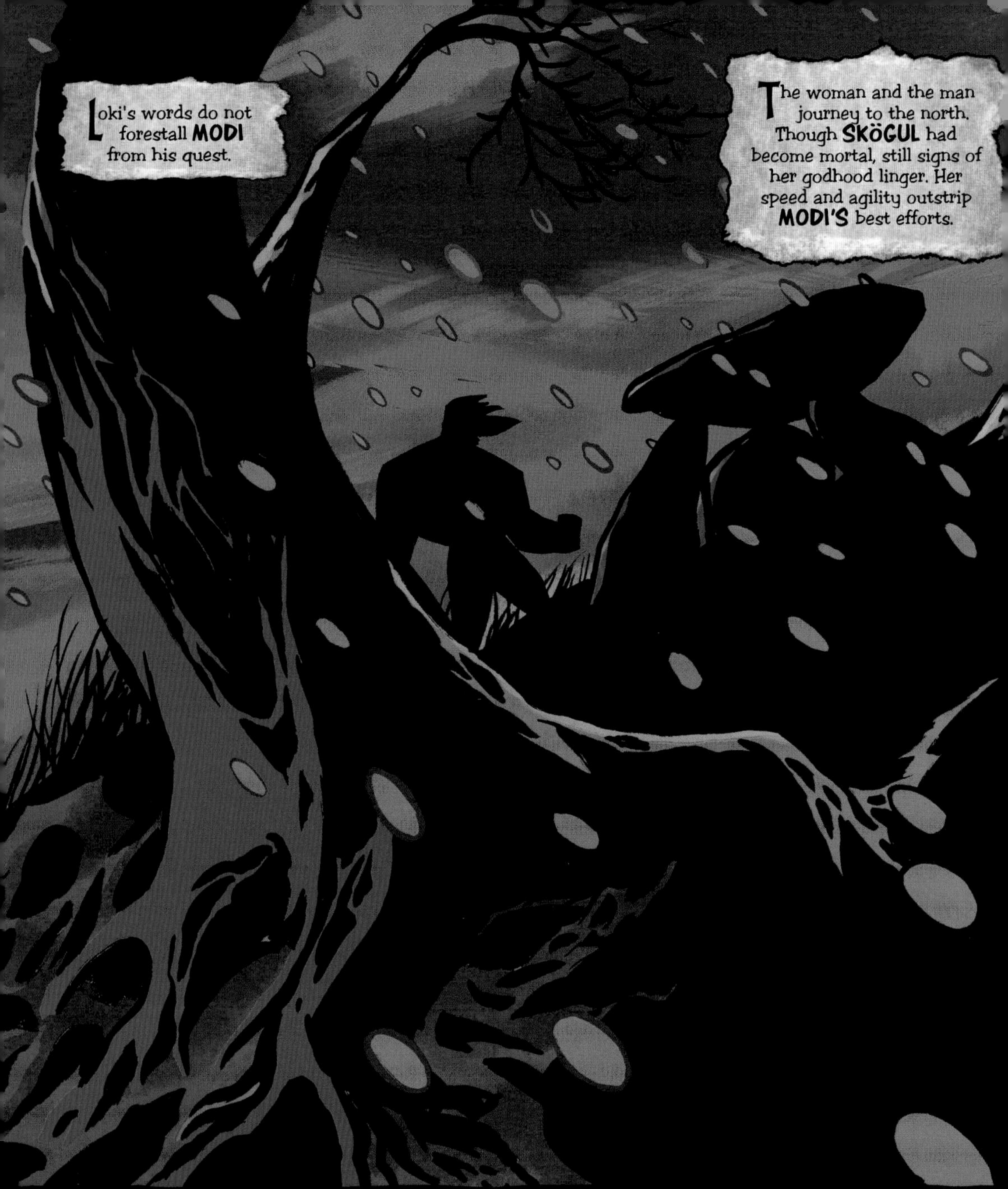
Loki's words do not forestall MODI from his quest.
The woman and the man journey to the north. Though SKÖGUL had become mortal, still signs of her godhood linger. Her speed and agility outstrip MODI'S best efforts.
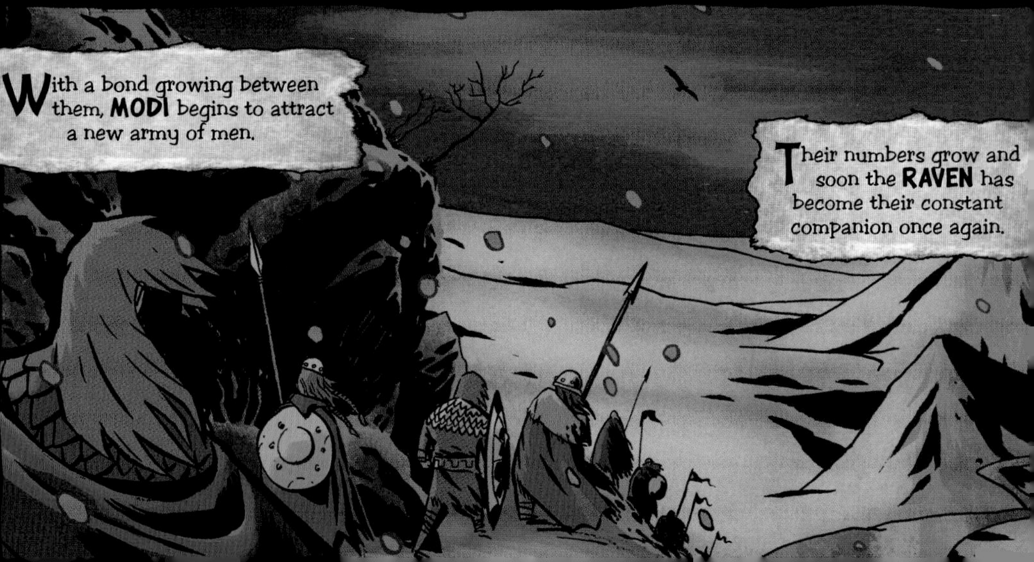
With a bond growing between them, MODI begins to attract a new army of men.
Their numbers grow and soon the RAVEN has become their constant companion once again.

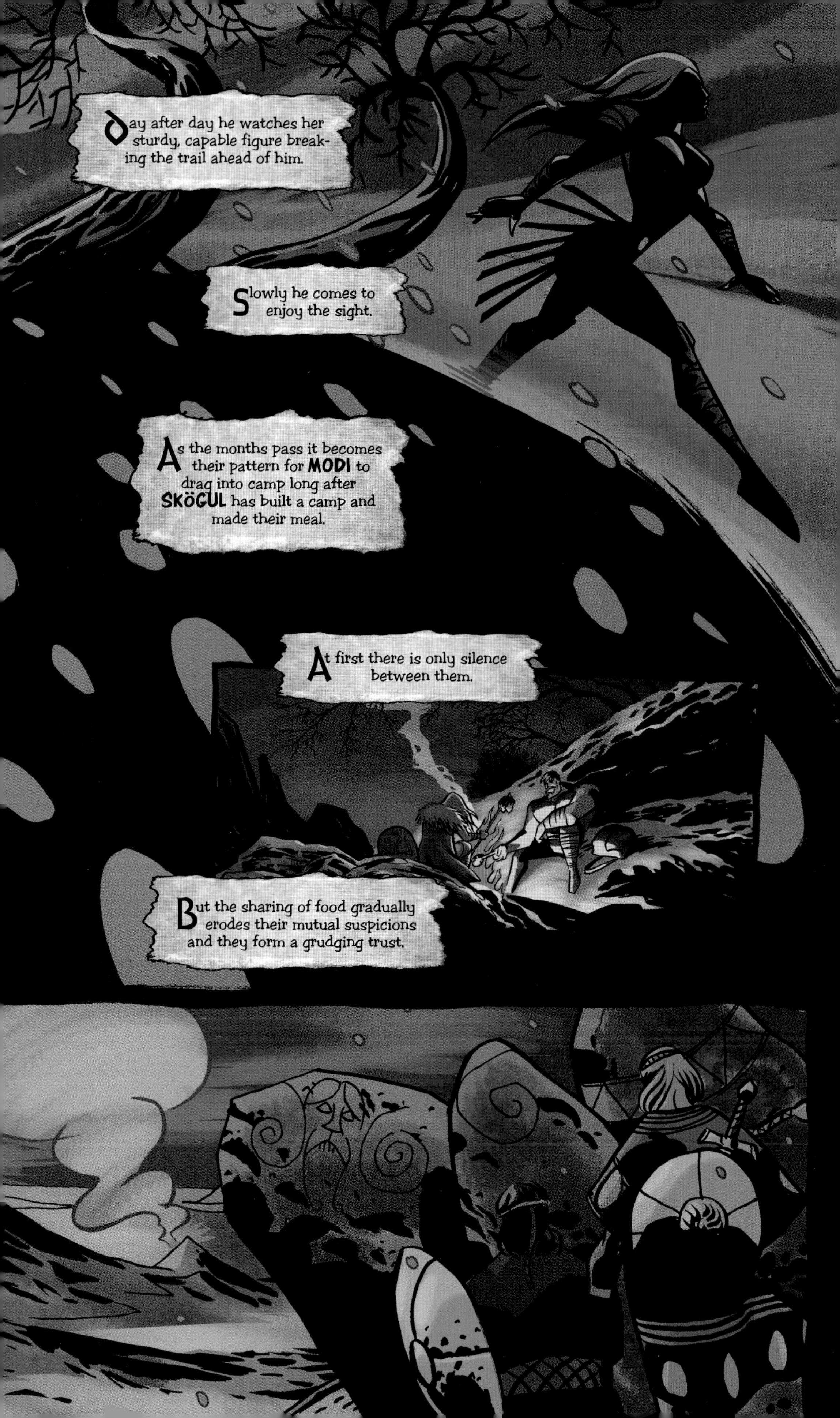
Day after day he watches her sturdy, capable figure breaking the trail ahead of him.
Slowly he comes to enjoy the sight.
As the months pass it becomes their pattern for MODI to drag into camp long after SKÖGUL has built a camp and made their meal.
At first there is only silence between them.
But the sharing of food gradually erodes their mutual suspicions and they form a grudging trust.

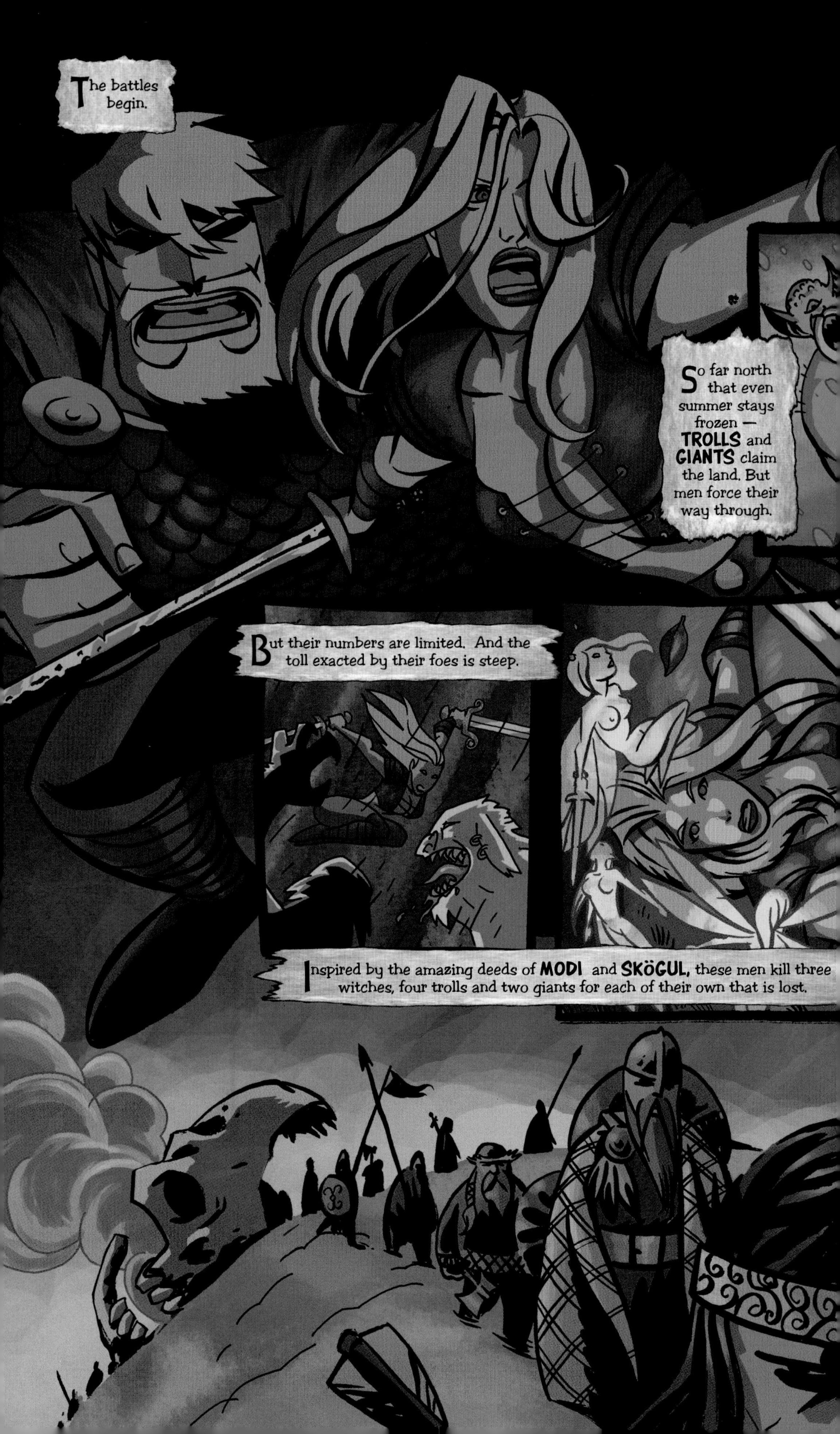
The battles begin.
So far north that even summer stays frozen — TROLLS and GIANTS claim the land. But men force their way through.
But their numbers are limited. And the toll exacted by their foes is steep.
Inspired by the amazing deeds of MODI and SKÖGUL, these men kill three witches, four trolls and two giants for each of their own that is lost.

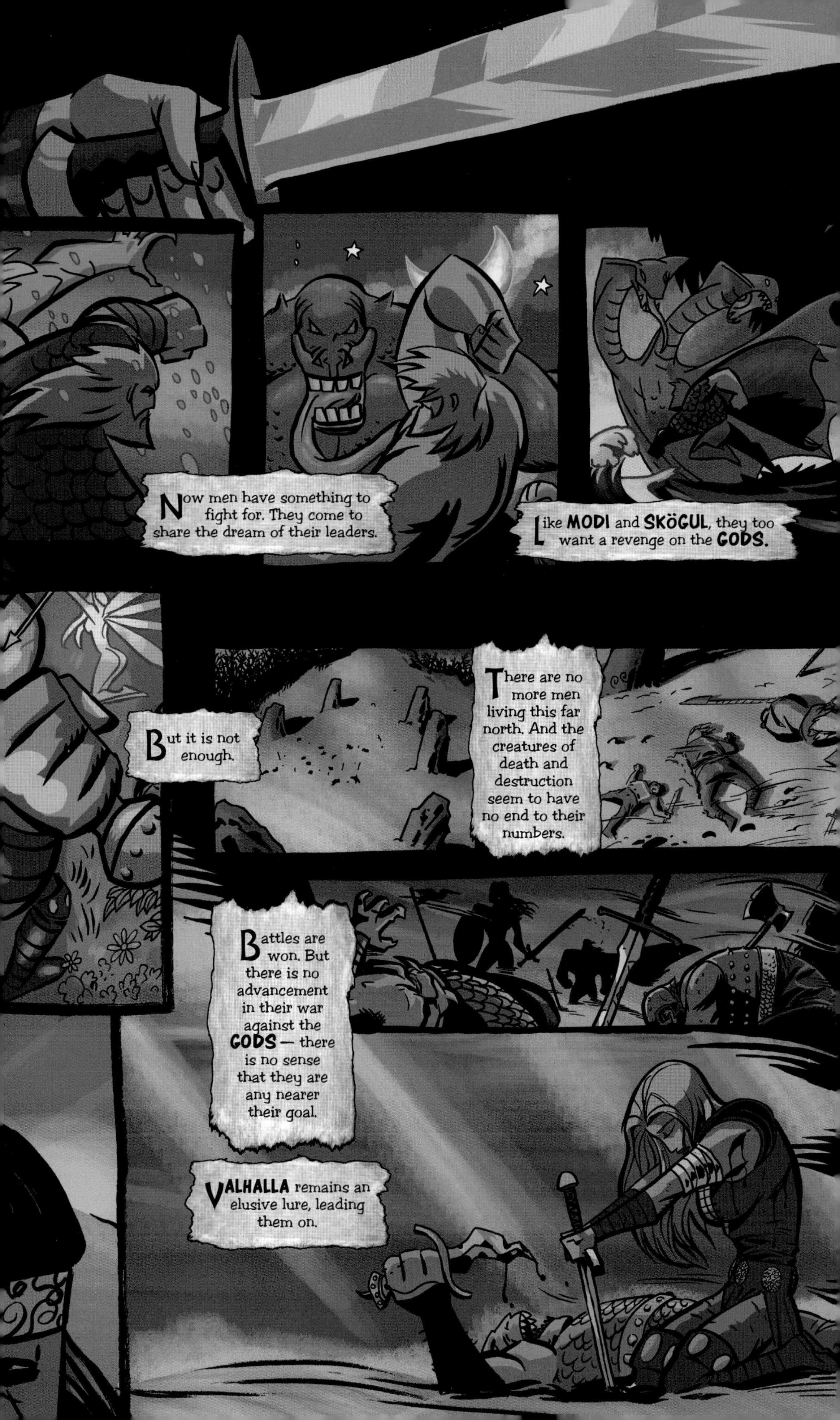
Now men have something to fight for. They come to share the dream of their leaders.
Like MODI and SKÖGUL, they too want a revenge on the GODS.
But it is not enough.
There are no more men living this far north. And the creatures of death and destruction seem to have no end to their numbers.
Battles are won. But there is no advancement in their war against the GODS — there is no sense that they are any nearer their goal.
VALHALLA remains an elusive lure, leading them on.

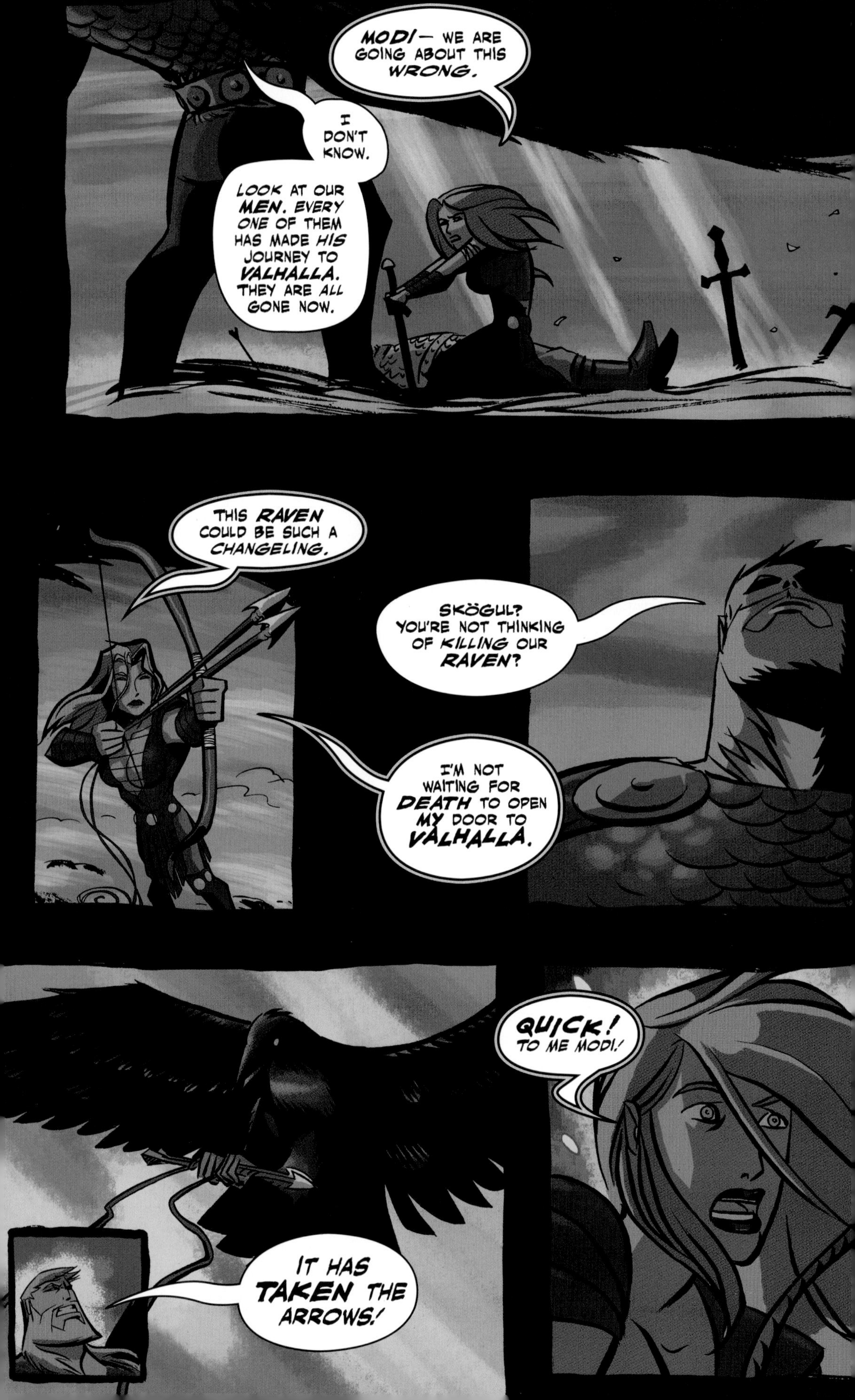
MODI— WE ARE GOING ABOUT THIS WRONG.
I DON'T KNOW.
LOOK AT OUR MEN. EVERY ONE OF THEM HAS MADE HIS JOURNEY TO VALHALLA. THEY ARE ALL GONE NOW.
THIS RAVEN COULD BE SUCH A CHANGELING.
SKÖGUL? YOU'RE NOT THINKING OF KILLING OUR RAVEN?
I'M NOT WAITING FOR DEATH TO OPEN MY DOOR TO VALHALLA.
QUICK! TO ME MODI!
IT HAS TAKEN THE ARROWS!

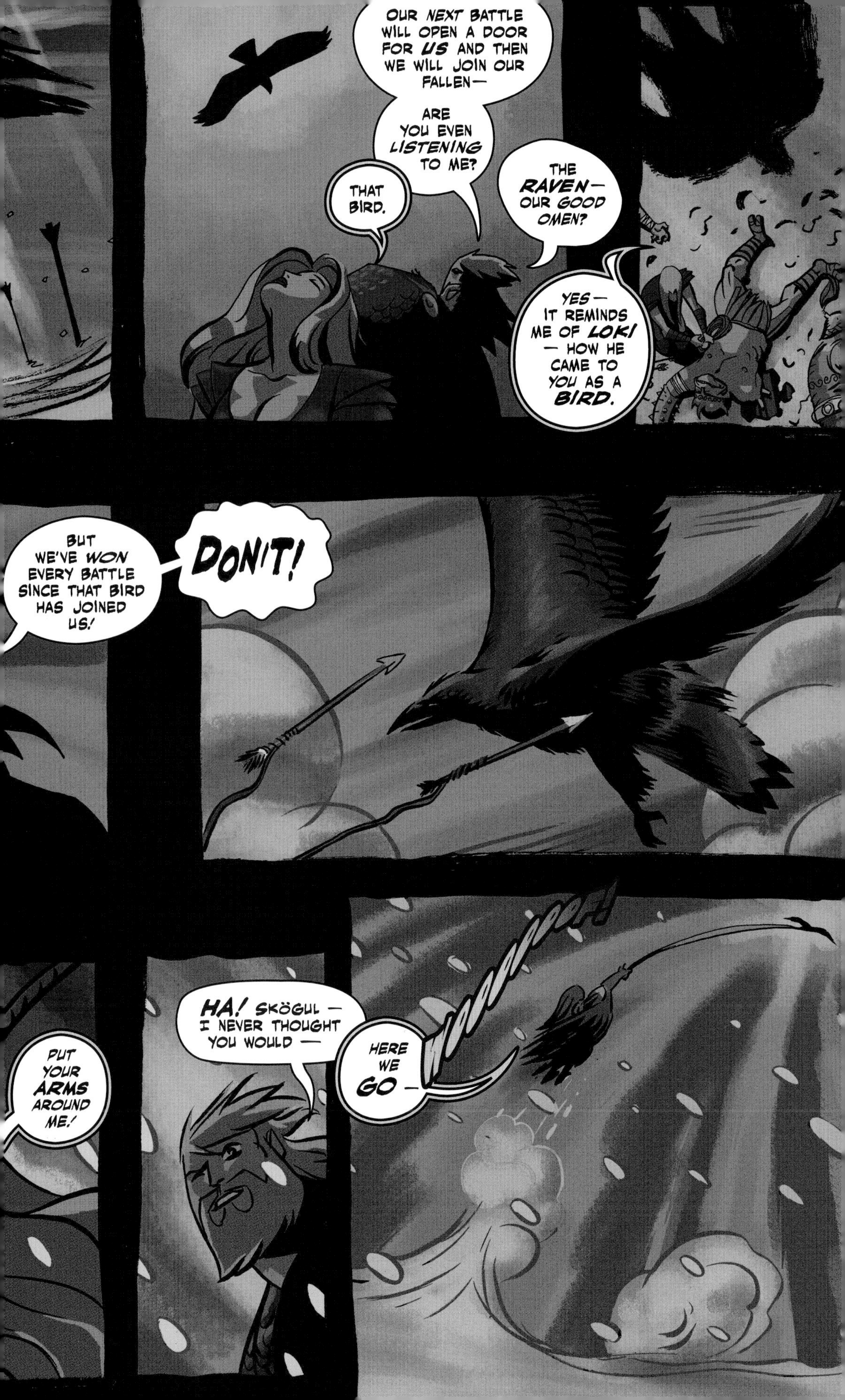

OUR NEXT BATTLE WILL OPEN A DOOR FOR US AND THEN WE WILL JOIN OUR FALLEN—
ARE YOU EVEN LISTENING TO ME?
THAT BIRD.
THE RAVEN— OUR GOOD OMEN?
YES— IT REMINDS ME OF LOKI — HOW HE CAME TO YOU AS A BIRD.
BUT WE'VE WON EVERY BATTLE SINCE THAT BIRD HAS JOINED US!
DON'T!
HA! SKÖGUL — I NEVER THOUGHT YOU WOULD —
HERE WE GO —
PUT YOUR ARMS AROUND ME!

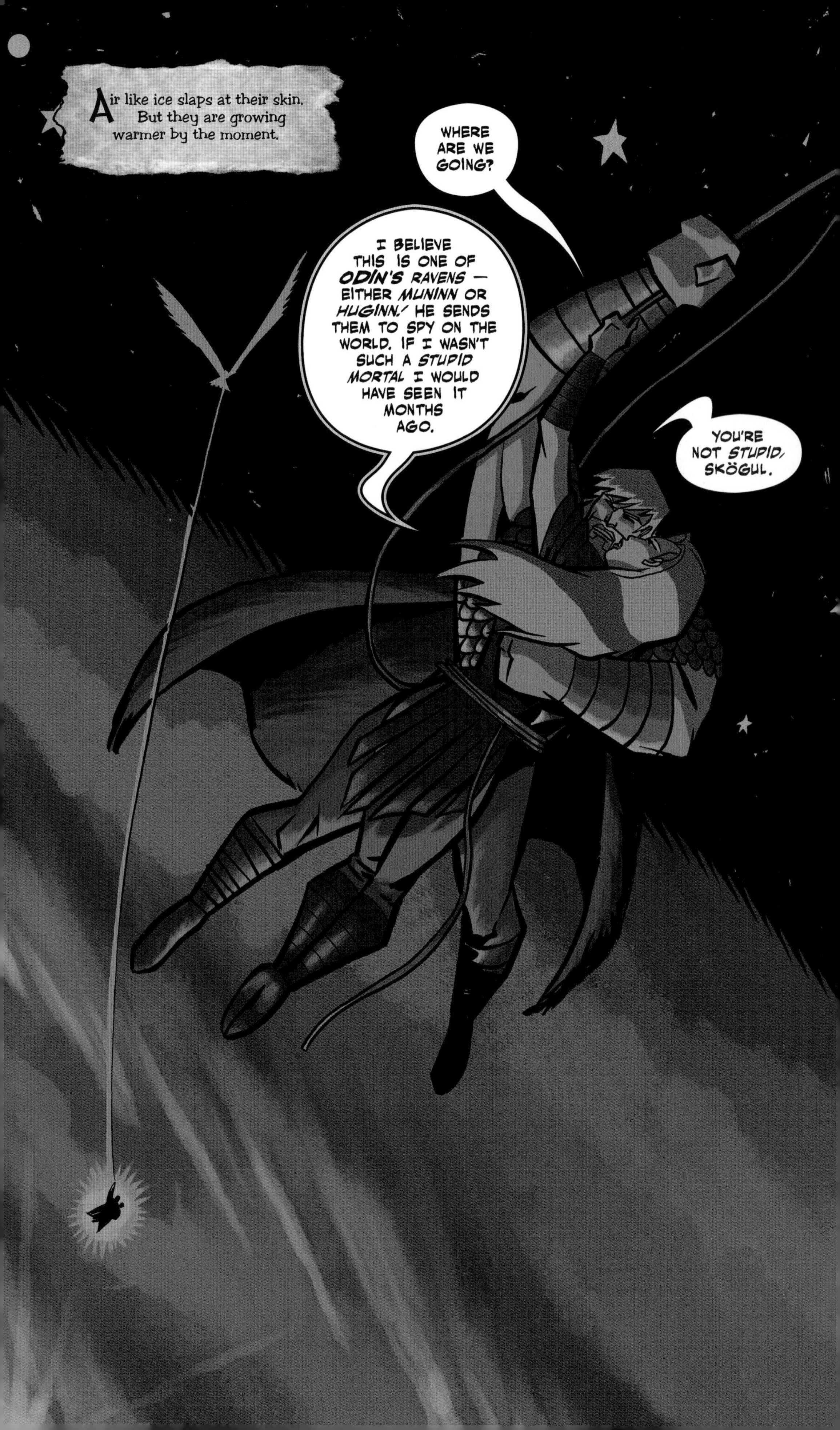
Air like ice slaps at their skin. But they are growing warmer by the moment.
WHERE ARE WE GOING?
I BELIEVE THIS IS ONE OF ODIN'S RAVENS — EITHER MUNINN OR HUGINN! HE SENDS THEM TO SPY ON THE WORLD. IF I WASN'T SUCH A STUPID MORTAL I WOULD HAVE SEEN IT MONTHS AGO.
YOU'RE NOT STUPID, SKÖGUL.

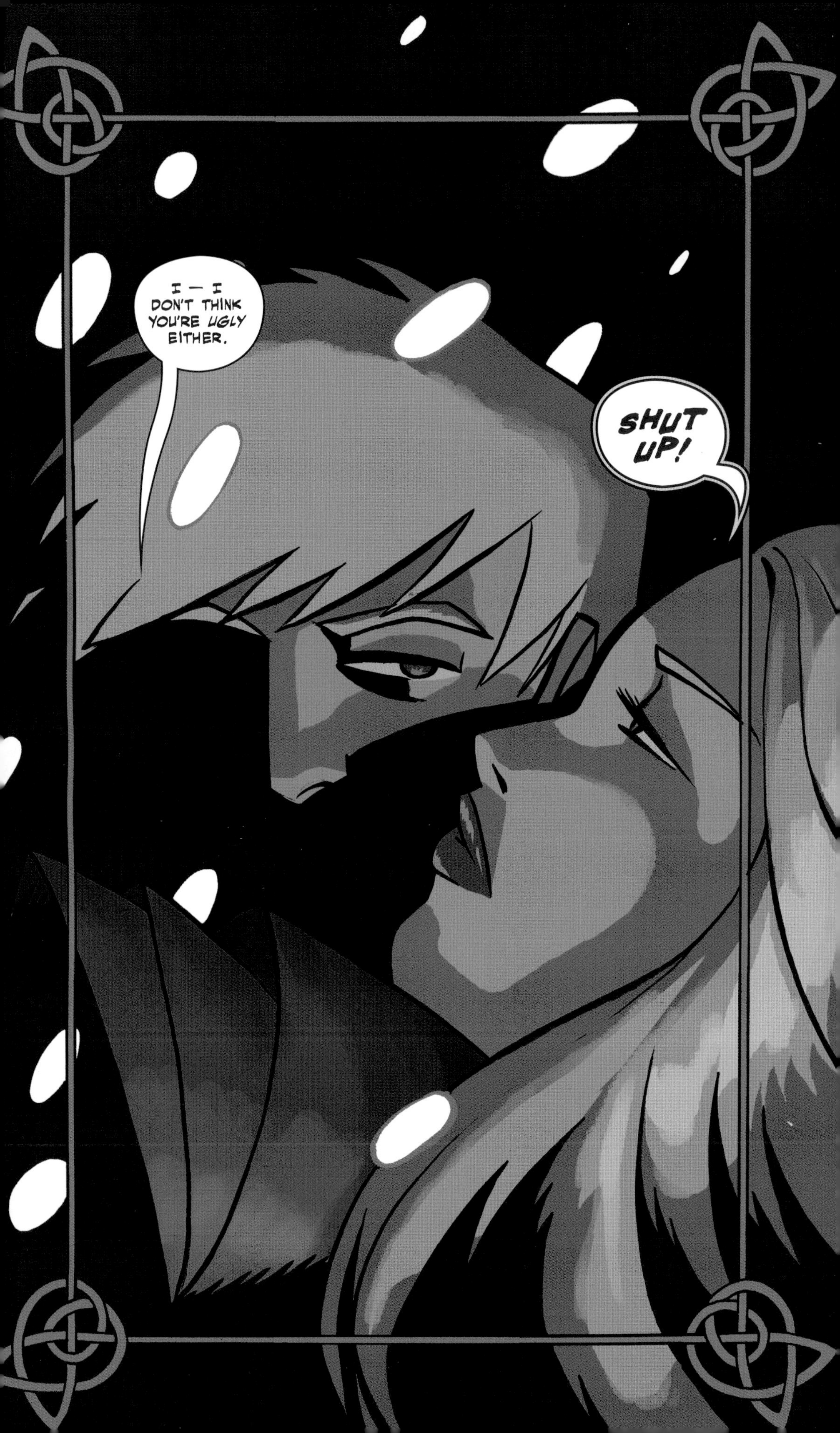
I — I DON'T THINK YOU'RE UGLY EITHER.
SHUT UP!

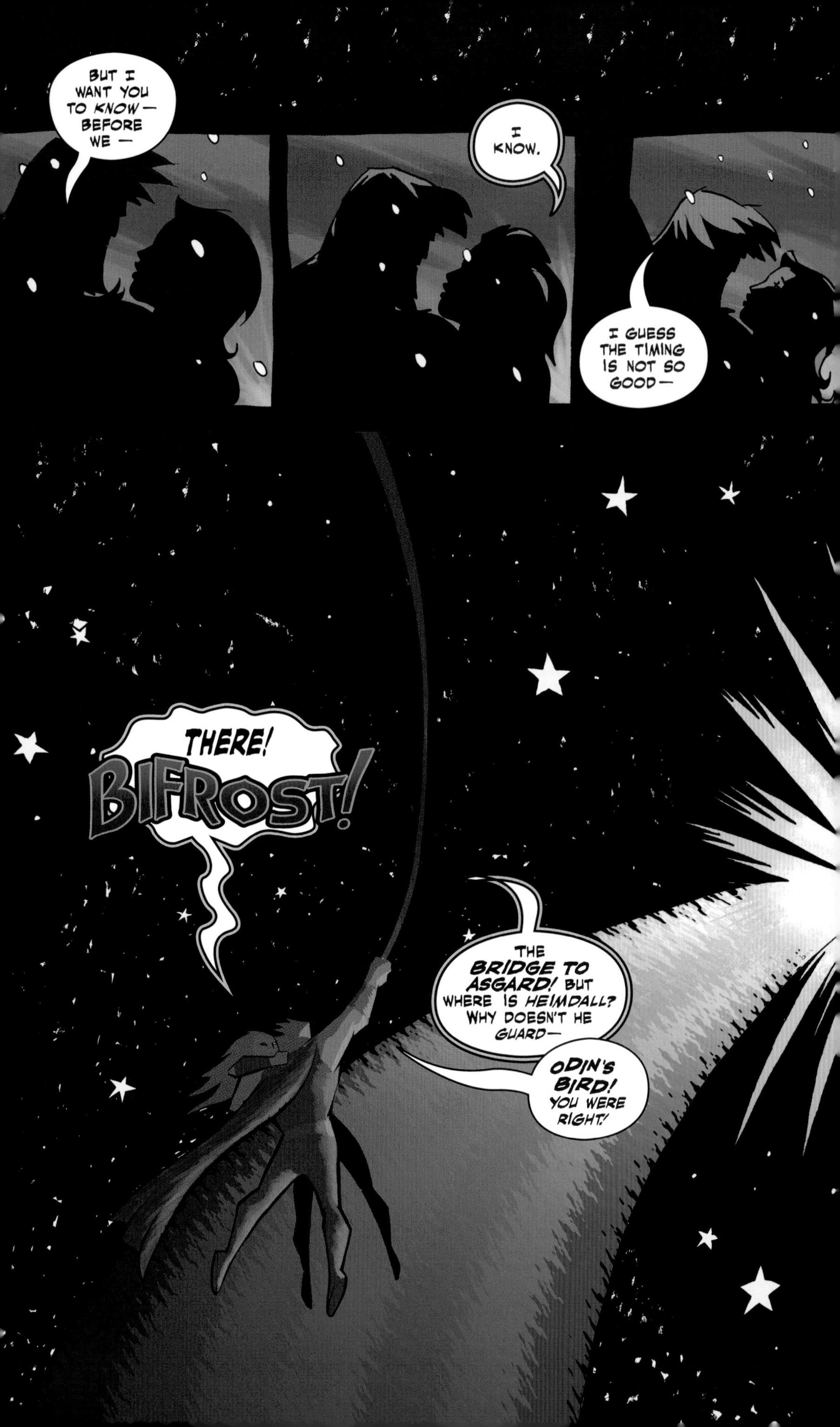

BUT I WANT YOU TO *KNOW*— BEFORE WE —
I KNOW.
I GUESS THE TIMING IS NOT SO GOOD—
THERE! BIFROST!
THE *BRIDGE TO ASGARD!* BUT WHERE IS *HEIMDALL?* WHY DOESN'T HE *GUARD*—
ODIN'S BIRD! YOU WERE *RIGHT!*

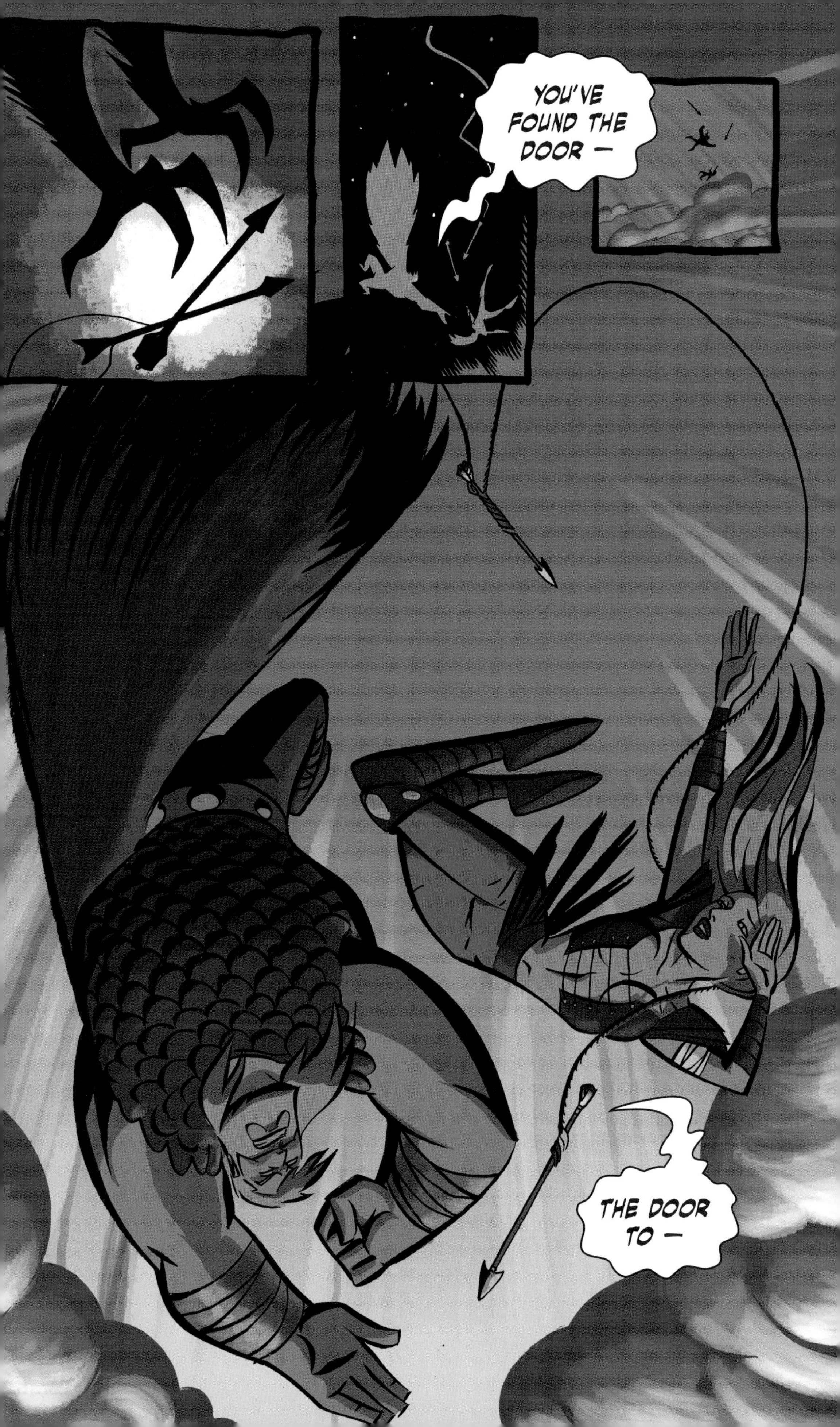
YOU'VE FOUND THE DOOR —
THE DOOR TO —

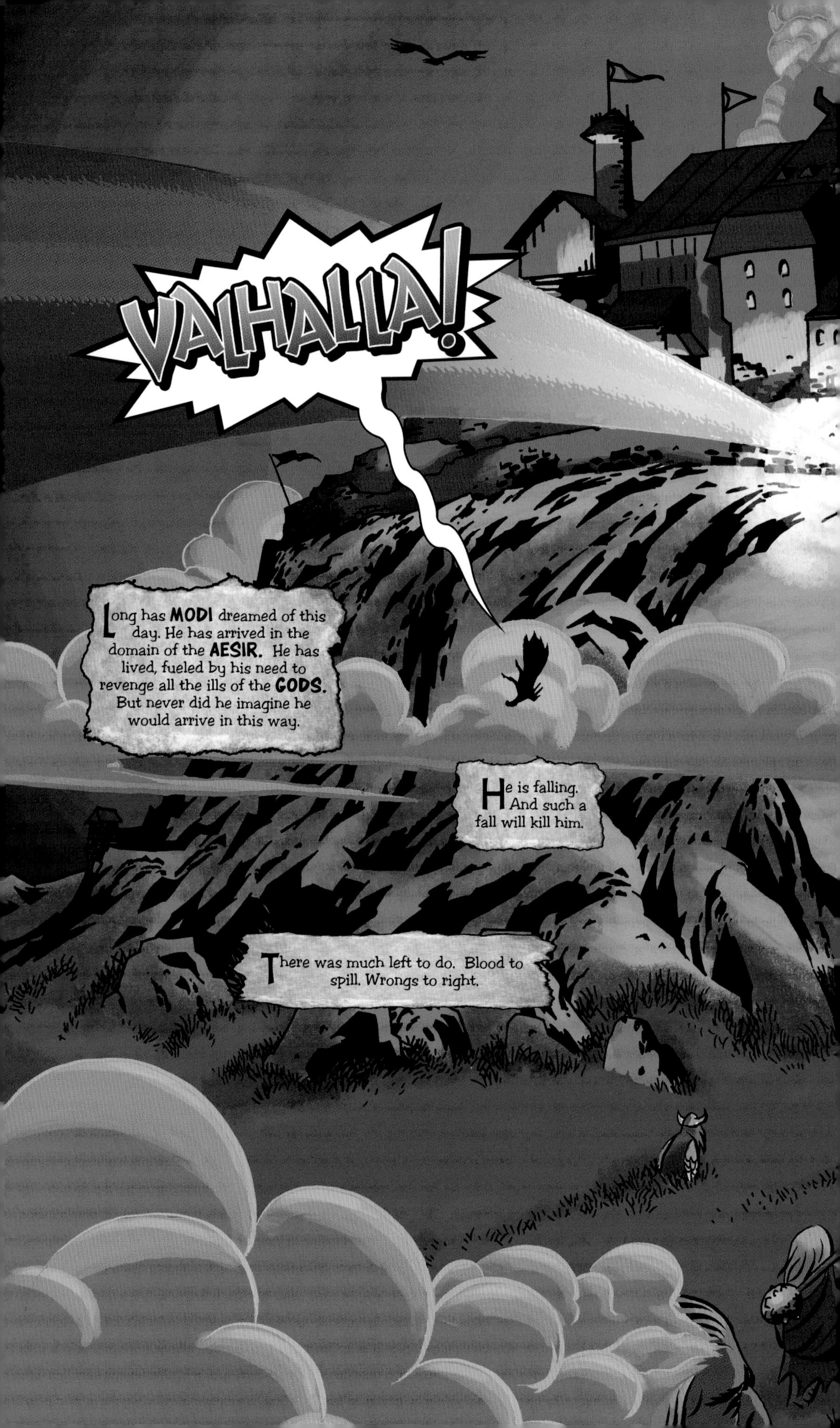
VALHALLA!
Long has MODI dreamed of this day. He has arrived in the domain of the AESIR. He has lived, fueled by his need to revenge all the ills of the GODS. But never did he imagine he would arrive in this way.
He is falling. And such a fall will kill him.
There was much left to do. Blood to spill. Wrongs to right.

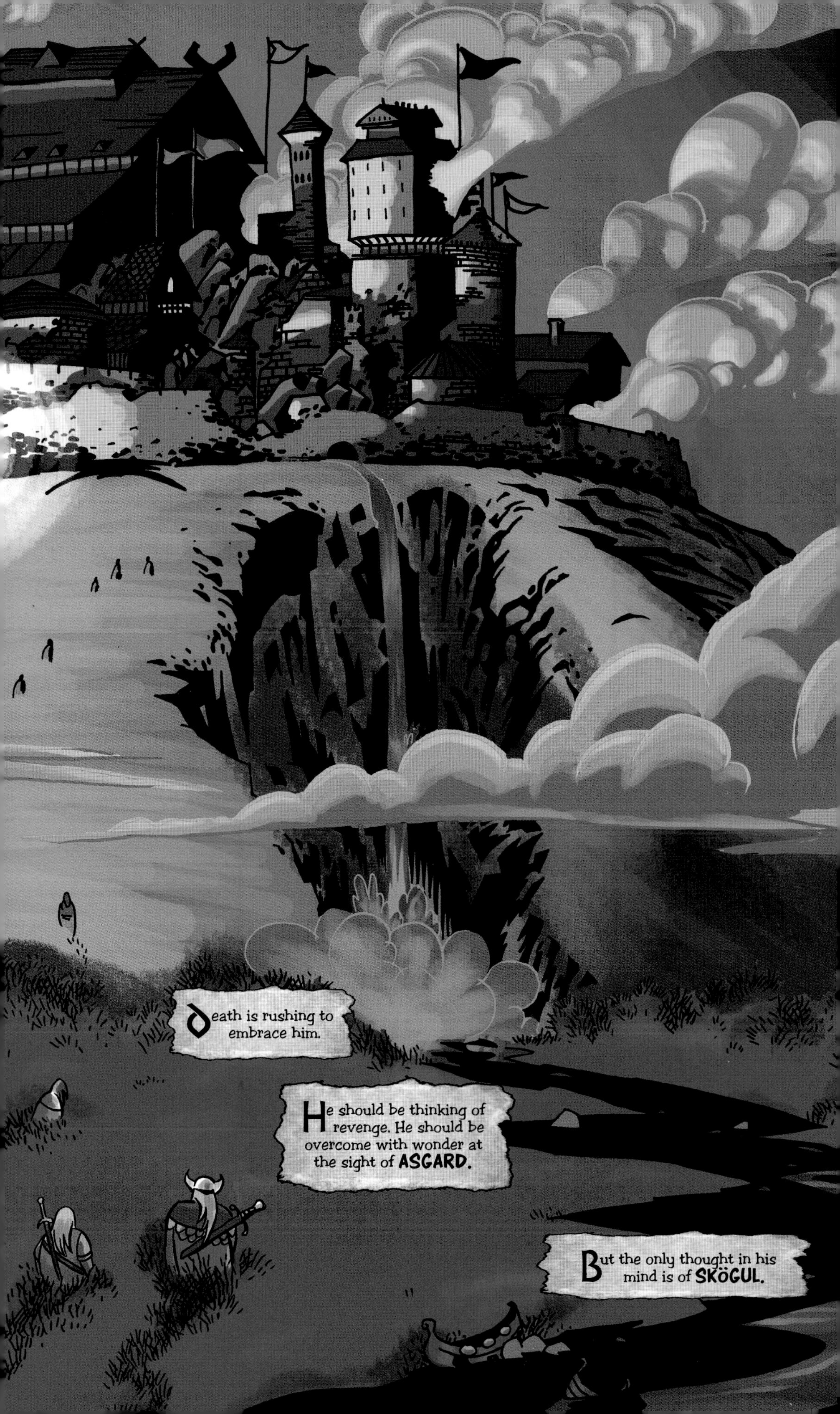
Death is rushing to embrace him.
He should be thinking of revenge. He should be overcome with wonder at the sight of ASGARD.
But the only thought in his mind is of SKÖGUL.

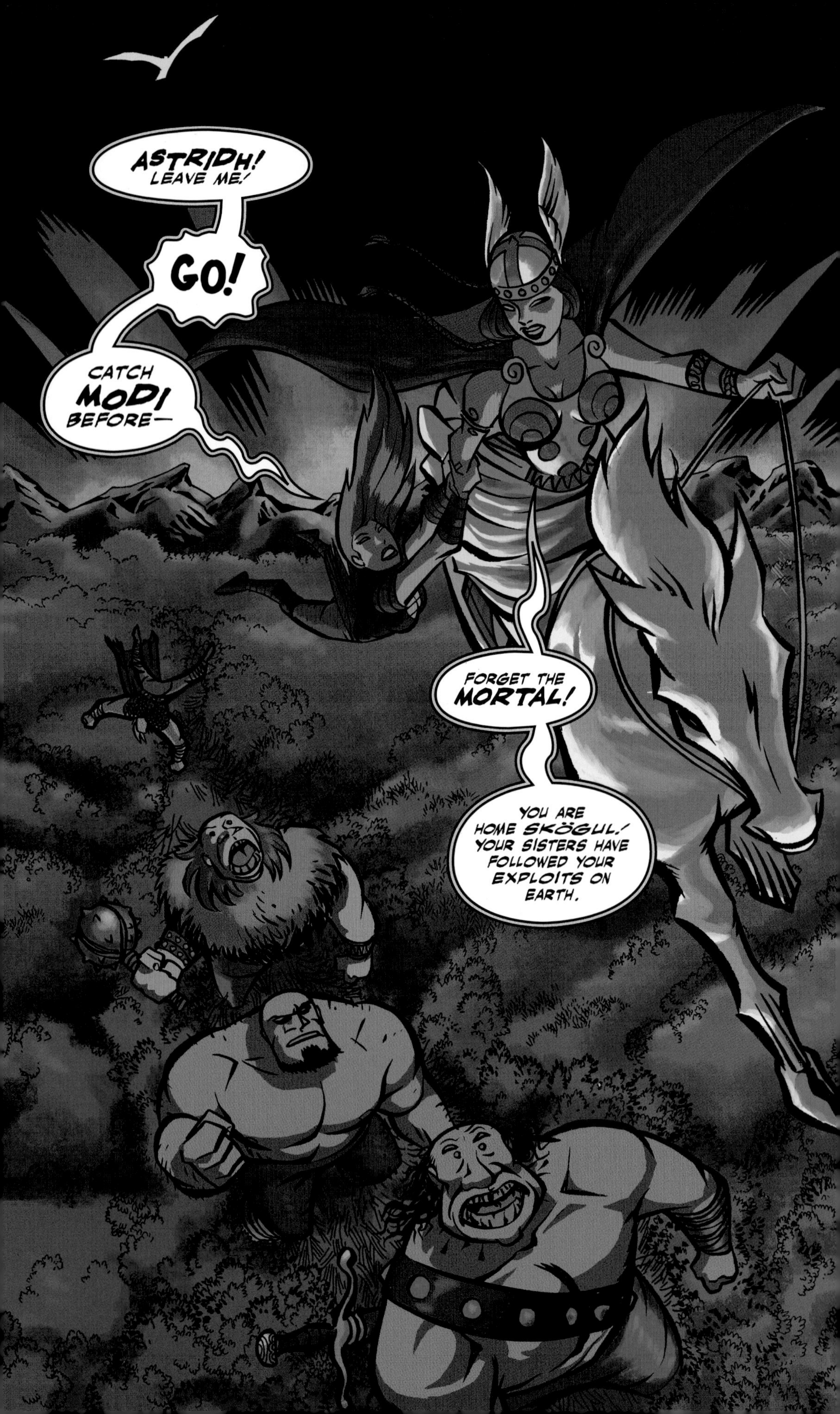
ASTRIDH! LEAVE ME!
GO!
CATCH MODI BEFORE—
FORGET THE MORTAL!
YOU ARE HOME SKÖGUL! YOUR SISTERS HAVE FOLLOWED YOUR EXPLOITS ON EARTH.

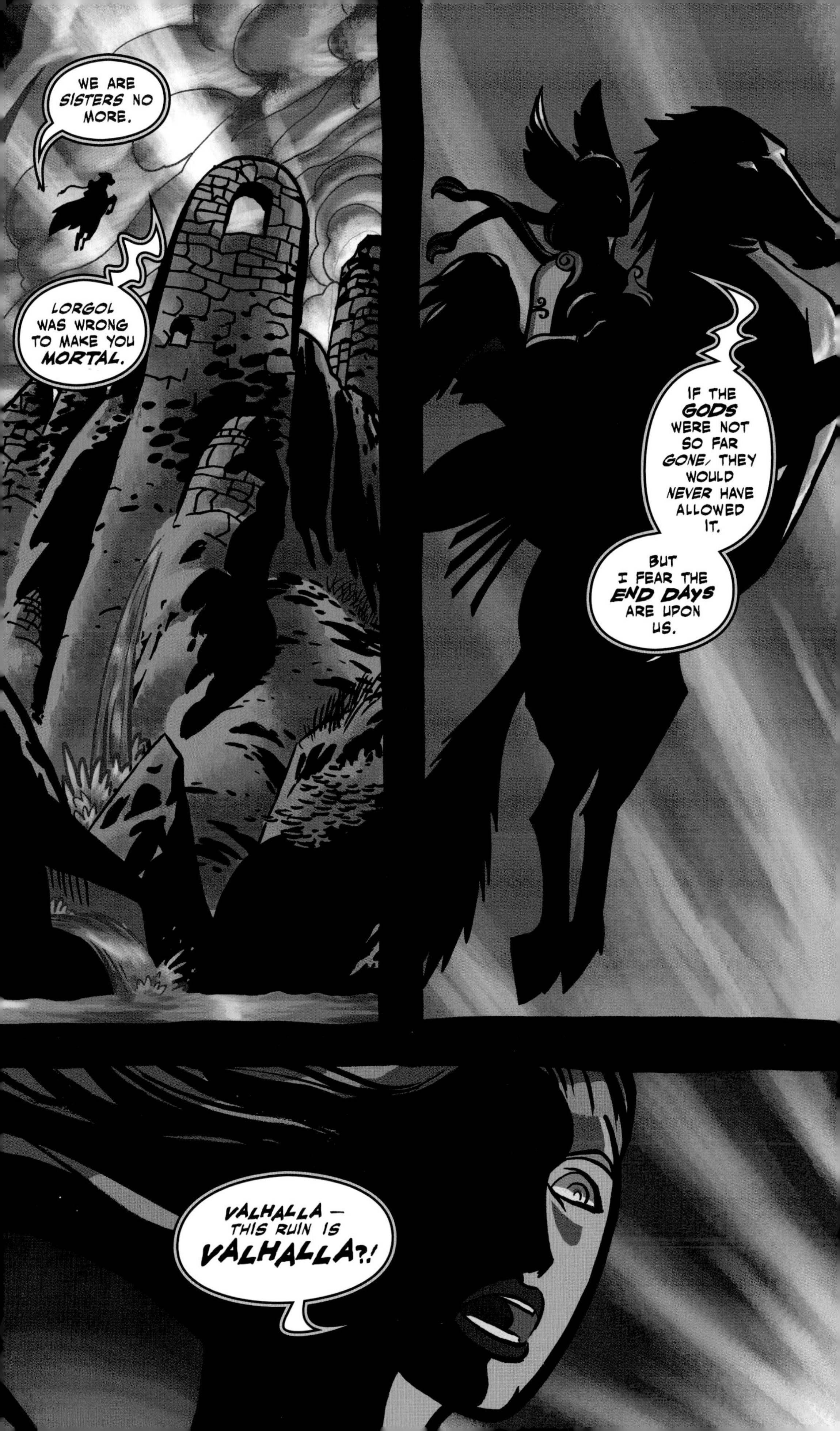
WE ARE SISTERS NO MORE.
LORGOL WAS WRONG TO MAKE YOU MORTAL.
IF THE GODS WERE NOT SO FAR GONE, THEY WOULD NEVER HAVE ALLOWED IT.
BUT I FEAR THE END DAYS ARE UPON US.
VALHALLA— THIS RUIN IS VALHALLA?!

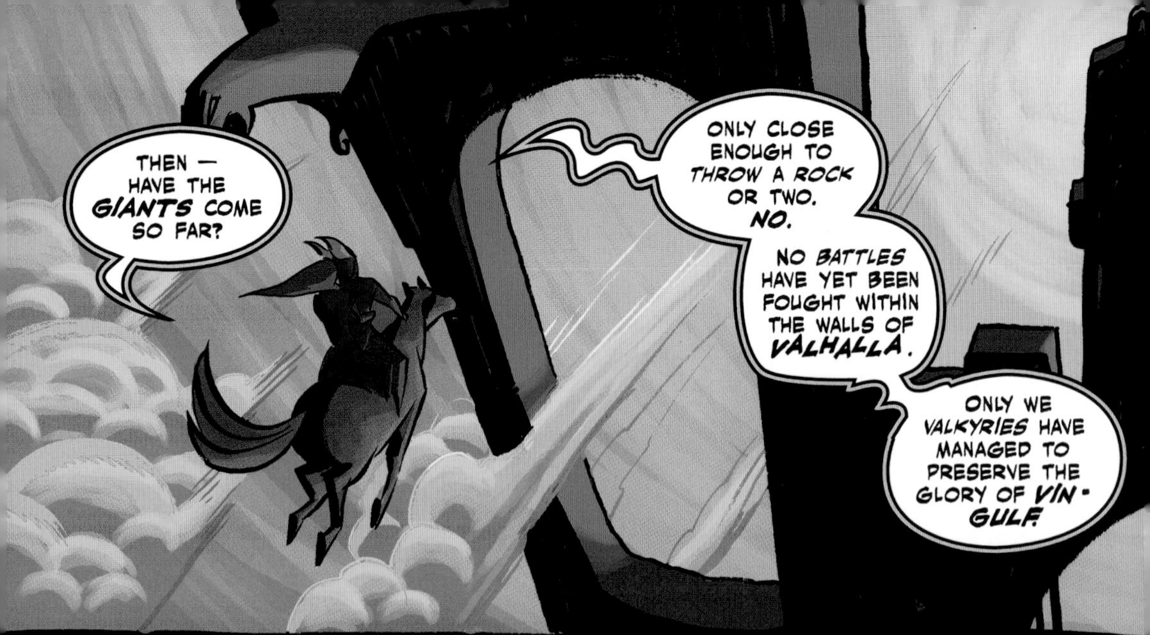
THEN — HAVE THE GIANTS COME SO FAR?
ONLY CLOSE ENOUGH TO THROW A ROCK OR TWO. NO.
NO BATTLES HAVE YET BEEN FOUGHT WITHIN THE WALLS OF VALHALLA.
ONLY WE VALKYRIES HAVE MANAGED TO PRESERVE THE GLORY OF VIN-GULF.

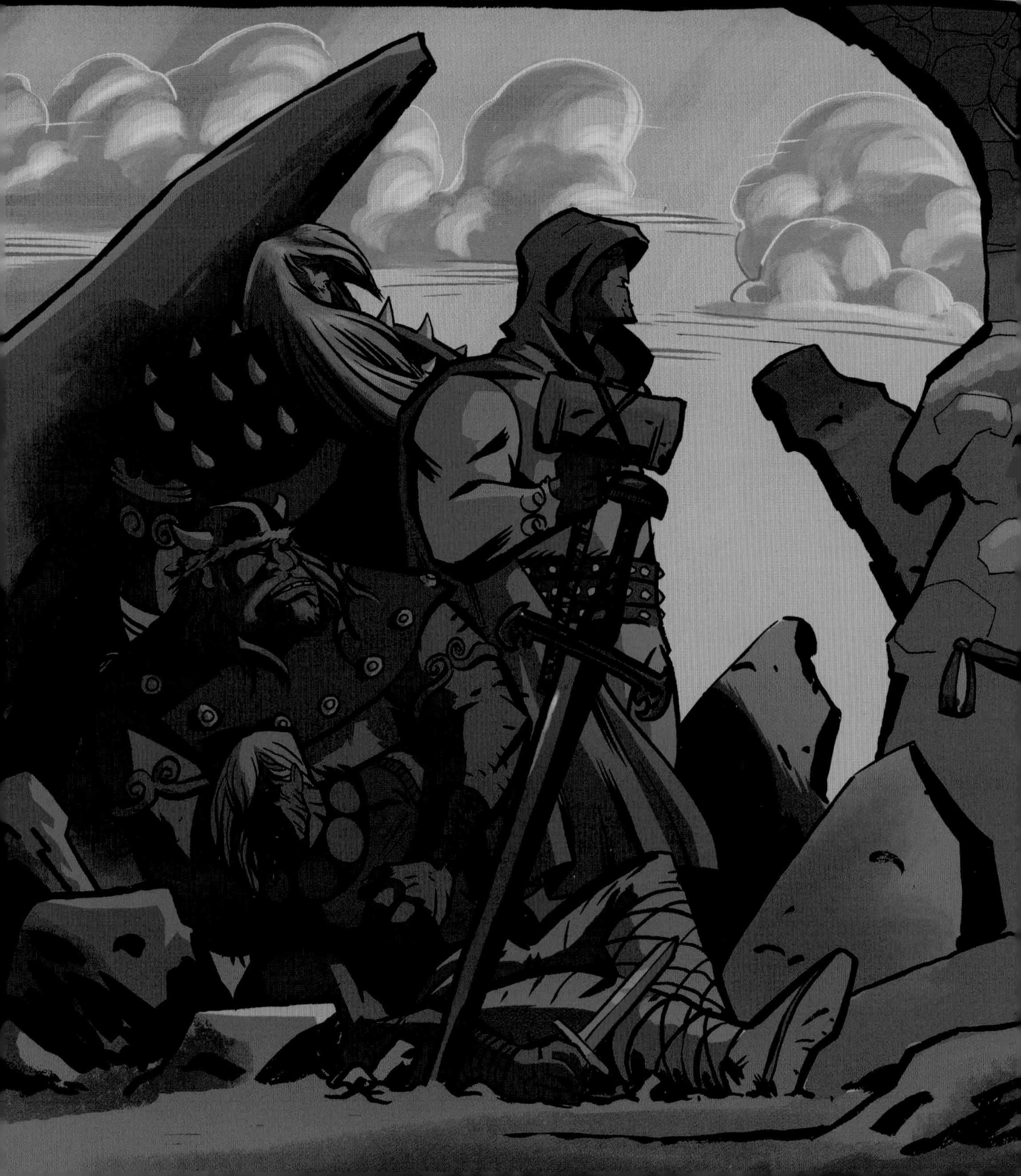

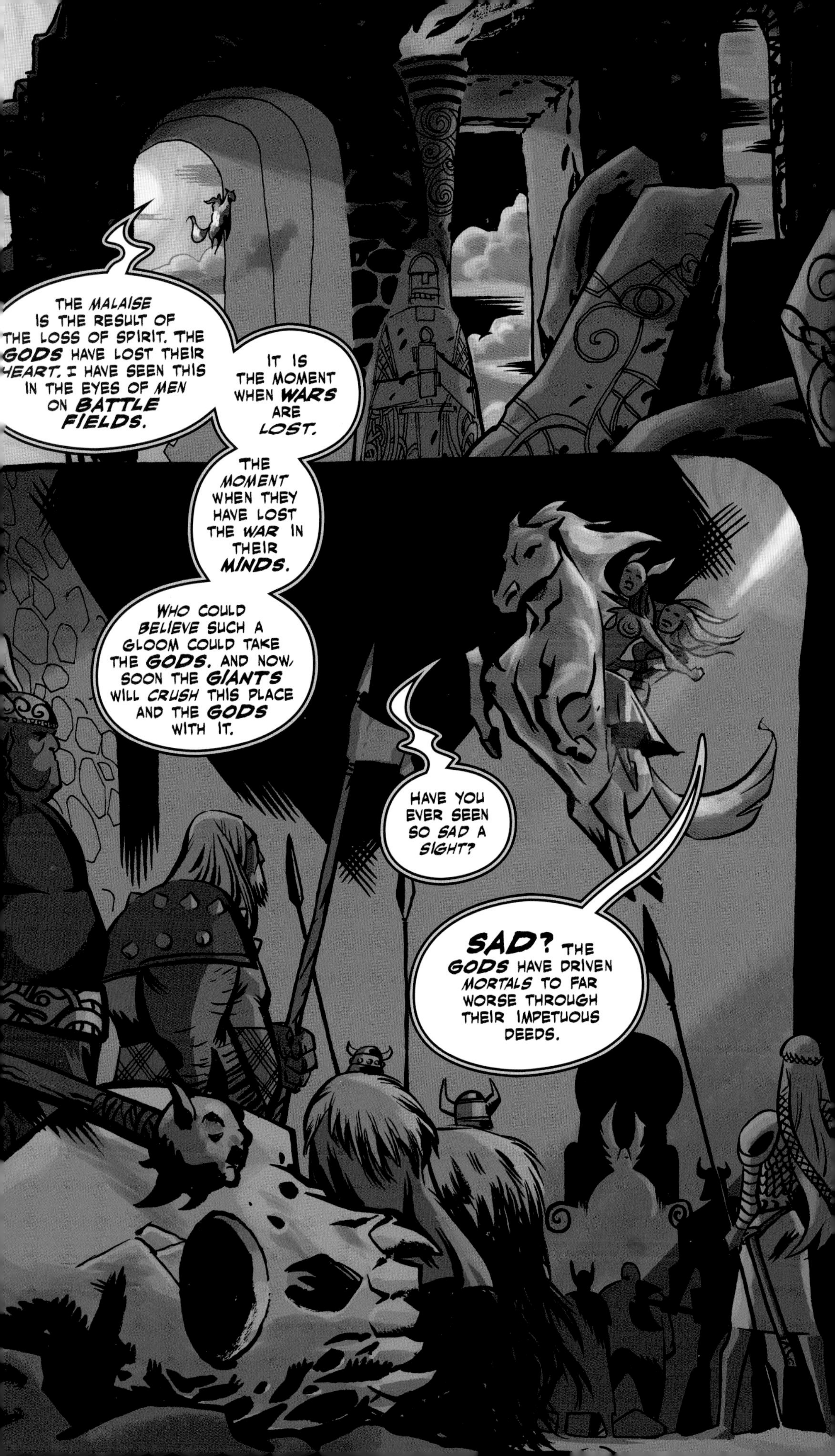
THE MALAISE IS THE RESULT OF THE LOSS OF SPIRIT. THE GODS HAVE LOST THEIR HEART. I HAVE SEEN THIS IN THE EYES OF MEN ON BATTLE FIELDS.
IT IS THE MOMENT WHEN WARS ARE LOST.
THE MOMENT WHEN THEY HAVE LOST THE WAR IN THEIR MINDS.
WHO COULD BELIEVE SUCH A GLOOM COULD TAKE THE GODS. AND NOW, SOON THE GIANTS WILL CRUSH THIS PLACE AND THE GODS WITH IT.
HAVE YOU EVER SEEN SO SAD A SIGHT?
SAD? THE GODS HAVE DRIVEN MORTALS TO FAR WORSE THROUGH THEIR IMPETUOUS DEEDS.

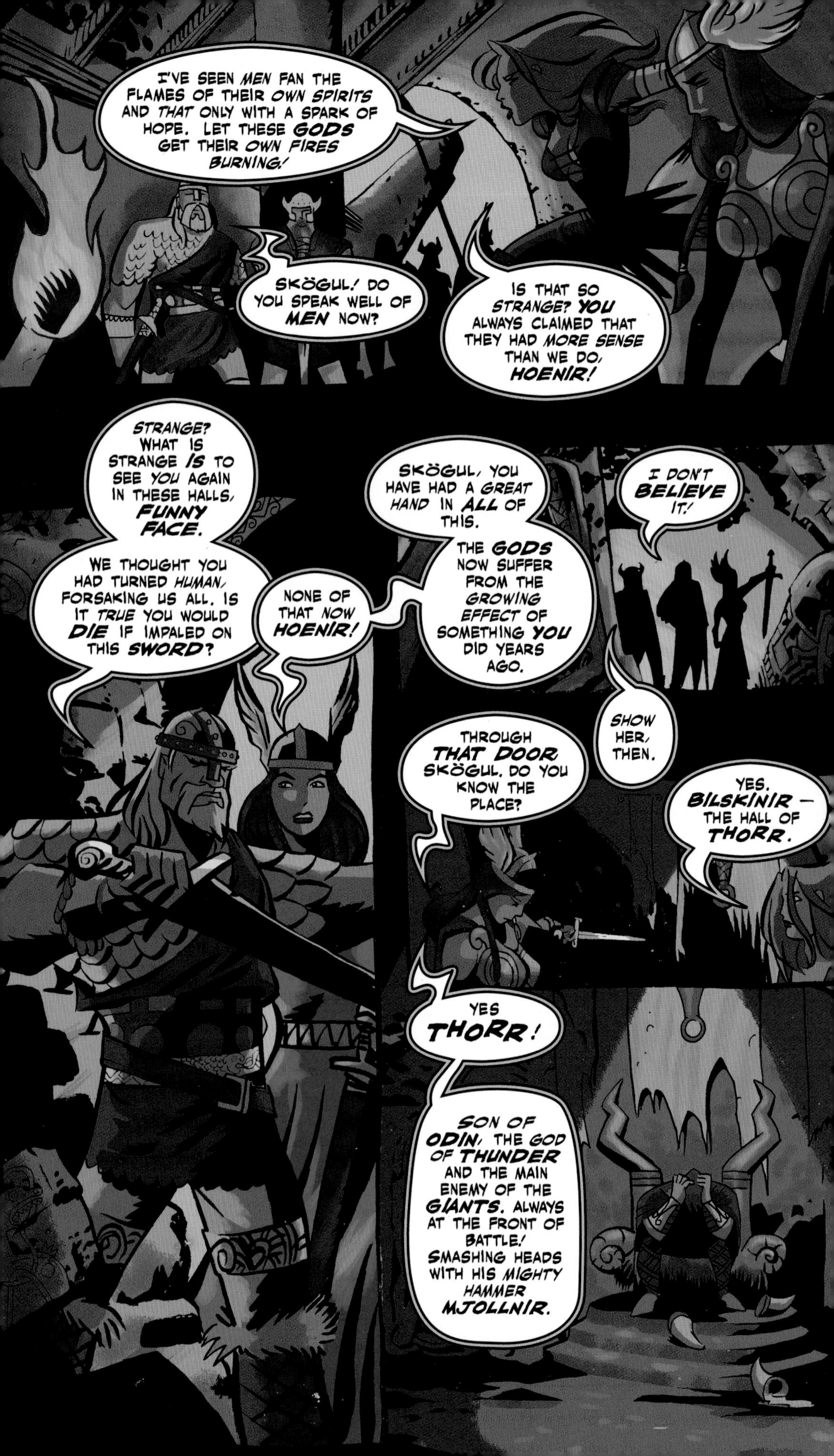

I'VE SEEN MEN FAN THE FLAMES OF THEIR OWN SPIRITS AND THAT ONLY WITH A SPARK OF HOPE. LET THESE GODS GET THEIR OWN FIRES BURNING!
SKÖGUL! DO YOU SPEAK WELL OF MEN NOW?
IS THAT SO STRANGE? YOU ALWAYS CLAIMED THAT THEY HAD MORE SENSE THAN WE DO, HOENIR!
STRANGE? WHAT IS STRANGE IS TO SEE YOU AGAIN IN THESE HALLS, FUNNY FACE.
WE THOUGHT YOU HAD TURNED HUMAN, FORSAKING US ALL. IS IT TRUE YOU WOULD DIE IF IMPALED ON THIS SWORD?
NONE OF THAT NOW HOENIR!
SKÖGUL, YOU HAVE HAD A GREAT HAND IN ALL OF THIS.
THE GODS NOW SUFFER FROM THE GROWING EFFECT OF SOMETHING YOU DID YEARS AGO.
I DON'T BELIEVE IT!
SHOW HER, THEN.
THROUGH THAT DOOR SKÖGUL. DO YOU KNOW THE PLACE?
YES. BILSKINIR — THE HALL OF THORR.
YES THORR!
SON OF ODIN, THE GOD OF THUNDER AND THE MAIN ENEMY OF THE GIANTS. ALWAYS AT THE FRONT OF BATTLE! SMASHING HEADS WITH HIS MIGHTY HAMMER MJOLLNIR.

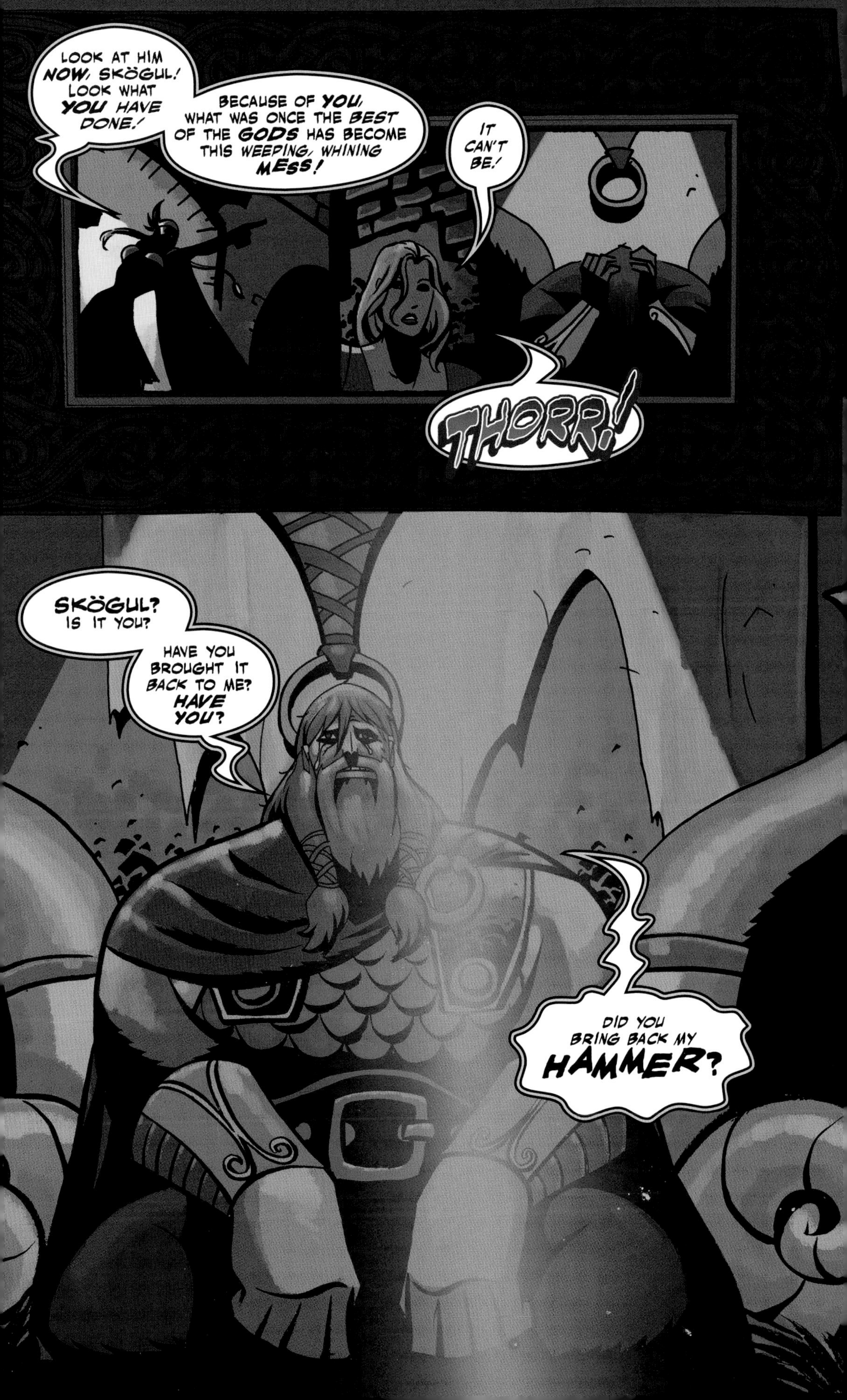
LOOK AT HIM NOW, SKÖGUL! LOOK WHAT YOU HAVE DONE!
BECAUSE OF YOU, WHAT WAS ONCE THE BEST OF THE GODS HAS BECOME THIS WEEPING, WHINING MESS!
IT CAN'T BE!
THORR!
SKÖGUL? IS IT YOU?
HAVE YOU BROUGHT IT BACK TO ME? HAVE YOU?
DID YOU BRING BACK MY HAMMER?

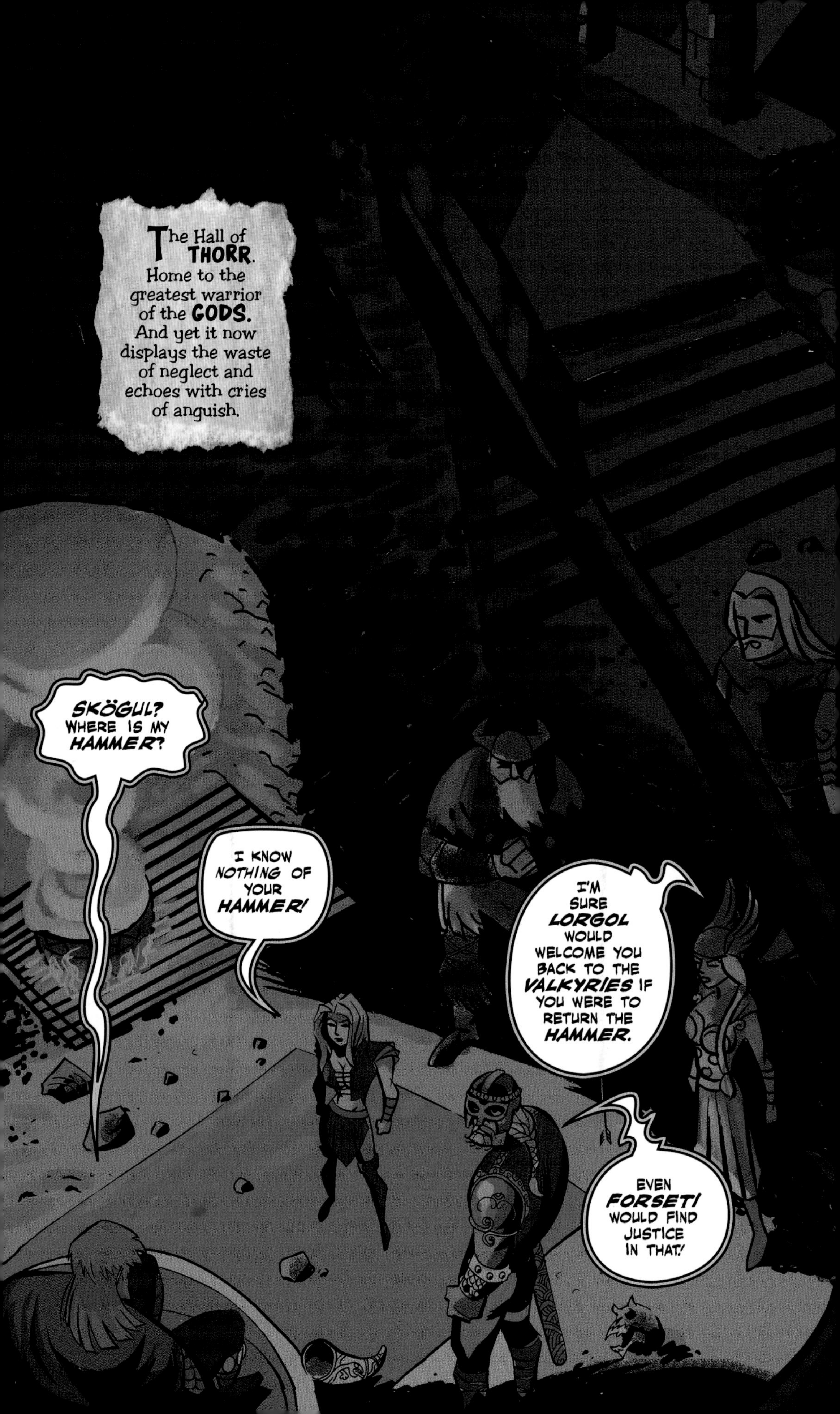
The Hall of THORR. Home to the greatest warrior of the GODS. And yet it now displays the waste of neglect and echoes with cries of anguish.
SKÖGUL? WHERE IS MY HAMMER?
I KNOW NOTHING OF YOUR HAMMER!
I'M SURE LORGOL WOULD WELCOME YOU BACK TO THE VALKYRIES IF YOU WERE TO RETURN THE HAMMER.
EVEN FORSETI WOULD FIND JUSTICE IN THAT!

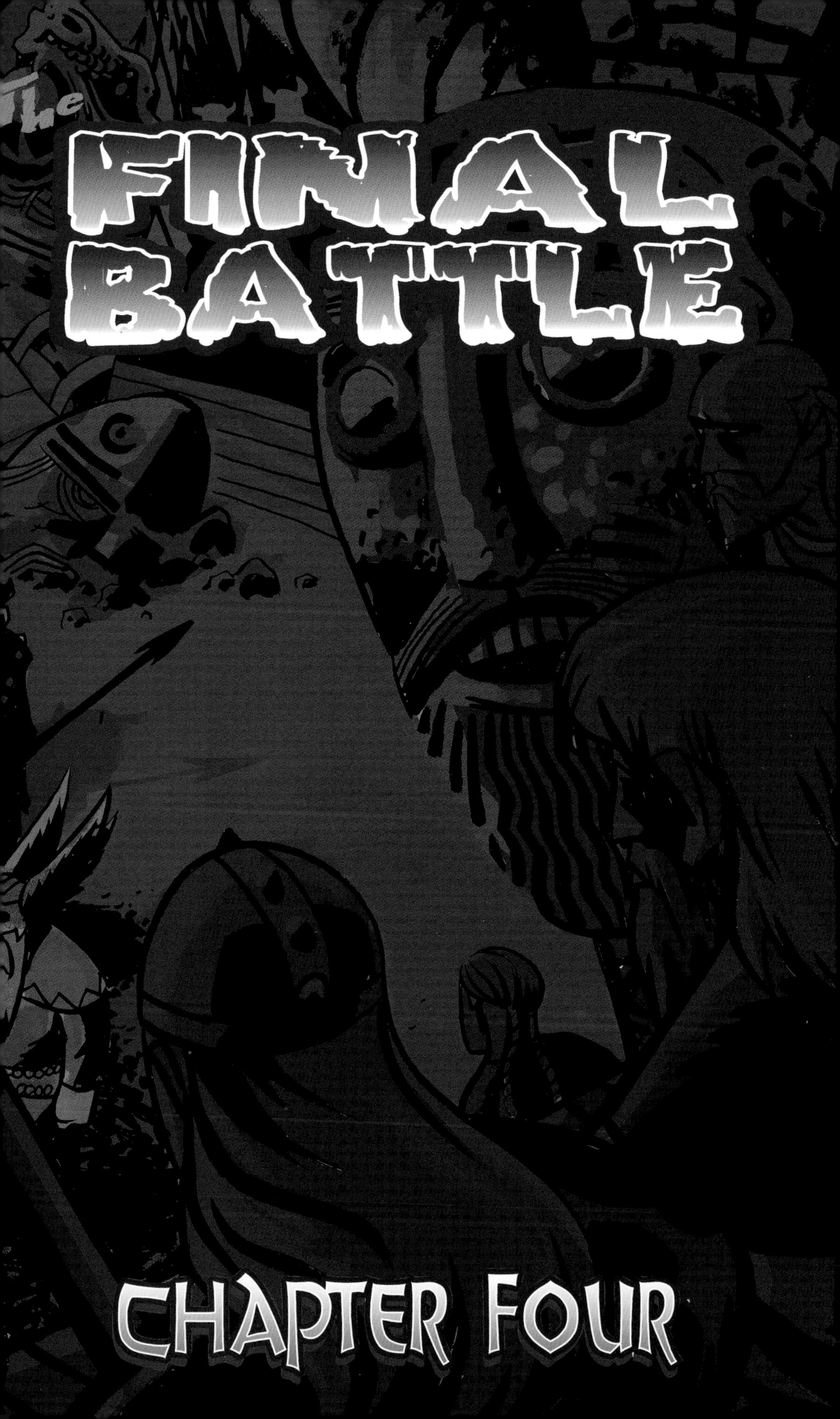
The
FINAL
BATTLE
CHAPTER FOUR

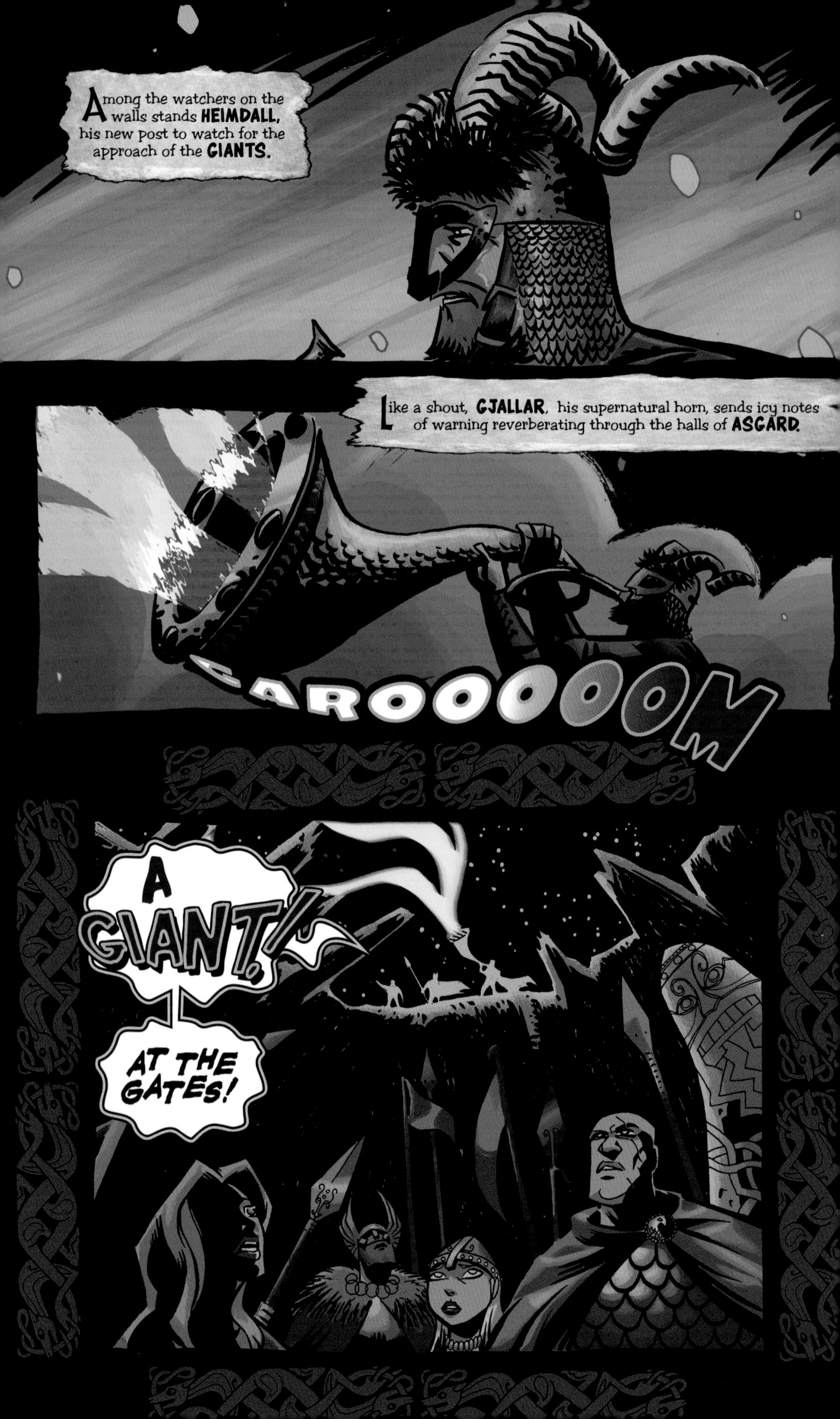
Among the watchers on the walls stands HEIMDALL, his new post to watch for the approach of the GIANTS.
Like a shout, GJALLAR, his supernatural horn, sends icy notes of warning reverberating through the halls of ASGARD.
AROOOOOOM
A GIANT!
AT THE GATES!

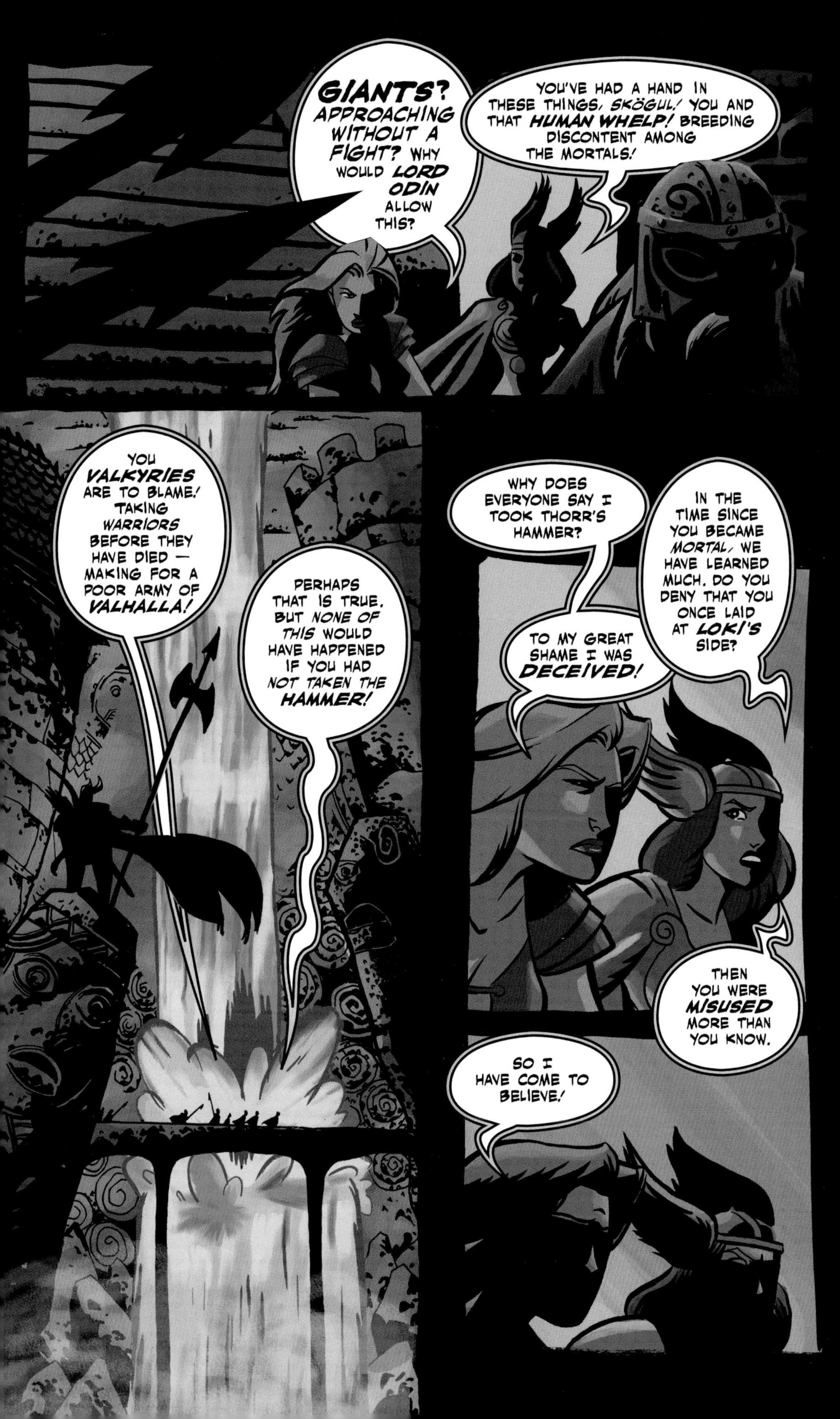

GIANTS? APPROACHING WITHOUT A FIGHT? WHY WOULD LORD ODIN ALLOW THIS?
YOU'VE HAD A HAND IN THESE THINGS, SKÖGUL! YOU AND THAT HUMAN WHELP! BREEDING DISCONTENT AMONG THE MORTALS!
YOU VALKYRIES ARE TO BLAME! TAKING WARRIORS BEFORE THEY HAVE DIED — MAKING FOR A POOR ARMY OF VALHALLA!
PERHAPS THAT IS TRUE. BUT NONE OF THIS WOULD HAVE HAPPENED IF YOU HAD NOT TAKEN THE HAMMER!
WHY DOES EVERYONE SAY I TOOK THORR'S HAMMER?
IN THE TIME SINCE YOU BECAME MORTAL, WE HAVE LEARNED MUCH. DO YOU DENY THAT YOU ONCE LAID AT LOKI'S SIDE?
TO MY GREAT SHAME I WAS DECEIVED!
THEN YOU WERE MISUSED MORE THAN YOU KNOW.
SO I HAVE COME TO BELIEVE!

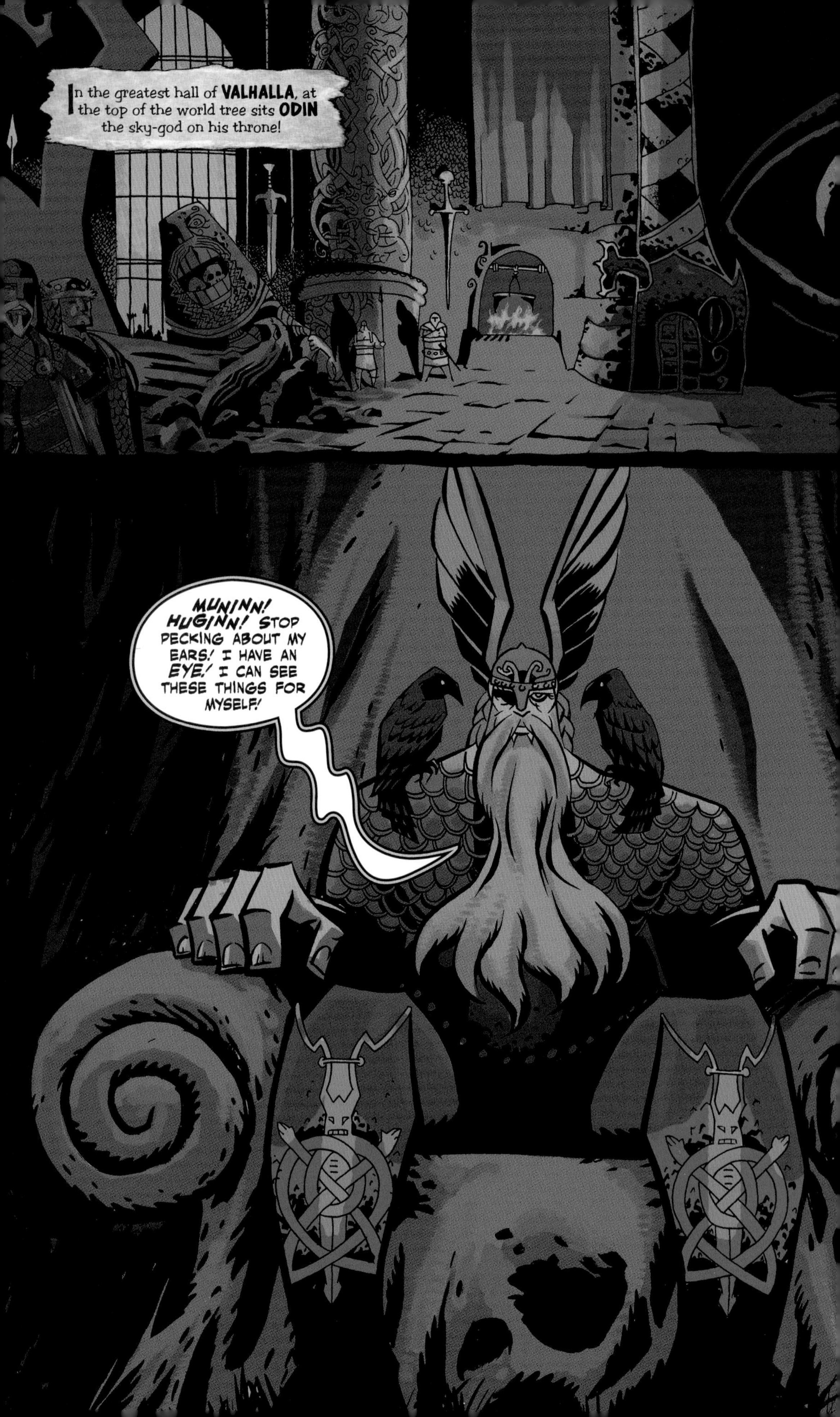
In the greatest hall of VALHALLA, at the top of the world tree sits ODIN the sky-god on his throne!
MUNINN! HUGINN! STOP PECKING ABOUT MY EARS! I HAVE AN EYE! I CAN SEE THESE THINGS FOR MYSELF!

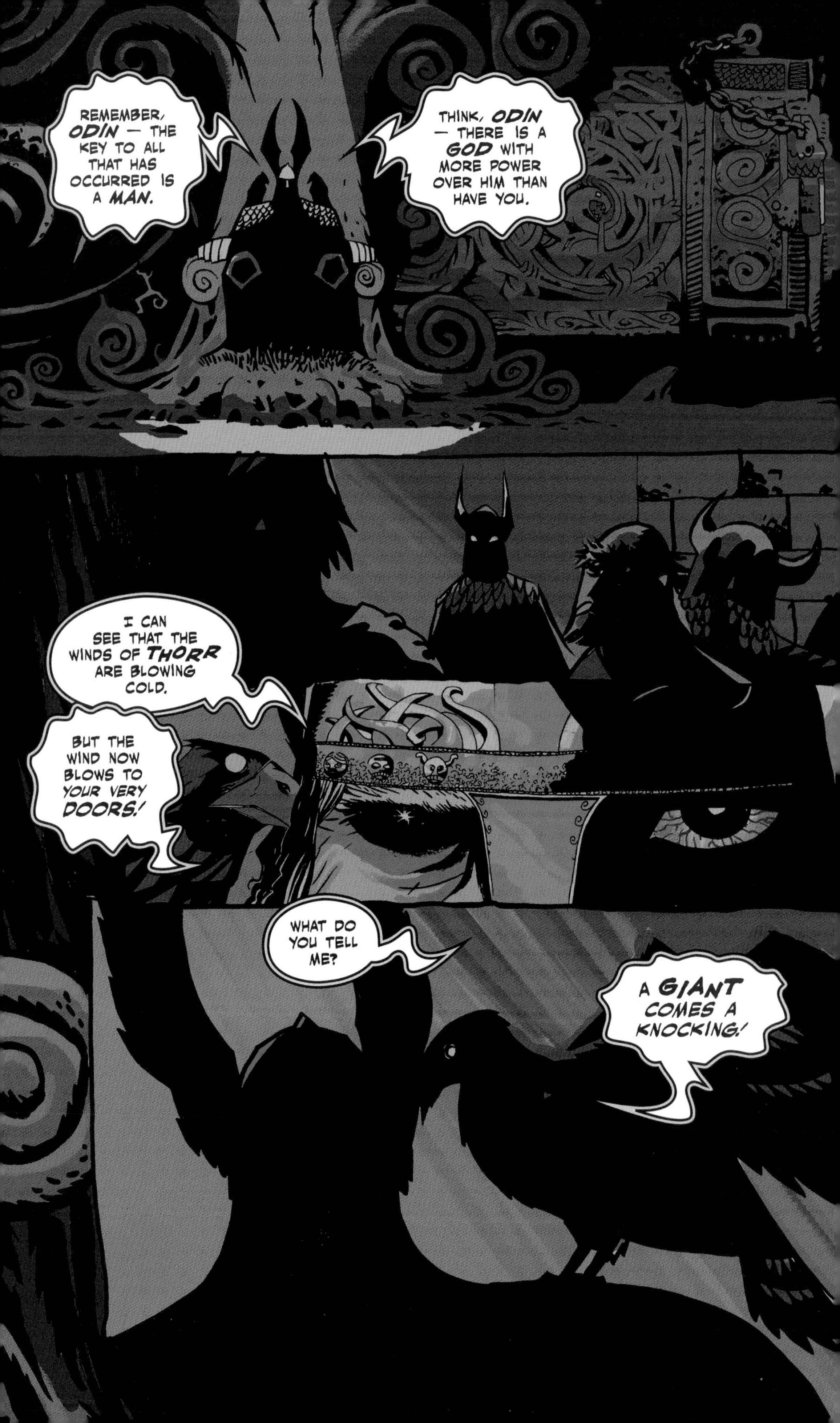
REMEMBER, ODIN — THE KEY TO ALL THAT HAS OCCURRED IS A MAN.
THINK, ODIN — THERE IS A GOD WITH MORE POWER OVER HIM THAN HAVE YOU.
I CAN SEE THAT THE WINDS OF THORR ARE BLOWING COLD.
BUT THE WIND NOW BLOWS TO YOUR VERY DOORS!
WHAT DO YOU TELL ME?
A GIANT COMES A KNOCKING!

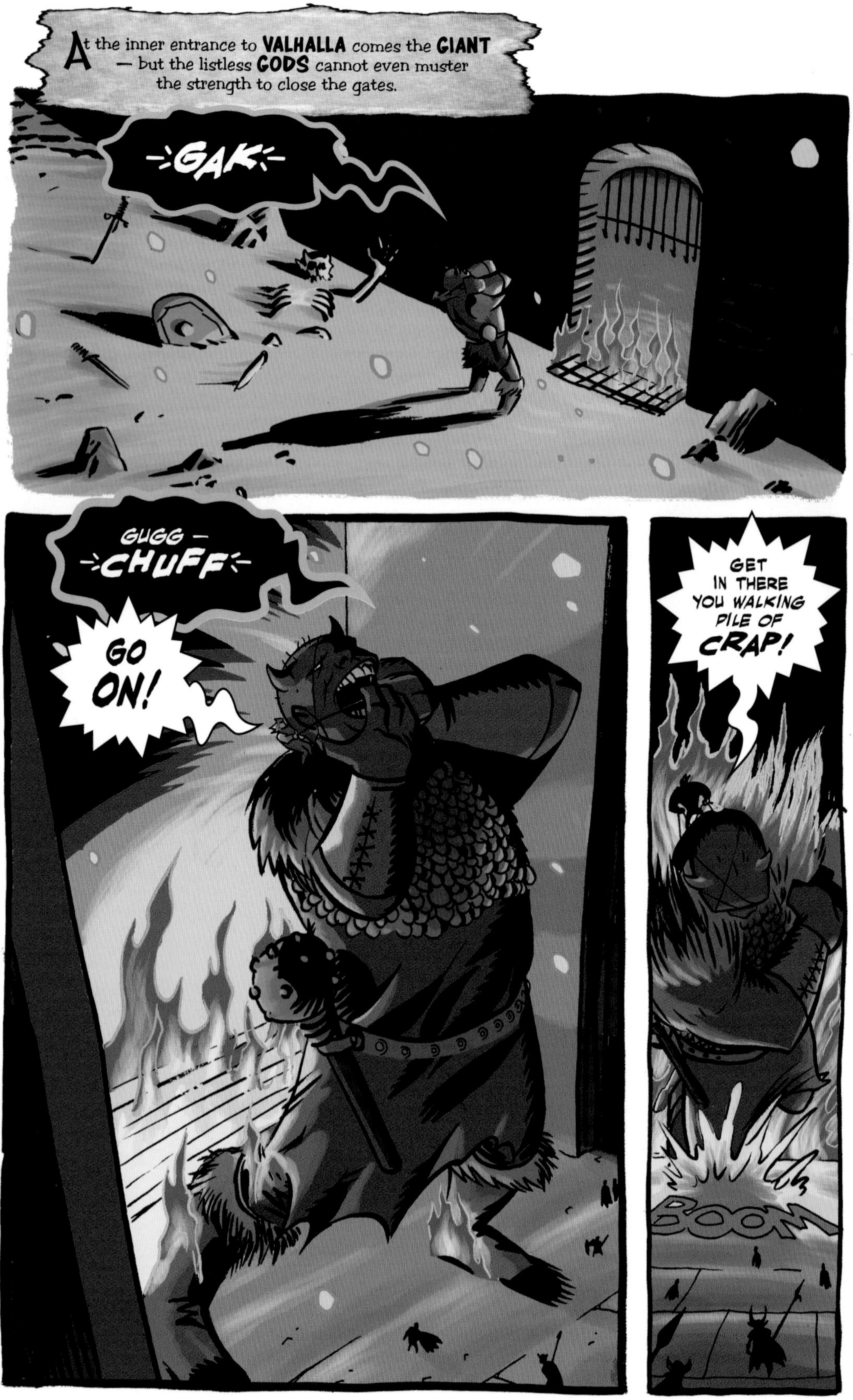
At the inner entrance to VALHALLA comes the GIANT — but the listless GODS cannot even muster the strength to close the gates.
GAK
GUGG — CHUFF
GO ON!
GET IN THERE YOU WALKING PILE OF CRAP!
BOOM

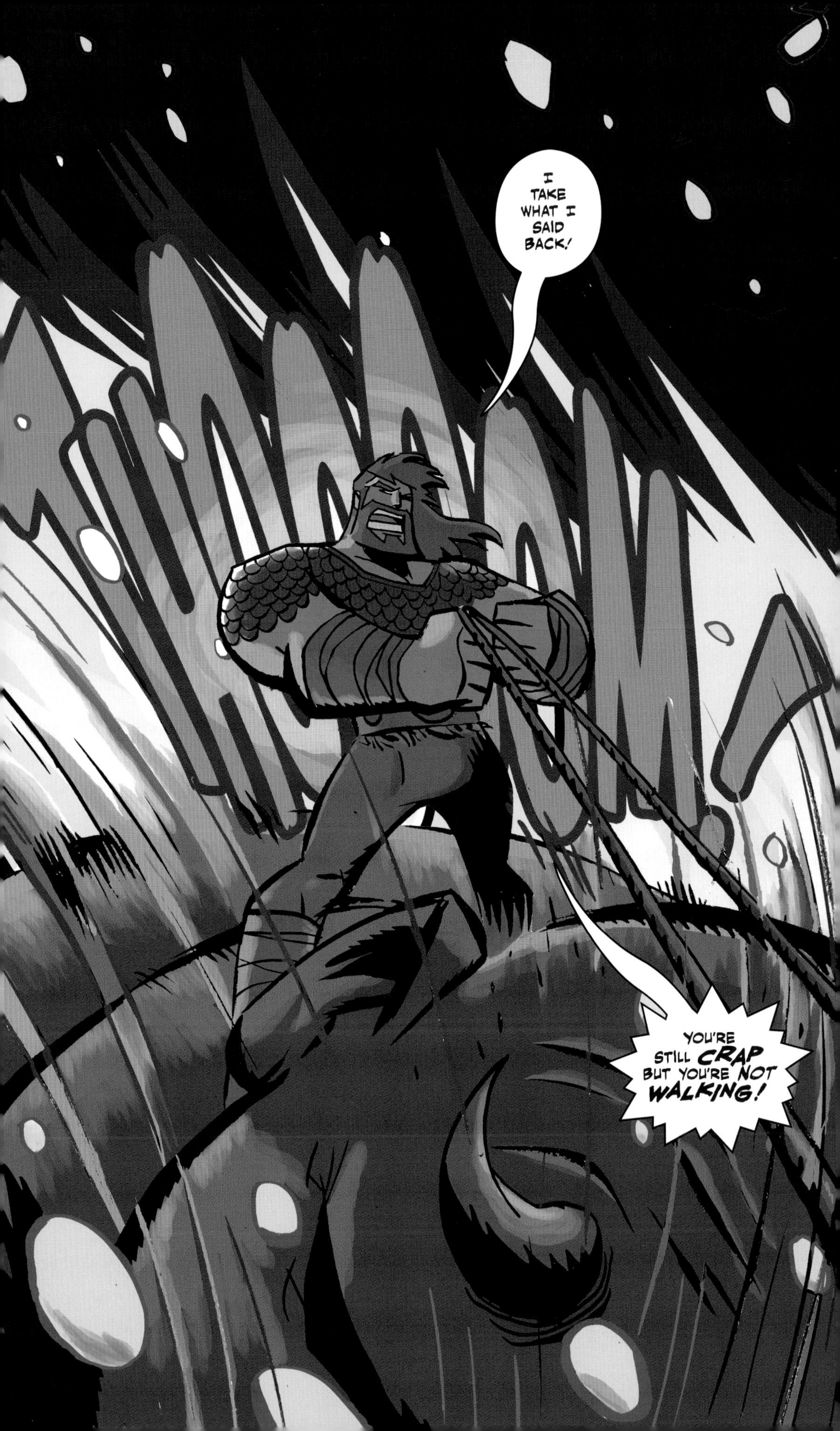
I TAKE WHAT I SAID BACK!
YOU'RE STILL CRAP BUT YOU'RE NOT WALKING!

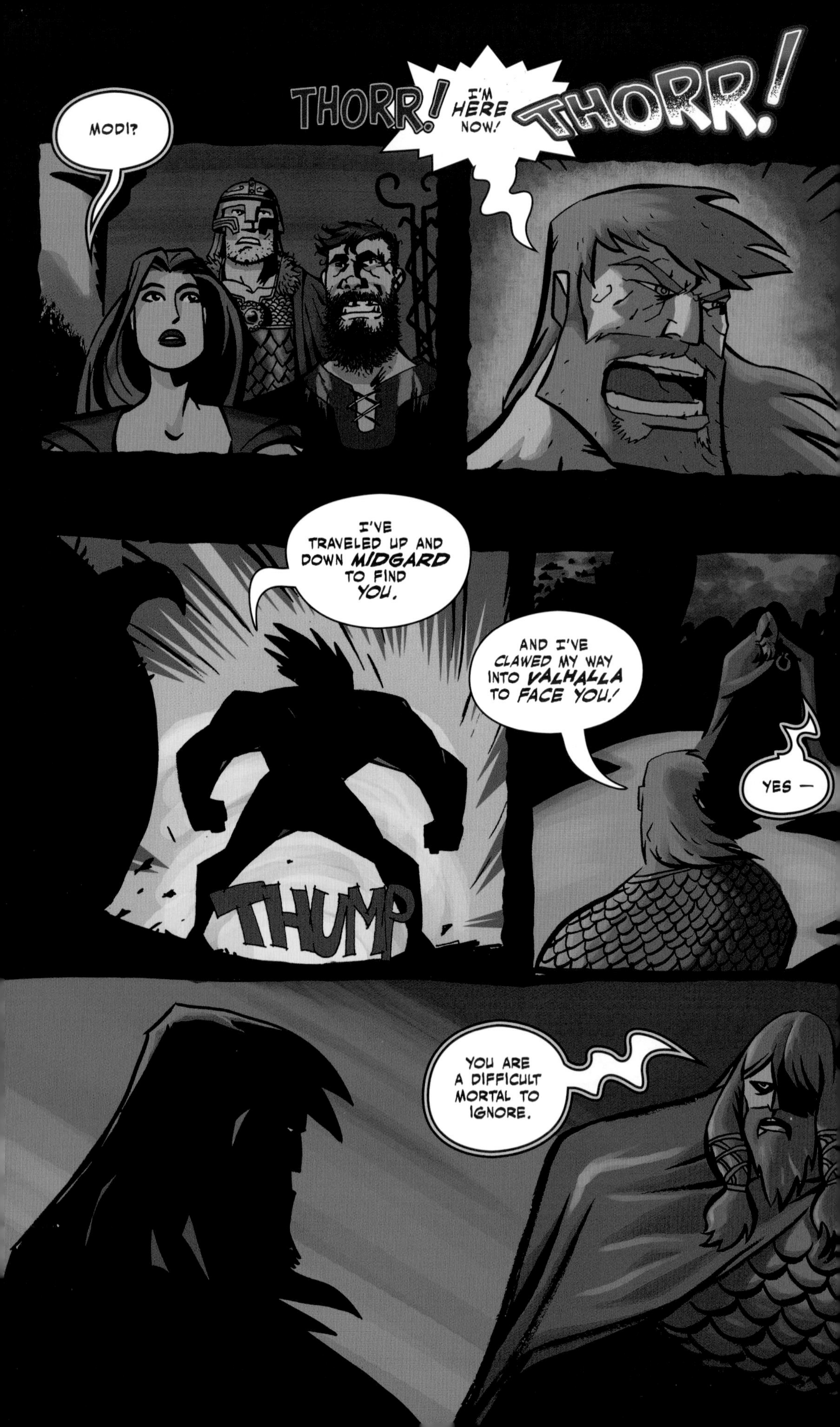

MODI?
THORR!
I'M HERE NOW!
THORR!
I'VE TRAVELED UP AND DOWN MIDGARD TO FIND YOU.
THUMP
AND I'VE CLAWED MY WAY INTO VALHALLA TO FACE YOU!
YES —
YOU ARE A DIFFICULT MORTAL TO IGNORE.

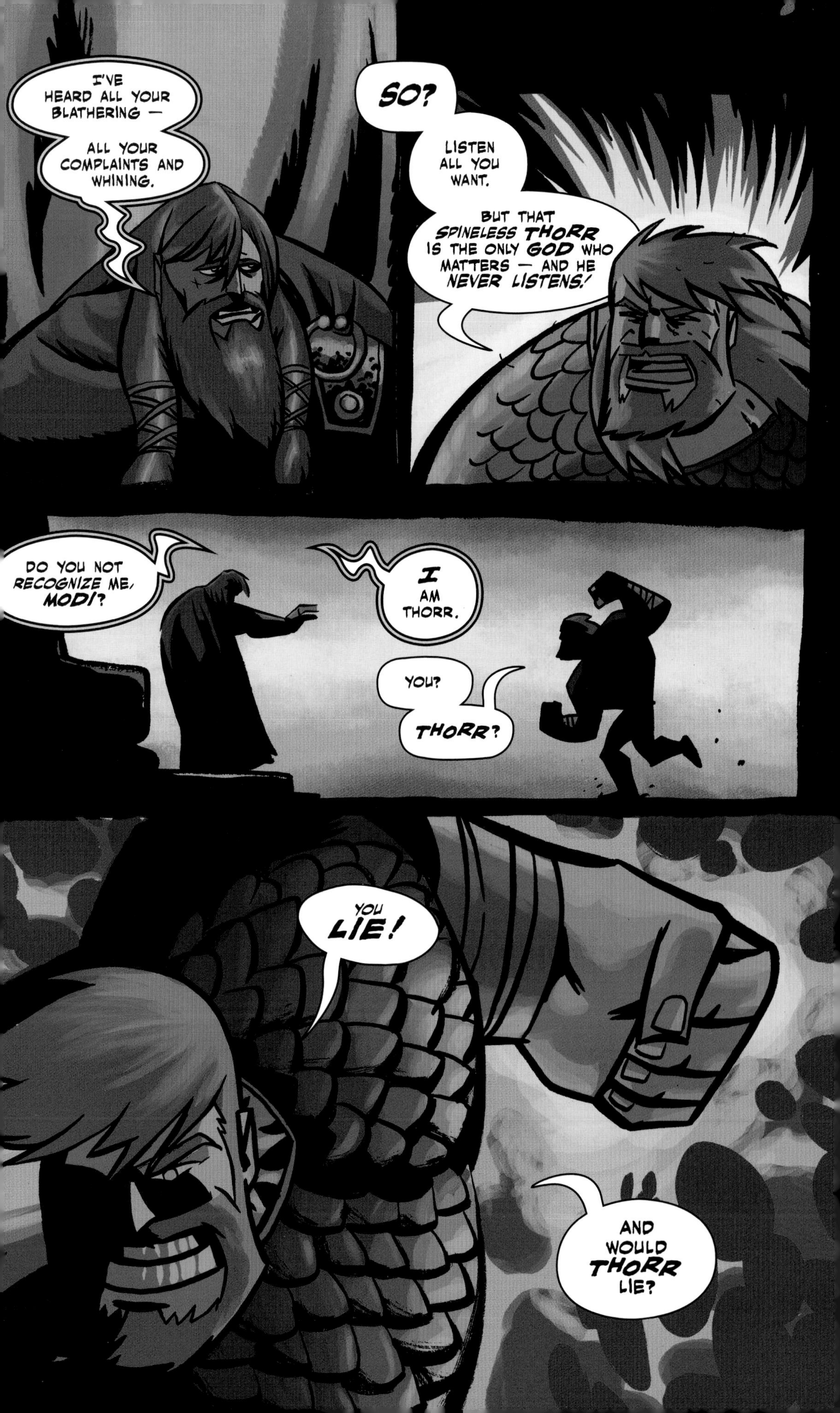
I'VE HEARD ALL YOUR BLATHERING —
ALL YOUR COMPLAINTS AND WHINING.
SO?
LISTEN ALL YOU WANT.
BUT THAT SPINELESS THORR IS THE ONLY GOD WHO MATTERS — AND HE NEVER LISTENS!
DO YOU NOT RECOGNIZE ME, MODI?
I AM THORR.
YOU?
THORR?
YOU LIE!
AND WOULD THORR LIE?

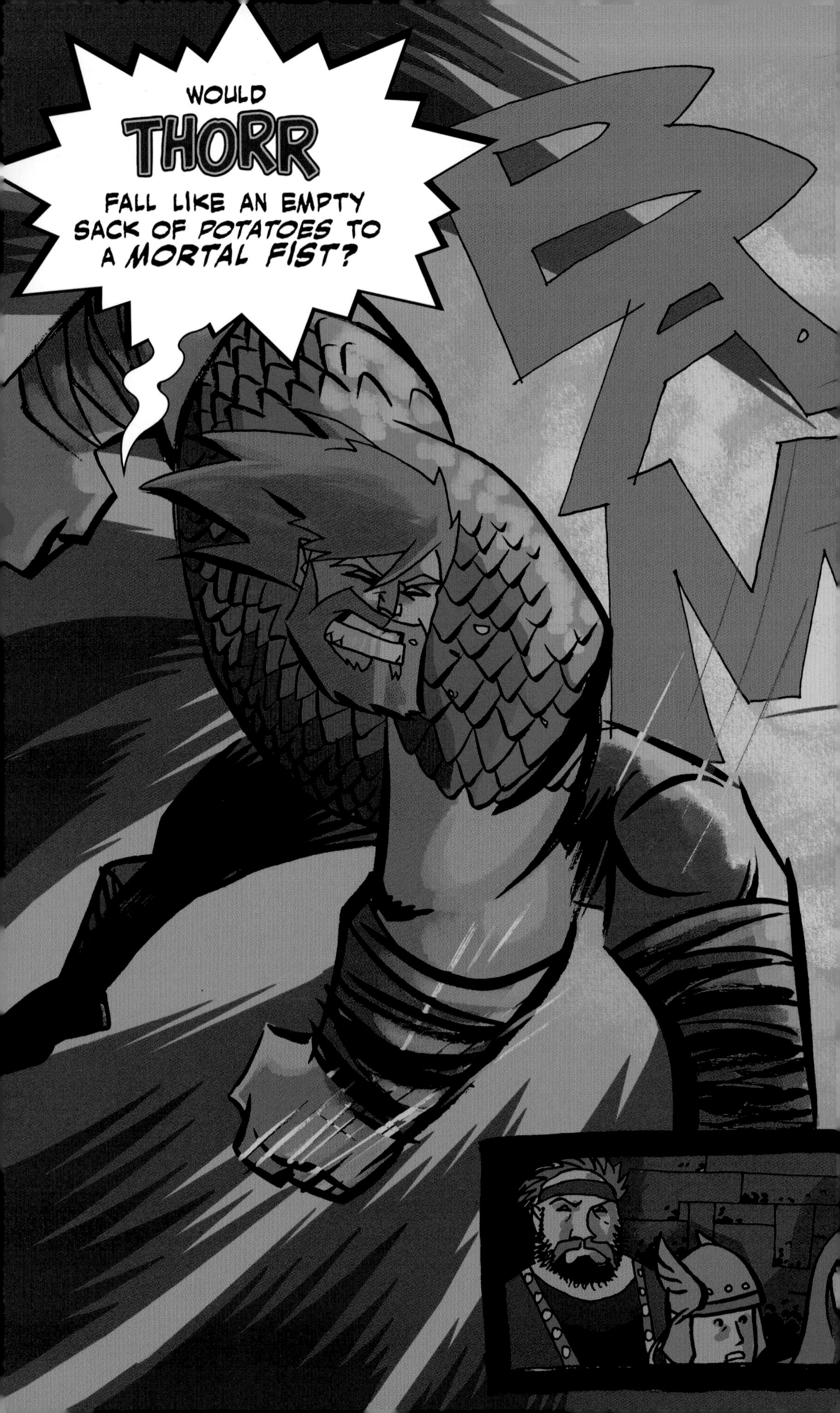
WOULD THORR FALL LIKE AN EMPTY SACK OF POTATOES TO A MORTAL FIST?
BAM

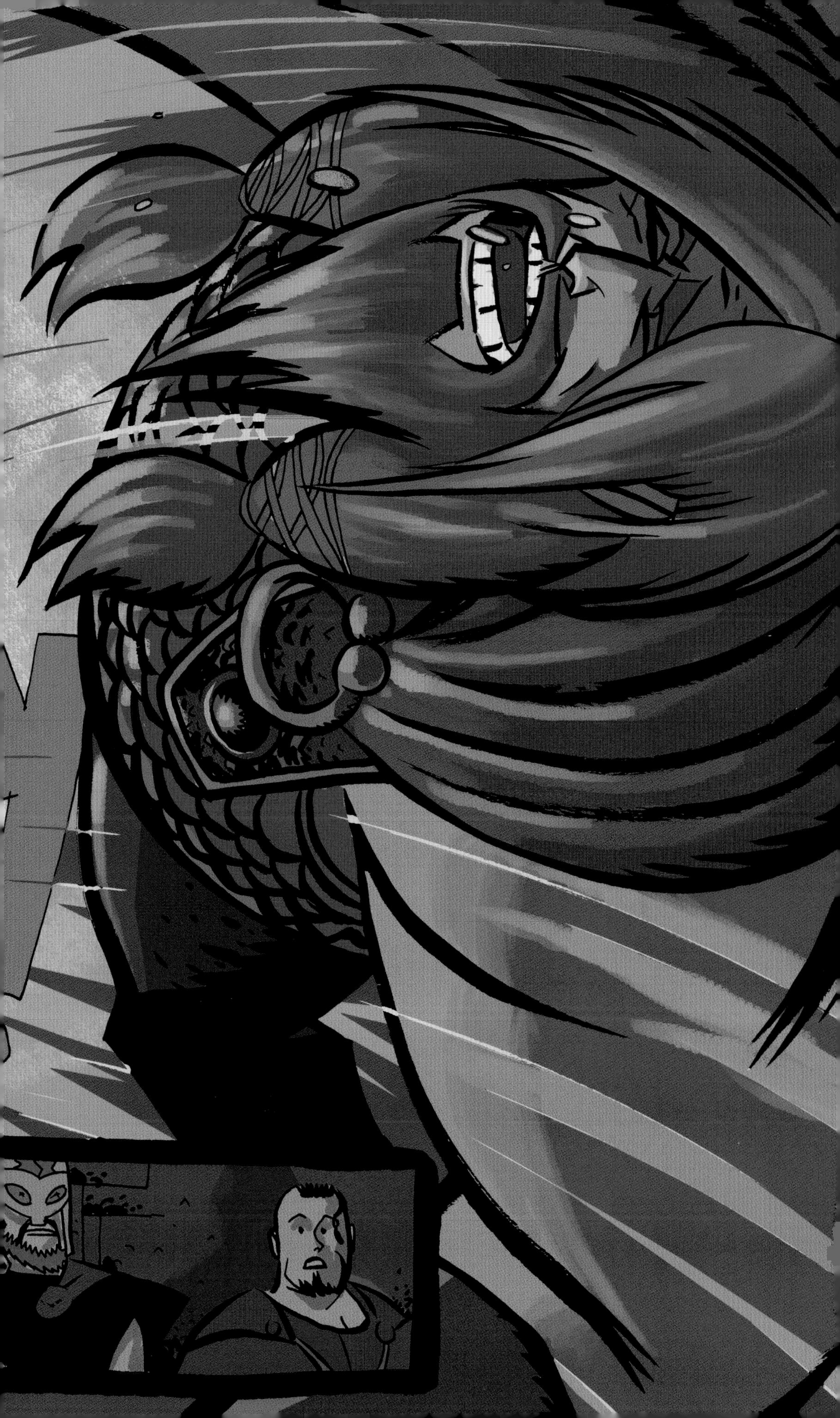

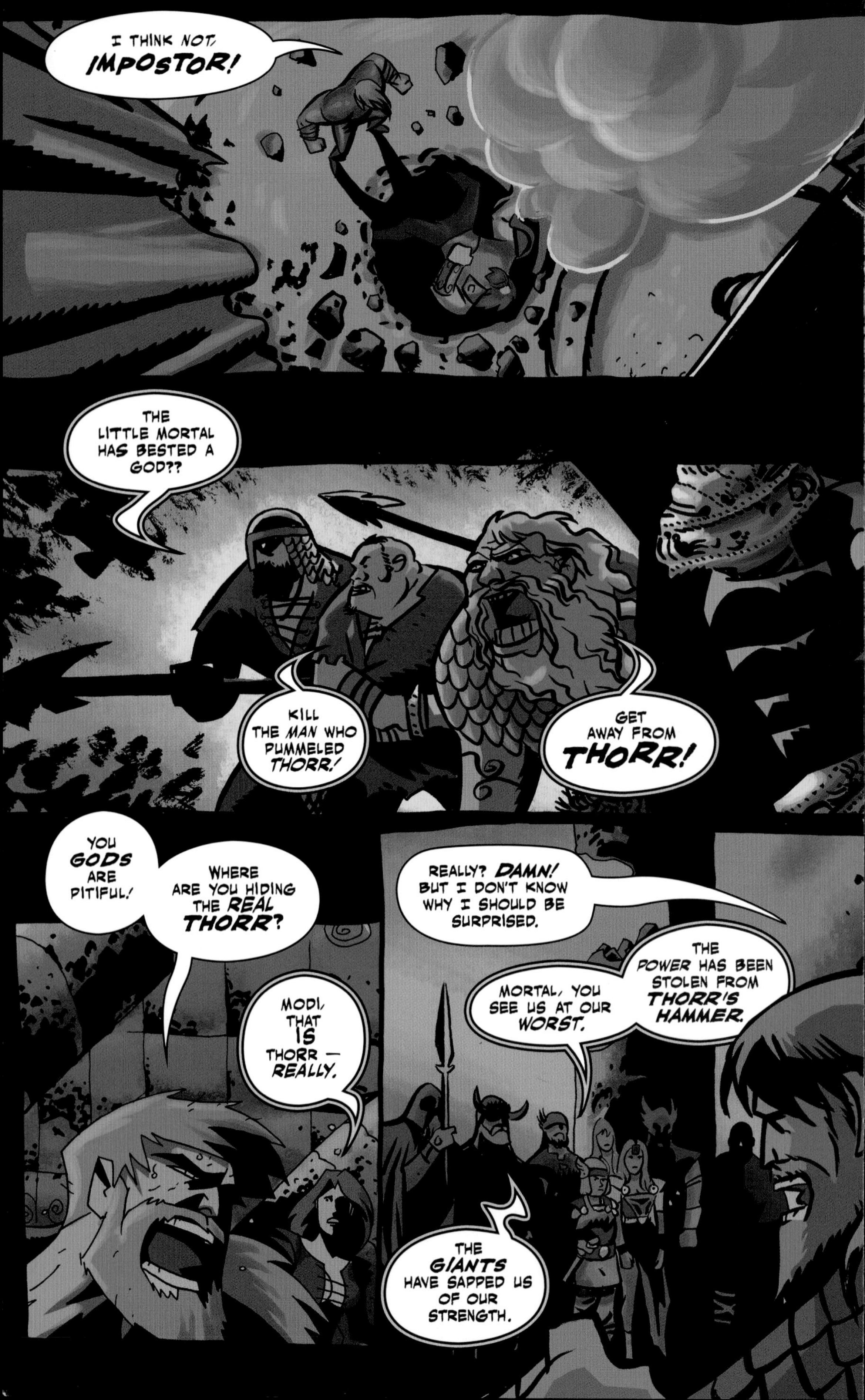

I THINK NOT, IMPOSTOR!
THE LITTLE MORTAL HAS BESTED A GOD??
KILL THE MAN WHO PUMMELED THORR!
GET AWAY FROM THORR!
YOU GODS ARE PITIFUL!
WHERE ARE YOU HIDING THE REAL THORR?
MODI, THAT IS THORR — REALLY.
REALLY? DAMN! BUT I DON'T KNOW WHY I SHOULD BE SURPRISED.
THE POWER HAS BEEN STOLEN FROM THORR'S HAMMER.
MORTAL, YOU SEE US AT OUR WORST.
THE GIANTS HAVE SAPPED US OF OUR STRENGTH.

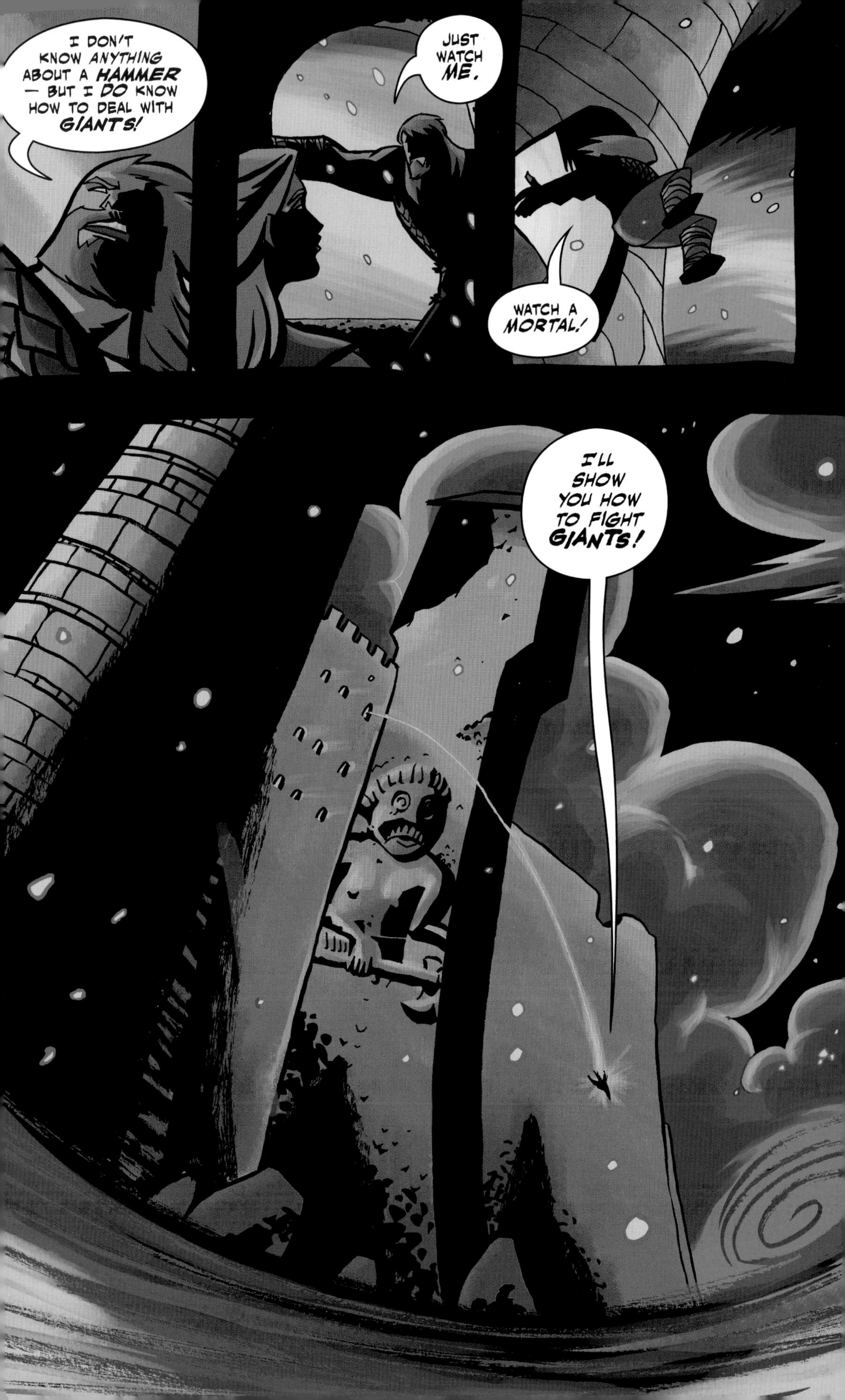
I DON'T KNOW ANYTHING ABOUT A HAMMER — BUT I DO KNOW HOW TO DEAL WITH GIANTS!
JUST WATCH ME.
WATCH A MORTAL!
I'LL SHOW YOU HOW TO FIGHT GIANTS!

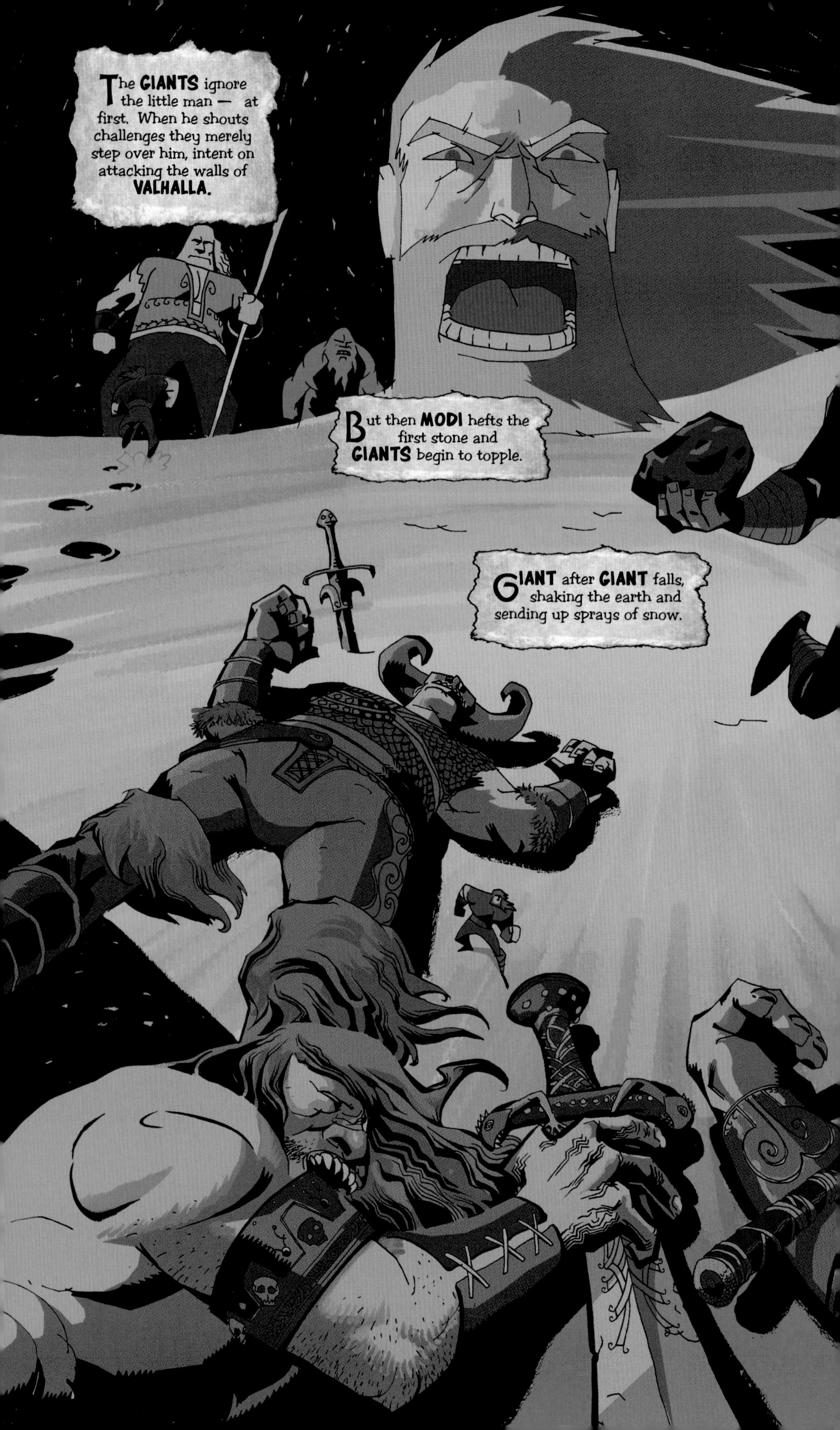
The GIANTS ignore the little man — at first. When he shouts challenges they merely step over him, intent on attacking the walls of VALHALLA.
But then MODI hefts the first stone and GIANTS begin to topple.
GIANT after GIANT falls, shaking the earth and sending up sprays of snow.

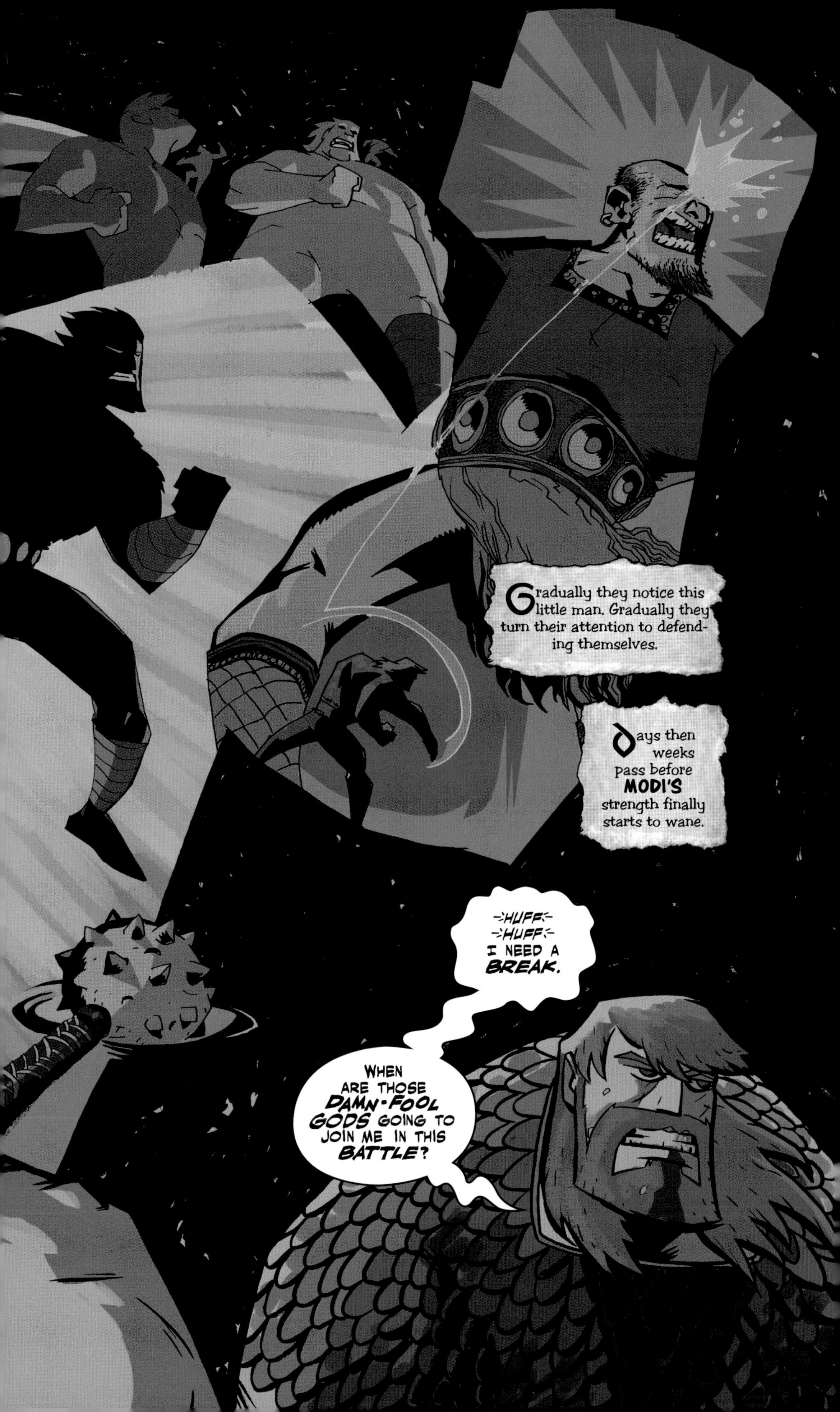
Gradually they notice this little man. Gradually they turn their attention to defending themselves.
Days then weeks pass before MODI'S strength finally starts to wane.
-HUFF- -HUFF- I NEED A BREAK.
WHEN ARE THOSE DAMN-FOOL GODS GOING TO JOIN ME IN THIS BATTLE?

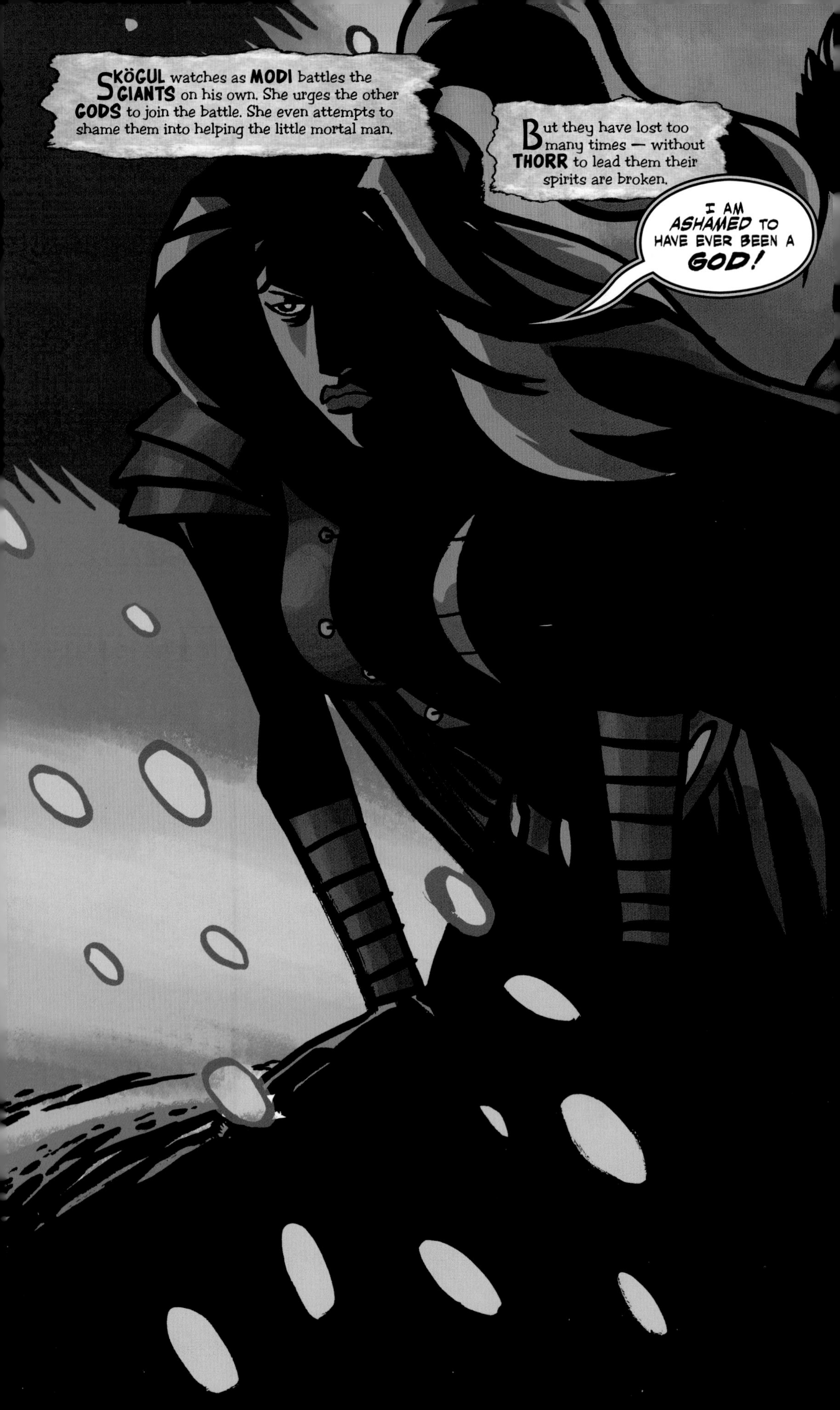
SKÖGUL watches as MODI battles the GIANTS on his own. She urges the other GODS to join the battle. She even attempts to shame them into helping the little mortal man.
But they have lost too many times — without THORR to lead them their spirits are broken.
I AM ASHAMED TO HAVE EVER BEEN A GOD!

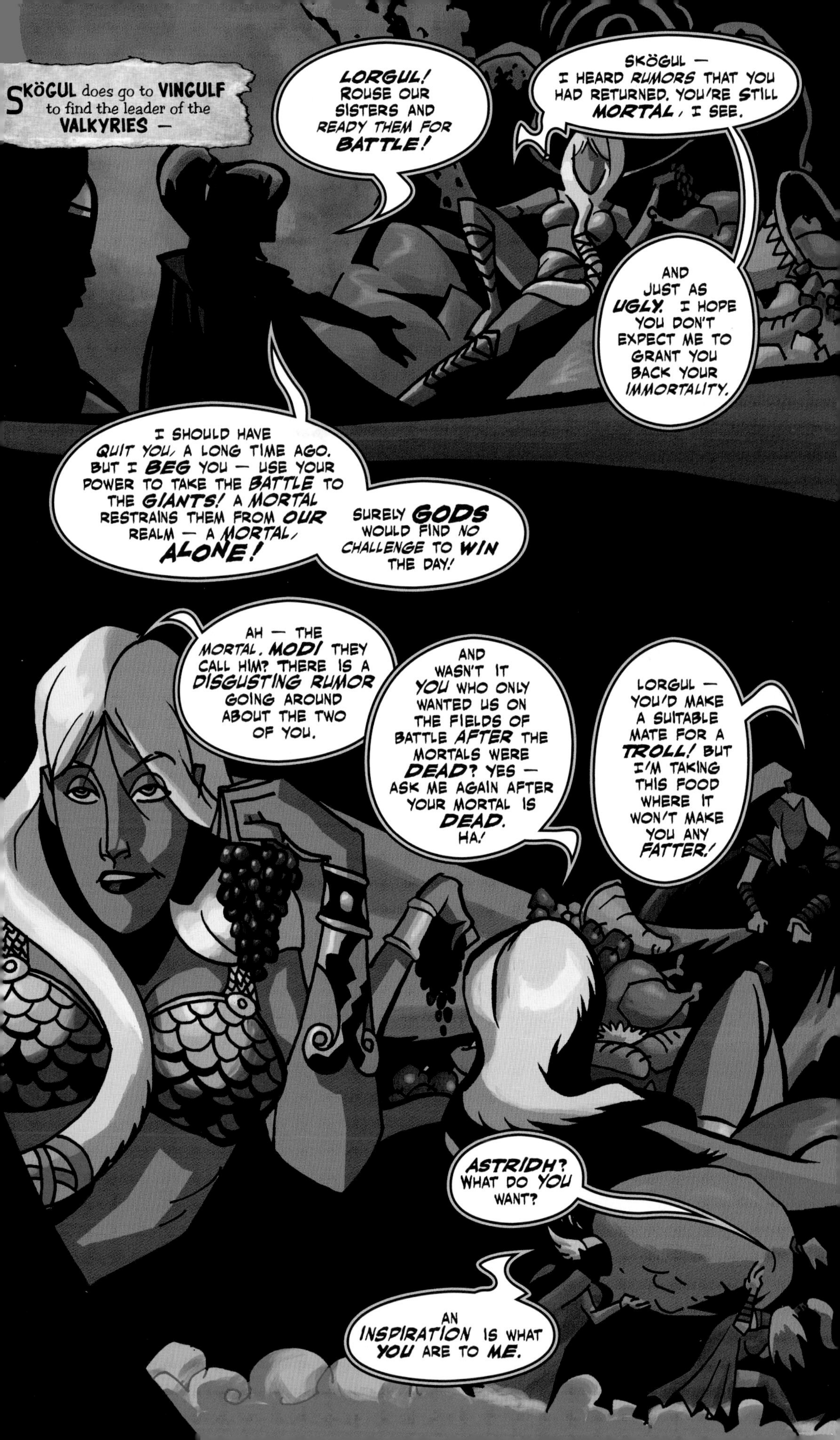
SKÖGUL does go to VINGULF to find the leader of the VALKYRIES —
LORGUL! ROUSE OUR SISTERS AND READY THEM FOR BATTLE!
SKÖGUL — I HEARD RUMORS THAT YOU HAD RETURNED. YOU'RE STILL MORTAL, I SEE.
AND JUST AS UGLY. I HOPE YOU DON'T EXPECT ME TO GRANT YOU BACK YOUR IMMORTALITY.
I SHOULD HAVE QUIT YOU, A LONG TIME AGO. BUT I BEG YOU — USE YOUR POWER TO TAKE THE BATTLE TO THE GIANTS! A MORTAL RESTRAINS THEM FROM OUR REALM — A MORTAL, ALONE!
SURELY GODS WOULD FIND NO CHALLENGE TO WIN THE DAY!
AH — THE MORTAL. MODI THEY CALL HIM? THERE IS A DISGUSTING RUMOR GOING AROUND ABOUT THE TWO OF YOU.
AND WASN'T IT YOU WHO ONLY WANTED US ON THE FIELDS OF BATTLE AFTER THE MORTALS WERE DEAD? YES — ASK ME AGAIN AFTER YOUR MORTAL IS DEAD. HA!
LORGUL — YOU'D MAKE A SUITABLE MATE FOR A TROLL! BUT I'M TAKING THIS FOOD WHERE IT WON'T MAKE YOU ANY FATTER!
ASTRIDH? WHAT DO YOU WANT?
AN INSPIRATION IS WHAT YOU ARE TO ME.

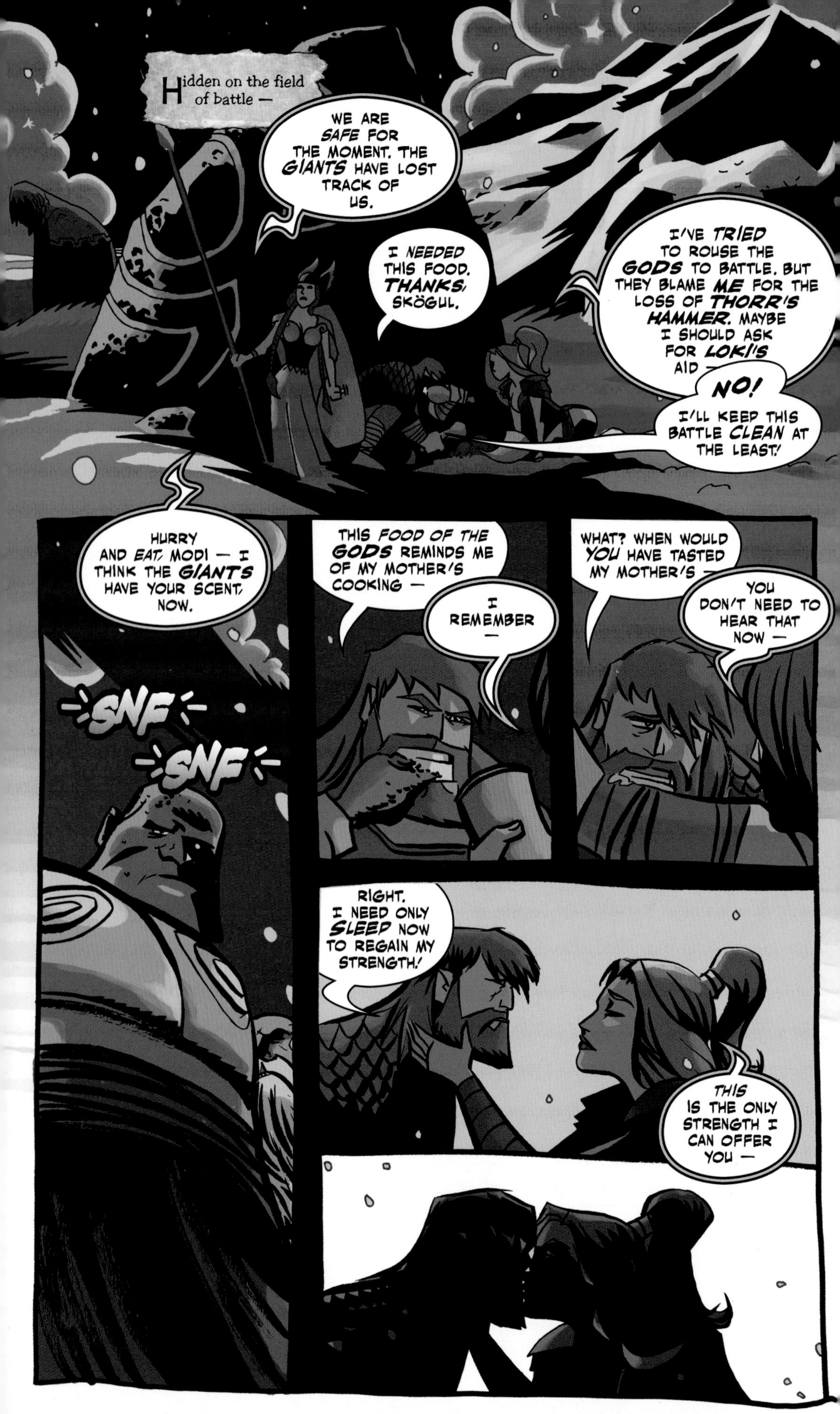
Hidden on the field of battle —
WE ARE SAFE FOR THE MOMENT. THE GIANTS HAVE LOST TRACK OF US.
I NEEDED THIS FOOD. THANKS, SKÖGUL.
I'VE TRIED TO ROUSE THE GODS TO BATTLE. BUT THEY BLAME ME FOR THE LOSS OF THORR'S HAMMER. MAYBE I SHOULD ASK FOR LOKI'S AID —
NO!
I'LL KEEP THIS BATTLE CLEAN AT THE LEAST!
HURRY AND EAT, MODI — I THINK THE GIANTS HAVE YOUR SCENT NOW.
SNF
SNF
THIS FOOD OF THE GODS REMINDS ME OF MY MOTHER'S COOKING —
I REMEMBER —
WHAT? WHEN WOULD YOU HAVE TASTED MY MOTHER'S —
YOU DON'T NEED TO HEAR THAT NOW —
RIGHT. I NEED ONLY SLEEP NOW TO REGAIN MY STRENGTH!
THIS IS THE ONLY STRENGTH I CAN OFFER YOU —

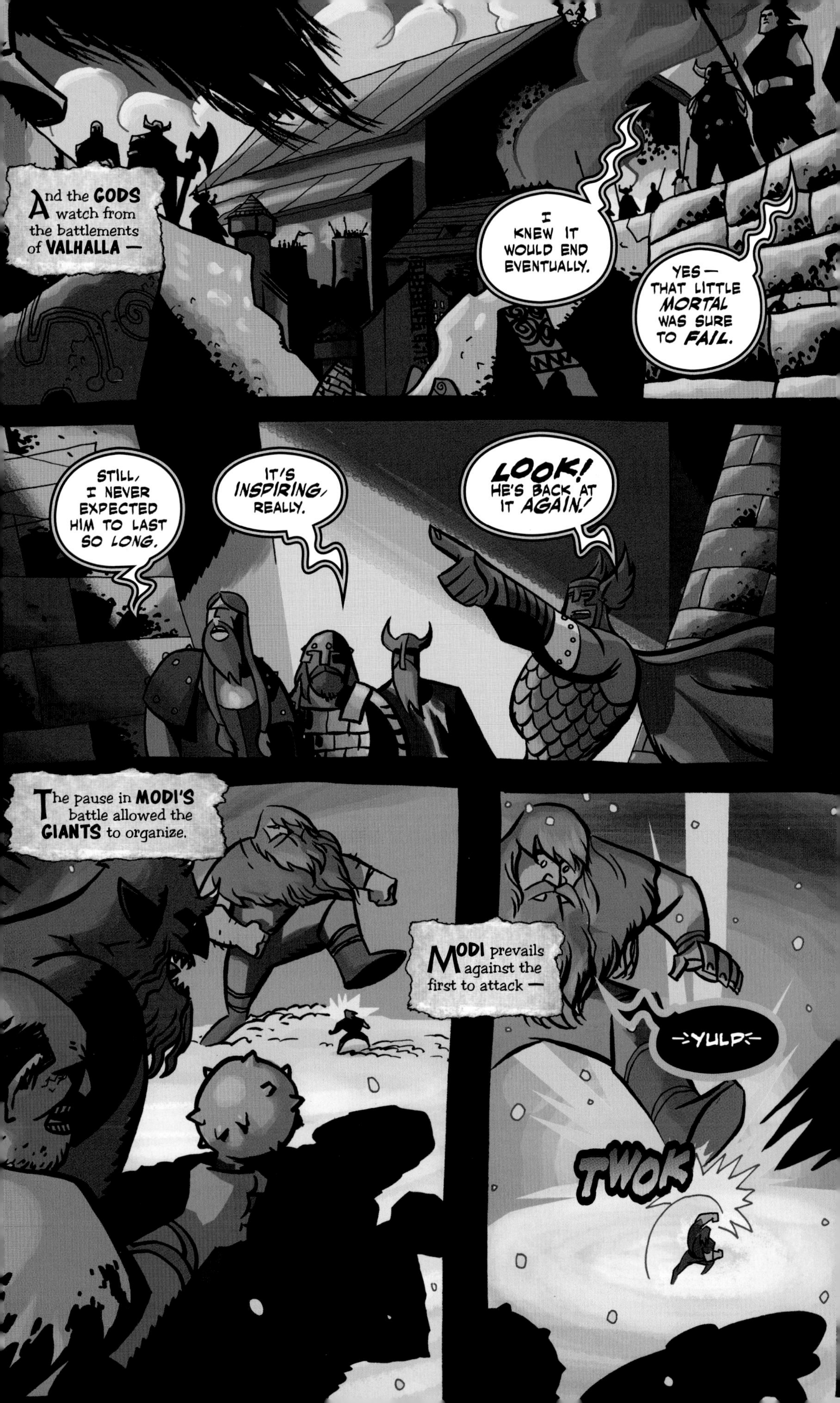
And the GODS watch from the battlements of VALHALLA —
I KNEW IT WOULD END EVENTUALLY.
YES — THAT LITTLE MORTAL WAS SURE TO FAIL.
STILL, I NEVER EXPECTED HIM TO LAST SO LONG.
IT'S INSPIRING, REALLY.
LOOK! HE'S BACK AT IT AGAIN!
The pause in MODI'S battle allowed the GIANTS to organize.
MODI prevails against the first to attack —
YULP
TWOK

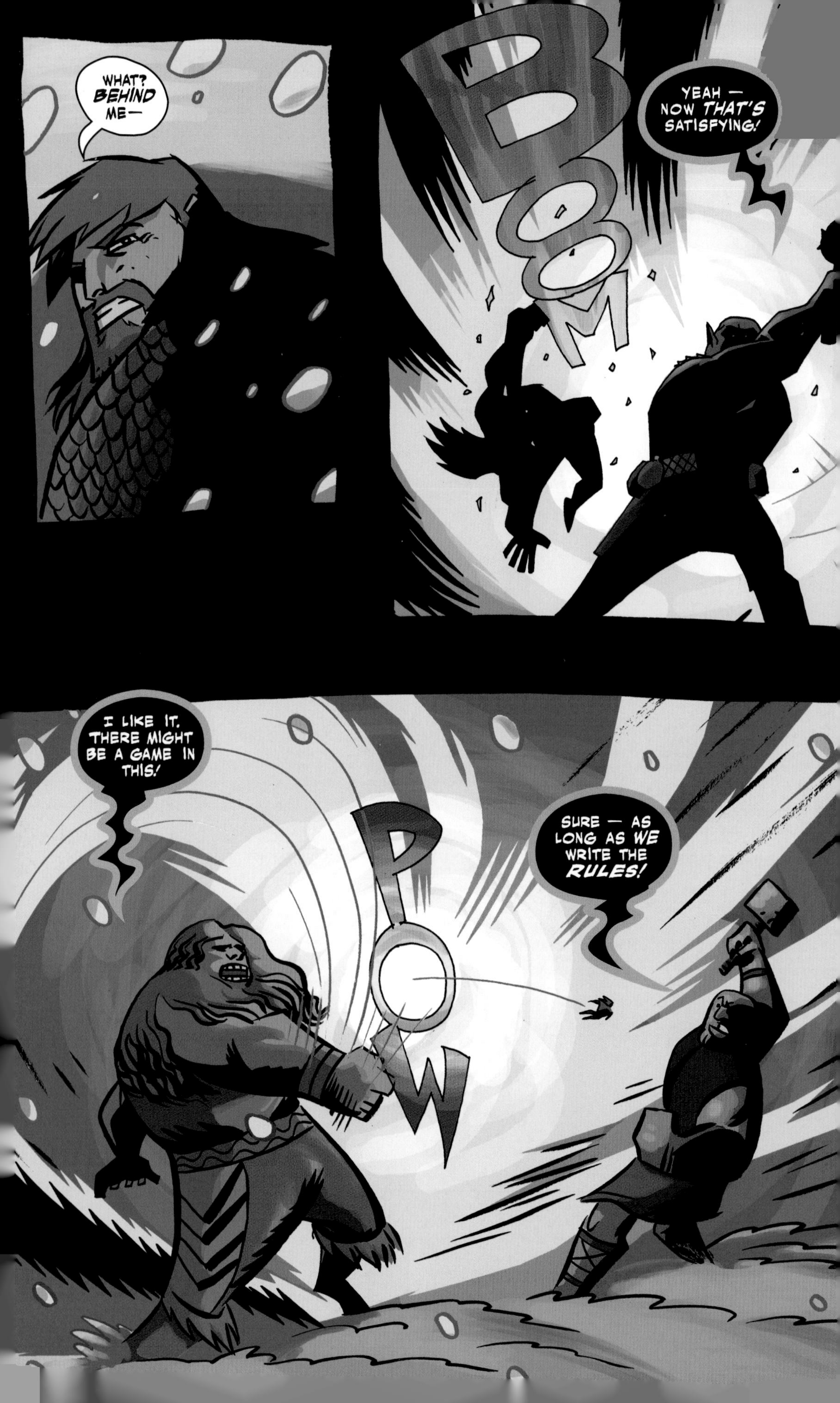

WHAT? BEHIND ME—
BOOM
YEAH — NOW THAT'S SATISFYING!
I LIKE IT. THERE MIGHT BE A GAME IN THIS!
POW
SURE — AS LONG AS WE WRITE THE RULES!

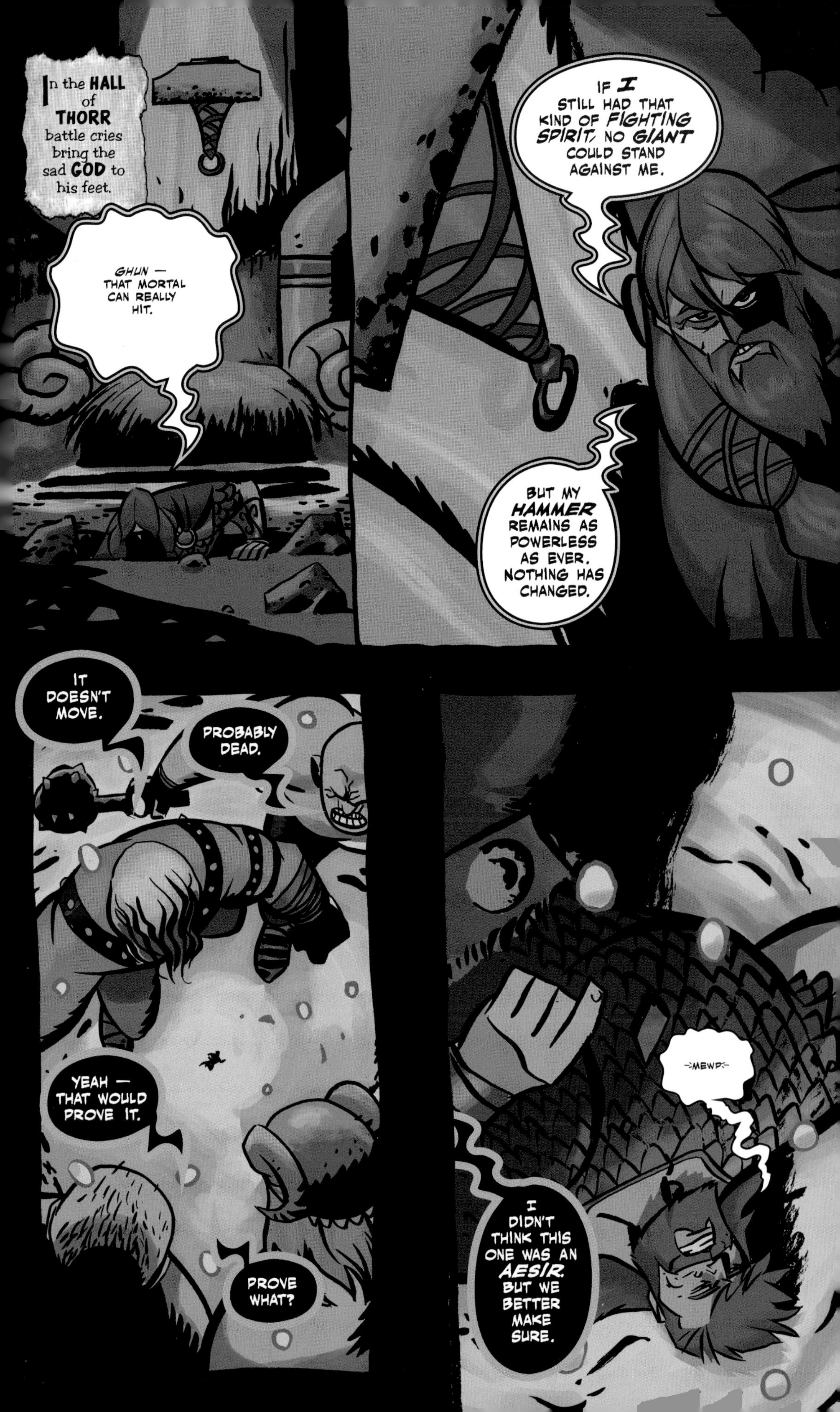
In the HALL of THORR battle cries bring the sad GOD to his feet.
GHUN — THAT MORTAL CAN REALLY HIT.
IF I STILL HAD THAT KIND OF FIGHTING SPIRIT, NO GIANT COULD STAND AGAINST ME.
BUT MY HAMMER REMAINS AS POWERLESS AS EVER. NOTHING HAS CHANGED.
IT DOESN'T MOVE.
PROBABLY DEAD.
YEAH — THAT WOULD PROVE IT.
PROVE WHAT?
-MEWP-
I DIDN'T THINK THIS ONE WAS AN AESIR. BUT WE BETTER MAKE SURE.

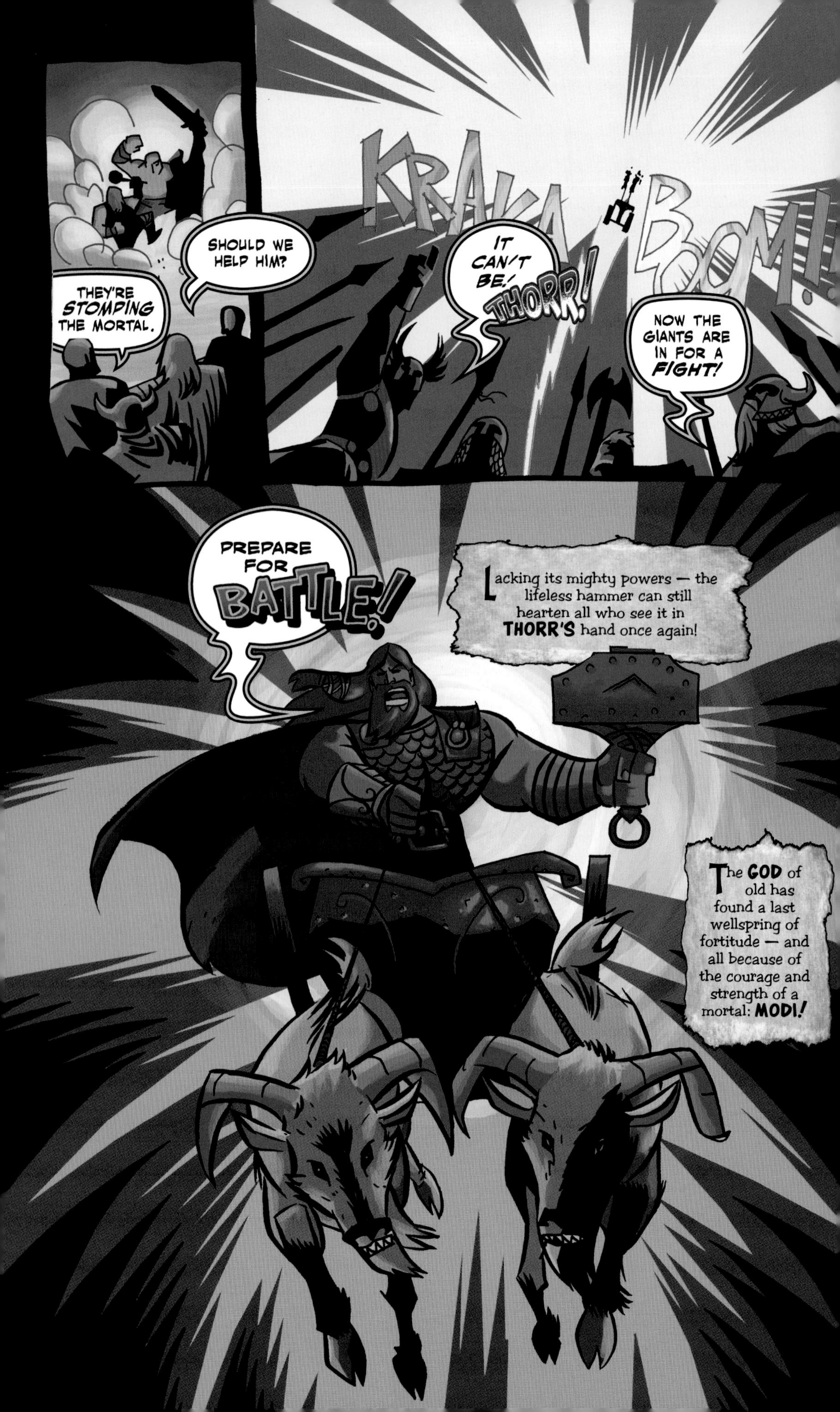
THEY'RE STOMPING THE MORTAL.
SHOULD WE HELP HIM?
KRAKA BOOM!!
IT CAN'T BE! THORR!
NOW THE GIANTS ARE IN FOR A FIGHT!
PREPARE FOR BATTLE!
Lacking its mighty powers — the lifeless hammer can still hearten all who see it in THORR'S hand once again!
The GOD of old has found a last wellspring of fortitude — and all because of the courage and strength of a mortal: MODI!

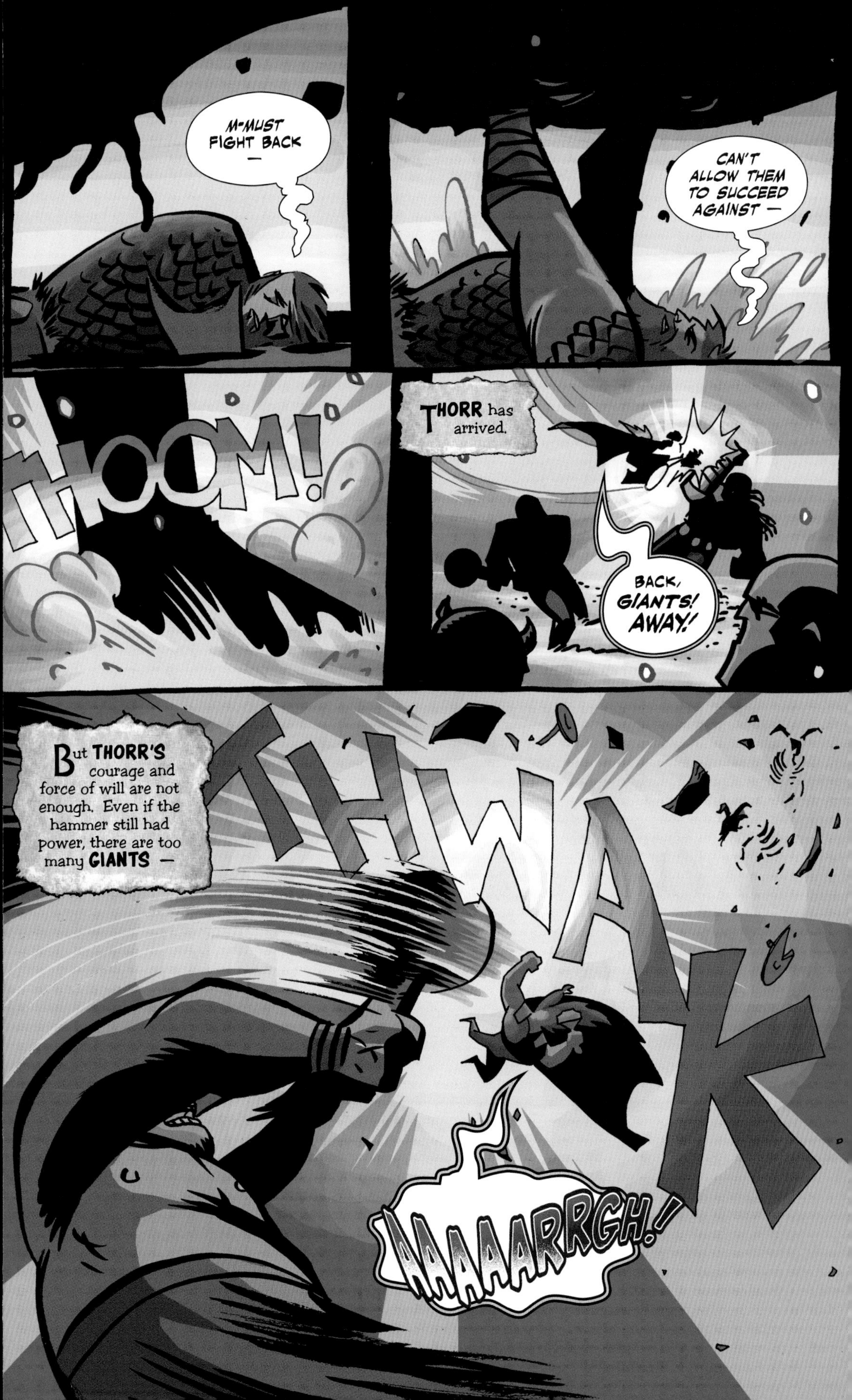

M-MUST FIGHT BACK —
CAN'T ALLOW THEM TO SUCCEED AGAINST —
THOOM!
THORR has arrived.
BACK, GIANTS! AWAY!
But THORR'S courage and force of will are not enough. Even if the hammer still had power, there are too many GIANTS —
THWAK
AAAAARRGH!

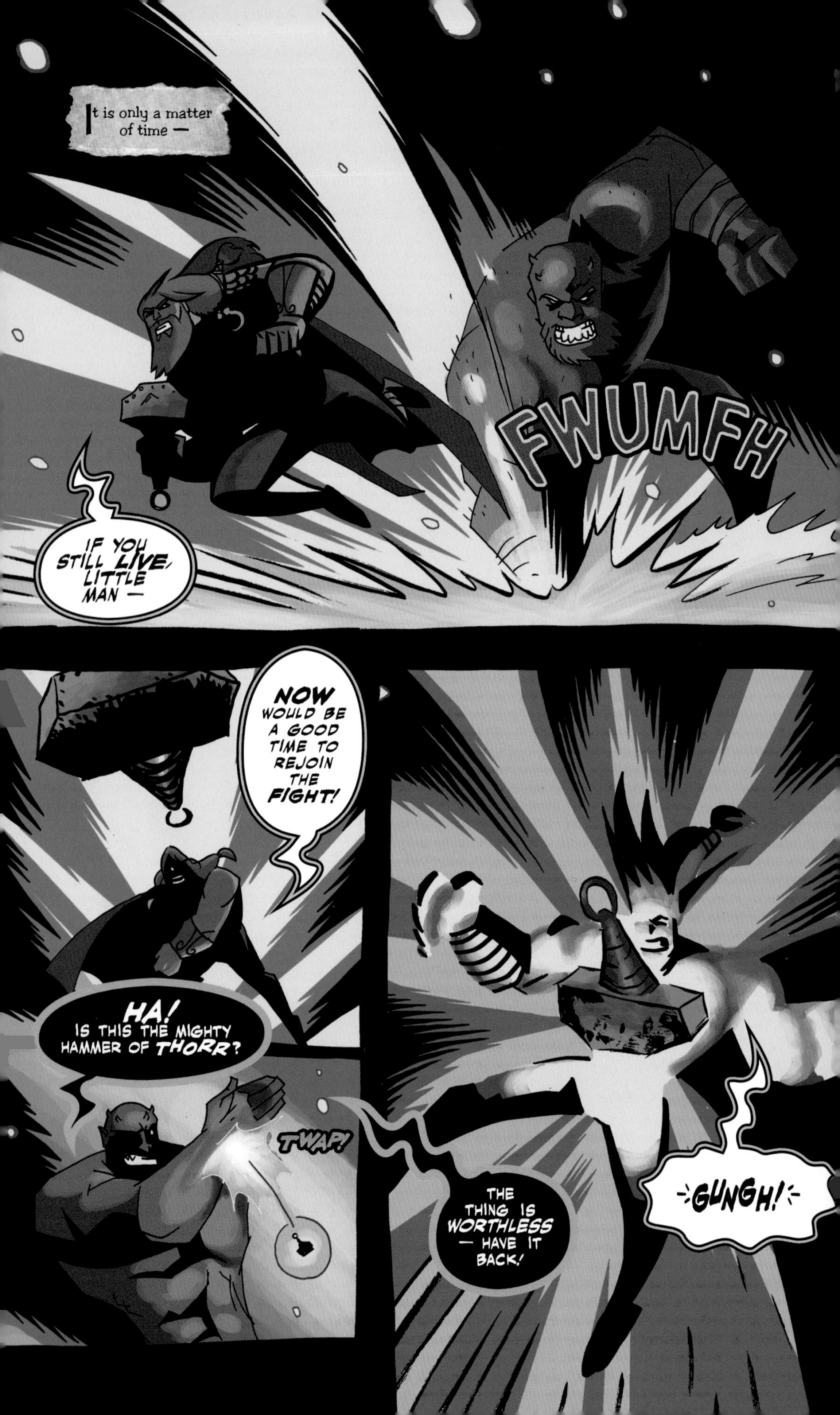
It is only a matter of time —
FWUMFH
IF YOU STILL LIVE, LITTLE MAN —
NOW WOULD BE A GOOD TIME TO REJOIN THE FIGHT!
HA! IS THIS THE MIGHTY HAMMER OF THORR?
TWAP!
THE THING IS WORTHLESS — HAVE IT BACK!
GUNGH!

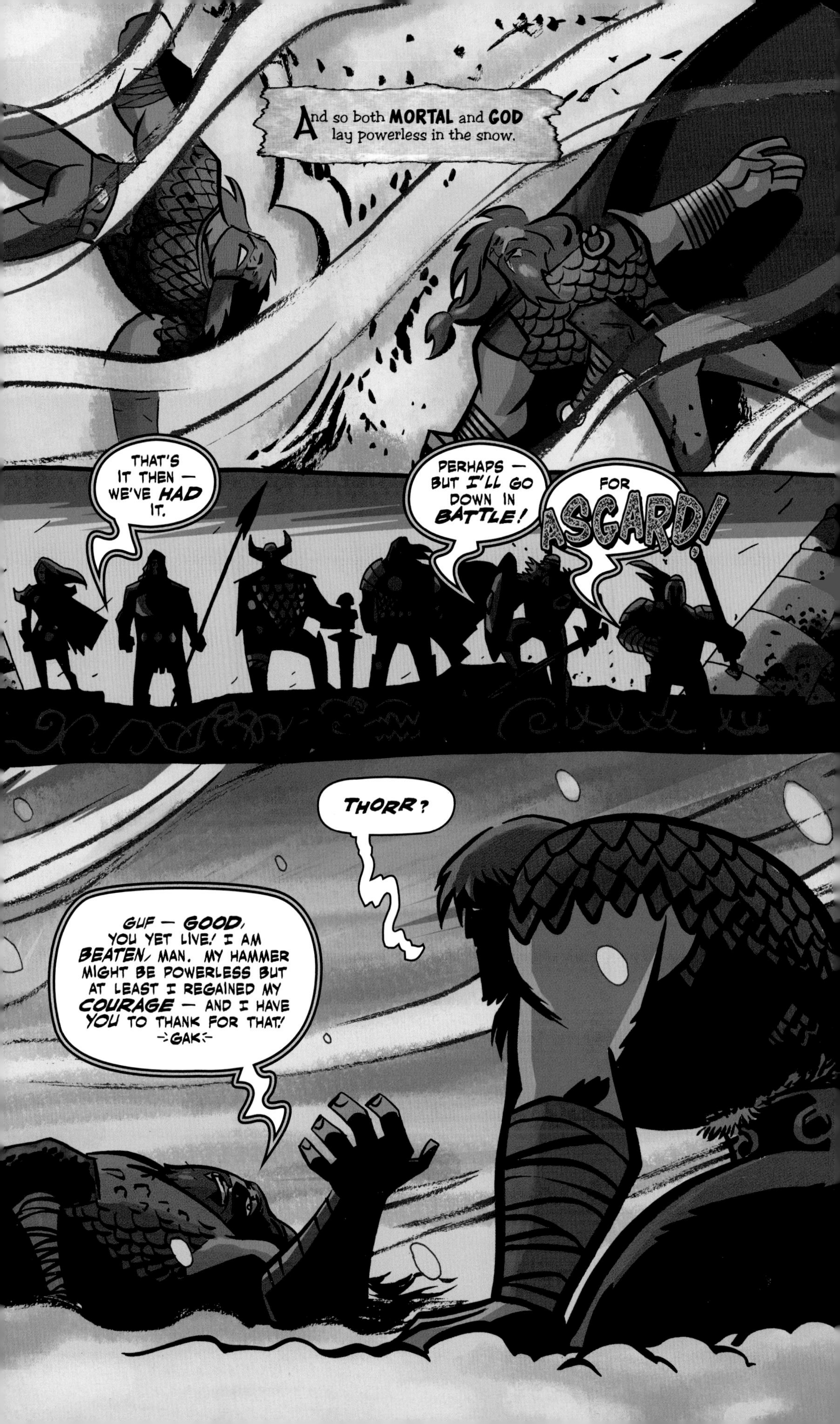
And so both MORTAL and GOD lay powerless in the snow.
THAT'S IT THEN — WE'VE HAD IT.
PERHAPS — BUT I'LL GO DOWN IN BATTLE!
FOR ASGARD!
THORR?
GUF — GOOD, YOU YET LIVE! I AM BEATEN, MAN. MY HAMMER MIGHT BE POWERLESS BUT AT LEAST I REGAINED MY COURAGE — AND I HAVE YOU TO THANK FOR THAT! -GAK-

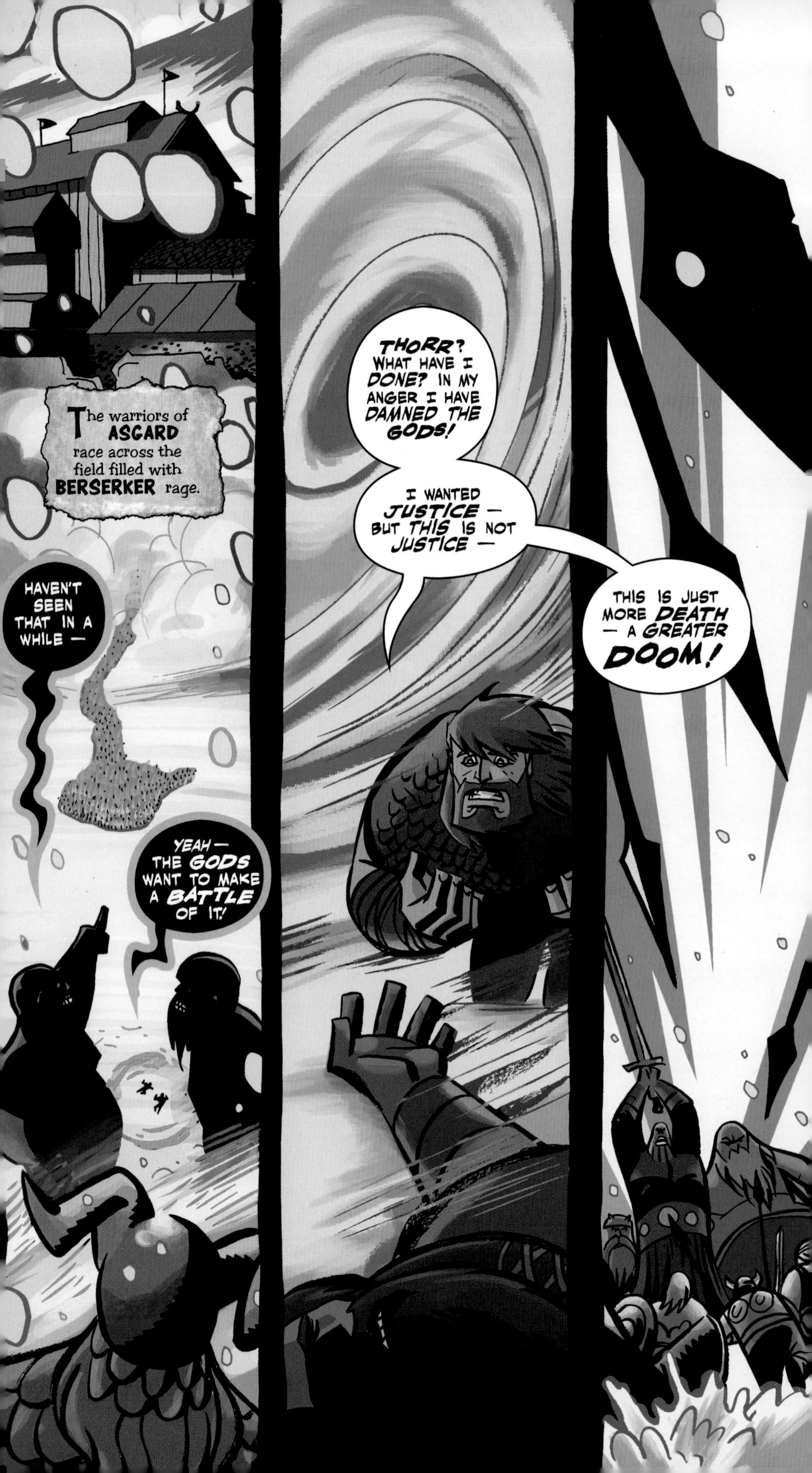
The warriors of ASGARD race across the field filled with BERSERKER rage.
HAVEN'T SEEN THAT IN A WHILE —
YEAH — THE GODS WANT TO MAKE A BATTLE OF IT!
THORR? WHAT HAVE I DONE? IN MY ANGER I HAVE DAMNED THE GODS!
I WANTED JUSTICE — BUT THIS IS NOT JUSTICE —
THIS IS JUST MORE DEATH — A GREATER DOOM!

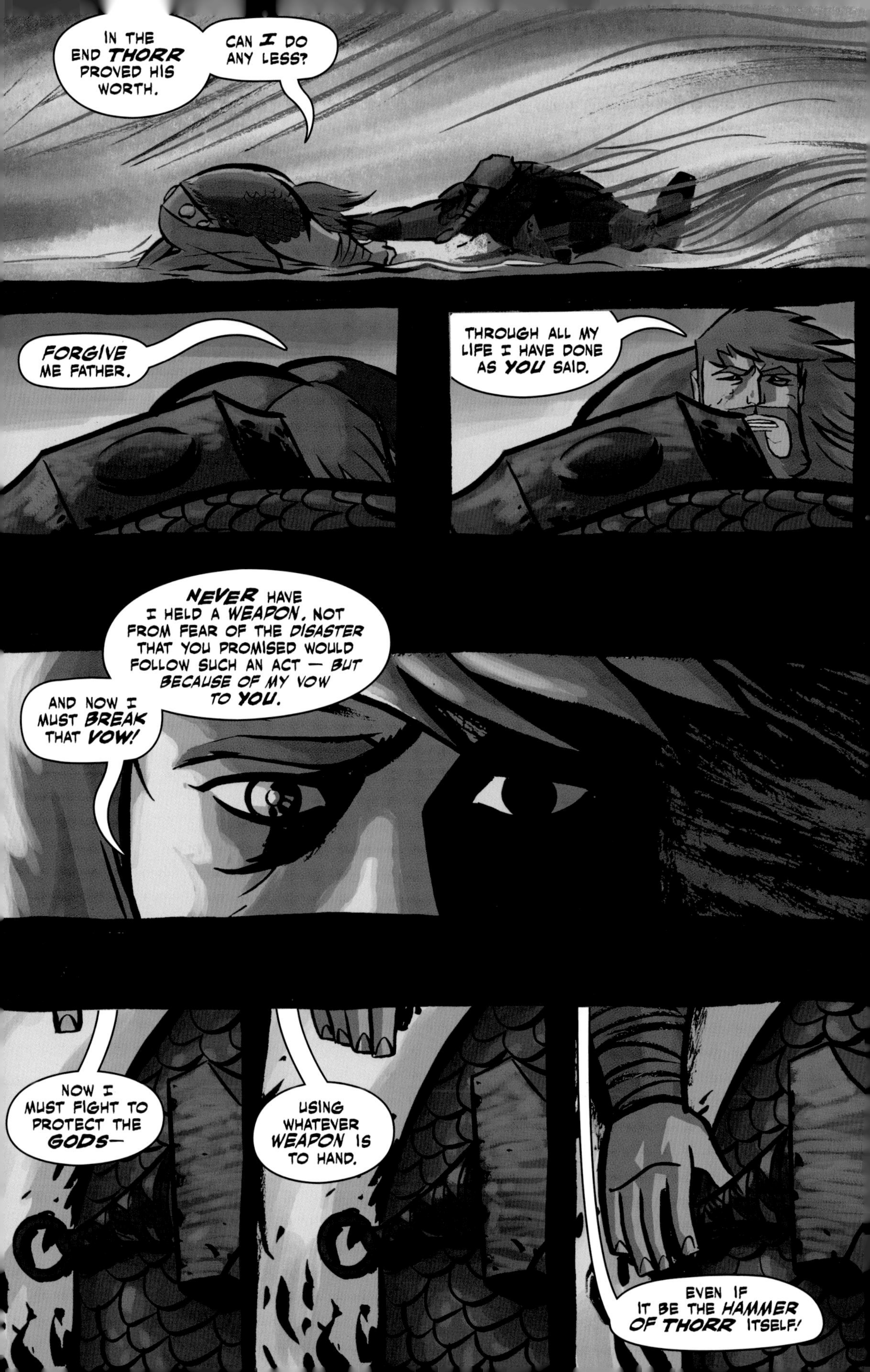
IN THE END THORR PROVED HIS WORTH.
CAN I DO ANY LESS?
FORGIVE ME FATHER.
THROUGH ALL MY LIFE I HAVE DONE AS YOU SAID.
NEVER HAVE I HELD A WEAPON, NOT FROM FEAR OF THE DISASTER THAT YOU PROMISED WOULD FOLLOW SUCH AN ACT — BUT BECAUSE OF MY VOW TO YOU.
AND NOW I MUST BREAK THAT VOW!
NOW I MUST FIGHT TO PROTECT THE GODS—
USING WHATEVER WEAPON IS TO HAND.
EVEN IF IT BE THE HAMMER OF THORR ITSELF!

THOUGH I MOST SURELY SEAL MY OWN DOOM!
In MODI'S hand the HAMMER comes to life.
Power surges between mortal man and a weapon born of an arcane forge.
Yet it should not be. THORR'S HAMMER had no power.

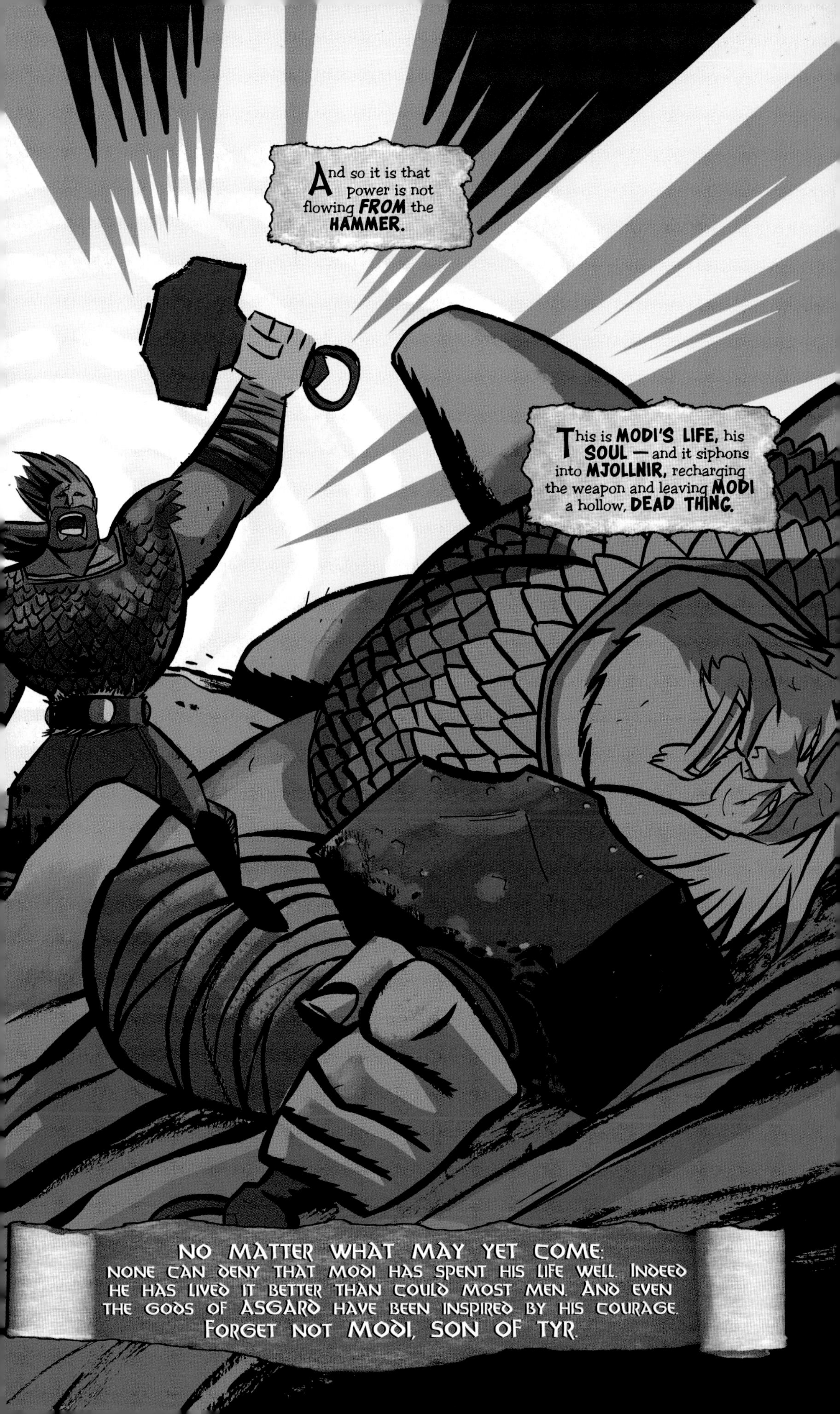
And so it is that power is not flowing FROM the HAMMER.
This is MODI'S LIFE, his SOUL — and it siphons into MJOLLNIR, recharging the weapon and leaving MODI a hollow, DEAD THING.
NO MATTER WHAT MAY YET COME:
NONE CAN DENY THAT MODI HAS SPENT HIS LIFE WELL. INDEED HE HAS LIVED IT BETTER THAN COULD MOST MEN. AND EVEN THE GODS OF ASGARD HAVE BEEN INSPIRED BY HIS COURAGE.
FORGET NOT MODI, SON OF TYR.

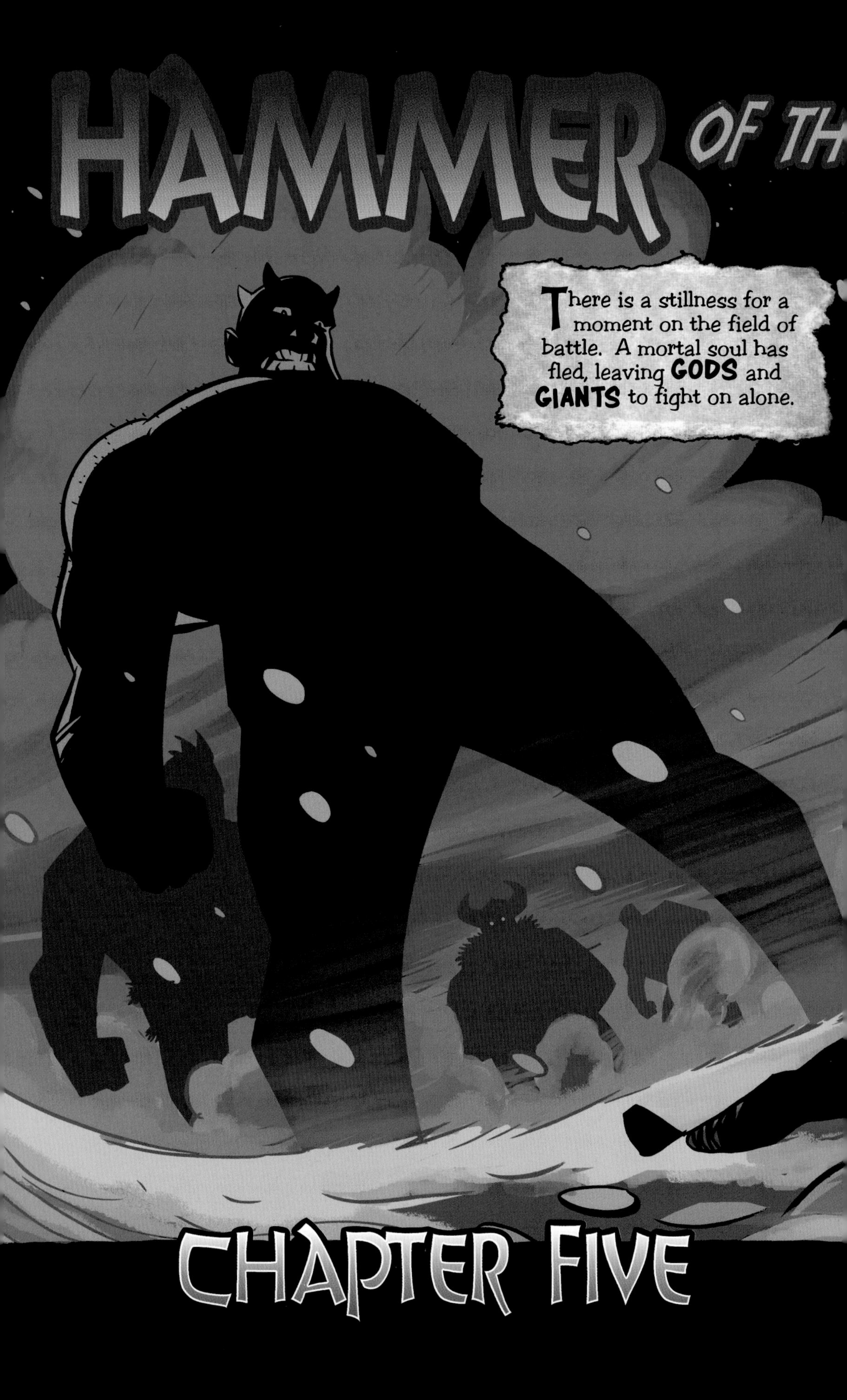
HAMMER OF TH
There is a stillness for a moment on the field of battle. A mortal soul has fled, leaving GODS and GIANTS to fight on alone.
CHAPTER FIVE

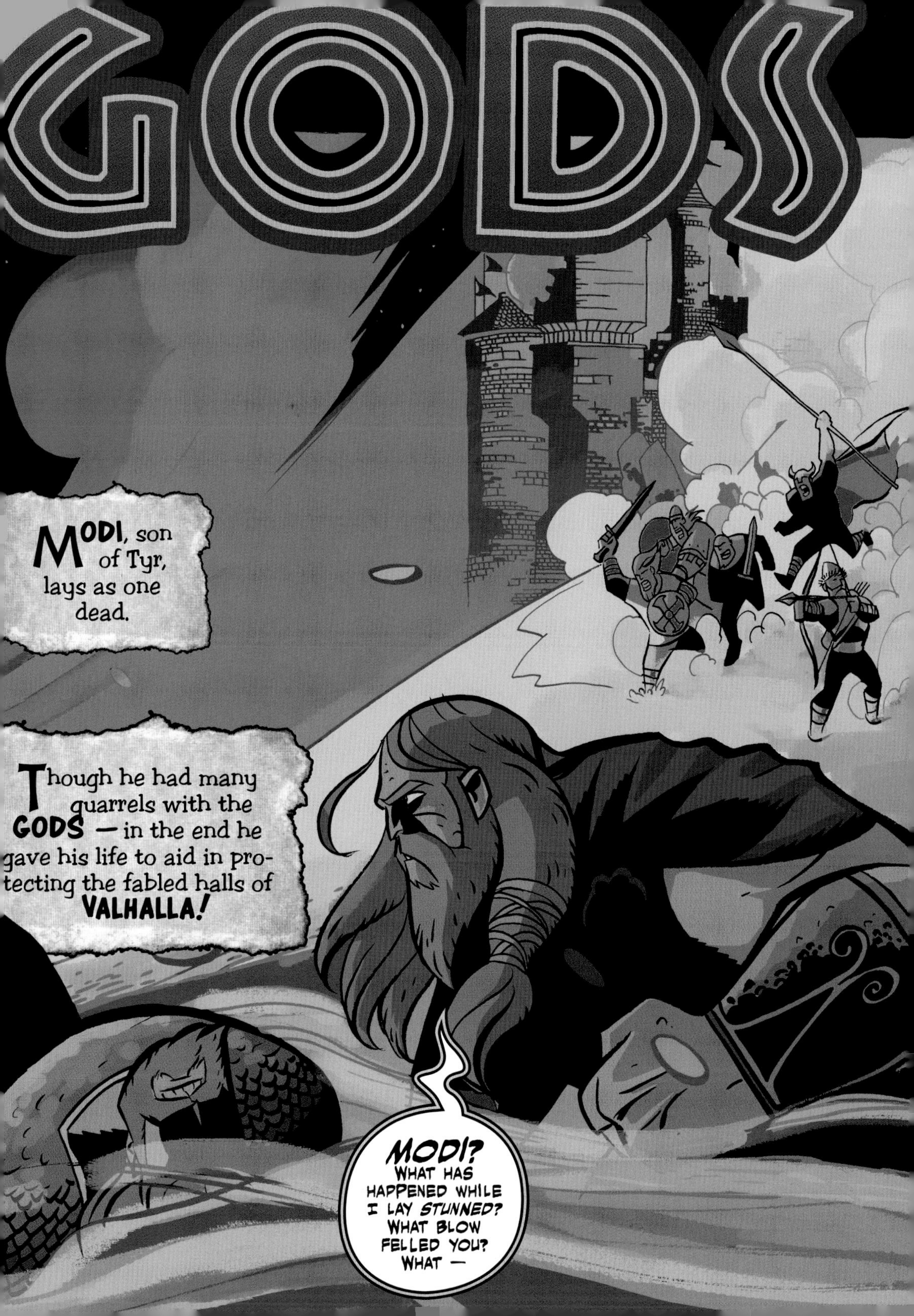
GODS
MODI, son of Tyr, lays as one dead.
Though he had many quarrels with the GODS — in the end he gave his life to aid in protecting the fabled halls of VALHALLA!
MODI? WHAT HAS HAPPENED WHILE I LAY STUNNED? WHAT BLOW FELLED YOU? WHAT —

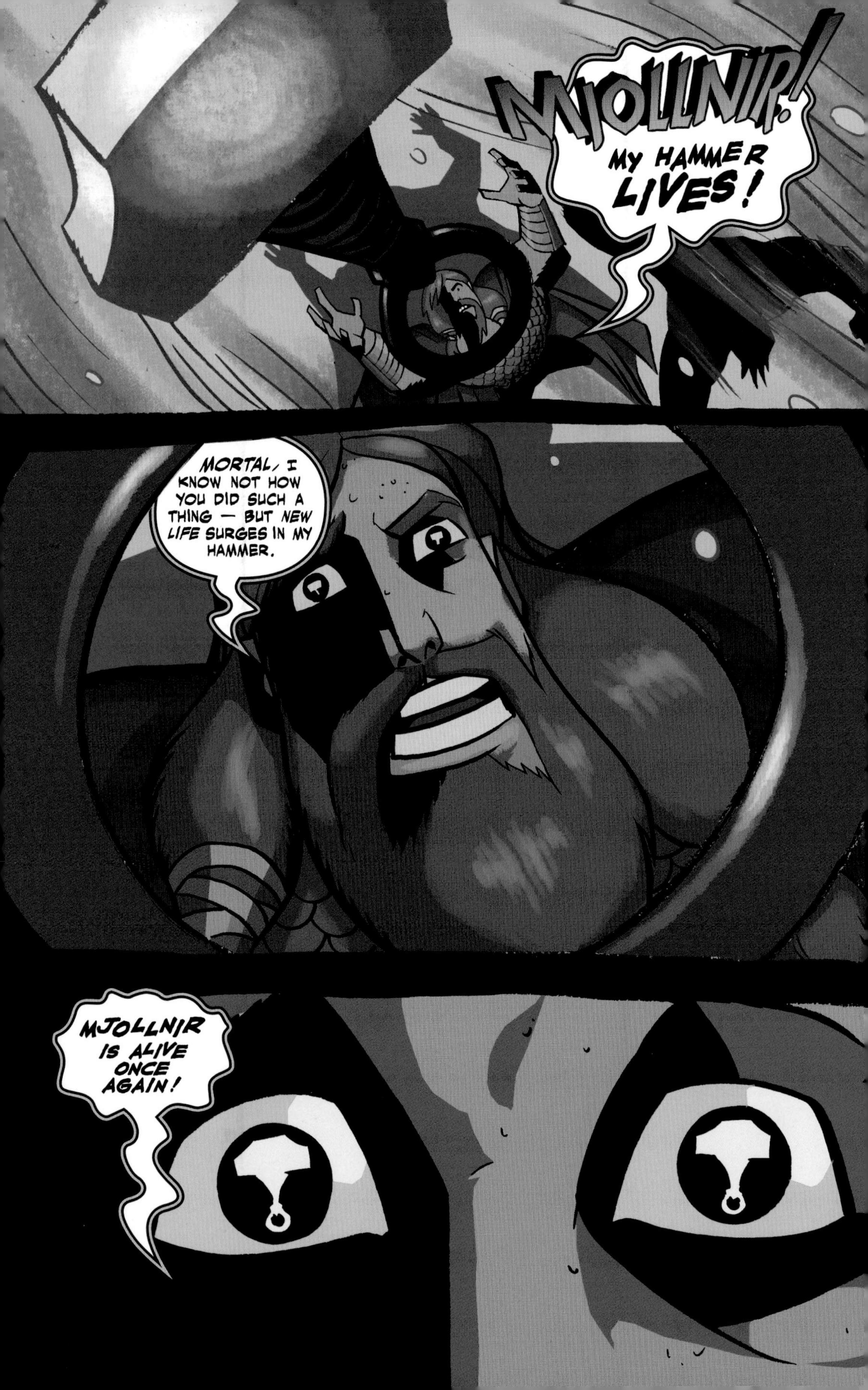
MJOLLNIR!
MY HAMMER LIVES!
MORTAL, I KNOW NOT HOW YOU DID SUCH A THING — BUT NEW LIFE SURGES IN MY HAMMER.
MJOLLNIR IS ALIVE ONCE AGAIN!

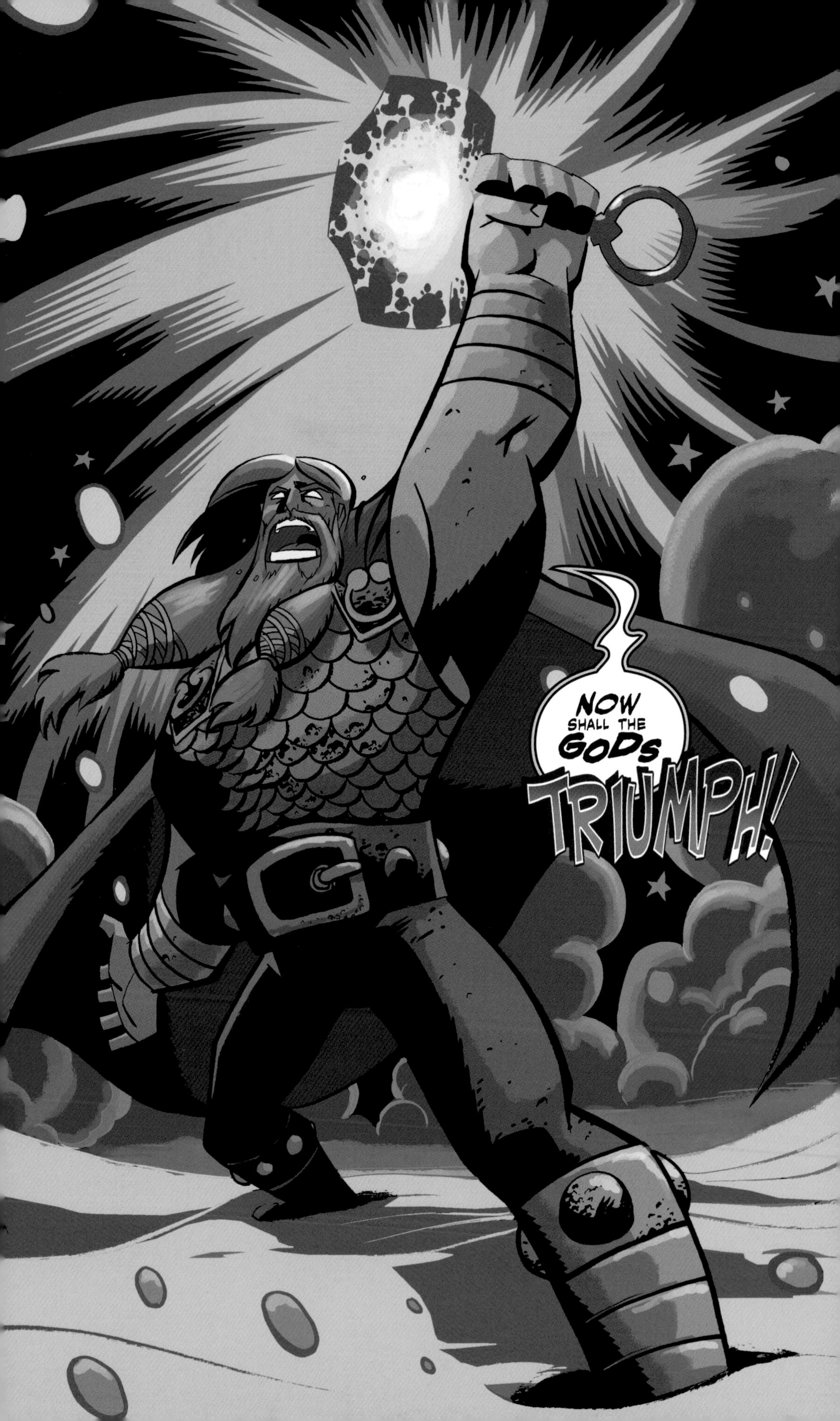
NOW SHALL THE GODS TRIUMPH!

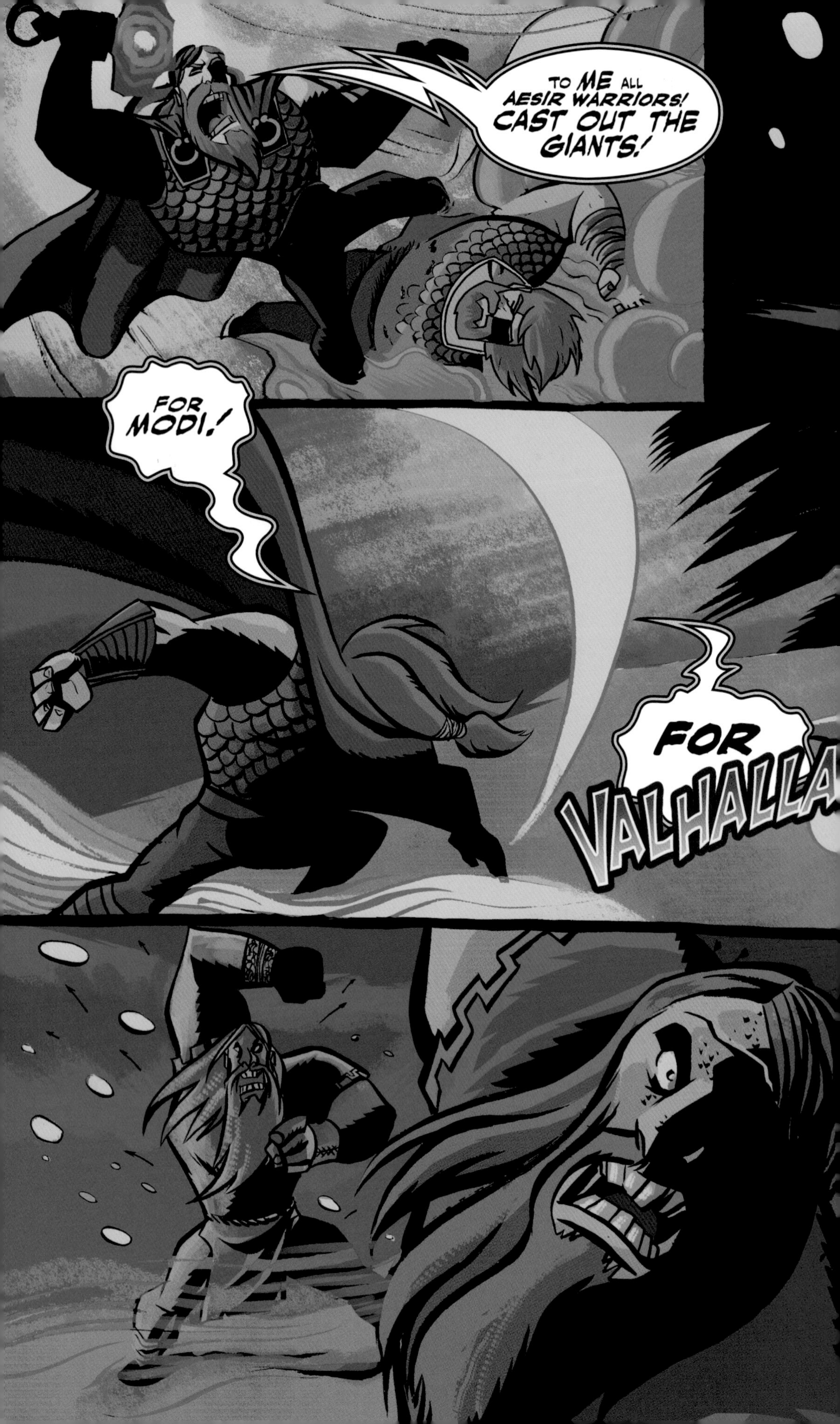
TO ME ALL AESIR WARRIORS! CAST OUT THE GIANTS!
FOR MODI!
FOR VALHALLA

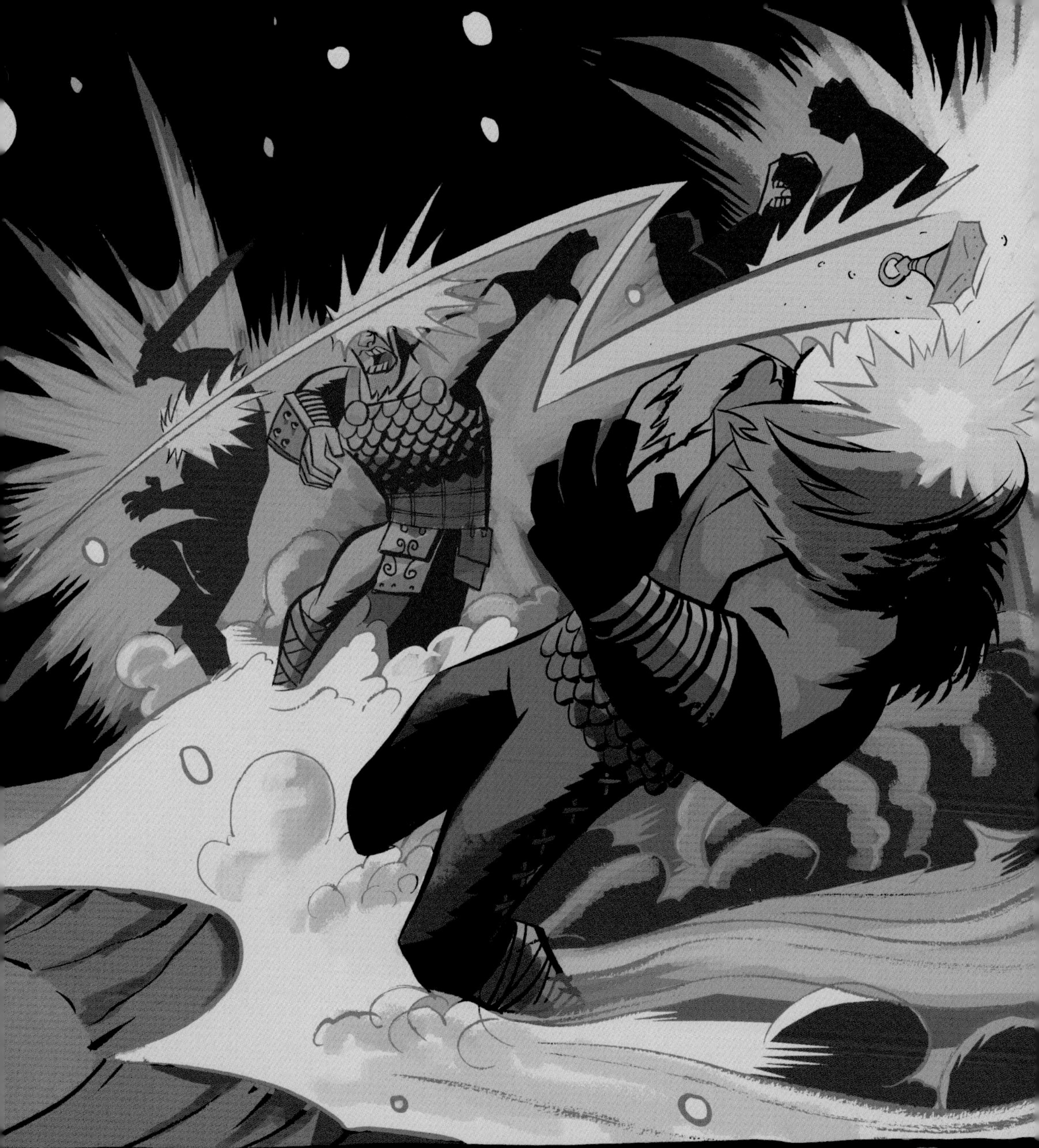

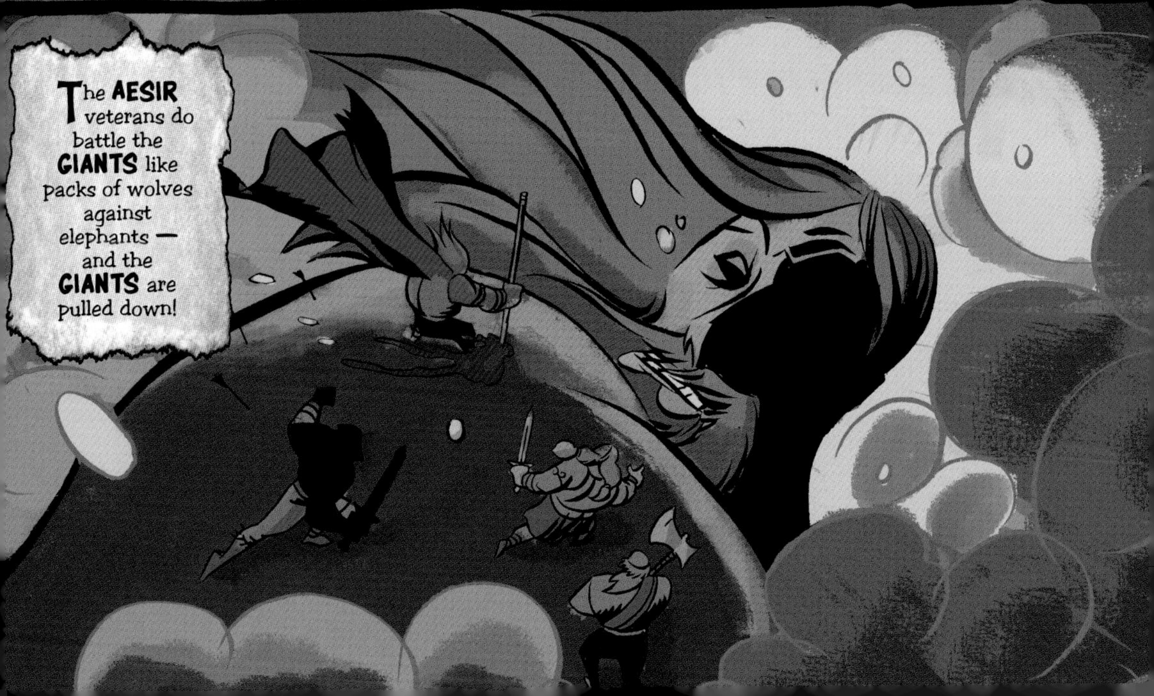
The AESIR veterans do battle the GIANTS like packs of wolves against elephants — and the GIANTS are pulled down!

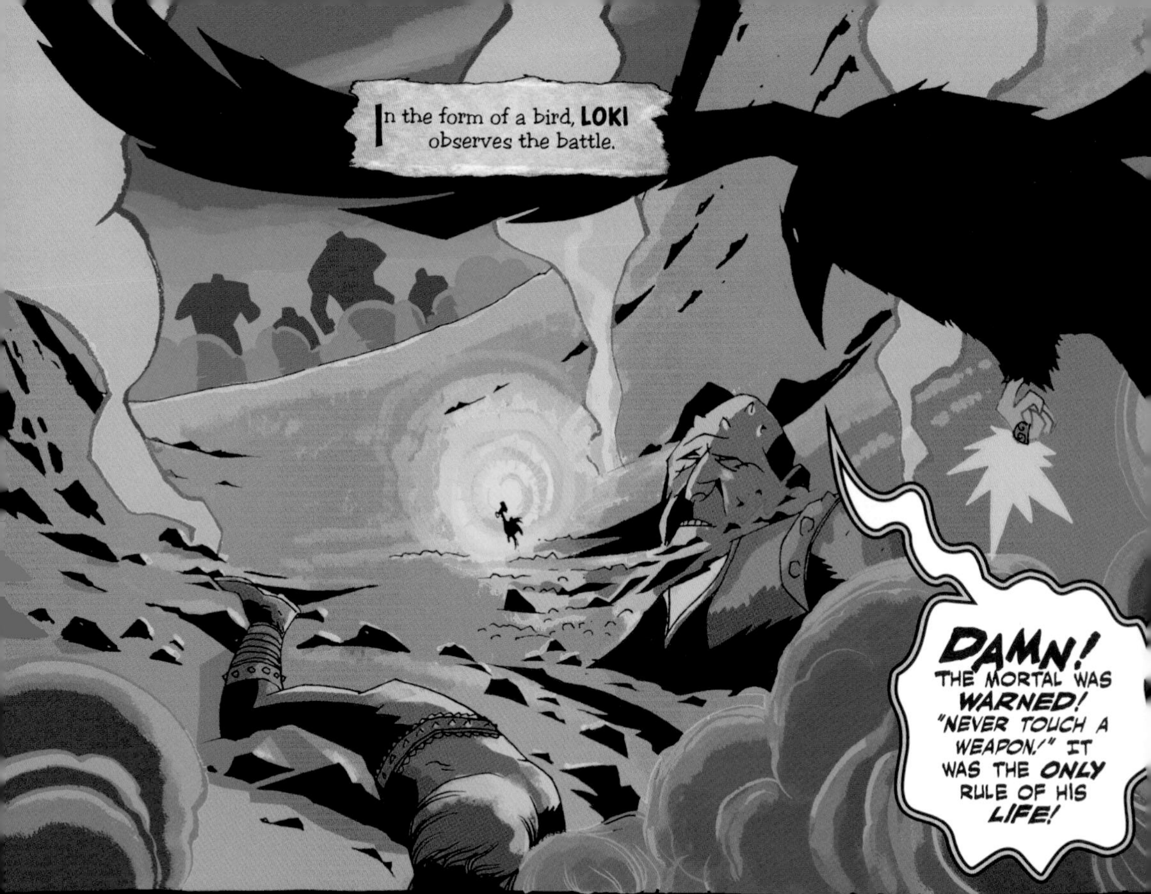
In the form of a bird, LOKI observes the battle.
DAMN! THE MORTAL WAS WARNED! "NEVER TOUCH A WEAPON." IT WAS THE ONLY RULE OF HIS LIFE!

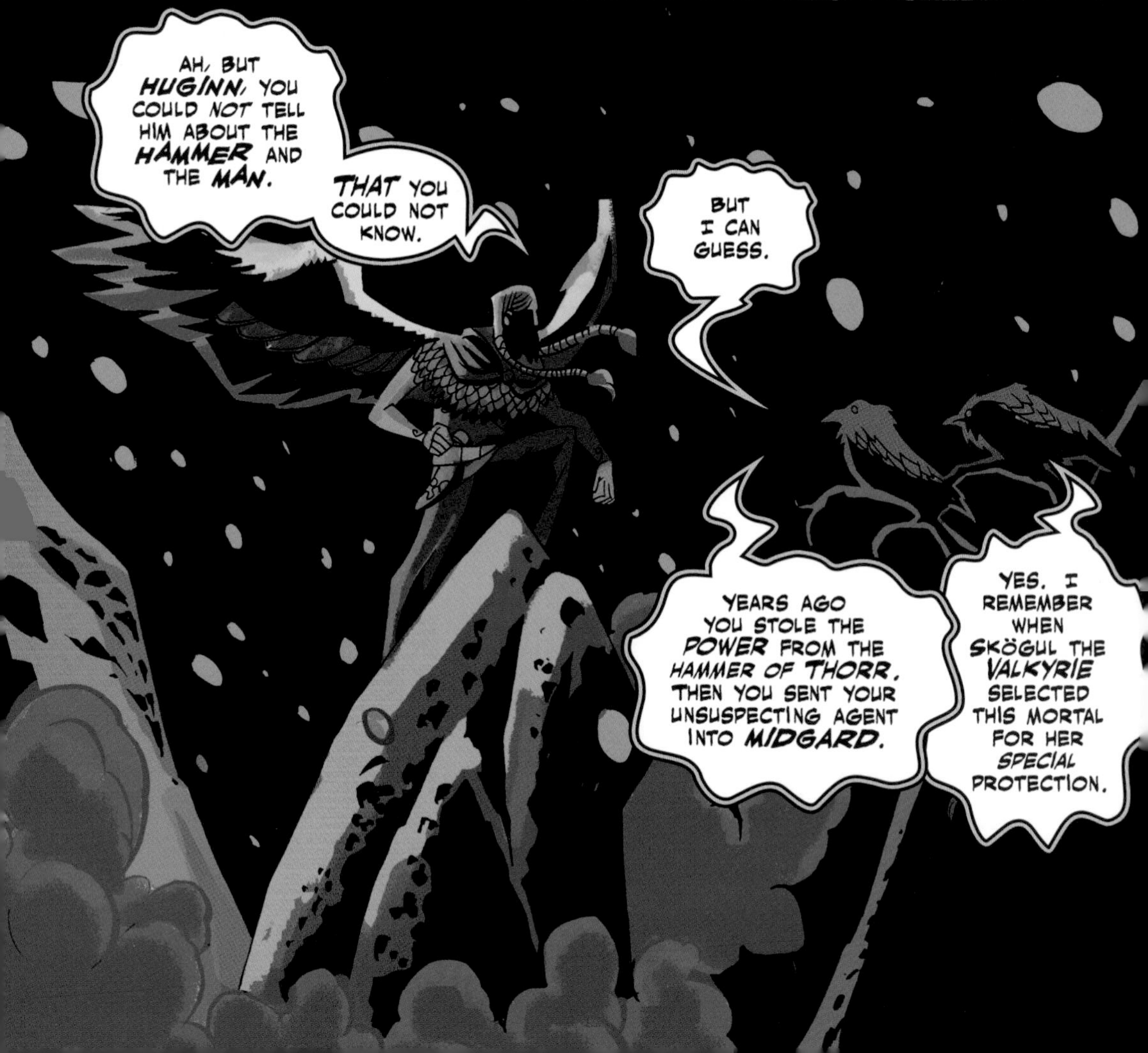
AH, BUT HUGINN, YOU COULD NOT TELL HIM ABOUT THE HAMMER AND THE MAN.
THAT YOU COULD NOT KNOW.
BUT I CAN GUESS.
YEARS AGO YOU STOLE THE POWER FROM THE HAMMER OF THORR. THEN YOU SENT YOUR UNSUSPECTING AGENT INTO MIDGARD.
YES. I REMEMBER WHEN SKÖGUL THE VALKYRIE SELECTED THIS MORTAL FOR HER SPECIAL PROTECTION.

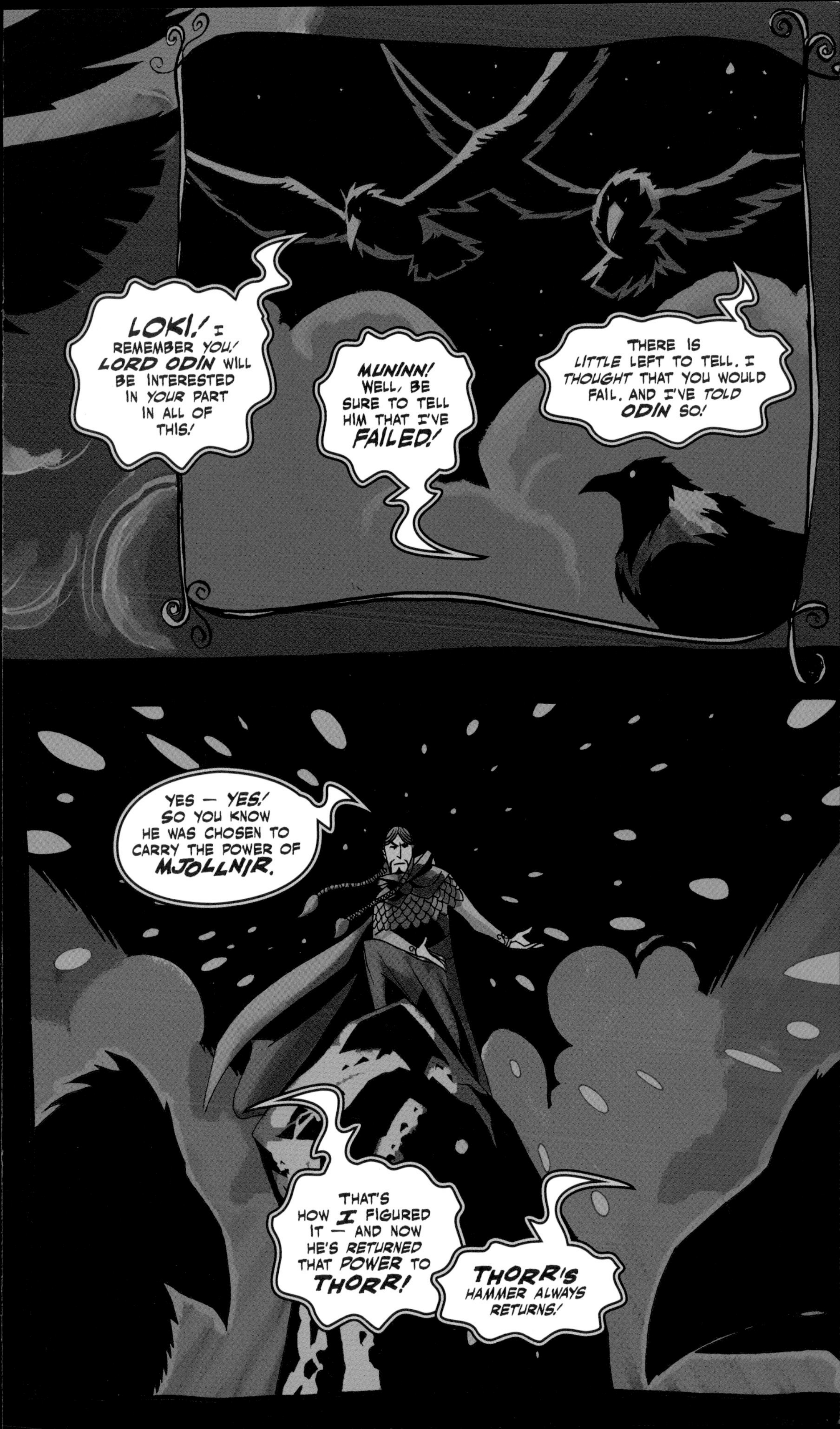
LOKI! I REMEMBER YOU! LORD ODIN WILL BE INTERESTED IN YOUR PART IN ALL OF THIS!
MUNINN! WELL, BE SURE TO TELL HIM THAT I'VE FAILED!
THERE IS LITTLE LEFT TO TELL. I THOUGHT THAT YOU WOULD FAIL. AND I'VE TOLD ODIN SO!
YES — YES! SO YOU KNOW HE WAS CHOSEN TO CARRY THE POWER OF MJOLLNIR.
THAT'S HOW I FIGURED IT — AND NOW HE'S RETURNED THAT POWER TO THORR!
THORR'S HAMMER ALWAYS RETURNS!

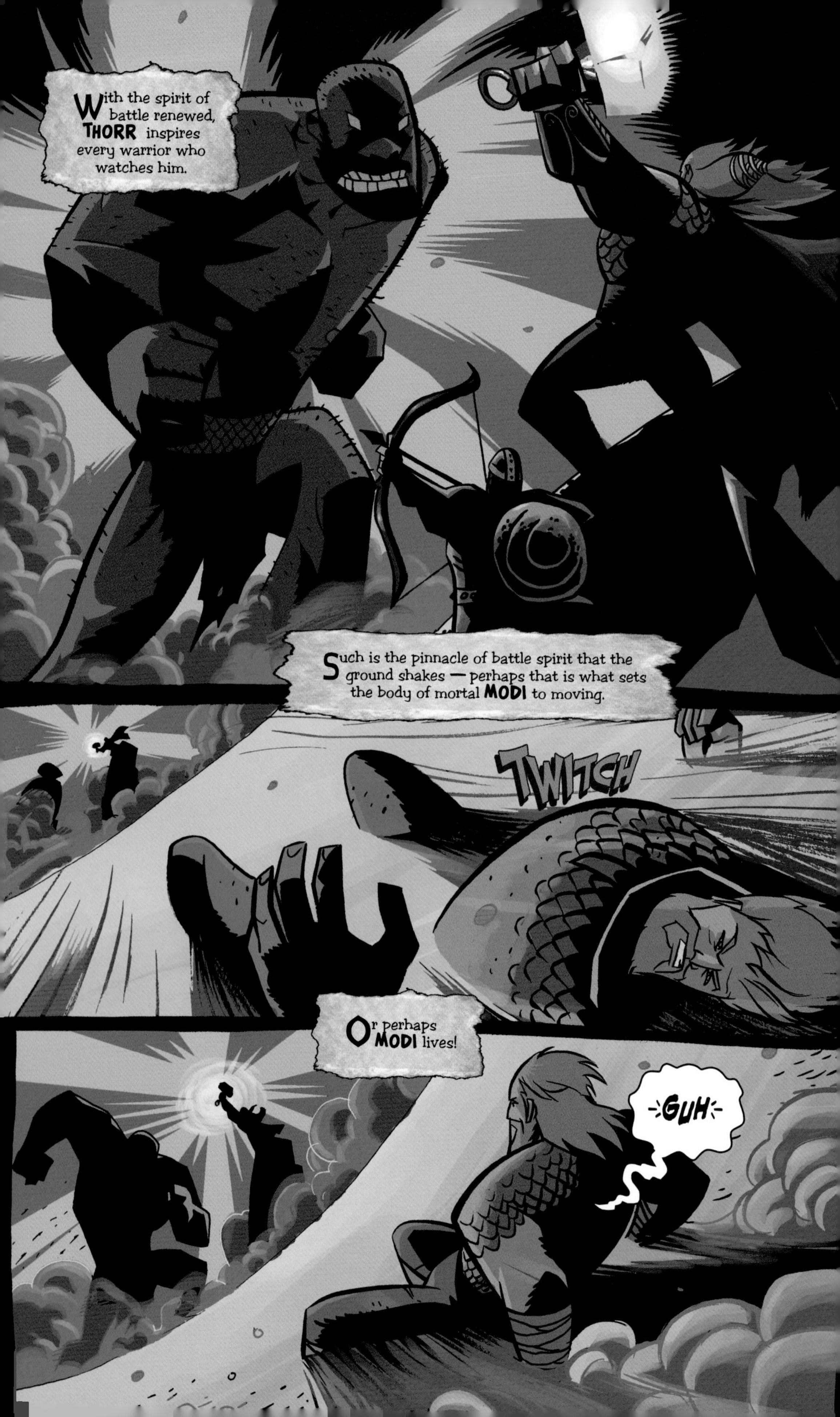
With the spirit of battle renewed, THORR inspires every warrior who watches him.
Such is the pinnacle of battle spirit that the ground shakes — perhaps that is what sets the body of mortal MODI to moving.
TWITCH
Or perhaps MODI lives!
GUH

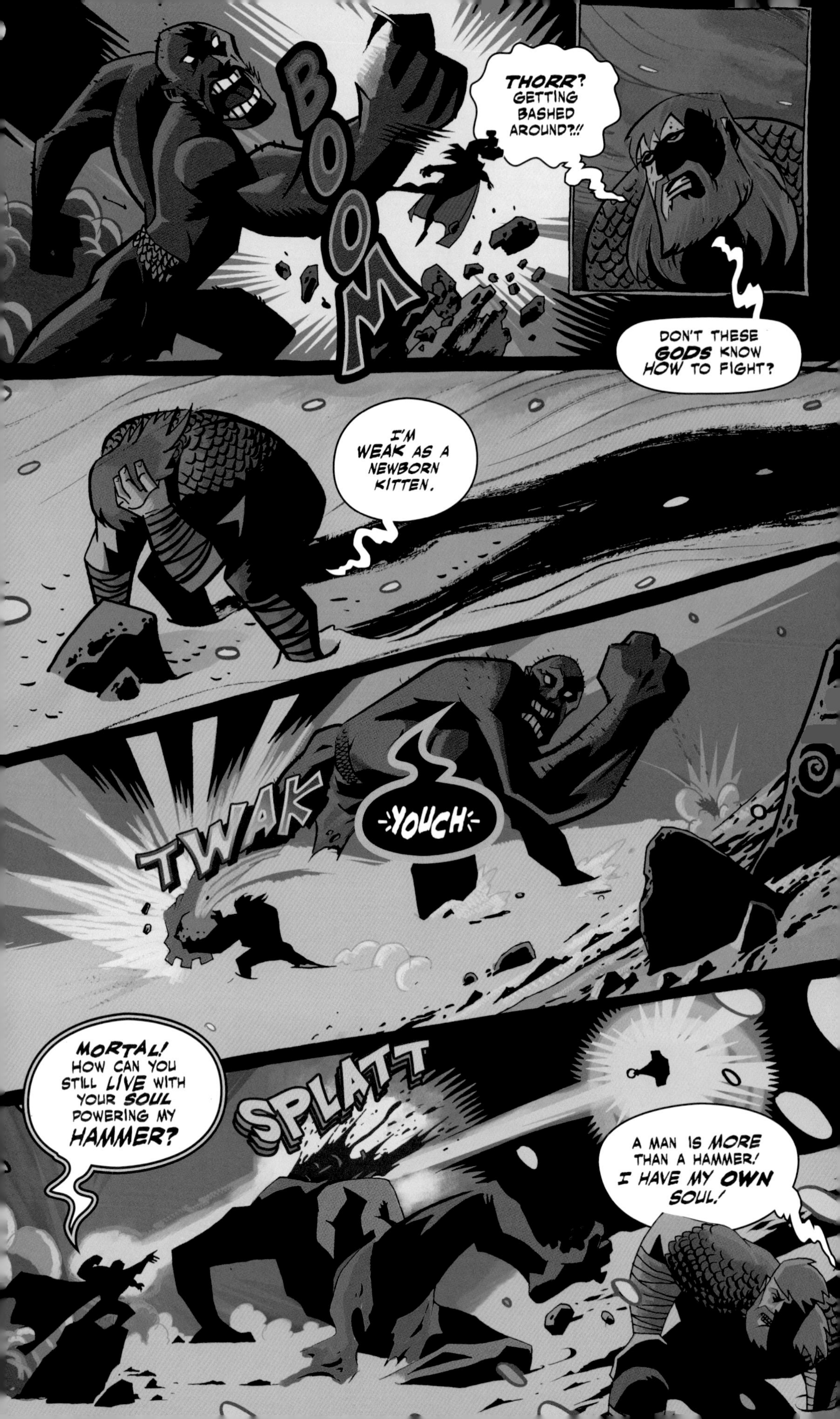
BOOM
THORR? GETTING BASHED AROUND?!!
DON'T THESE GODS KNOW HOW TO FIGHT?
I'M WEAK AS A NEWBORN KITTEN.
TWAK
YOUCH
MORTAL! HOW CAN YOU STILL LIVE WITH YOUR SOUL POWERING MY HAMMER?
SPLATT
A MAN IS MORE THAN A HAMMER! I HAVE MY OWN SOUL!

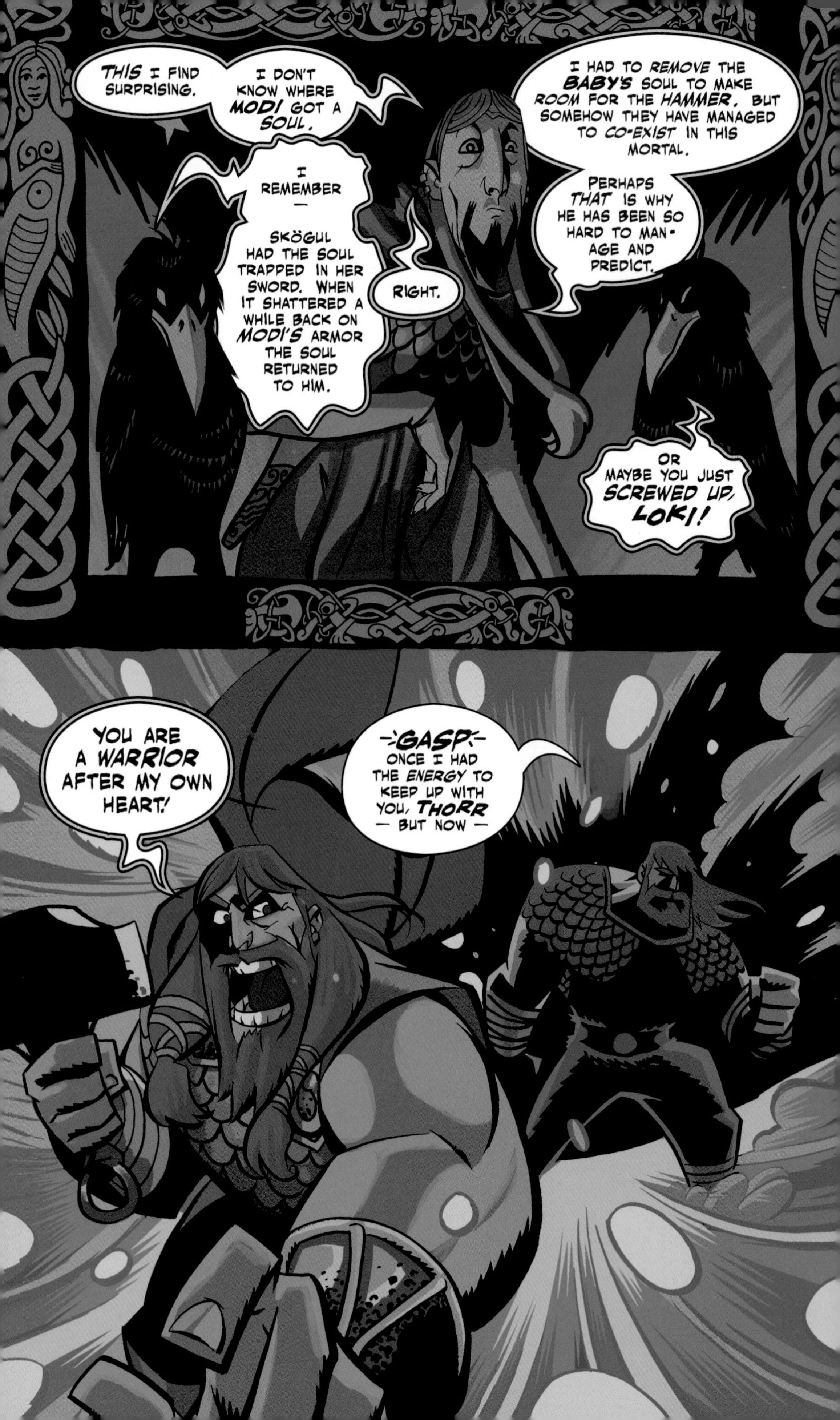
THIS I FIND SURPRISING.
I DON'T KNOW WHERE MODI GOT A SOUL.
I HAD TO REMOVE THE BABY'S SOUL TO MAKE ROOM FOR THE HAMMER. BUT SOMEHOW THEY HAVE MANAGED TO CO-EXIST IN THIS MORTAL.
PERHAPS THAT IS WHY HE HAS BEEN SO HARD TO MAN-AGE AND PREDICT.
I REMEMBER — SKÖGUL HAD THE SOUL TRAPPED IN HER SWORD. WHEN IT SHATTERED A WHILE BACK ON MODI'S ARMOR THE SOUL RETURNED TO HIM.
RIGHT.
OR MAYBE YOU JUST SCREWED UP, LOKI!
YOU ARE A WARRIOR AFTER MY OWN HEART!
GASP ONCE I HAD THE ENERGY TO KEEP UP WITH YOU, THORR — BUT NOW —

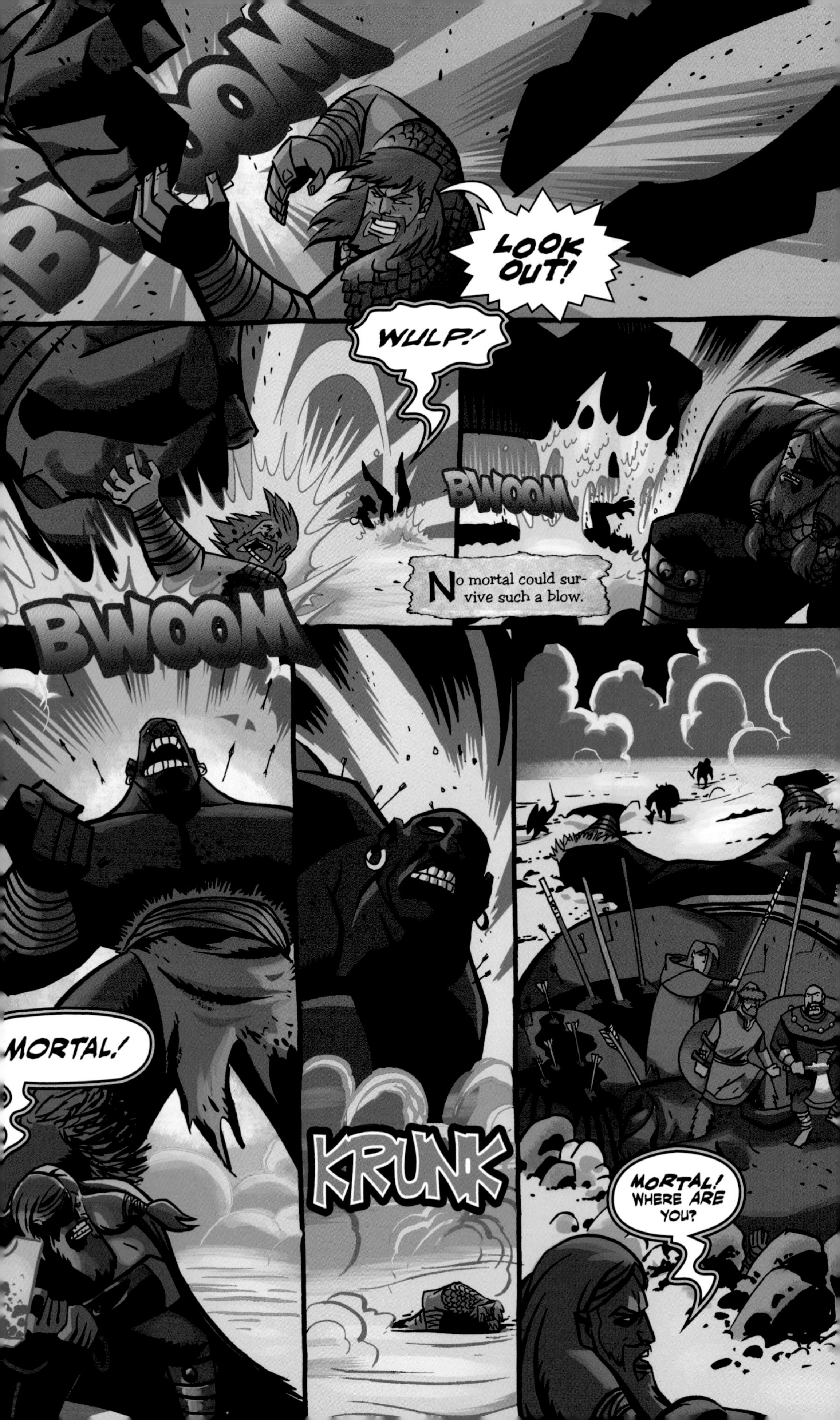
BOOM
LOOK OUT!
WULP!
BWOOM
No mortal could survive such a blow.
BWOOM
MORTAL!
KRUNK
MORTAL! WHERE ARE YOU?

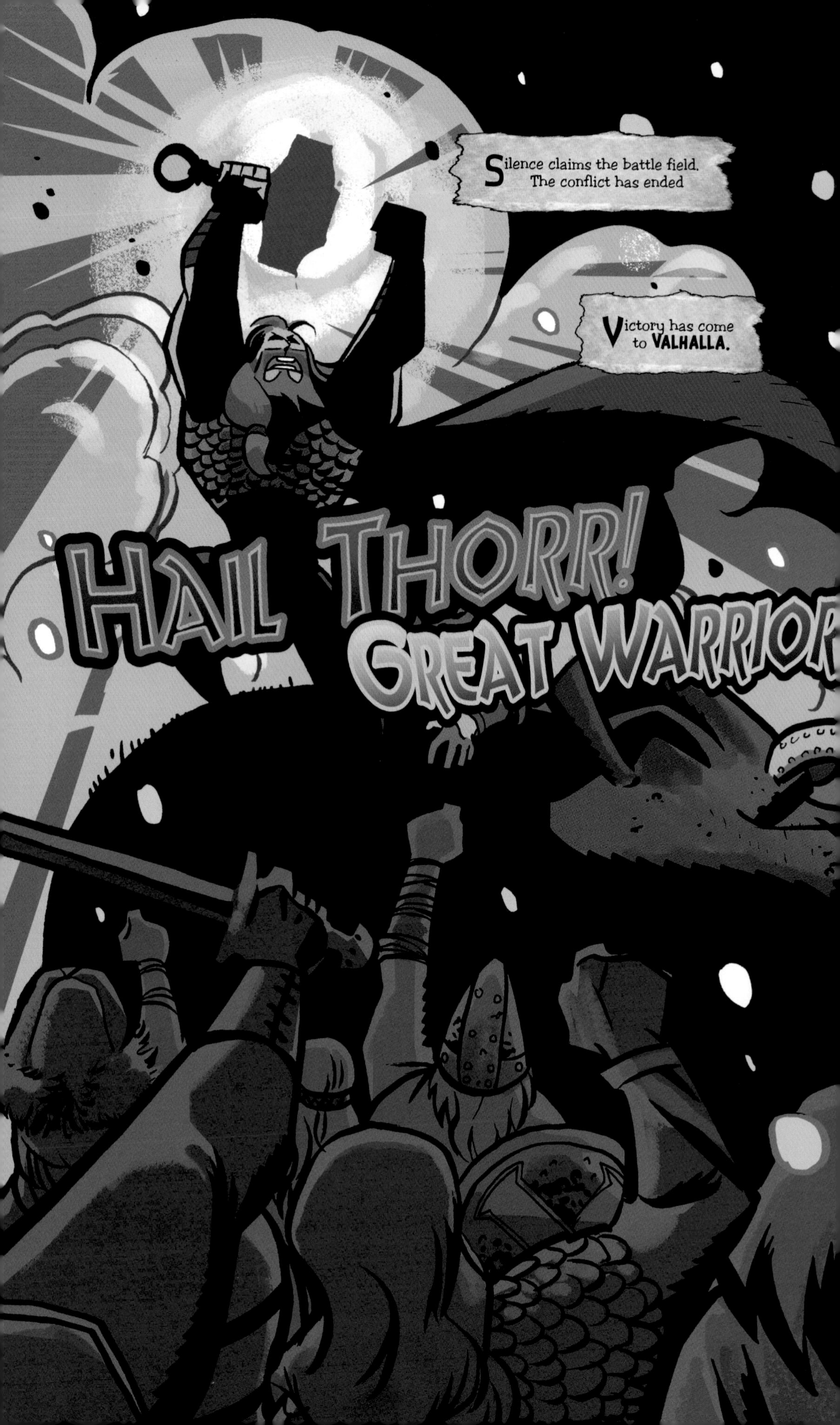
Silence claims the battle field. The conflict has ended
Victory has come to VALHALLA.
HAIL THORR! GREAT WARRIOR

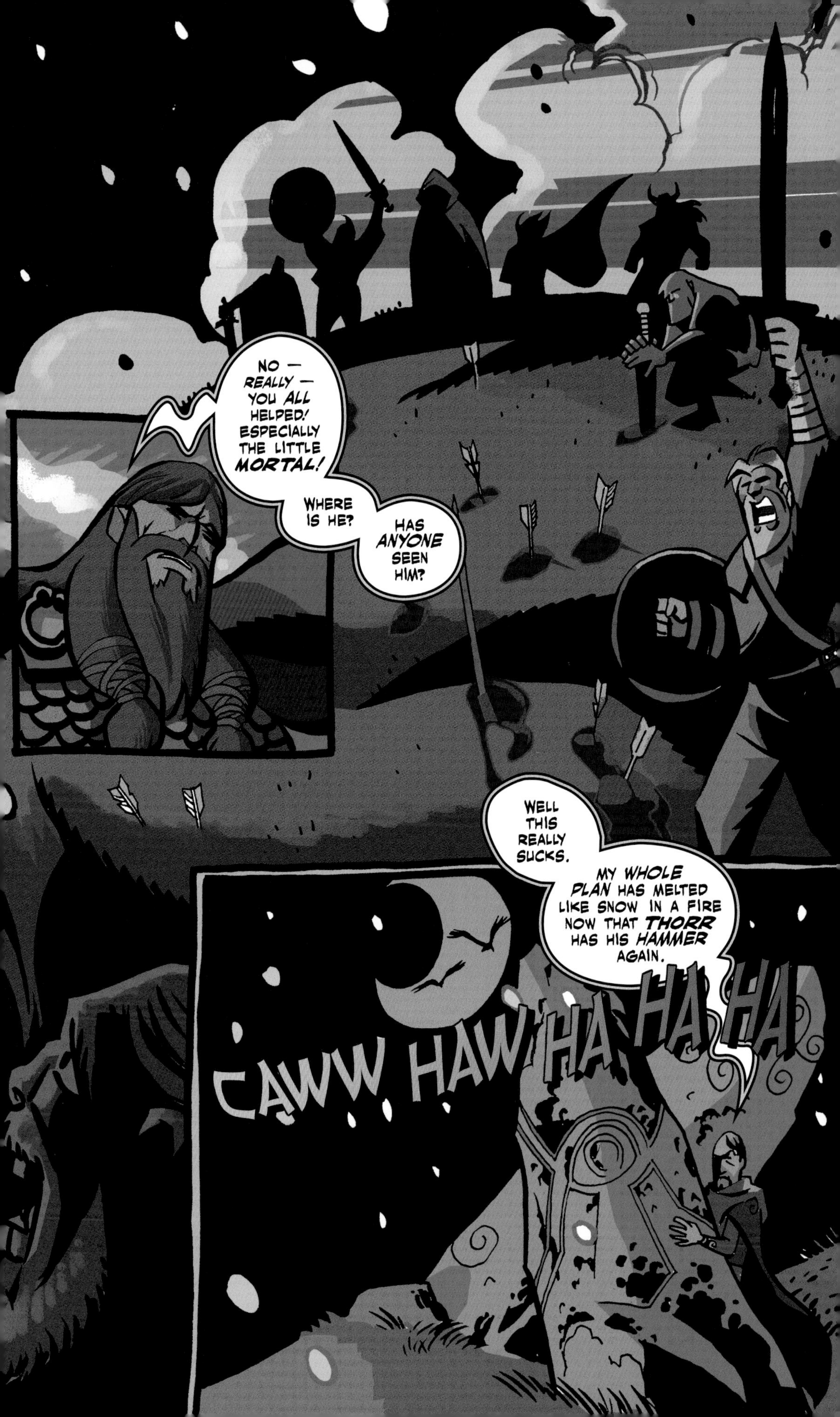
NO — REALLY — YOU ALL HELPED! ESPECIALLY THE LITTLE MORTAL!
WHERE IS HE?
HAS ANYONE SEEN HIM?
WELL THIS REALLY SUCKS.
MY WHOLE PLAN HAS MELTED LIKE SNOW IN A FIRE NOW THAT THORR HAS HIS HAMMER AGAIN.
CAWW HAW HA HA HA HA

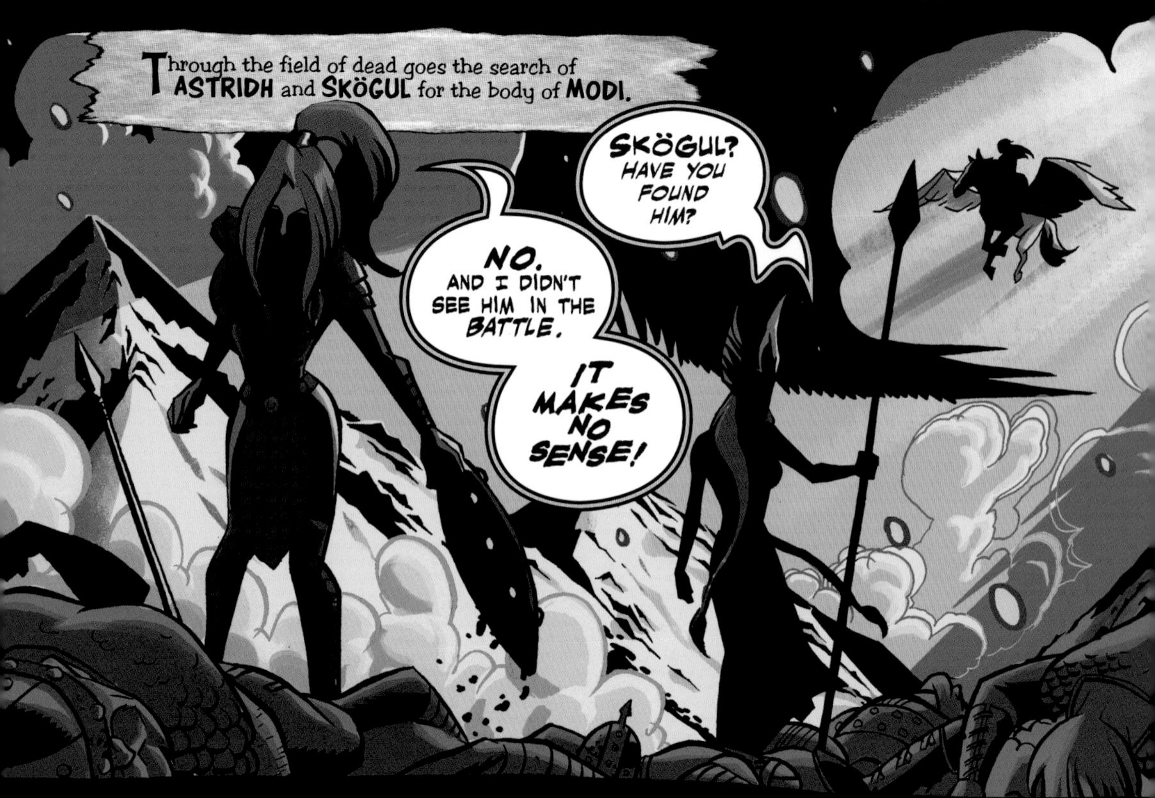
Through the field of dead goes the search of ASTRIDH and SKÖGUL for the body of MODI.
SKÖGUL? HAVE YOU FOUND HIM?
NO. AND I DIDN'T SEE HIM IN THE BATTLE.
IT MAKES NO SENSE!

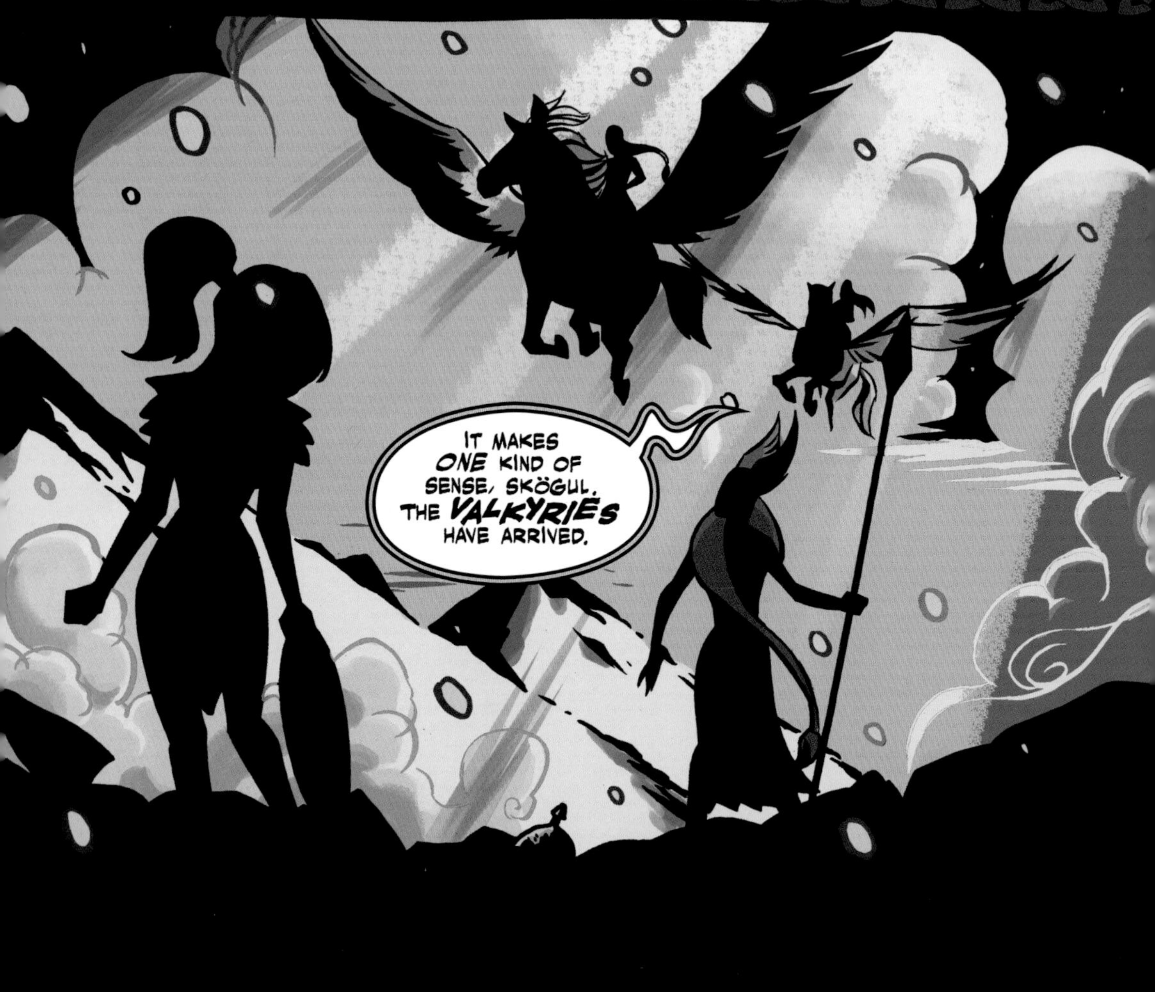
IT MAKES ONE KIND OF SENSE, SKÖGUL. THE VALKYRIES HAVE ARRIVED.

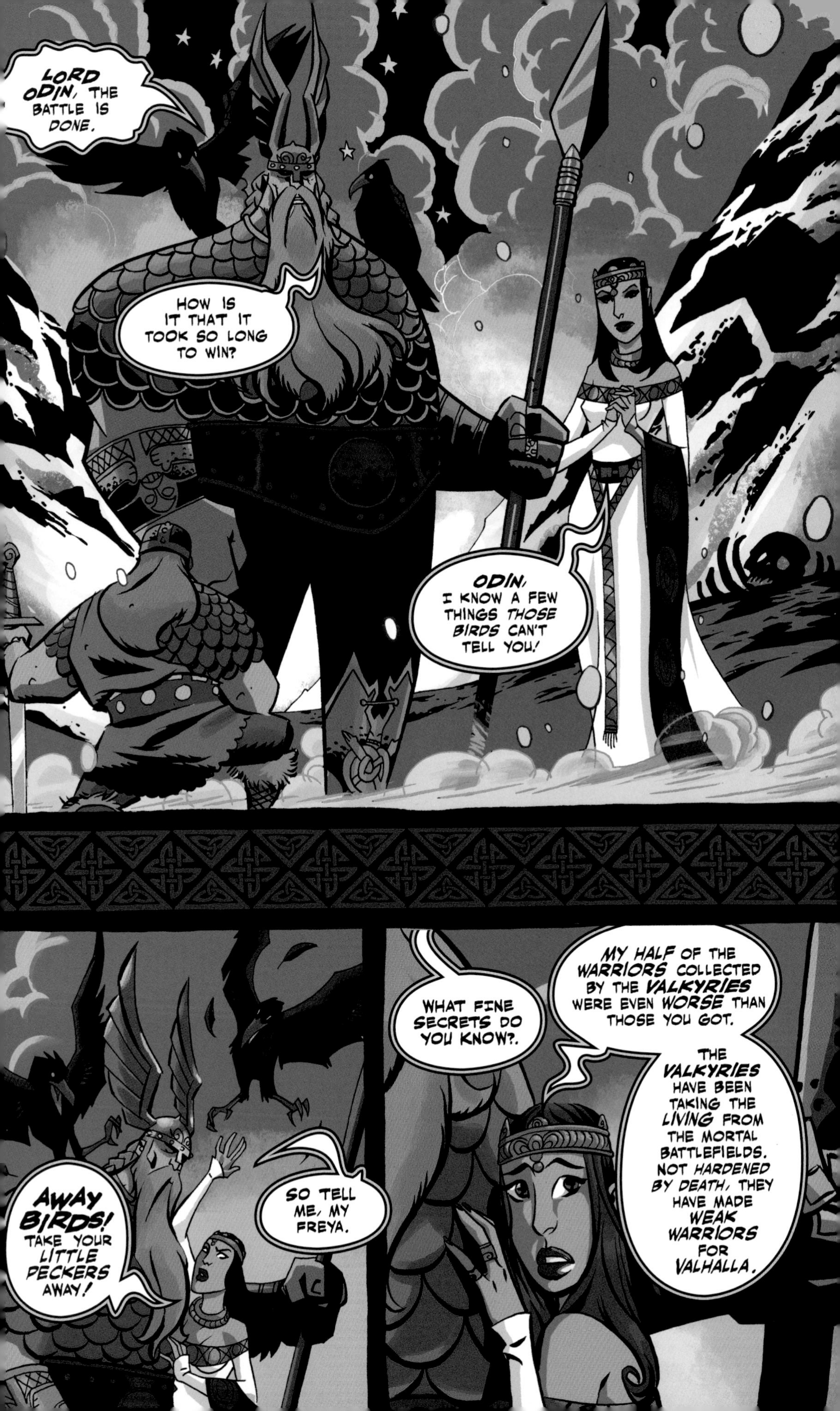

LORD ODIN, THE BATTLE IS DONE.
HOW IS IT THAT IT TOOK SO LONG TO WIN?
ODIN, I KNOW A FEW THINGS THOSE BIRDS CAN'T TELL YOU!
AWAY BIRDS! TAKE YOUR LITTLE PECKERS AWAY!
SO TELL ME, MY FREYA.
WHAT FINE SECRETS DO YOU KNOW?.
MY HALF OF THE WARRIORS COLLECTED BY THE VALKYRIES WERE EVEN WORSE THAN THOSE YOU GOT.
THE VALKYRIES HAVE BEEN TAKING THE LIVING FROM THE MORTAL BATTLEFIELDS. NOT HARDENED BY DEATH, THEY HAVE MADE WEAK WARRIORS FOR VALHALLA.

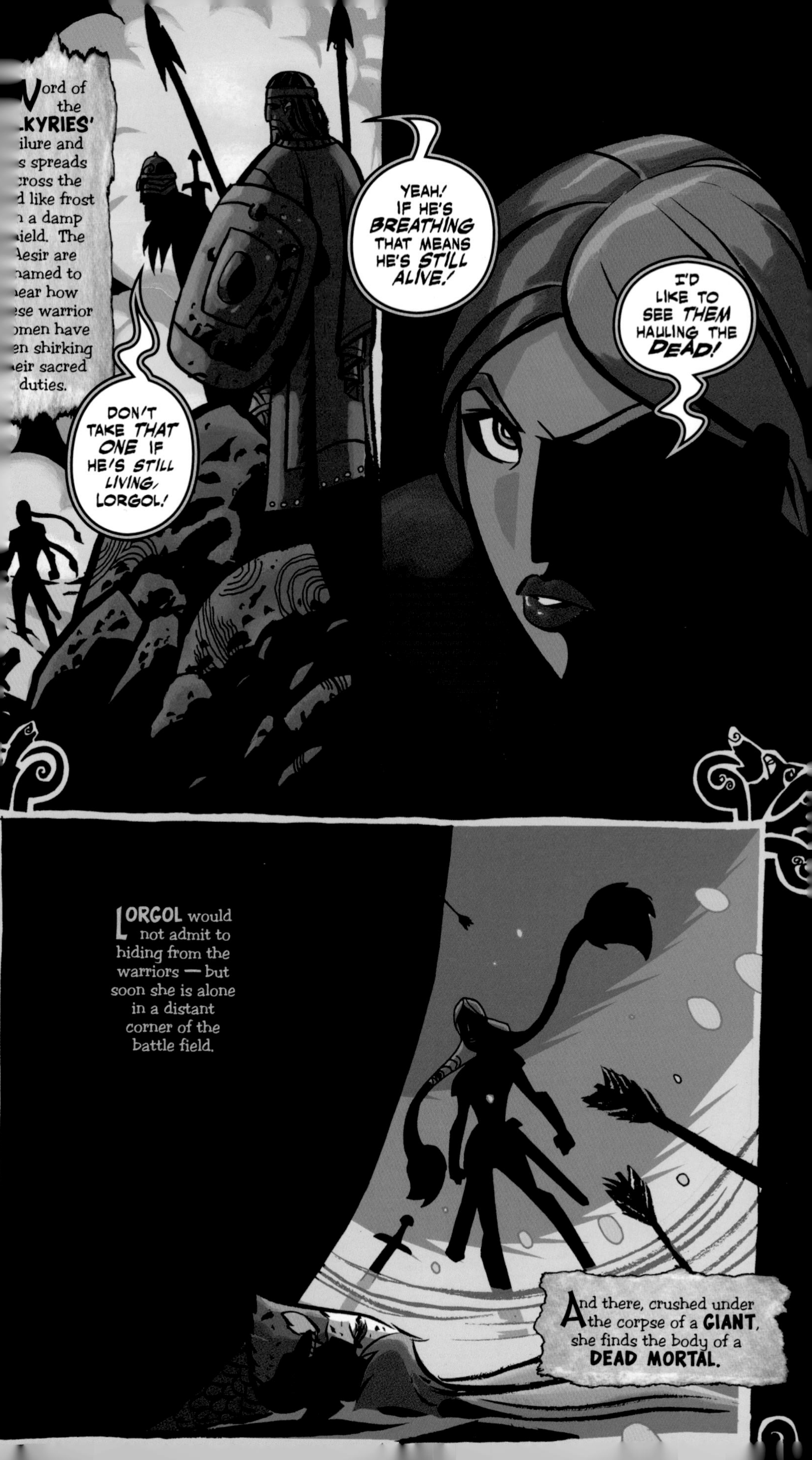

Word of the
LKYRIES'
ilure and
s spreads
cross the
d like frost
n a damp
ield. The
Aesir are
hamed to
ear how
ese warrior
omen have
en shirking
eir sacred
duties.
DON'T TAKE THAT ONE IF HE'S STILL LIVING, LORGOL!
YEAH! IF HE'S BREATHING THAT MEANS HE'S STILL ALIVE!
I'D LIKE TO SEE THEM HAULING THE DEAD!
LORGOL would not admit to hiding from the warriors — but soon she is alone in a distant corner of the battle field.
And there, crushed under the corpse of a GIANT, she finds the body of a DEAD MORTAL.

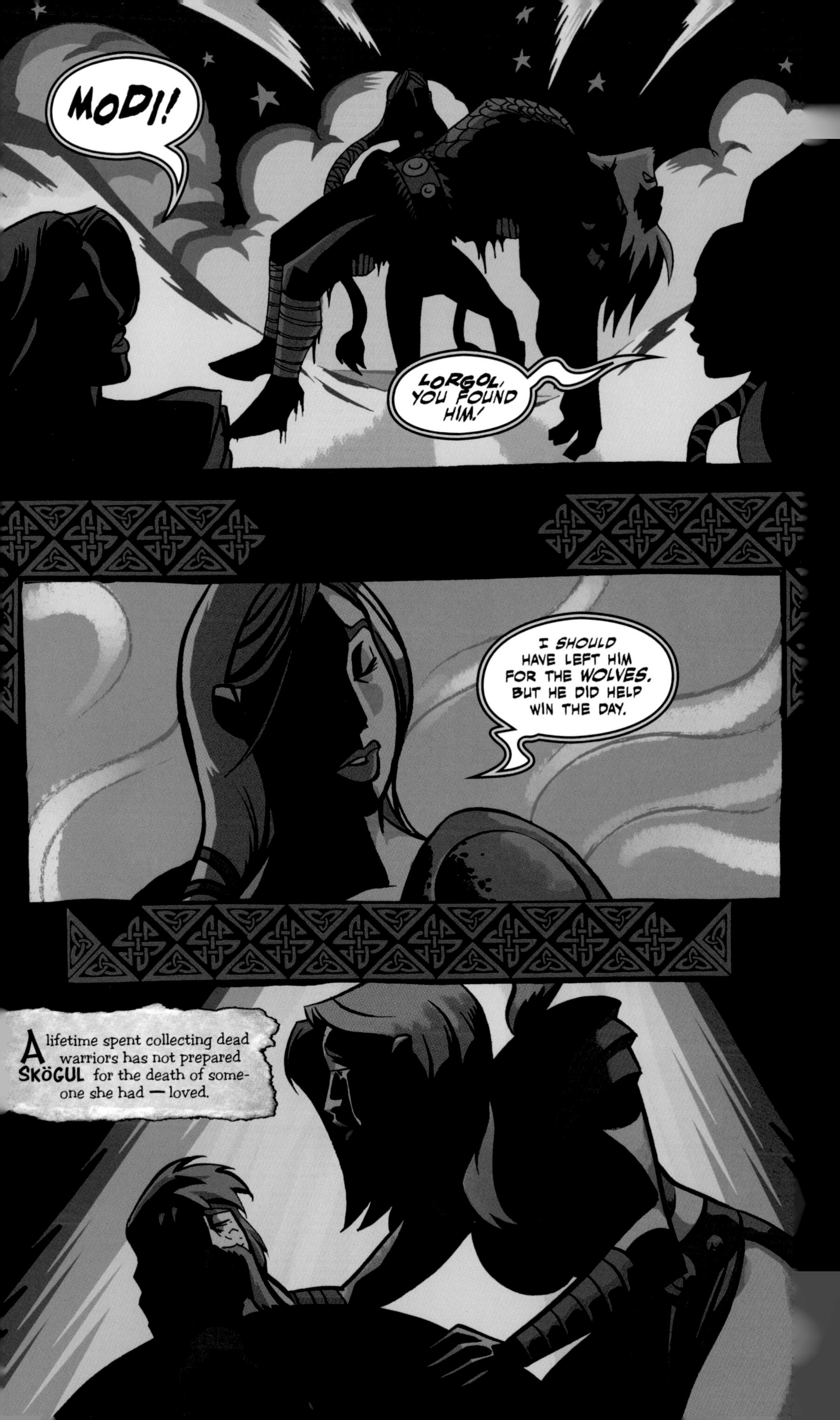
MODI!
LORGOL, YOU FOUND HIM!
I SHOULD HAVE LEFT HIM FOR THE WOLVES. BUT HE DID HELP WIN THE DAY.
A lifetime spent collecting dead warriors has not prepared SKÖGUL for the death of someone she had — loved.

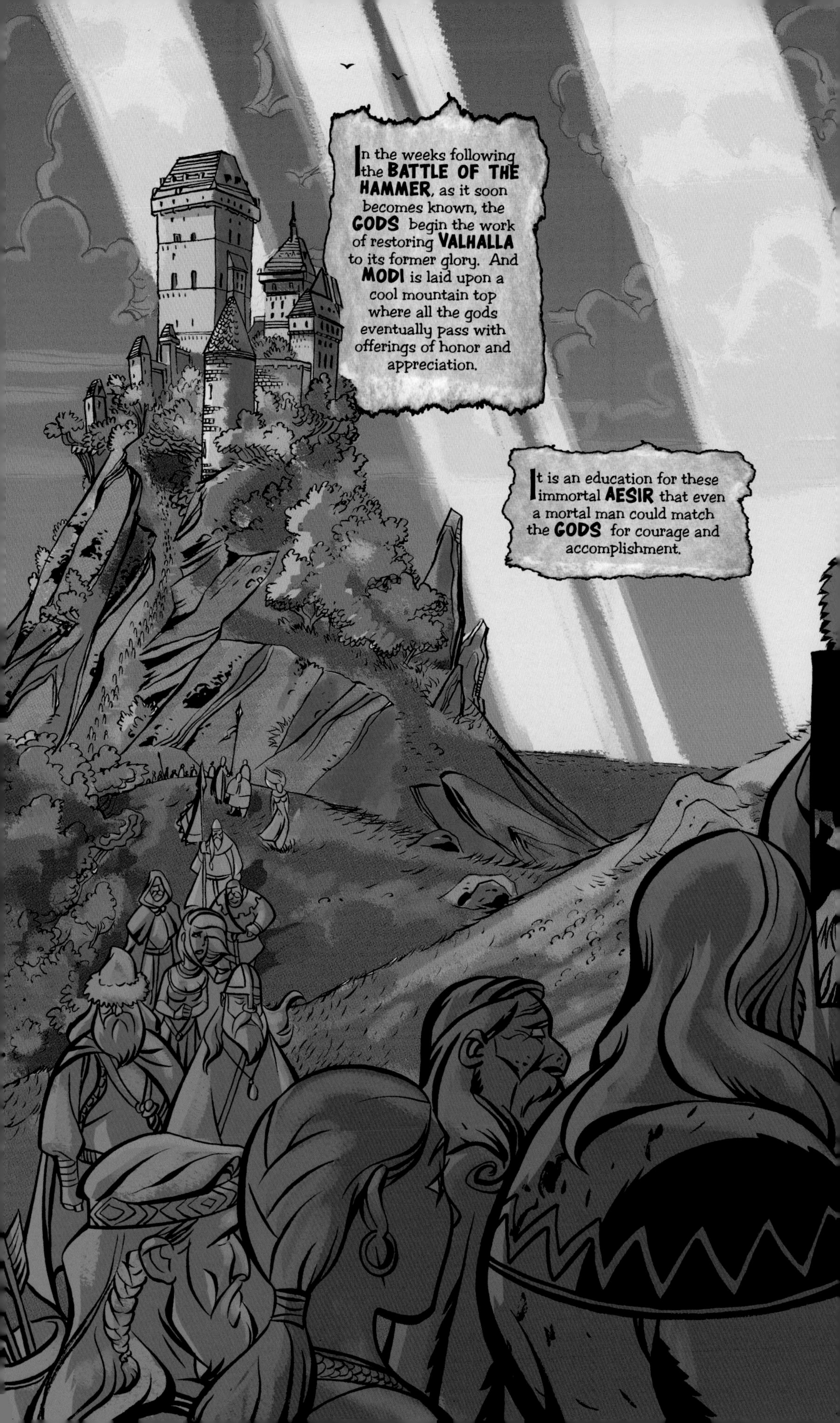
In the weeks following the BATTLE OF THE HAMMER, as it soon becomes known, the GODS begin the work of restoring VALHALLA to its former glory. And MODI is laid upon a cool mountain top where all the gods eventually pass with offerings of honor and appreciation.
It is an education for these immortal AESIR that even a mortal man could match the GODS for courage and accomplishment.

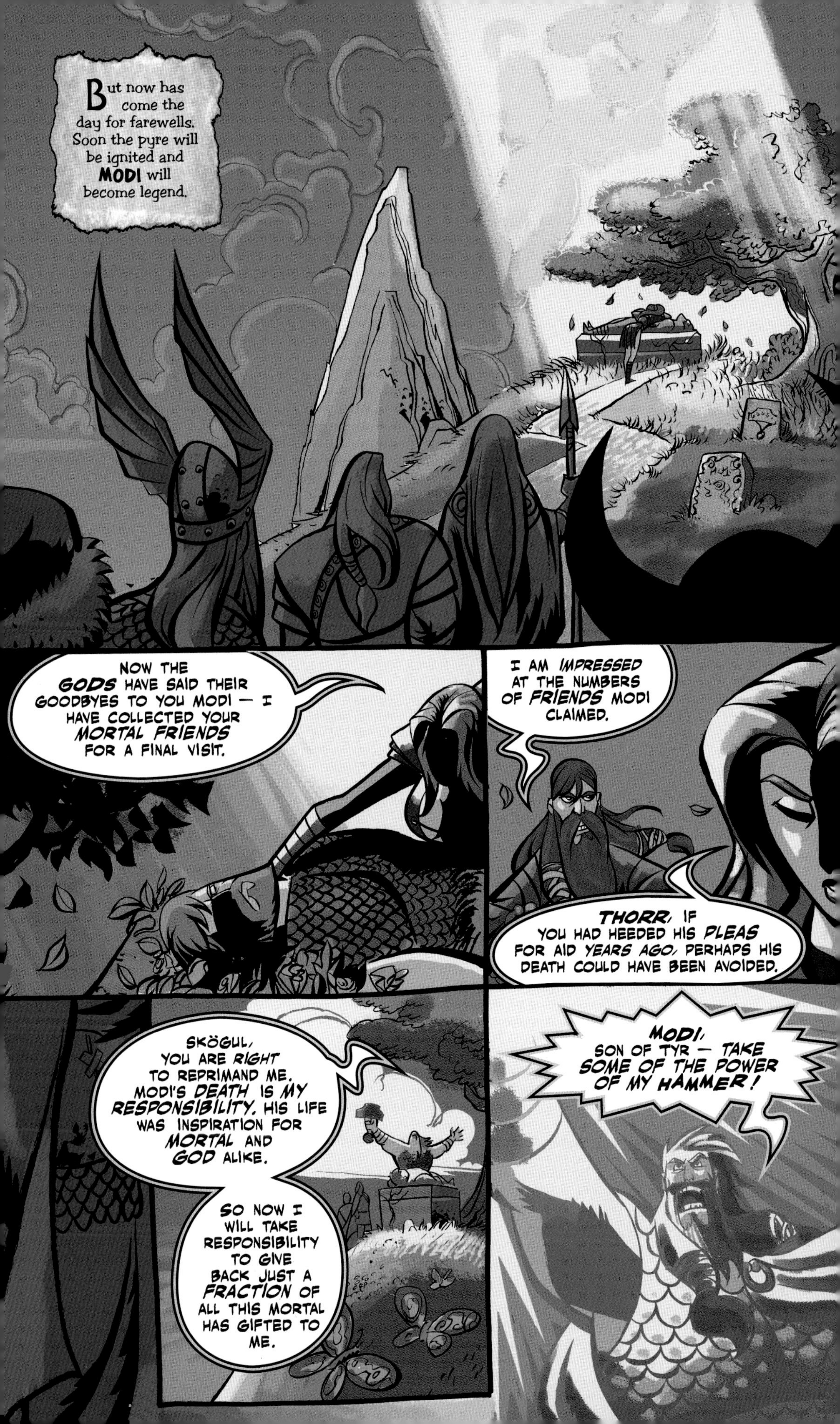

But now has come the day for farewells. Soon the pyre will be ignited and MODI will become legend.
NOW THE GODS HAVE SAID THEIR GOODBYES TO YOU MODI — I HAVE COLLECTED YOUR MORTAL FRIENDS FOR A FINAL VISIT.
I AM IMPRESSED AT THE NUMBERS OF FRIENDS MODI CLAIMED.
THORR, IF YOU HAD HEEDED HIS PLEAS FOR AID YEARS AGO, PERHAPS HIS DEATH COULD HAVE BEEN AVOIDED.
SKÖGUL, YOU ARE RIGHT TO REPRIMAND ME. MODI'S DEATH IS MY RESPONSIBILITY. HIS LIFE WAS INSPIRATION FOR MORTAL AND GOD ALIKE.
SO NOW I WILL TAKE RESPONSIBILITY TO GIVE BACK JUST A FRACTION OF ALL THIS MORTAL HAS GIFTED TO ME.
MODI, SON OF TYR — TAKE SOME OF THE POWER OF MY HAMMER!

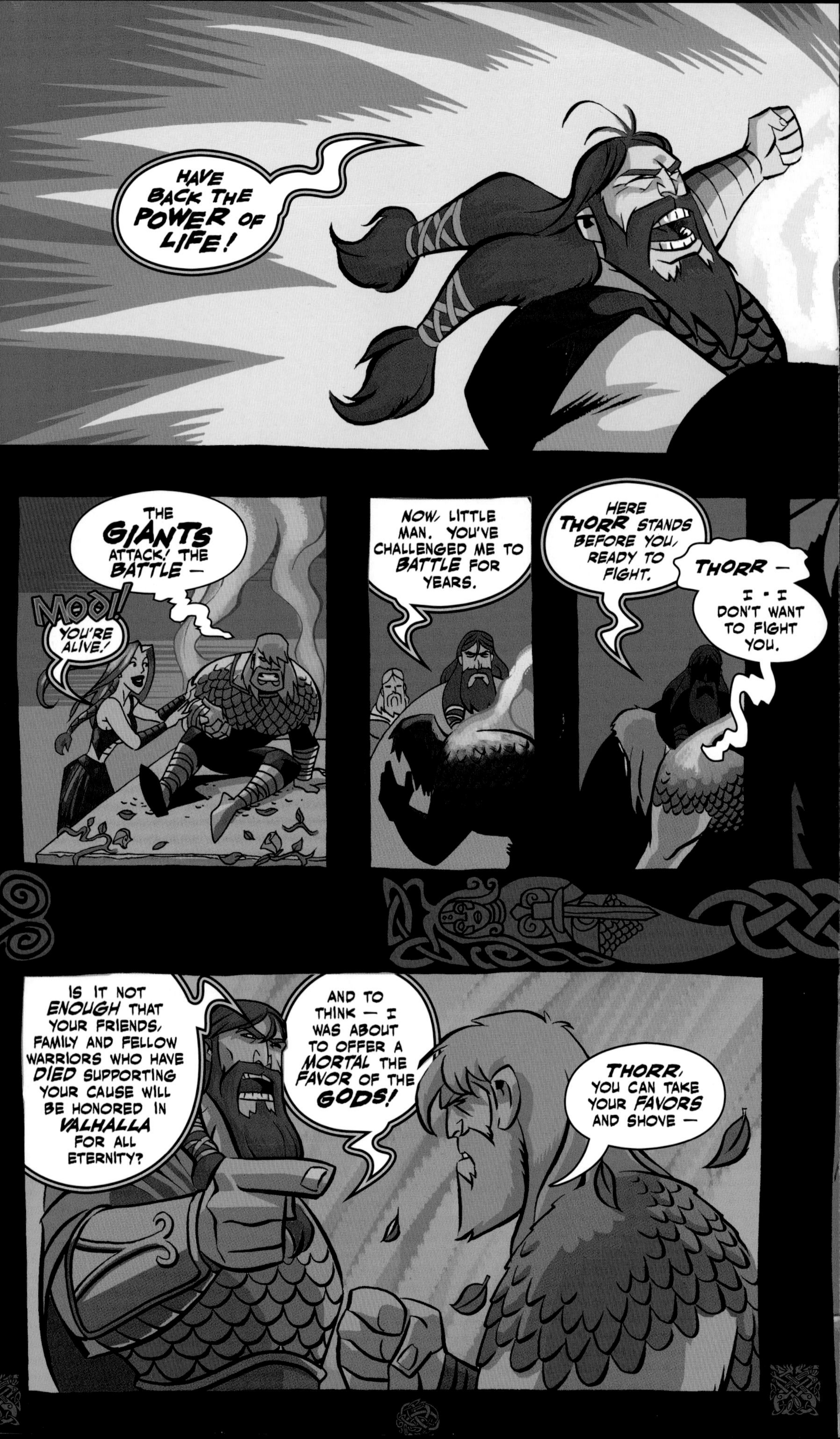
HAVE BACK THE POWER OF LIFE!
THE GIANTS ATTACK! THE BATTLE —
MOOI! YOU'RE ALIVE!
NOW, LITTLE MAN. YOU'VE CHALLENGED ME TO BATTLE FOR YEARS.
HERE THORR STANDS BEFORE YOU, READY TO FIGHT.
THORR — I - I DON'T WANT TO FIGHT YOU.
IS IT NOT ENOUGH THAT YOUR FRIENDS, FAMILY AND FELLOW WARRIORS WHO HAVE DIED SUPPORTING YOUR CAUSE WILL BE HONORED IN VALHALLA FOR ALL ETERNITY?
AND TO THINK — I WAS ABOUT TO OFFER A MORTAL THE FAVOR OF THE GODS!
THORR, YOU CAN TAKE YOUR FAVORS AND SHOVE —

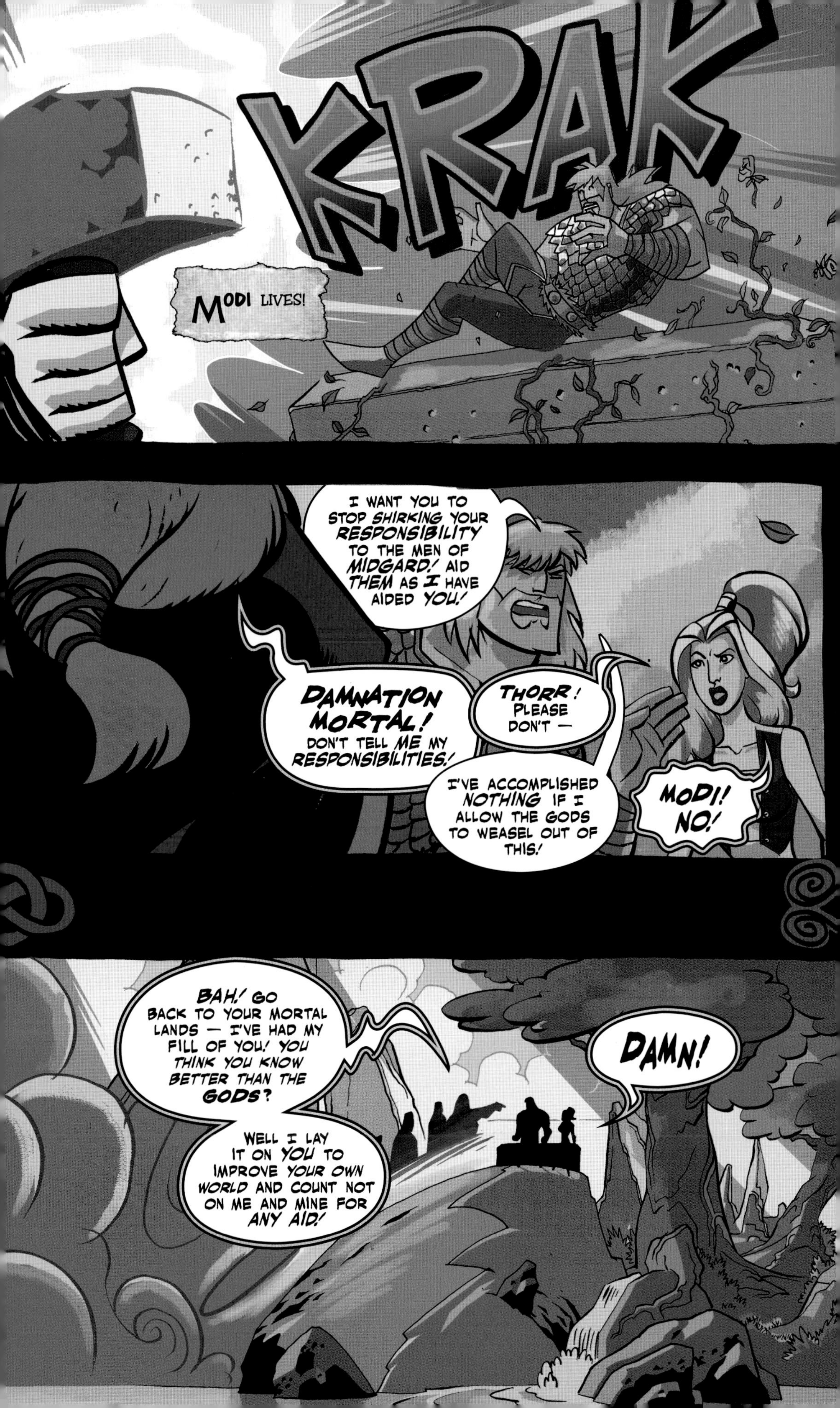
KRAK
MODI LIVES!
I WANT YOU TO STOP SHIRKING YOUR RESPONSIBILITY TO THE MEN OF MIDGARD! AID THEM AS I HAVE AIDED YOU!
DAMNATION MORTAL! DON'T TELL ME MY RESPONSIBILITIES!
THORR! PLEASE DON'T —
I'VE ACCOMPLISHED NOTHING IF I ALLOW THE GODS TO WEASEL OUT OF THIS!
MODI! NO!
BAH! GO BACK TO YOUR MORTAL LANDS — I'VE HAD MY FILL OF YOU! YOU THINK YOU KNOW BETTER THAN THE GODS?
WELL I LAY IT ON YOU TO IMPROVE YOUR OWN WORLD AND COUNT NOT ON ME AND MINE FOR ANY AID!
DAMN!

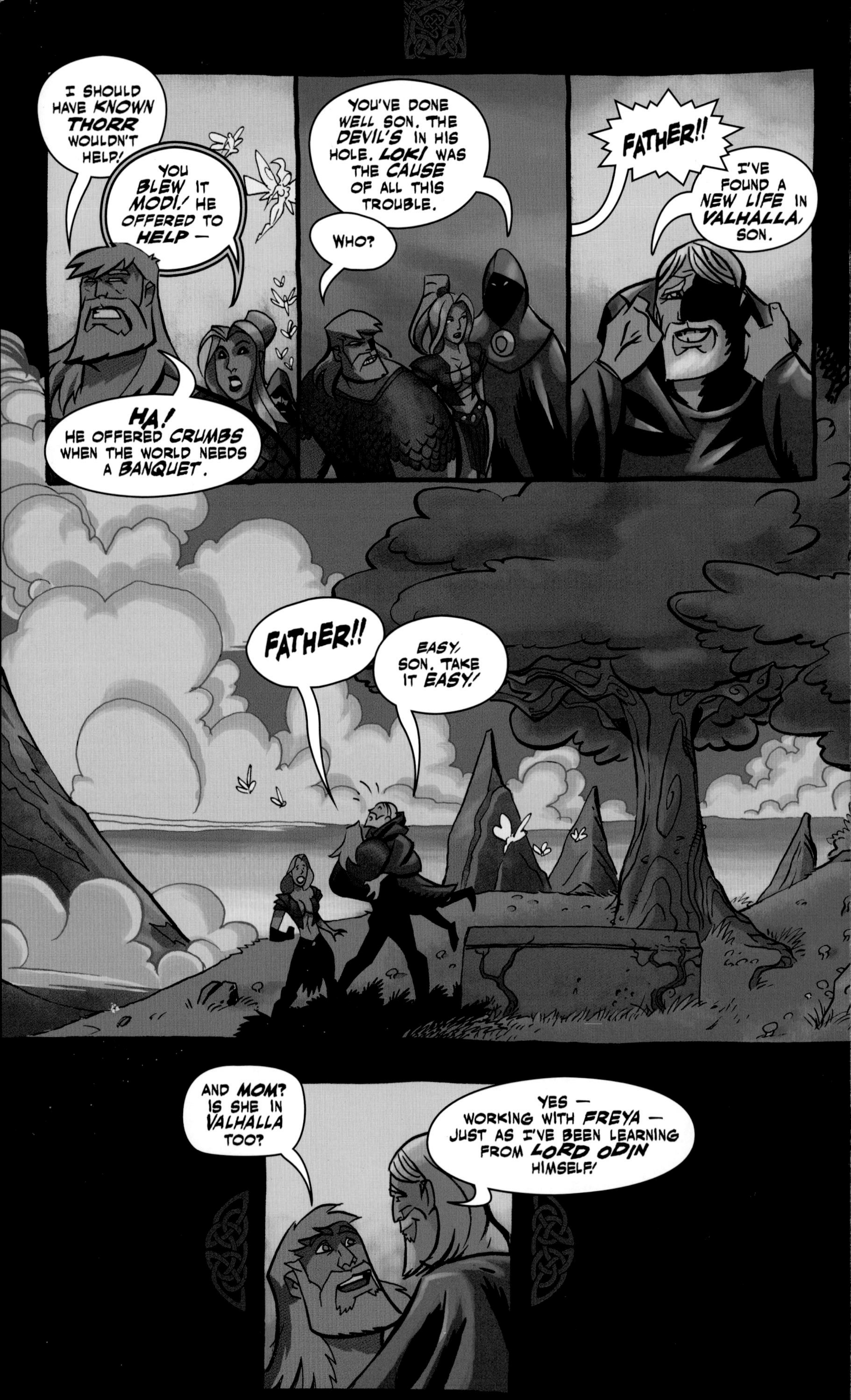
I SHOULD HAVE KNOWN THORR WOULDN'T HELP!
YOU BLEW IT MODI! HE OFFERED TO HELP —
HA! HE OFFERED CRUMBS WHEN THE WORLD NEEDS A BANQUET.
YOU'VE DONE WELL SON. THE DEVIL'S IN HIS HOLE. LOKI WAS THE CAUSE OF ALL THIS TROUBLE.
WHO?
FATHER!!
I'VE FOUND A NEW LIFE IN VALHALLA, SON.
FATHER!!
EASY, SON. TAKE IT EASY!
AND MOM? IS SHE IN VALHALLA TOO?
YES — WORKING WITH FREYA — JUST AS I'VE BEEN LEARNING FROM LORD ODIN HIMSELF!

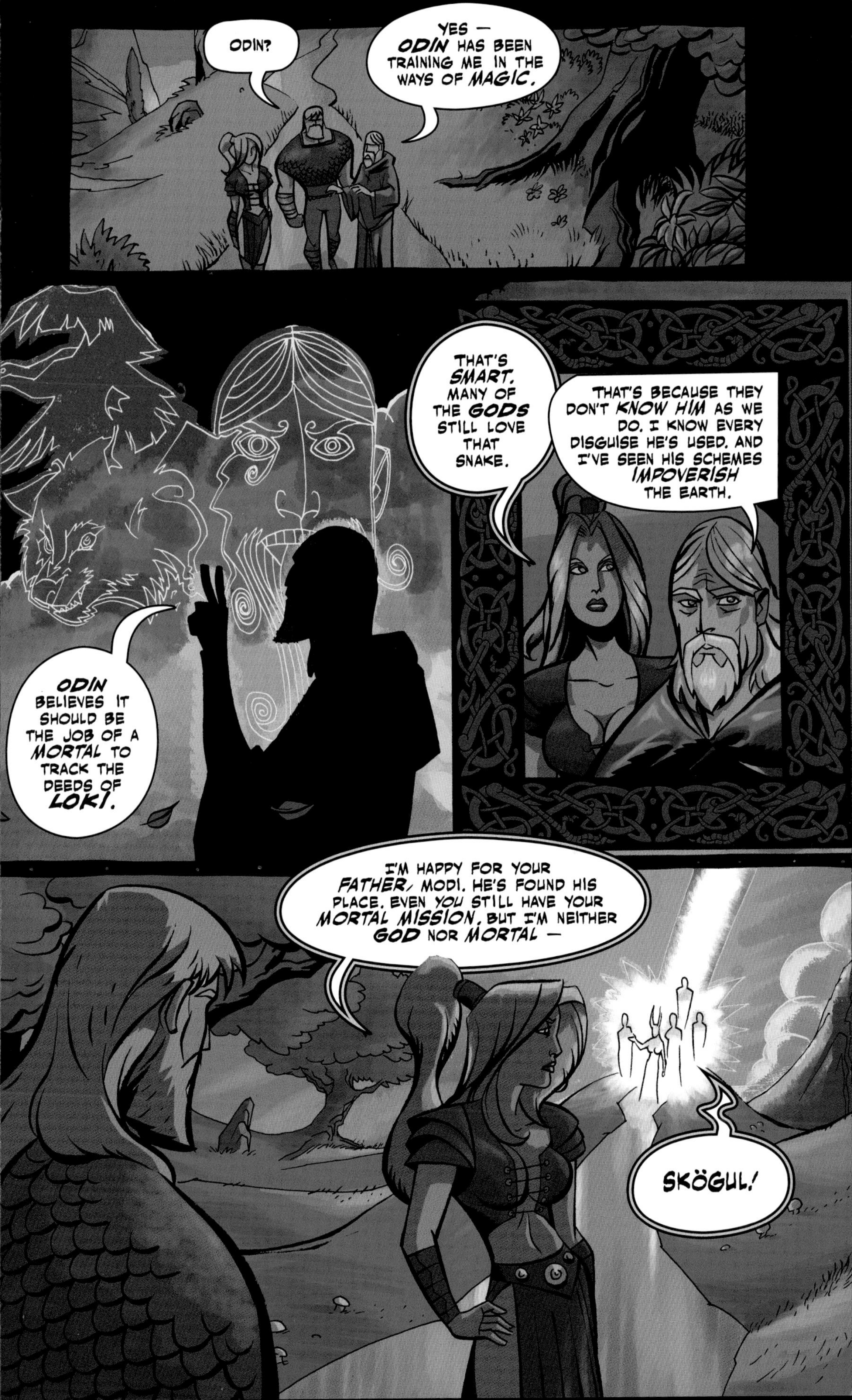
ODIN?
YES — ODIN HAS BEEN TRAINING ME IN THE WAYS OF MAGIC.
ODIN BELIEVES IT SHOULD BE THE JOB OF A MORTAL TO TRACK THE DEEDS OF LOKI.
THAT'S SMART. MANY OF THE GODS STILL LOVE THAT SNAKE.
THAT'S BECAUSE THEY DON'T KNOW HIM AS WE DO. I KNOW EVERY DISGUISE HE'S USED. AND I'VE SEEN HIS SCHEMES IMPOVERISH THE EARTH.
I'M HAPPY FOR YOUR FATHER, MODI. HE'S FOUND HIS PLACE. EVEN YOU STILL HAVE YOUR MORTAL MISSION. BUT I'M NEITHER GOD NOR MORTAL —
SKÖGUL!

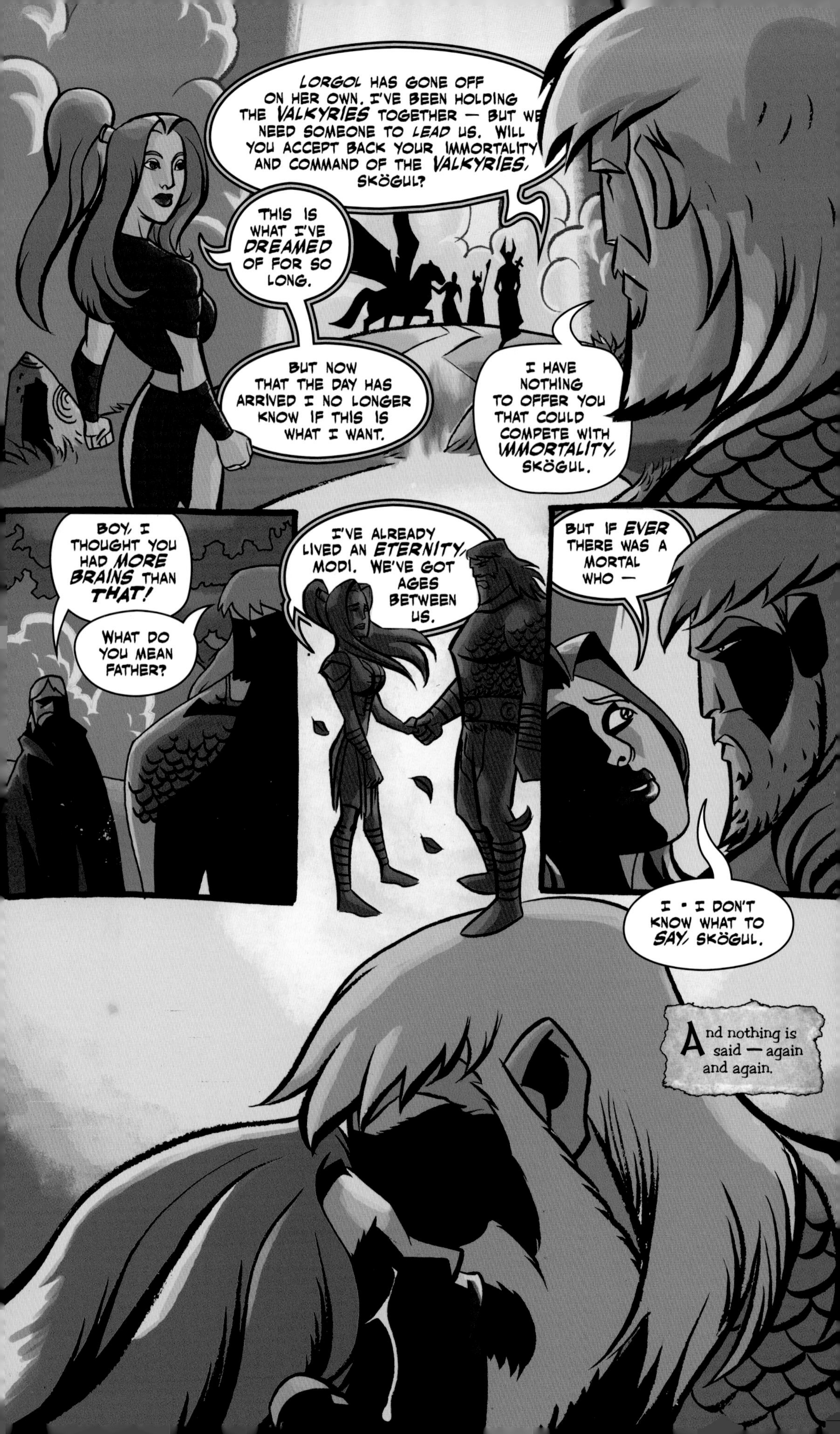
LORGOL HAS GONE OFF ON HER OWN. I'VE BEEN HOLDING THE VALKYRIES TOGETHER — BUT WE NEED SOMEONE TO LEAD US. WILL YOU ACCEPT BACK YOUR IMMORTALITY AND COMMAND OF THE VALKYRIES, SKÖGUL?
THIS IS WHAT I'VE DREAMED OF FOR SO LONG.
BUT NOW THAT THE DAY HAS ARRIVED I NO LONGER KNOW IF THIS IS WHAT I WANT.
I HAVE NOTHING TO OFFER YOU THAT COULD COMPETE WITH IMMORTALITY, SKÖGUL.
BOY, I THOUGHT YOU HAD MORE BRAINS THAN THAT!
WHAT DO YOU MEAN FATHER?
I'VE ALREADY LIVED AN ETERNITY, MODI. WE'VE GOT AGES BETWEEN US.
BUT IF EVER THERE WAS A MORTAL WHO —
I - I DON'T KNOW WHAT TO SAY, SKÖGUL.
And nothing is said — again and again.

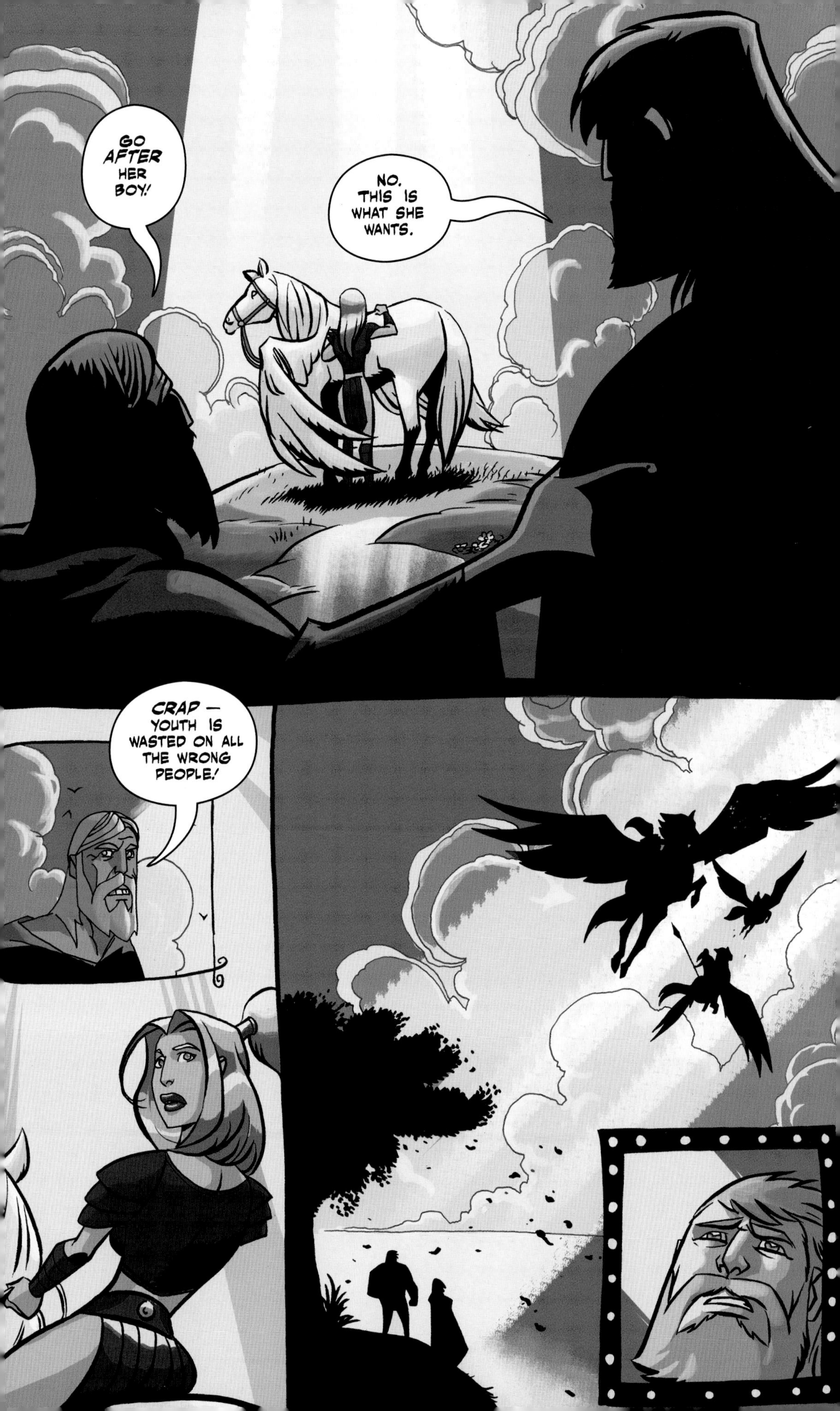
GO AFTER HER BOY!
NO. THIS IS WHAT SHE WANTS.
CRAP — YOUTH IS WASTED ON ALL THE WRONG PEOPLE!

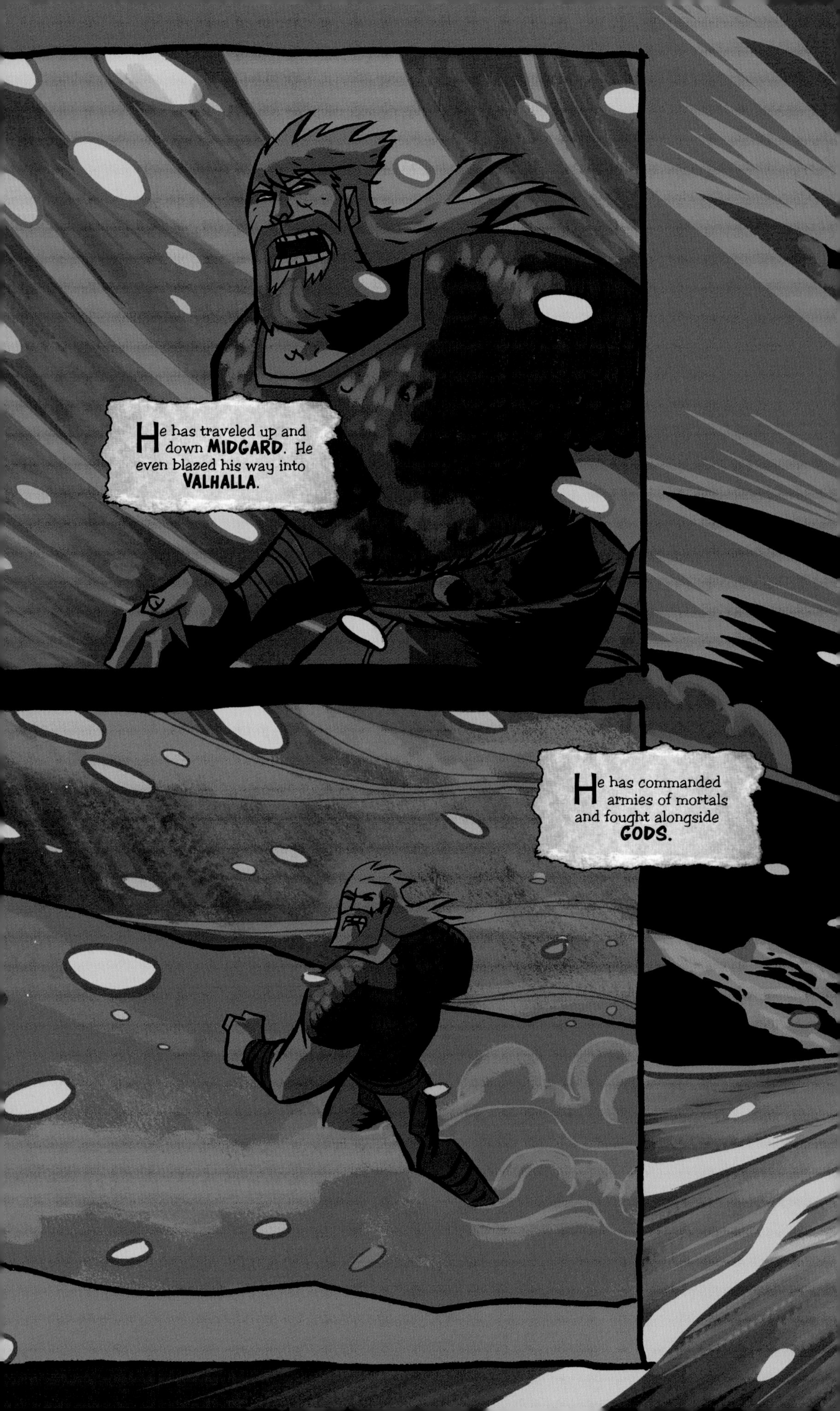
He has traveled up and down MIDGARD. He even blazed his way into VALHALLA.
He has commanded armies of mortals and fought alongside GODS.

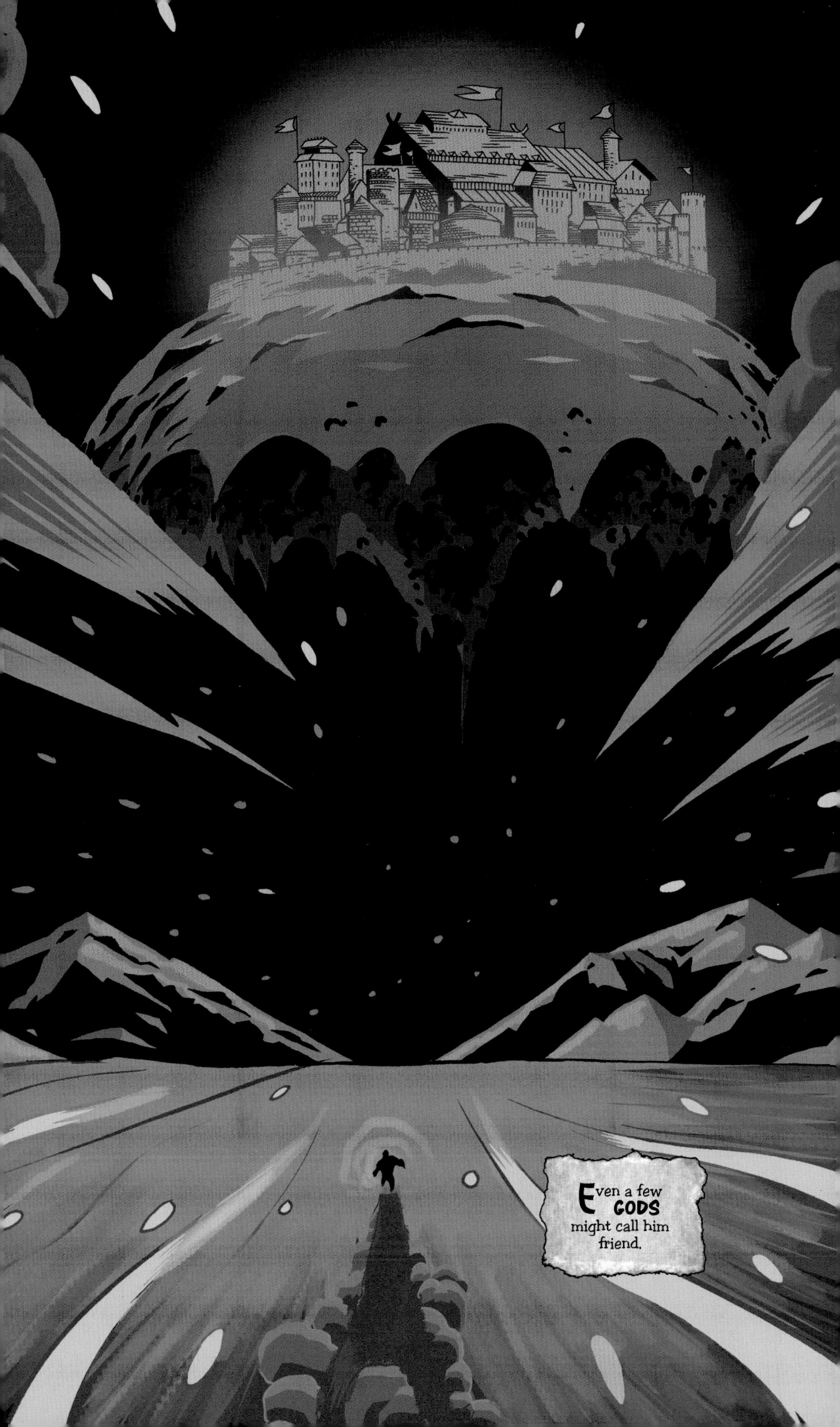
Even a few GODS might call him friend.

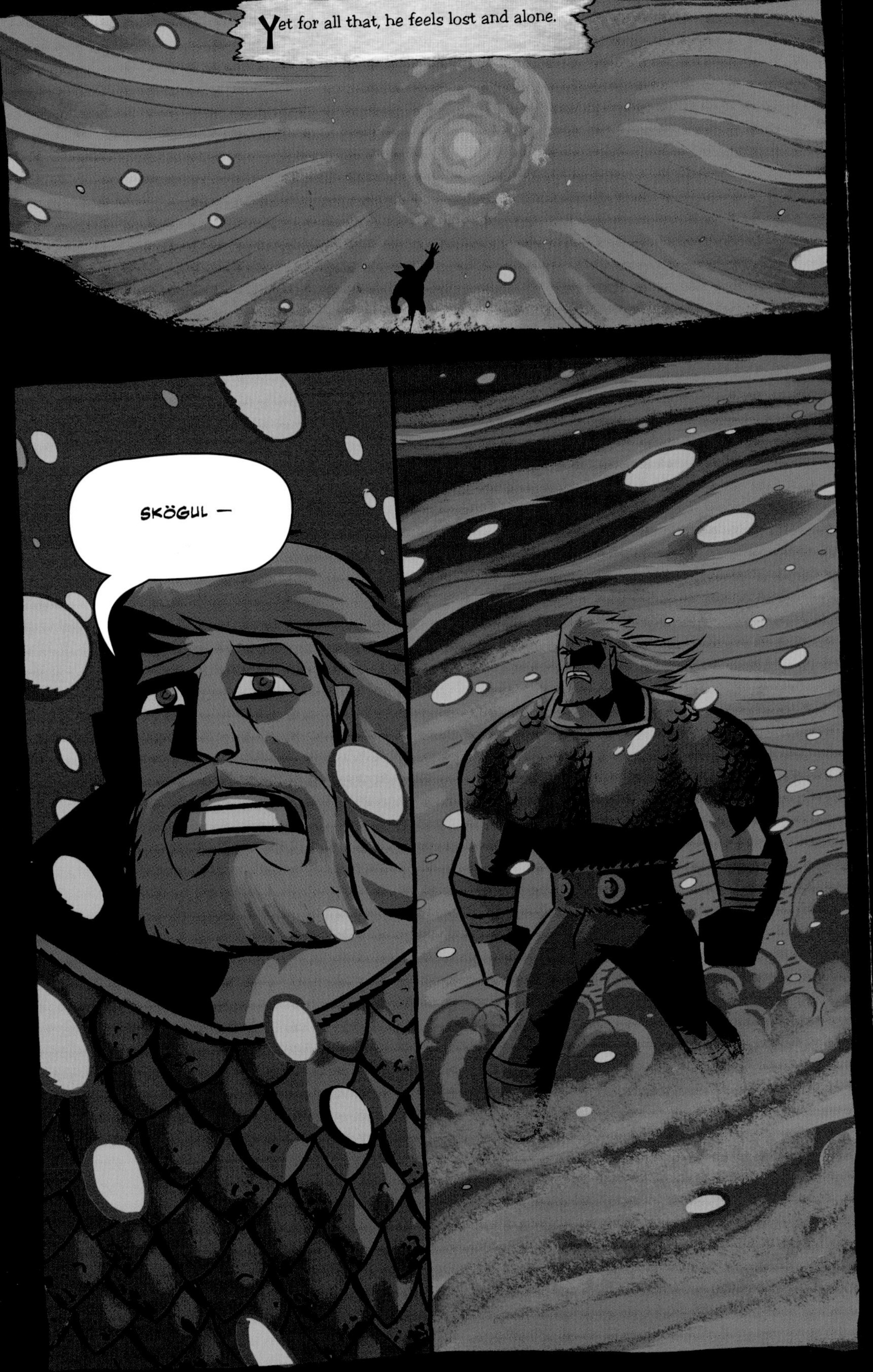
Yet for all that, he feels lost and alone.
SKÖGUL —

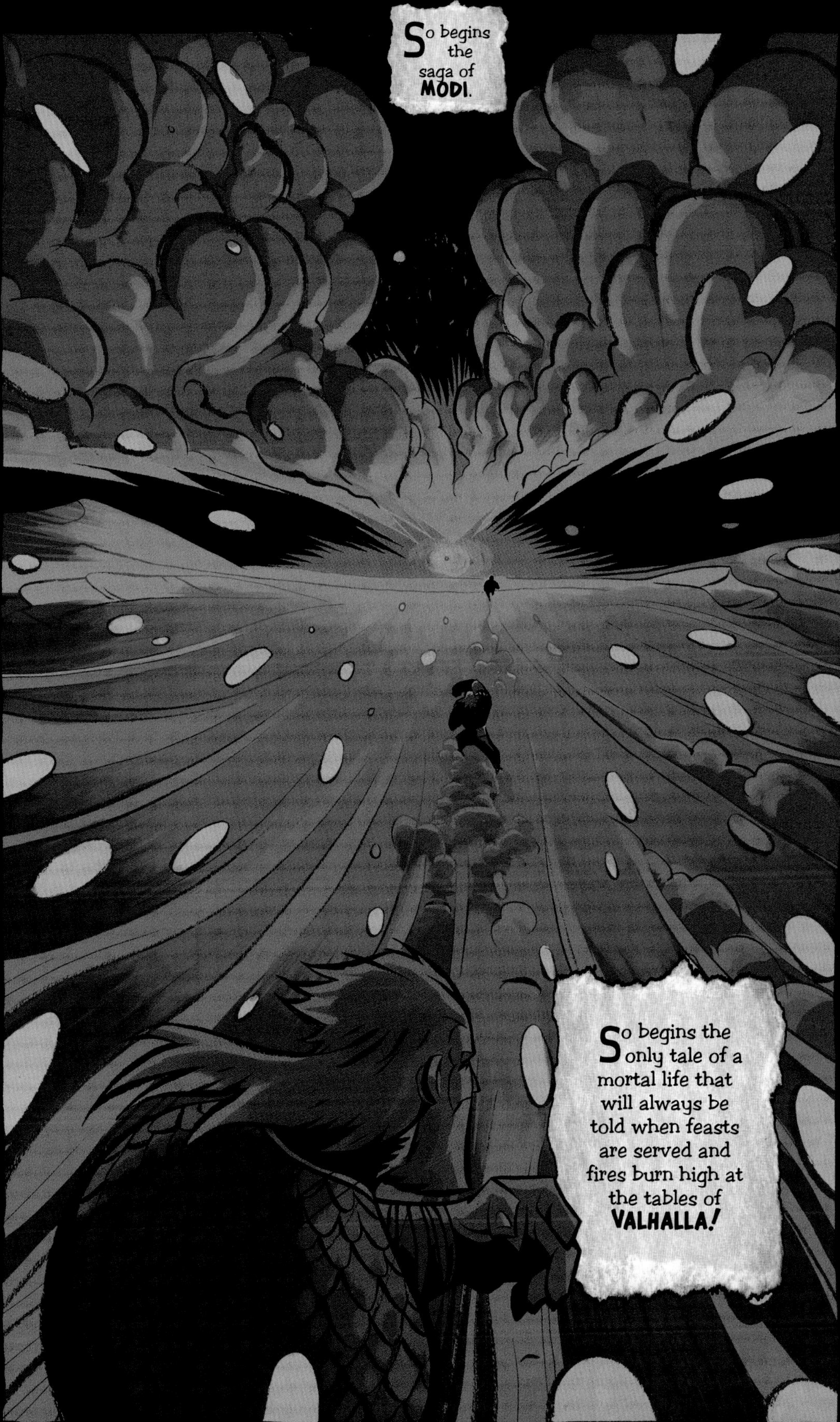
So begins the saga of MODI.
So begins the only tale of a mortal life that will always be told when feasts are served and fires burn high at the tables of VALHALLA!

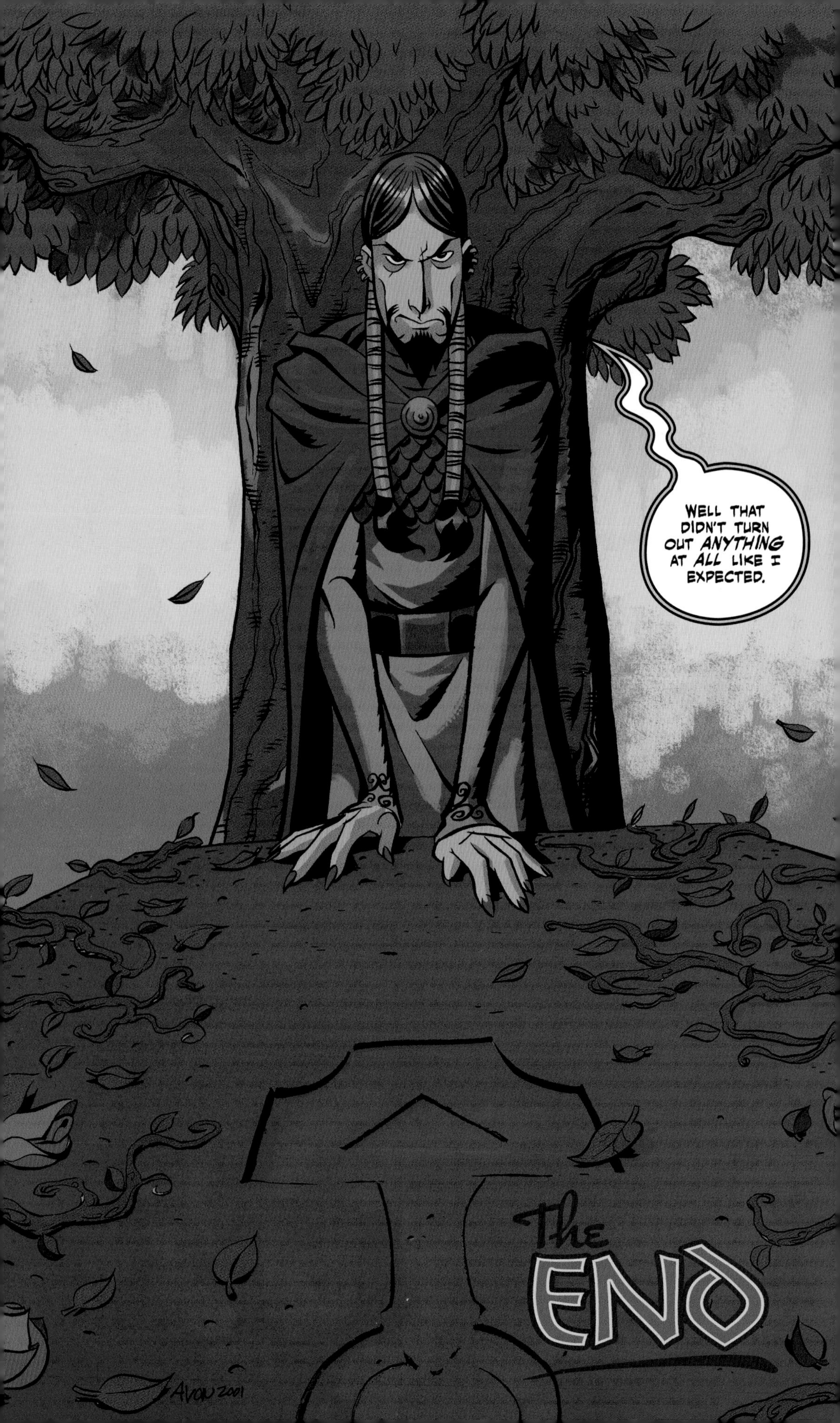
WELL THAT DIDN'T TURN OUT ANYTHING AT ALL LIKE I EXPECTED.
The END
AVON 2001

WORDS SPOKEN in A CAVE

*O*utside the cave, in a world forgotten by the gods, dark snow was stirred by a cold wind. Inside the cave the sounds of men building death echoed. Metal clanged against metal. Grunts and sighs sounded as shouts. It was sword against sword. Two valiant warriors, each with many battles to their credit, pitted their strength and skill against the other. Avon and Obie were their names, names that had been mingled with the history of the gods. Finally these two men were pressed close, the edges of their heavy weapons each holding the other at bay. Avon laughed and said, "Had enough?"

*O*bie grinned and answered, "Yeah – I think the readers get the idea." Setting their blades aside Avon and Obie broke out the mead, leaned against the cold stone in front of a roaring fire and began to talk about the battles of making comic books.

OBIE: You put up a good fight, Mike. It must have been tough for you to give up doing comics in the late 1990s and start a regular job as a night watchman. But I remember you said at the time that you were finally getting paid a good

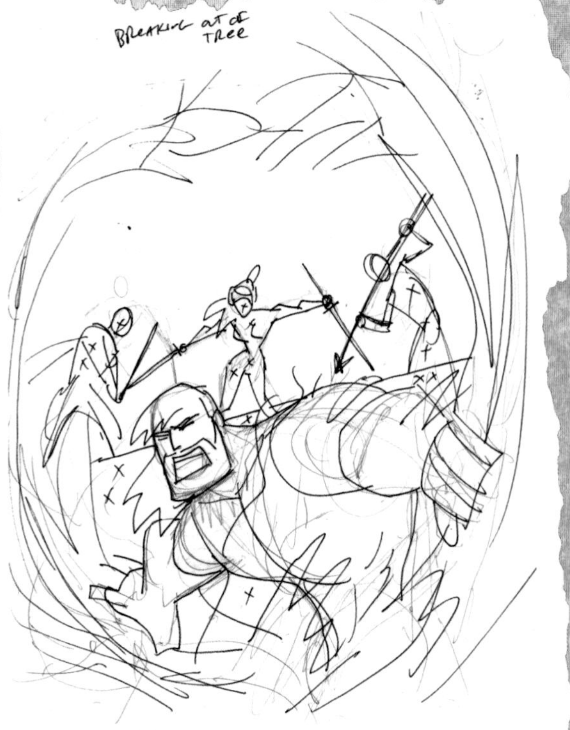
BREAKING OUT OF TREE

Rough layout for the cover to the second issue, by Avon.

wage to sit around and draw. What were you thinking about your comic business career when you started that job?

Avon: Mark, I was thinking that it was over! I honestly believed that all I would do from then on would be to keep the "real job" and then do some indie comics from time to time on the side. The plan was that I'd work in the car lot as a security guy, maybe get enough experience to get a better paying security job with benefits someday. During any spare time, I'd do mini series after mini series like **Hammer**, and enjoy a limited comics life, not counting on it to support me anymore.

Obie: Yeah. The late '90s sucked for the comic industry. A lot of guys were in the same boat you were. But not many of them had your guts to walk away from it.

Avon: Well, it was a very important time in my life. It was the first time *ever* that I had a real job. I left high school and went straight into doing comics. There were a few years of being unpublished at first, then I slowly broke into the field. But comics was all I knew. Getting the "real" job taught me that I didn't need to be working for Marvel or DC to be a "real artist," that no matter what I was doing for income, or how I was being published, I could always work for myself in the indie market and be happy. Once I let go of working for a career in comics, that's when I finally got one. Very Zen, and often the way things go in life.

Obie: Oh, I agree. I read a book on Zen years and years ago and the only thing that I embraced was that concept of letting it go. Insight Studios and I experienced much the same thing at about the same time – 1997 when I said, "screw it" and just started doing the books I wanted to do. We've been selling better ever since. We've been connecting with the readers by doing comics that really mattered to us. Not only Zen at work, but a strong commitment to creating comics as a complete artistic experience. And by artistic I don't mean being constantly over the edge and personal. You and I both like to communicate with an audience. But we're not following the trends. We're following our own interests. Still, you raise a few new subjects. Now you quit high school before you graduated. And yet you are constantly reading up on mythology and your craft of storytelling and I'll guess a lot more subjects that we just haven't talked about – yet. So obviously you don't find study to be a problem. Why did you drop out and how was that *not* a case of "letting it go"? Or was it?

The cover from issue two, drawn by Avon and colored by Obie.

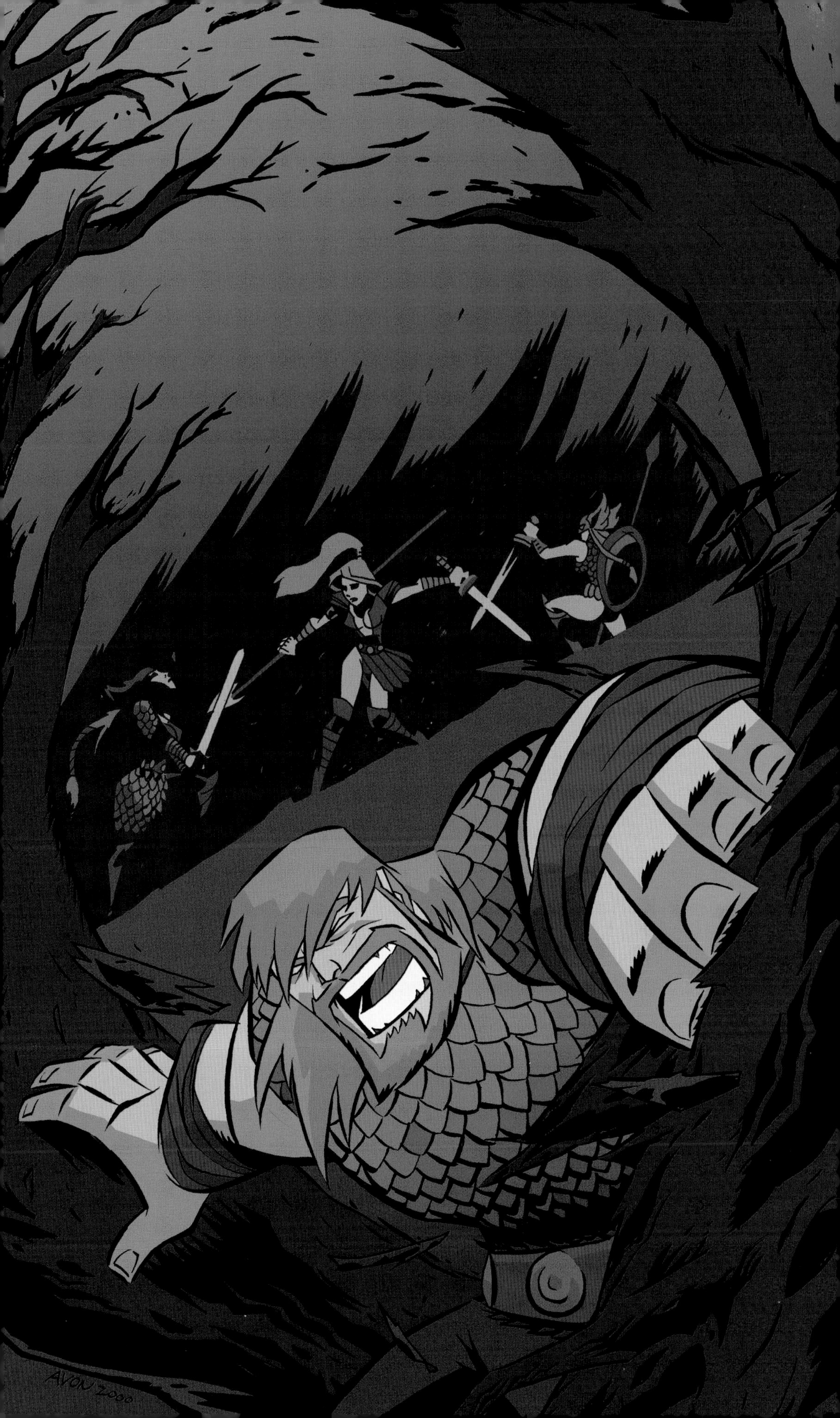
AVON 2000

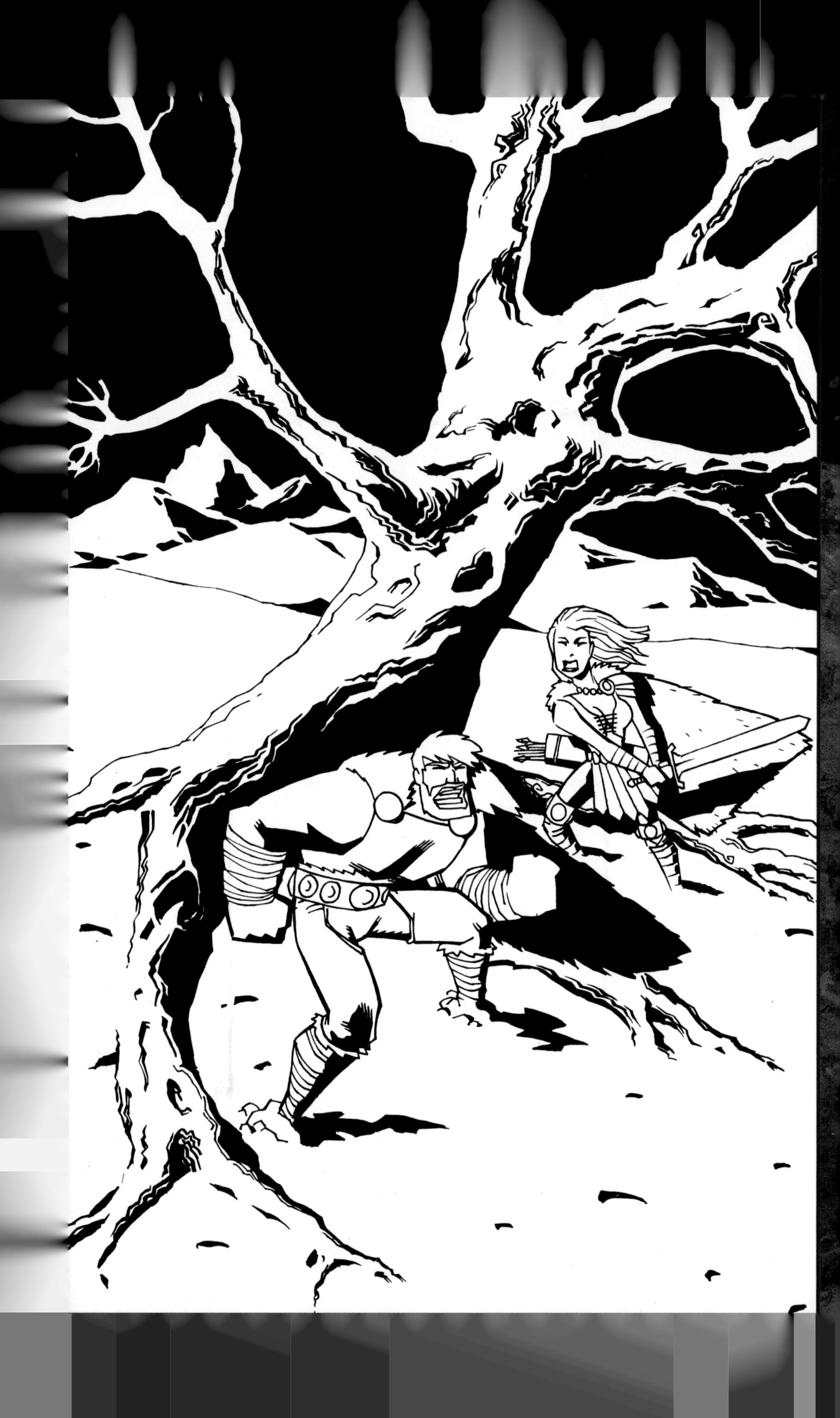

The original sketch by Avon, right out of his sketch book. The finished drawing appears to the left.

AVON: I'm not sure what the case was there. Mostly I was just young and impatient. I had skipped school so many times to stay home and draw that the school wanted me to repeat my junior year. I was passing my classes, but they thought because I had skipped so many days they wanted to hold me back. That made me really angry, I was passing my classes. So instead I just left and never looked back. It came back to bite me in the ass ten years later when I was looking for that "real" job. But I had no diploma. I just lied and said I did, no one ever checked, but it kept me from applying for better jobs.

OBIE: But maybe you ended up with the perfect job after all, because it gave you time to draw. How long did it take before you started working on HAMMER OF THE GODS during your night watch?

AVON: I started before I got the job. Some of the art in the first issue of

HAMMER OF THE GODS goes back to '98 or maybe even '97! I just worked on it whenever I had time, very slowly...

OBIE: What was it that first started you thinking about the Norse myths?

AVON: Early on, it was an episode of BEWITCHED where someone was reading a play about Thor.

OBIE: You mean I've got to start working a nosey neighbor into the saga?

AVON: Maybe, if it's a good idea! But I said, "Wow, there's a comic about Thor too." I went to the library and got some books on mythology and started reading. One of my earliest batches of pages was me drawing Odin and Loki being attacked by a bird. Then later, I got into LED ZEPPELIN and *POW!* It opened up that door and images came flooding in. HAMMER owes a lot to Zeppelin.

OBIE: So you're getting images from the music? I think that's a fairly common experience. I also think there is some kind of analog between music and comics. Lots of comic creators are musicians. Hell, I've got my own recording studio. Something about the way each discipline sets up the brain-paths that is the same. What do you think? Or have I been drinking too much mead?

AVON: I think that's true. Storytelling is storytelling wether it's on paper or music, it has beats, movements, acts. I think a lot of artists, like me, are frustrated musicians and vice versa.

OBIE: I don't know how frustrated – you've got a nice theme song for BASTARD SAMURAI on your website that you composed. Between us we should start planning that musical version of HAMMER! Maybe we could get Robert Plant to play Odin?

AVON: Let's do it!

OBIE: Careful now. This is how we got

started doing Moduck! How long were you cranking out HAMMER OF THE GODS material before you contacted me?

AVON: I think I was working on the concept for over a year. My outline that I sent you was pretty new. I did a four-page story that we cut up and used in the online strips, the stuff that became the lead story in COLOR SAGA, that was the first thing I showed you along with the outline. I was looking for help with the script.

Westfield comics is a very well run mail order source for all things comics. They publish a nice catalog every month. This was planned as their special holiday cover for December of 2000. But this version never saw print due to being in the wrong format! So you see it here for the first time, even if you have to lay on your side to get a good look at it. Drawn by Avon. Color and snow by Obie.

OBIE: Yeah and I remember when the pages started arriving for what eventually got broken up into the first three issues of MORTAL ENEMY. You had some amazing scenes and a fantastic concept. Yet you were very gracious about accepting my direction and changes and additions. I've had a lot of experience with collaborations, some very good experiences, but working with you has got to be the easiest and most fun of all of them. You seem to have left your ego at the door – or maybe you just have so much fun telling stories that you aren't concerned with forcing control on a project. What do you think?

AVON: A good idea is a good idea, and if you suggest something that's better than what I have, I want the better idea. I also know that just because I'm an artist who can tell a story, doesn't mean that I'm a writer.

OBIE: I think of myself as a storyteller. That covers all the different ways there are to get a story told. And you are a master of telling a story. You understand the important basics of character and scene structure. Words are just one part of the mix.

AVON: I've been working on the words over the past few years and I feel more confident as a writer, but when we started out, I knew I needed someone to guide the story beyond my capabilities.

OBIE: That's not all you've been working on. I see a sharp change in your drawing style and in your approach to telling a story between your "first comics career" and your current rise to fame. Since HAMMER OF THE GODS pre-dates your POWERS work, it would be good if you could talk a bit about how your transformation took place. Obviously Alex Toth and Bruce Timm had something to do with it.

AVON: A year, maybe two, before I started on POWERS with Brian, I started playing with HAMMER OF THE GODS and that simple style. When I got my security job, I knew my time would be limited. I realized if I wanted to do any comics, I'd have to simplify my drawing style. I started that some in BULLETPROOF MONK but that style was more "realistic." A year earlier, I started playing with the animated style, and got really strong positive reactions to it, and the style was really fast. So I decided I had to go that route, or else I'd never produce any work, because it would take so long. The simple, Toth/Timm style was very economical and fast, but still tricky and difficult to figure out at first. Once I had it, it flowed nicely and after a while, I wasn't imitating Timm but found my own style in that arena.

OBIE: So it was just an economy of time? I think it also changes the way an artist can tell a story. I think that simple style opens things wide to larger audience and to treatment of more subjects and genre. The eye can "read" a simple drawing with

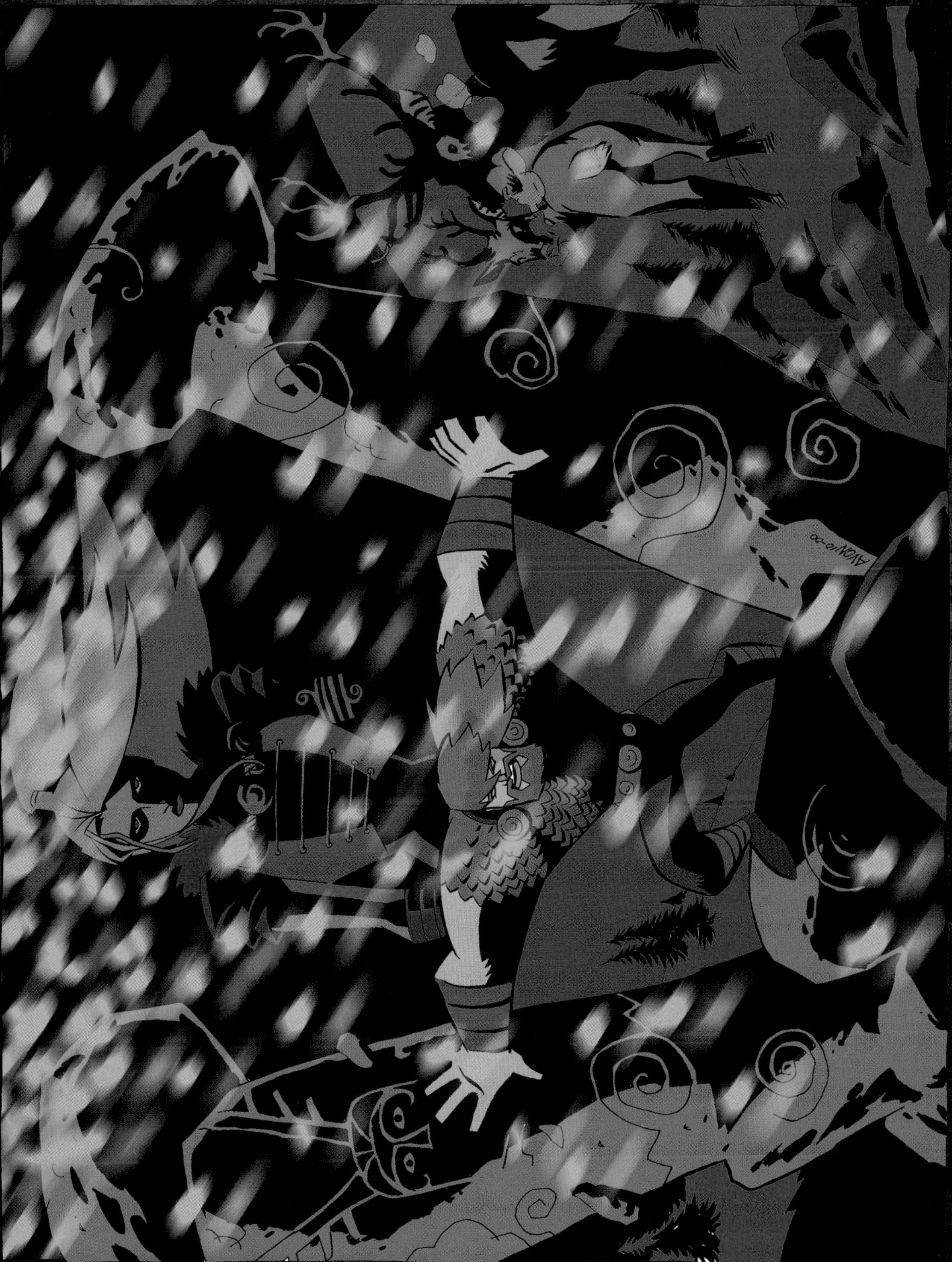

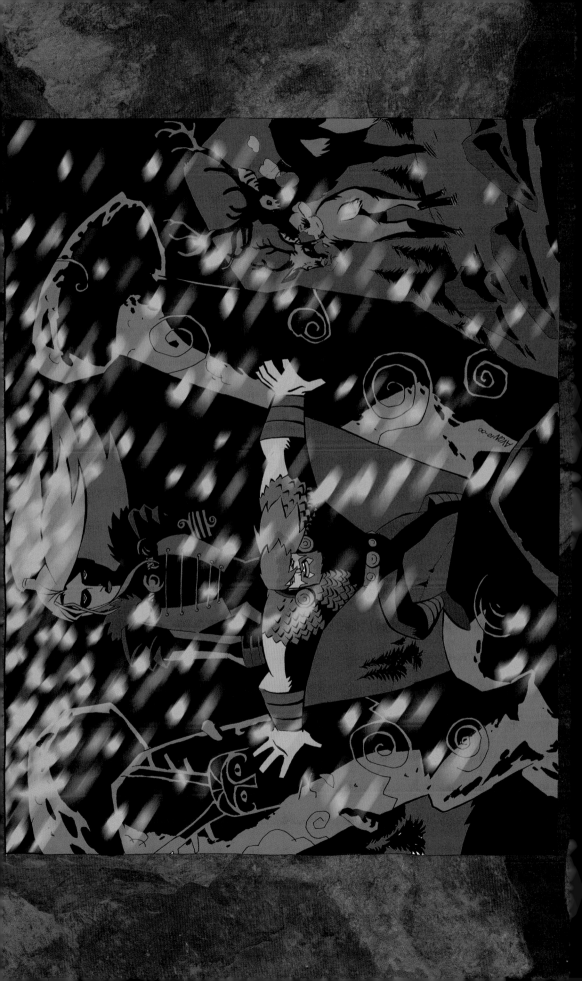

so much more ease. And the emotions portrayed become much more clear.

AVON: I agree. I think the simplicity brings out the intent much more. Things are so much more clear because there is less to get in the way.

OBIE: Well, let's talk about how you go about it. When you draw do you like to do a detailed drawing before you go to inks?

AVON: Not at all. In fact, there's not much on the page, usually. I do loose breakdowns and put them on a lightbox. I hardly use a pencil at that point, maybe just for faces and hands. Inks are where the page comes alive for me.

OBIE: And I think that is one of your "secrets" – you draw with the ink rather than trace. How is this different when you ink other artists?

AVON: When I ink another artist or someone inks me, I like to see the inker bring something to the art. I want to see them express the depth and form, not just copy the lines. Guys like Adam Hughes need really really tight inkers who can stay true to their lines, you have to be faithful to someone like that. But I prefer having a mix of artists when I'm inking or being inked. That said, I rarely ever have anyone ink me.

OBIE: I know many artists who use a process that involves sketching on the front of the paper, then re-sketching on the back of the paper, then going to rough ink or finished pencil or ink back on the front again. You sent me some examples of you working this way. I've worked that way myself. It has the advantage of redrawing the reversed image and there-by fixing any symmetry problems with the drawing. What led you to this approach?

AVON: Those layouts are old. I haven't done that in awhile. I go through phases when I work, working on different paper, different sizes, sometimes I draw on tracing paper, photocopy paper, sometimes I reverse the page.

OBIE: I know. You gave John a real workout scanning the pages, making everything fit the final format.

AVON: And he did a great job! But I do that to break up the everyday work pace so something different is going on and it keeps me fresh. Maybe I'll try it again now that you mentioned it. I never get bored with my work, but I like to feel "fresh," especially on an ongoing series like POWERS. POWERS is very thought intensive, very purposeful, but HAMMER isn't. HAMMER flows much more easily – like daydreaming on paper. I never know what's going to happen when I start. I like that.

B- REDO OF FRANKS WOMAN WITH SKYTHE
MOON
MOON
ROCKS

Inspired by a Frank Frazetta painting, this is the original sketch for the cover to issue number four, by Avon. The finished cover is on the facing page, colored by Obie.

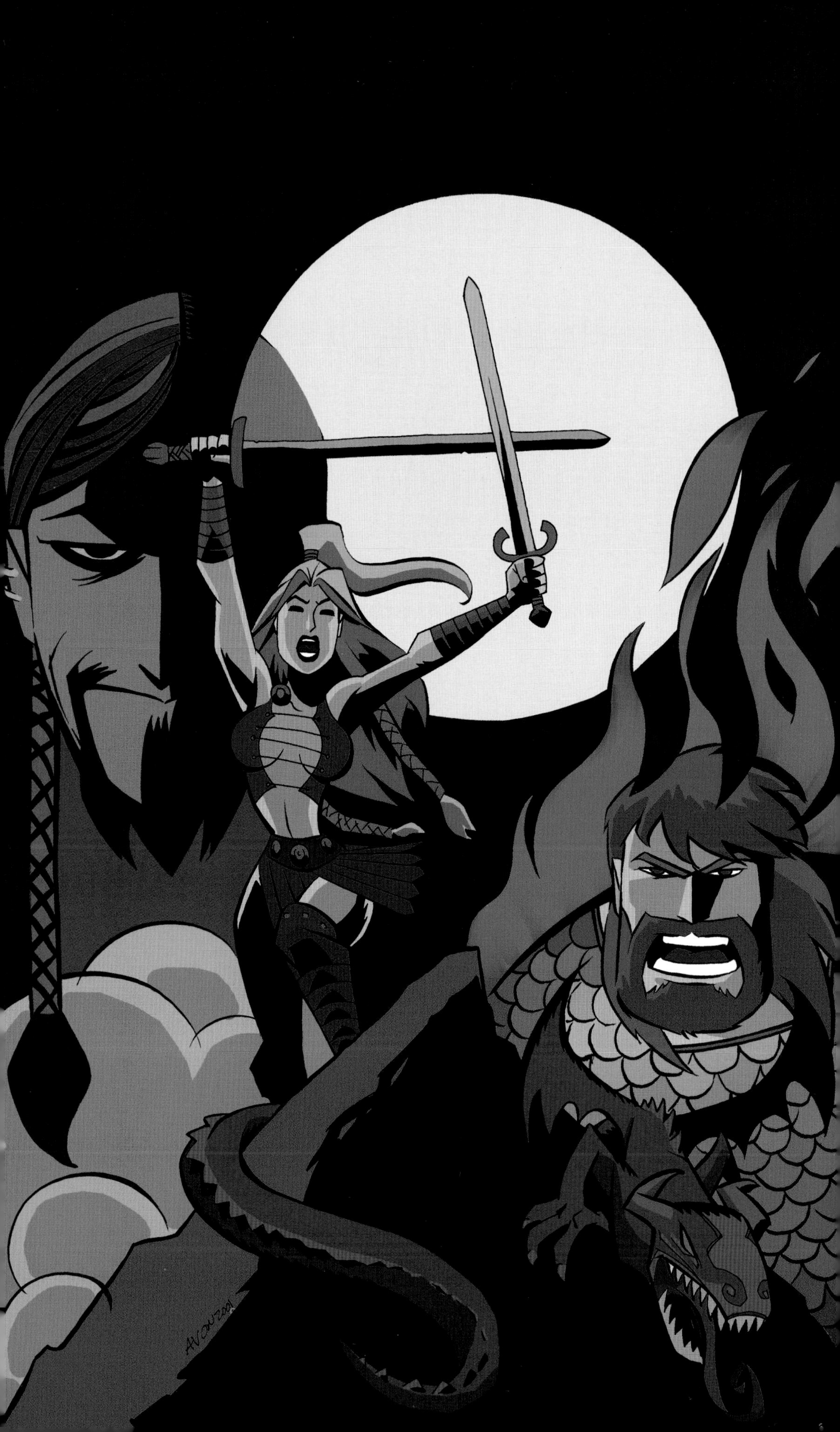

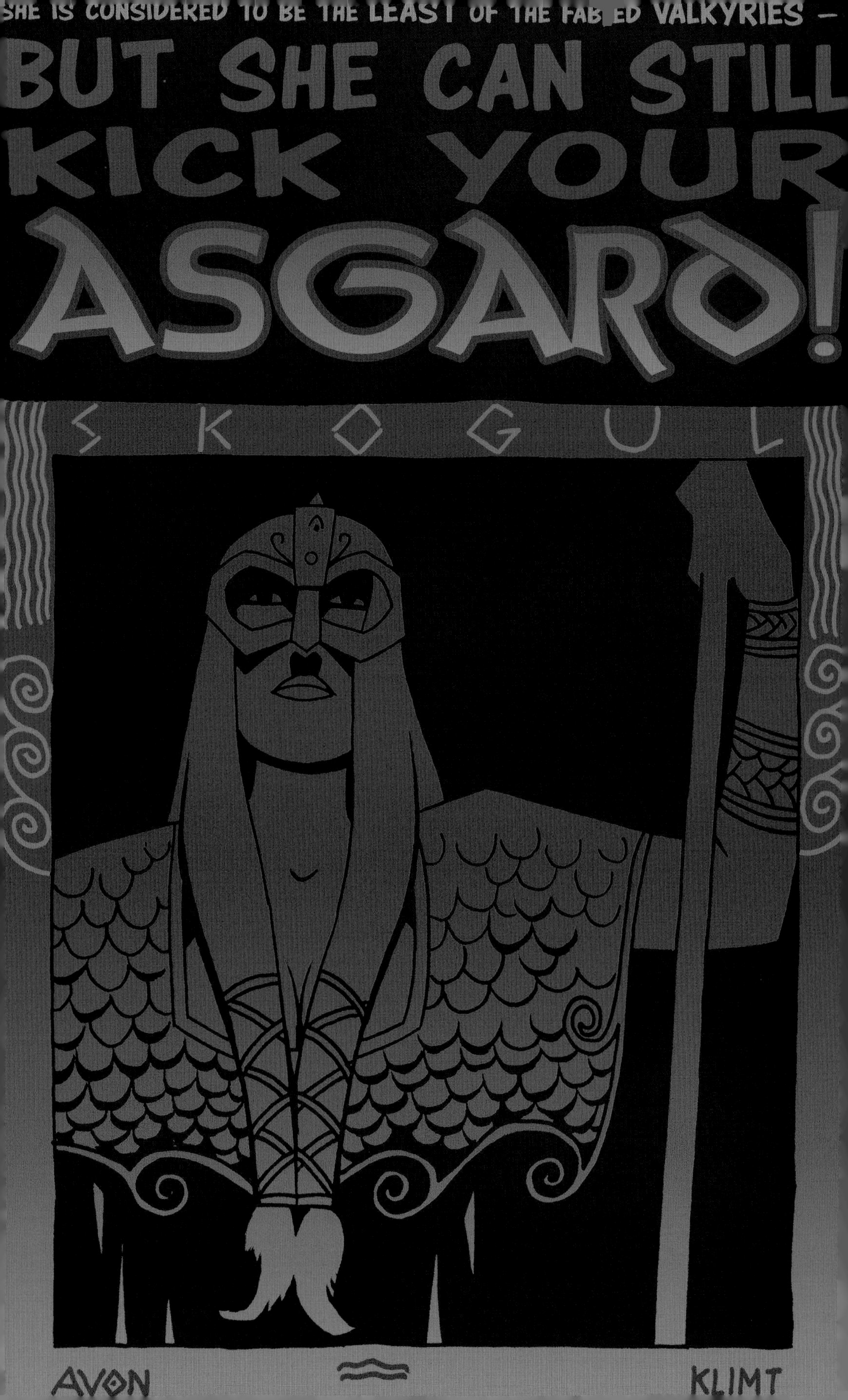
SHE IS CONSIDERED TO BE THE LEAST OF THE FABLED VALKYRIES –
BUT SHE CAN STILL KICK YOUR ASGARD!
SKOGUL
AVON
KLIMT

Back cover design from issue two and the birth of a catchphrase. This is the only known collaboration between Gustav Klimt (1862-1918) and Avon. Color by Obie.

Obie: And that might be one of the "secrets" of our collaboration since I've also written many stories that were expressions of my dreams. I've developed a knack for gently forcing a dream to make sense! Also your approach keeps the life

First draft penciled page from issue five, by Avon with an assist from Kelsey Shannon. Compare this to the finished page in chapter five of this collection.

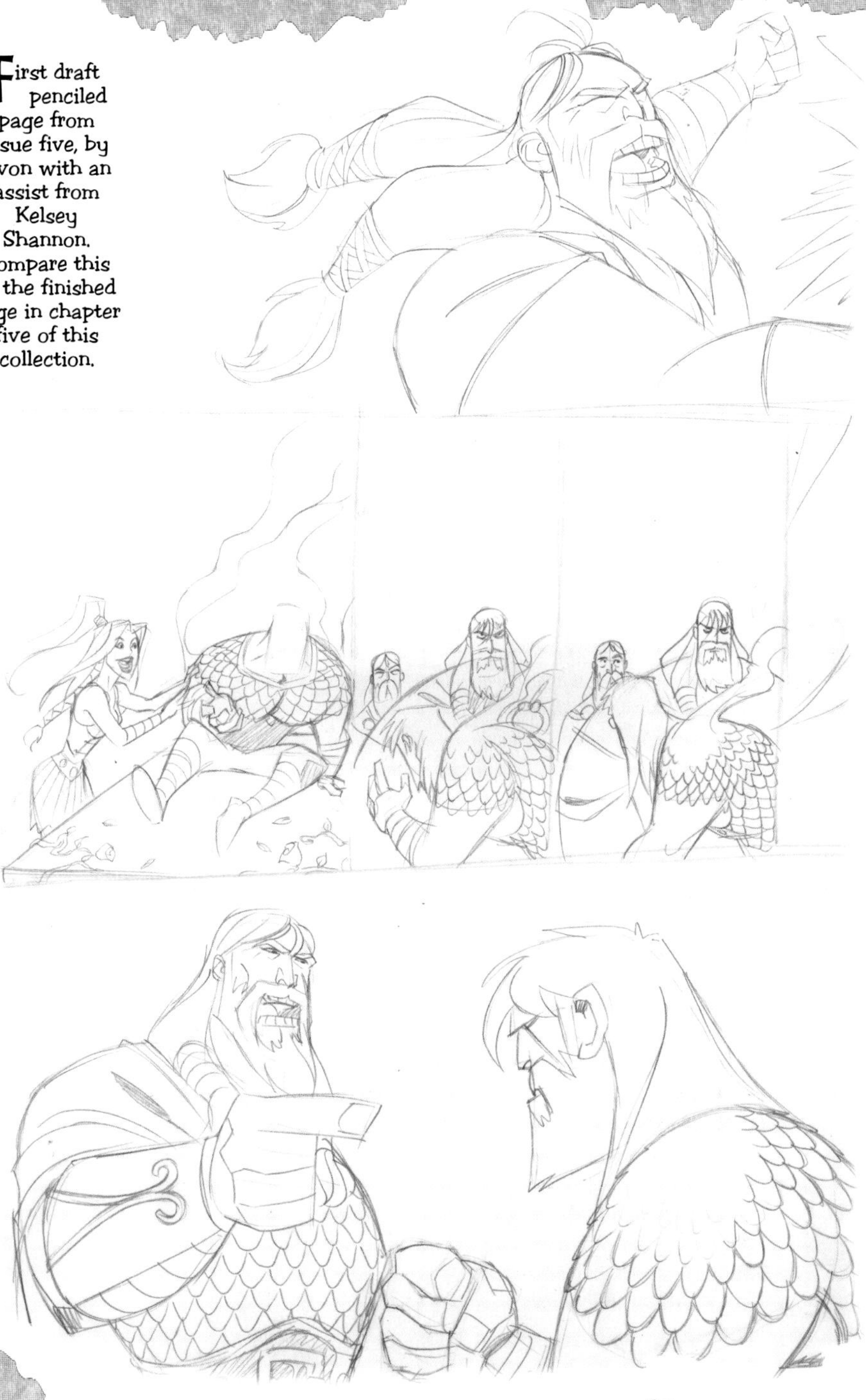

in the story, retaining a very strong sense of fun. For Norse myth, which can be so heavy and dark, I think the elements of fun and irreverence are some of my favorite parts for HAMMER. Are any aspects more attractive to you?

AVON: I'm going for mood. Snow, or dark twisted trees, the mountains and rocks. Mood and scenery.

OBIE: That's obvious. You've been doing an incredible job of creating a sense of wonder for HAMMER. Now, several of the art pages you sent for inclusion in this great big collected edition are on heavy art board and appear to be near-finished pages from issue five. Are these 100% Oeming or is there the hand of Kelsey Shannon in the mix?

The back cover from issue four, drawn by Avon and colored by Obie. Words by Led Zeppelin.

An untold saga of Modi! Perhaps some day more information about this strange encounter will be found in a forgotten manuscript! Sketch by Avon.

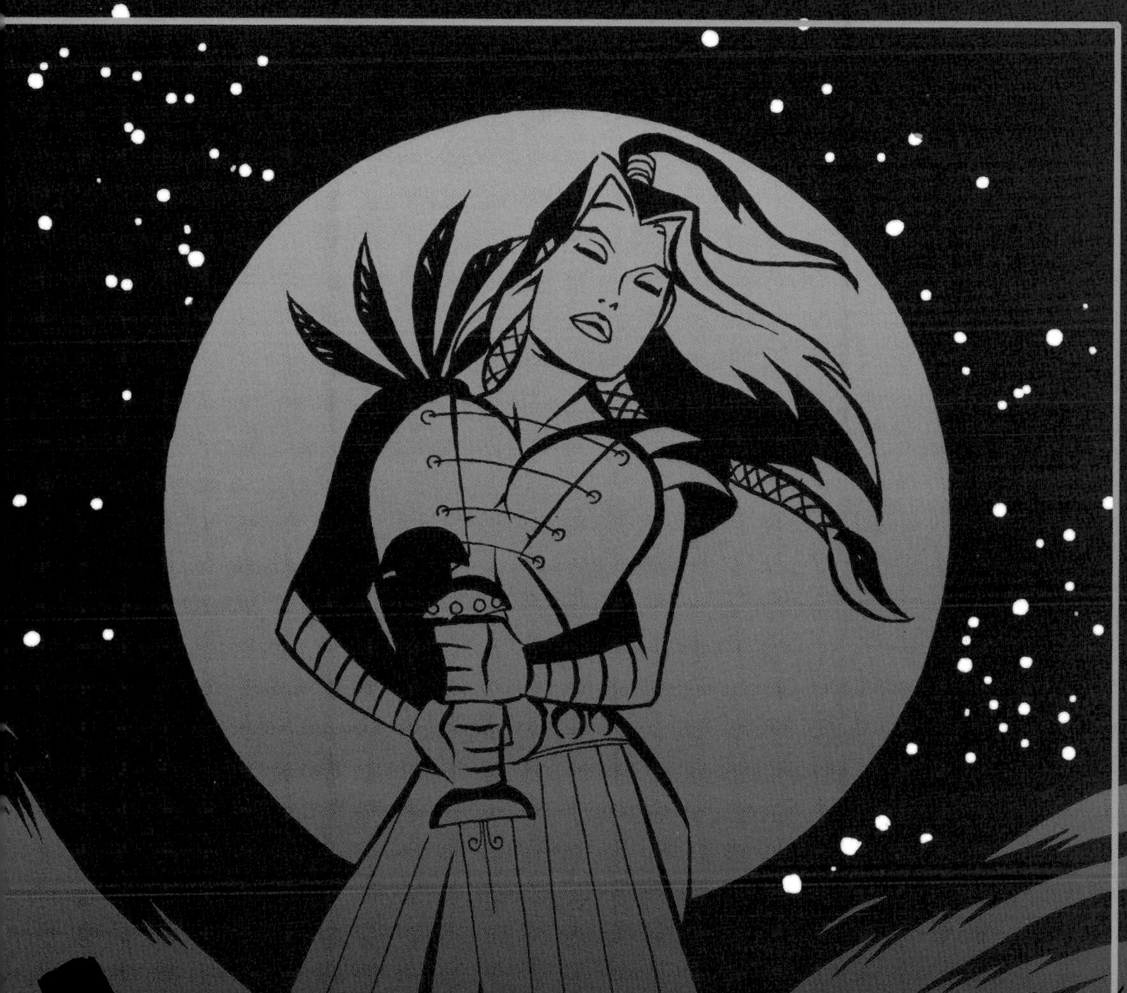

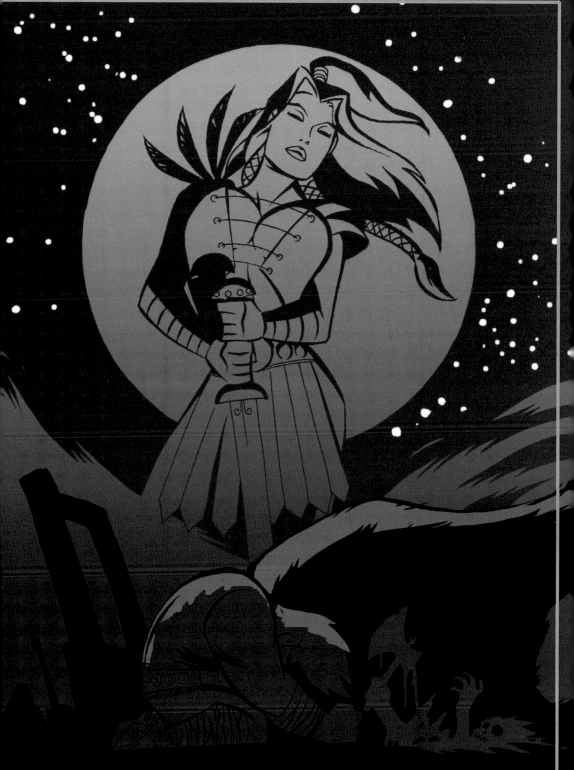

"THE WINDS OF THORR
ARE BLOWING COLD"
– LED ZEPPELIN –

AVON: Kesley helped with issue five as my schedules with POWERS, BLUNTMAN AND CHRONIC and HAMMER OF THE GODS collided last year. It was a horrible time. Kesley took my layouts, the kind you see here, and transferred those for me to art board, adding in details to clothing and background. Of course, his style crept in, and I let it. I love those elements. Kelsey is amazing and we'll be seeing more from him, including a Hammer back up at some point.

OBIE: I'm a big fan of Kelsey's work and I would love to work with him on a HAMMER story. So if I was going to put a caption under that page (and I *am* going to put a caption under that page) I should say that these are penciled by Kelsey over layouts by Oeming? Or –

AVON: I just say art assists because it could get confusing. He added a lot of detail to my layouts, including that animation pull and stretch I love so much.

Travel poster appeared as the back cover to issue three. Drawn by Avon. Designed and colored by Obie.

OBIE: Okay. This cave is getting cold now that the fire has died down. So one last question. From what you and I have talked about, the plans for stories, comic stories, epic tales, short stories, even novels – HAMMER OF THE GODS is looking like a saga that will carry us through the next decade. And yet you have been very clear from day one that there were three acts to Modi's story. At this point, we're still working on act one with our plans for HAMMER HITS CHINA scheduled for January. And we've written the first draft of the very long mini-saga, BIRTHRIGHT, that hasn't been scheduled yet. But BIRTHRIGHT begins the second act in the life and times of Modi, correct?

AVON: Technically, I guess it does. But I know it's going to be the start of a very long second act.

Dawn was breaking through the snow clouds when the two warriors came out of the cave. They shivered in their bearskins and then waded out into the deep white stuff. They had sagas to create.

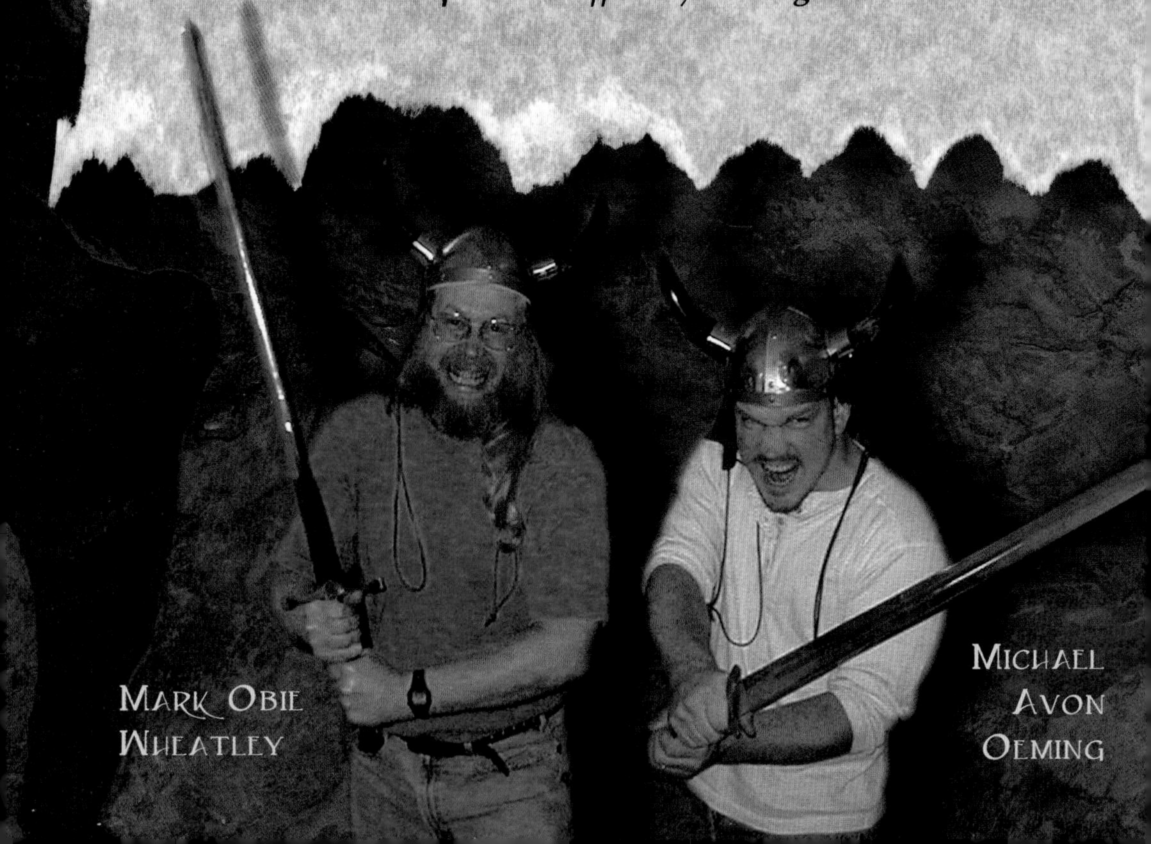

MARK OBIE WHEATLEY

MICHAEL AVON OEMING

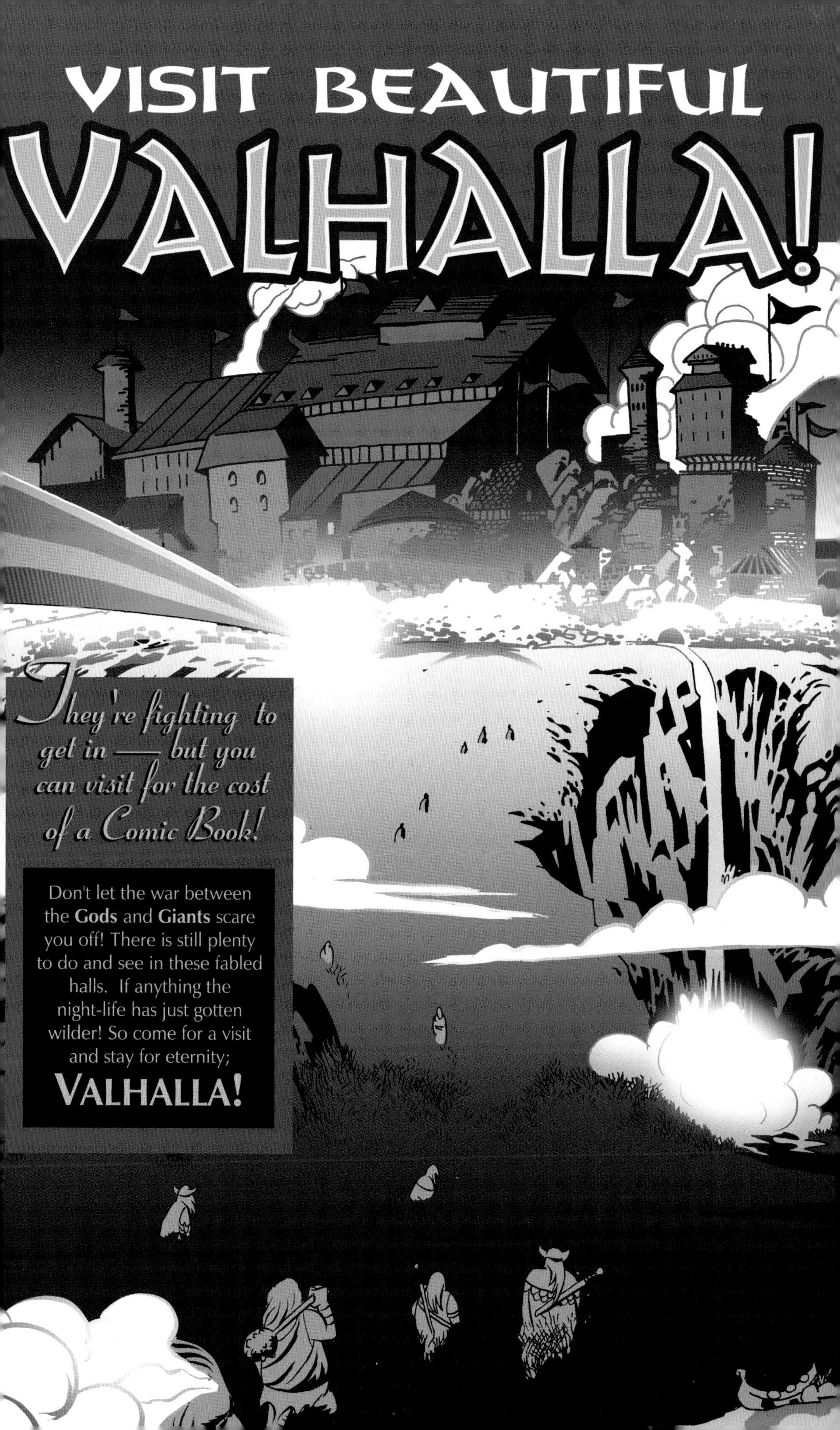
VISIT BEAUTIFUL
VALHALLA!
They're fighting to get in — but you can visit for the cost of a Comic Book!
Don't let the war between the **Gods** and **Giants** scare you off! There is still plenty to do and see in these fabled halls. If anything the night-life has just gotten wilder! So come for a visit and stay for eternity;
VALHALLA!

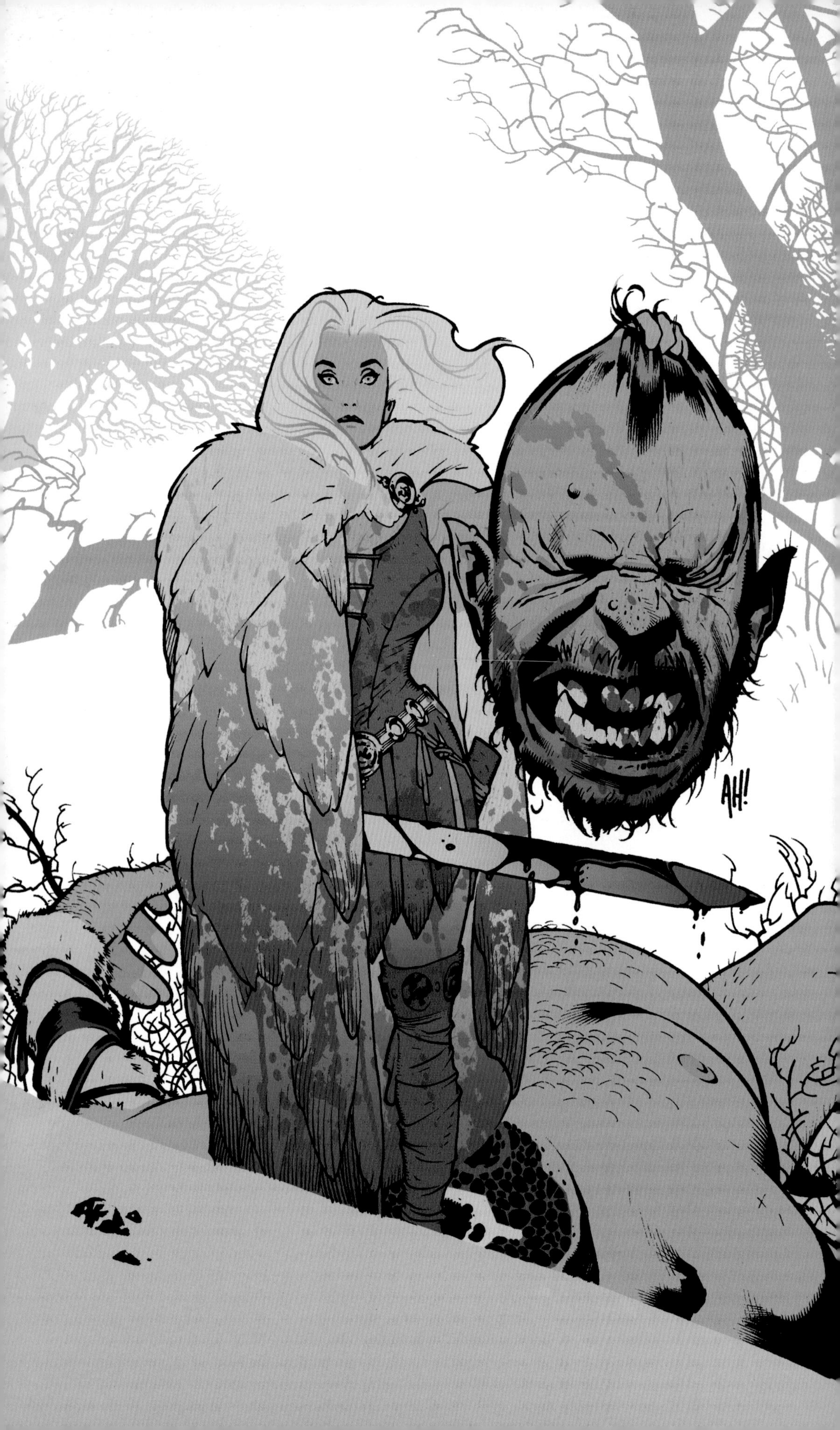
AH!

AFTER THE BATTLE

Where do I start?

If I were to start with my first impression, then this really wouldn't sound like the most flattering afterword ever written, but pay close attention, dear reader.

My first exposure to Avon Oeming's art was in the comic book POWERS. (Avon Oeming, an odd sounding name bordering on pretentious, I think that's why I like it.) I love Brian Bendis' writing, but I thought the art was very basic, cartoony, and a poor combination with such realistic writing.

On the facing page is the cover art for the third issue, drawn and colored by Adam Hughes. Adam posed for the giant's head.

Fast forward: Avon Oeming asked me to write a foreword to HAMMER OF THE GODS: MORTAL ENEMY. I got very excited even considering the job doesn't pay. I started to read the first issue, and I find it to be trite, formulaic and uh, well, you get the point.

Rewind: In high school, I could not stand the taste of beer. Hated it, hated it, hated it. However, if one wanted to get good and properly sauced, certain inconveniences could not be avoided. I tell you all this because I eventually became a rip roaring alcoholic, one of the great drunks of the late '80s and '90s. I loved beer so much I drank it from the moment I got up to the moment I went to bed. It was a love affair that was

AFTERWORD TO A SAGA BY
RAVEN

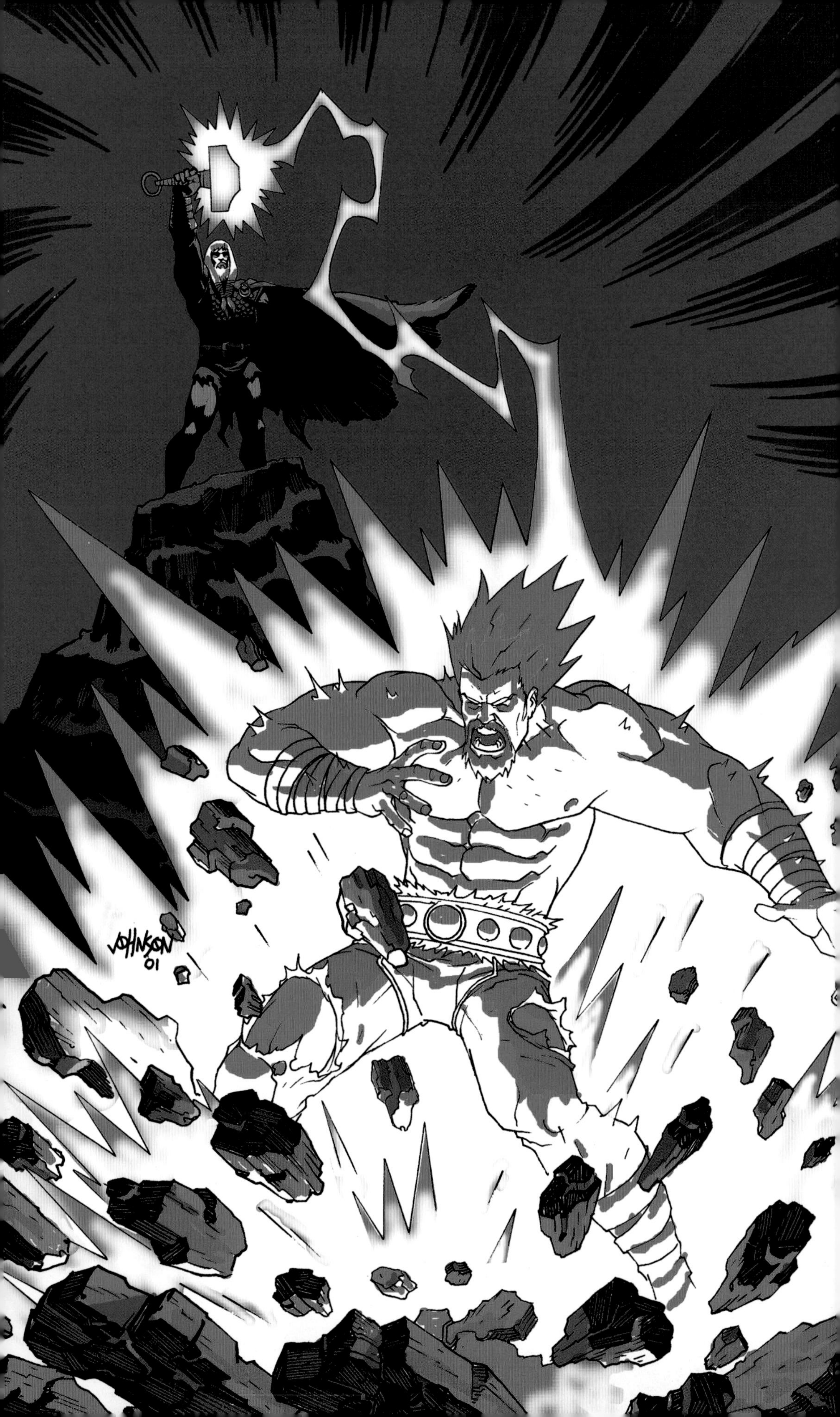
JOHNSON
'01

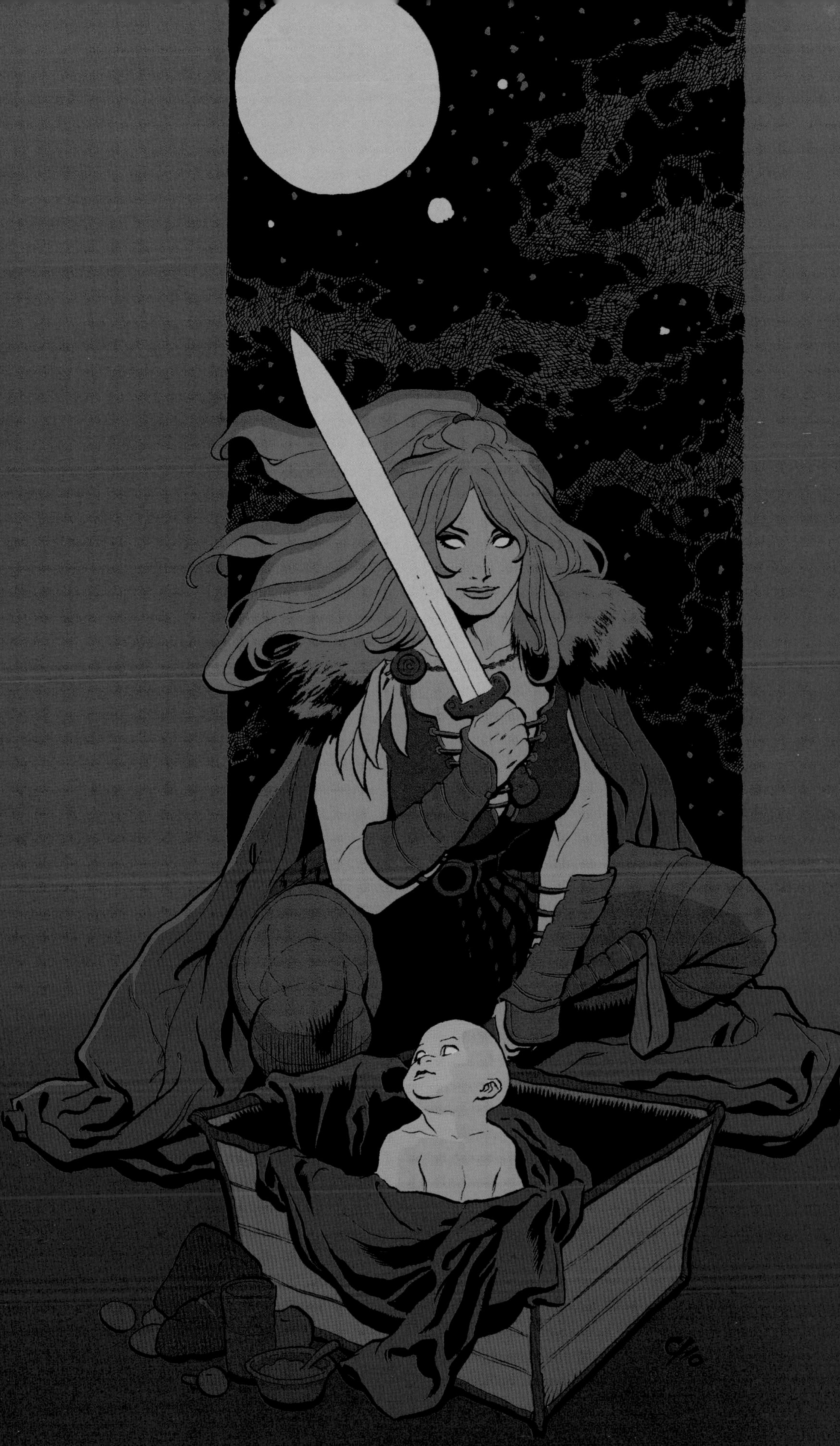

Art on the previous two pages is by two friends of Avon and Obie. The first is by Dave Johnson, done for the fifth issue. Second is the cover art from issue one by Frank Cho. Both covers were colored by Obie.

of course doomed from the start. Eventually a bout of pancreatitis and common sense sobered me up. I've been happily on the wagon for two years.

Thankfully I still have my comic book addiction.

If you haven't picked up on where I'm going with this yet, I will tell you in no uncertain terms that the more I read Powers, the more I realized that Bendis' vision could not have worked without Avon Oeming as the artist. It would not have been the same book and I'm proud to say that I'm currently having framed some Avon Oeming (I love that name) original art from Powers. For someone who's art is very cartoony, the more you look at it the more you realize that cartoony *is* the magic.

Avon Oeming's art conveys so much emotion, so much drama. He is able to do so much more by, oddly enough, doing so much less. If working in this simple style was easy or a secret formula anyone could use, my stick figures would be hanging in the Louvre.

On to Hammer of the Gods. (I know there's no verb in the previous sentence, but its my afterword not yours.) As I read the first issue, I worried about how to write a foreword if I didn't think much of the book. Well, I should know better than to underestimate Avon Oeming. The story goes nowhere I expected it to, is anything but trite or formulaic, in fact it's absolutely breathtaking.

Where Mortal Enemy goes and why it is so good can only be summed up by another analogy, something I once read about murder mysteries. It said the killer should be the last person you expect, but when you find out, it's the most obvious choice. This book does that without a murder mystery. If you've read the book you'll understand the analogy. If not, don't blame me, my brain is still a little bit addled, I've only been sober for two years. But I'm sure of one thing. The art and writing for Hammer of the Gods is epic in scope and beauty. Enjoy.

—Raven—

WWE superstar
reigning over 20 championships

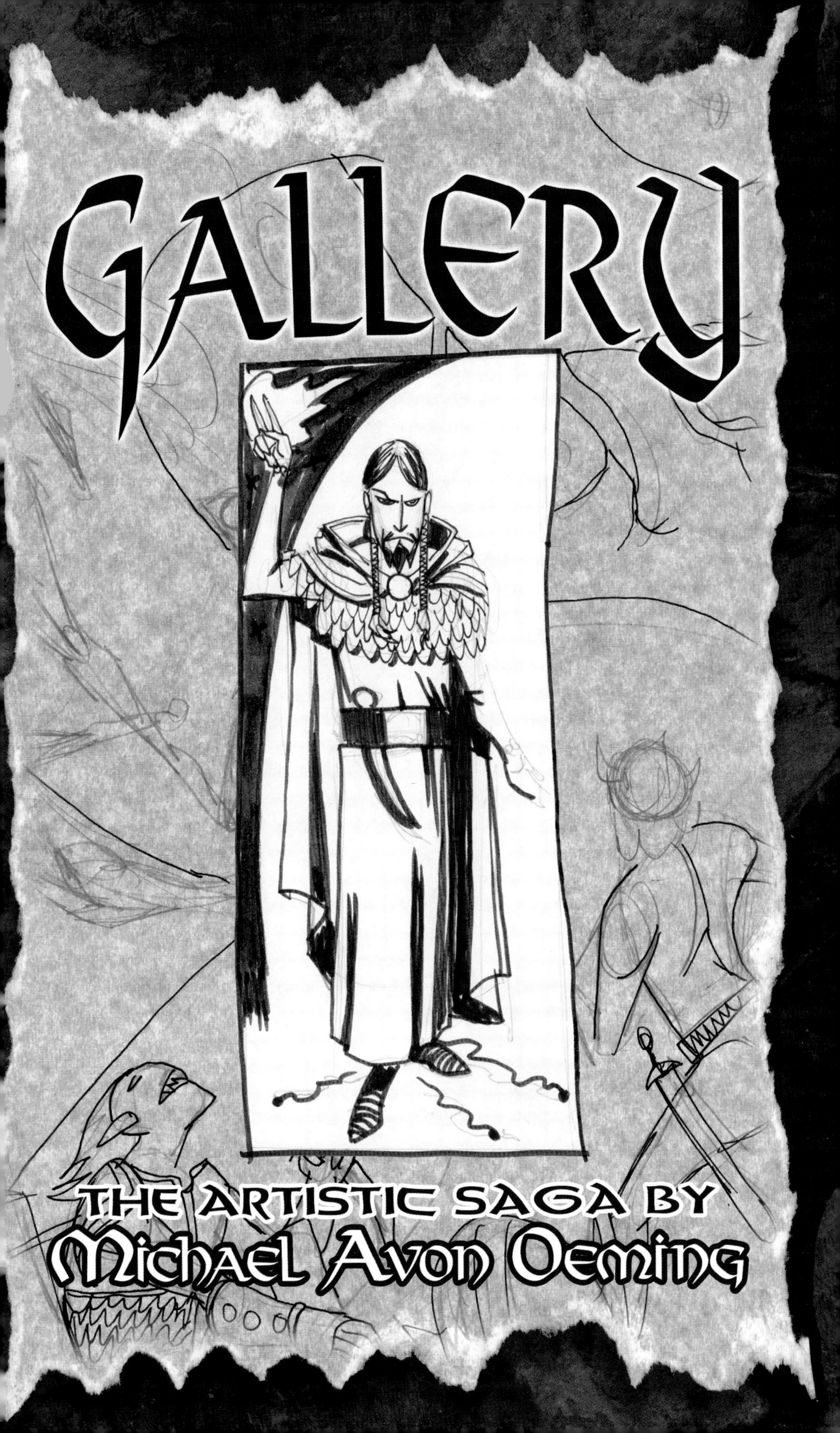
GALLERY
THE ARTISTIC SAGA BY
Michael Avon Oeming

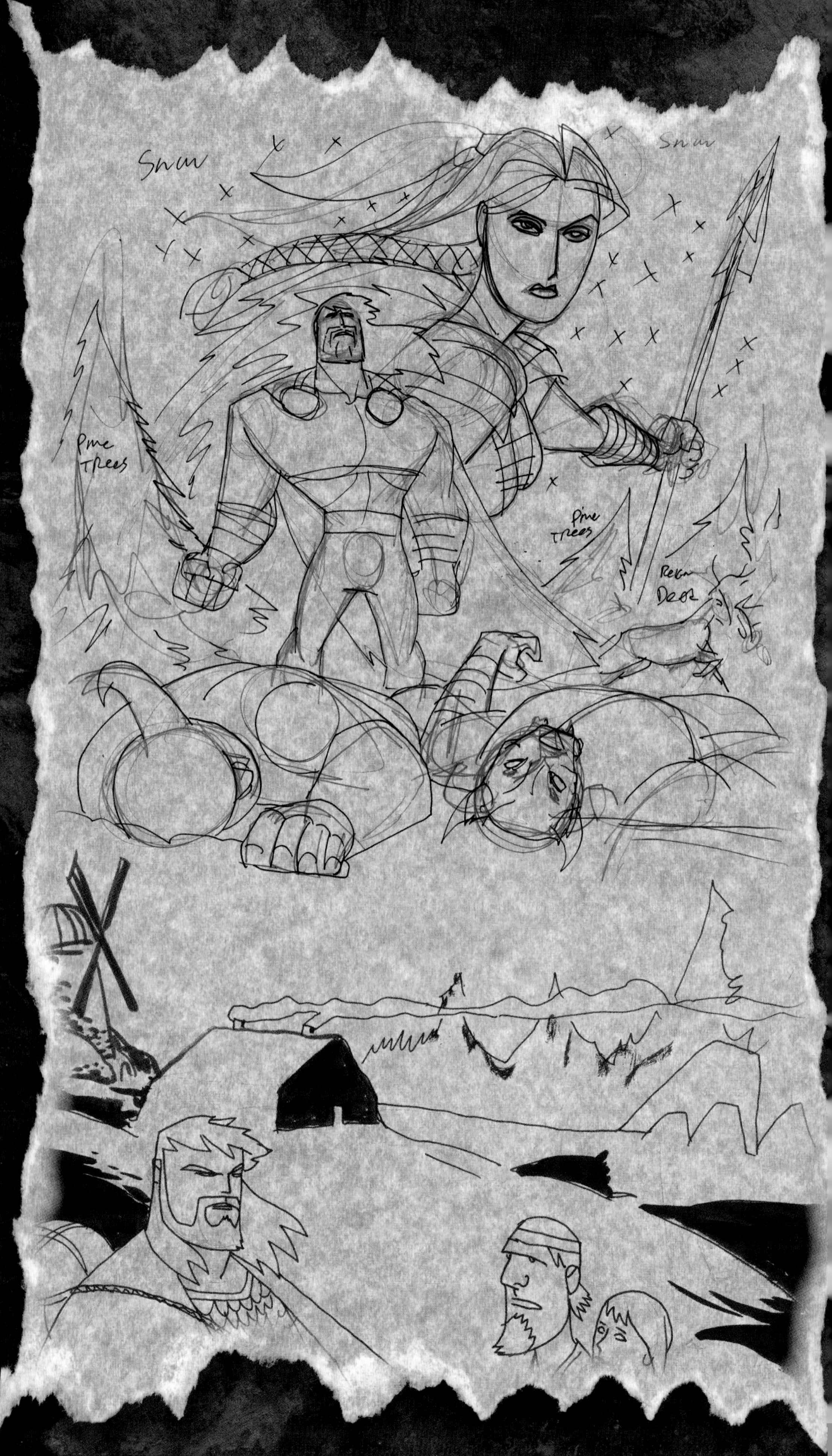
Snow
Snow
Pine Trees
Pine Trees
Reindeer

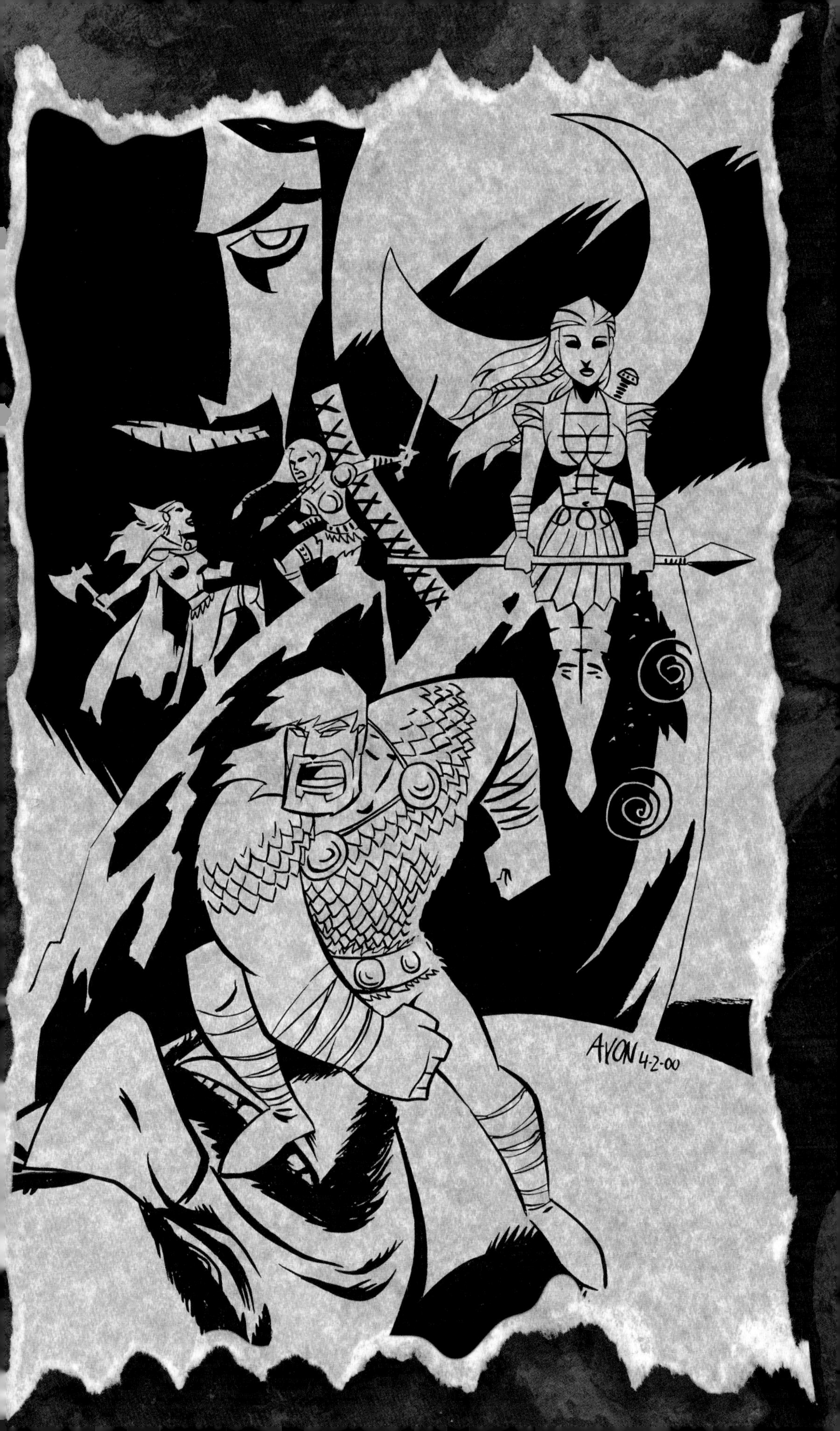
AVON 4-2-00

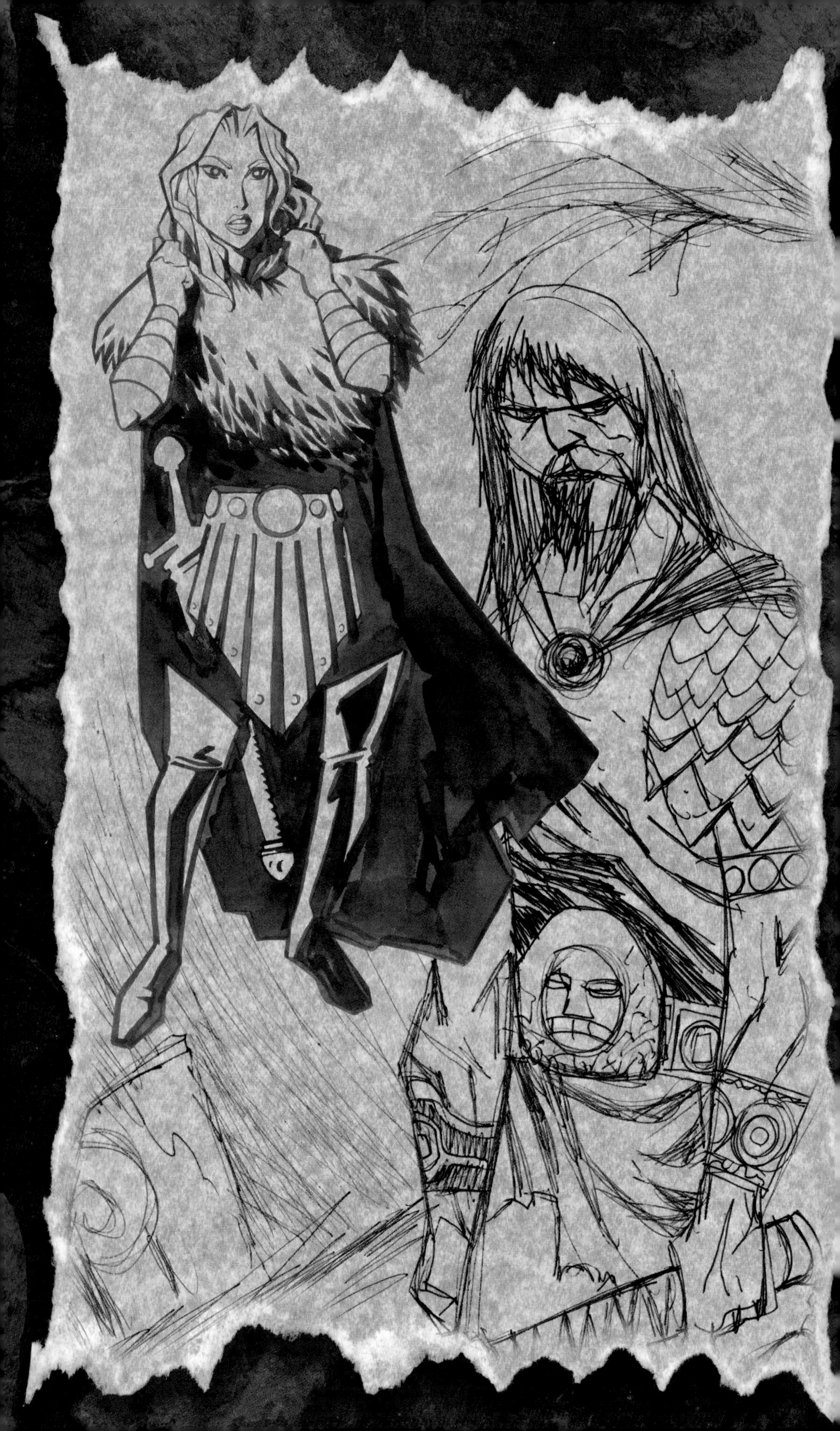

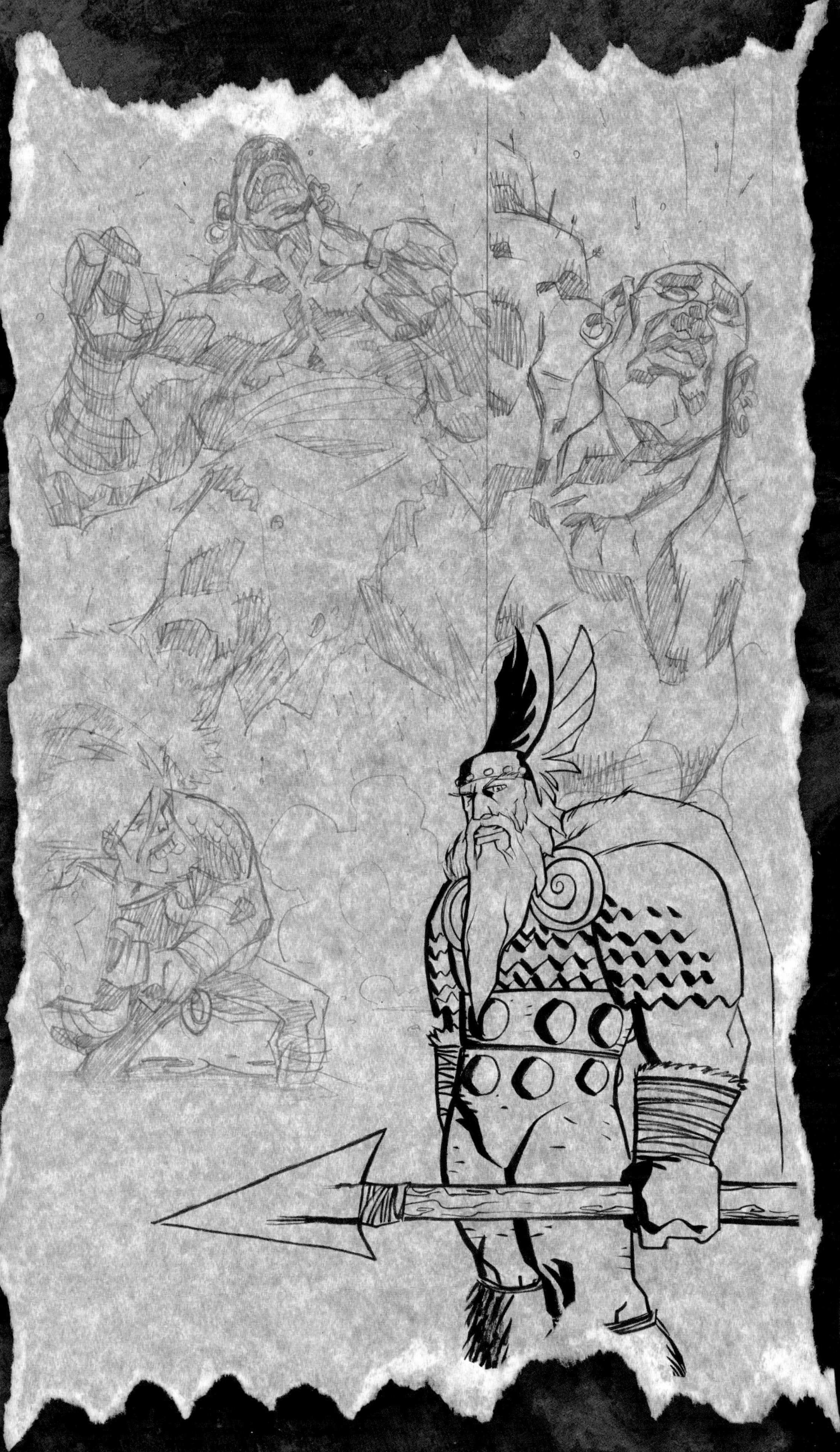

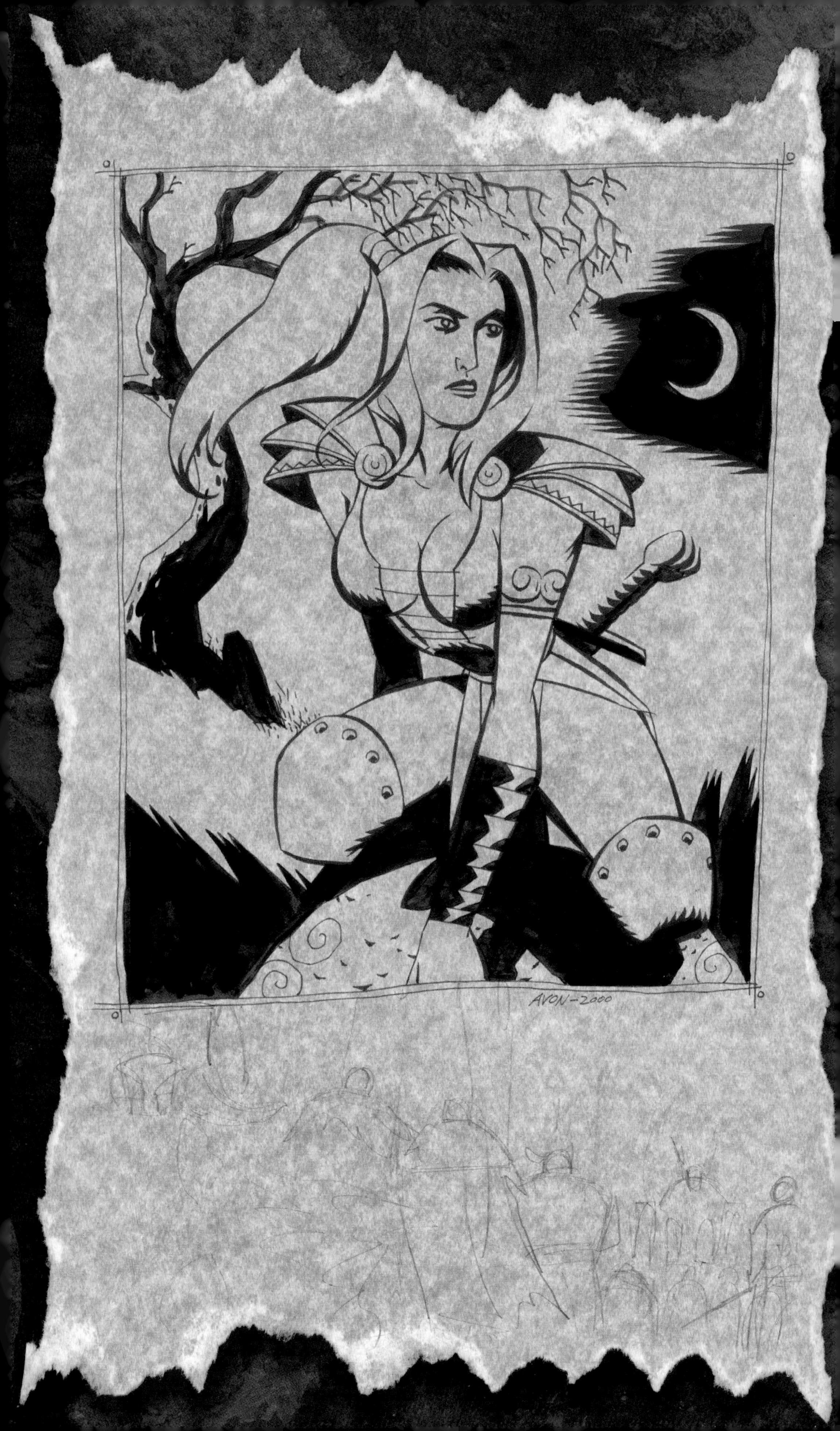
AVON-2000

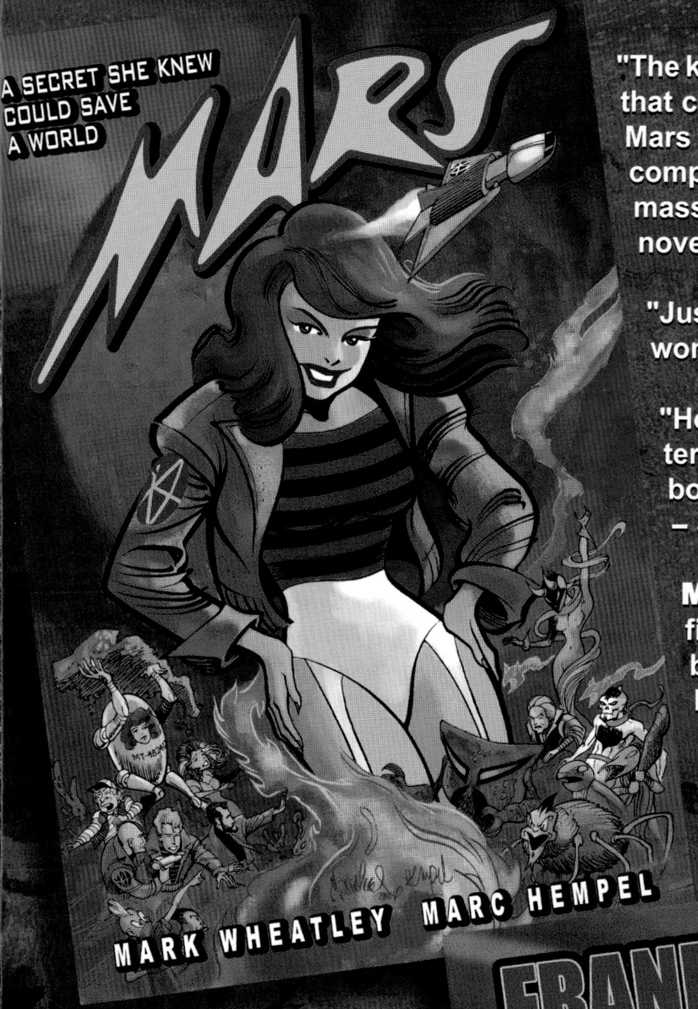
A SECRET SHE KNEW
COULD SAVE
A WORLD
MARS
MARK WHEATLEY MARC HEMPEL

"The kind of science fiction/fantasy that comics seldom venture into. Mars is an original work, just as complex as the best selling mass market science fiction novels." – **T. E. Pouncey**

"Just full of wonder and wonderment." – **Joe Sarno**

"How you got away with that terrific art style in this age of boring comics is beyond me." – **Jamie Hernandez**

MARS is a thoughtful science fiction action story told in a bold, unique style by two highly honored and multiple award winning creators, **Mark Wheatley** and **Marc Hempel**.

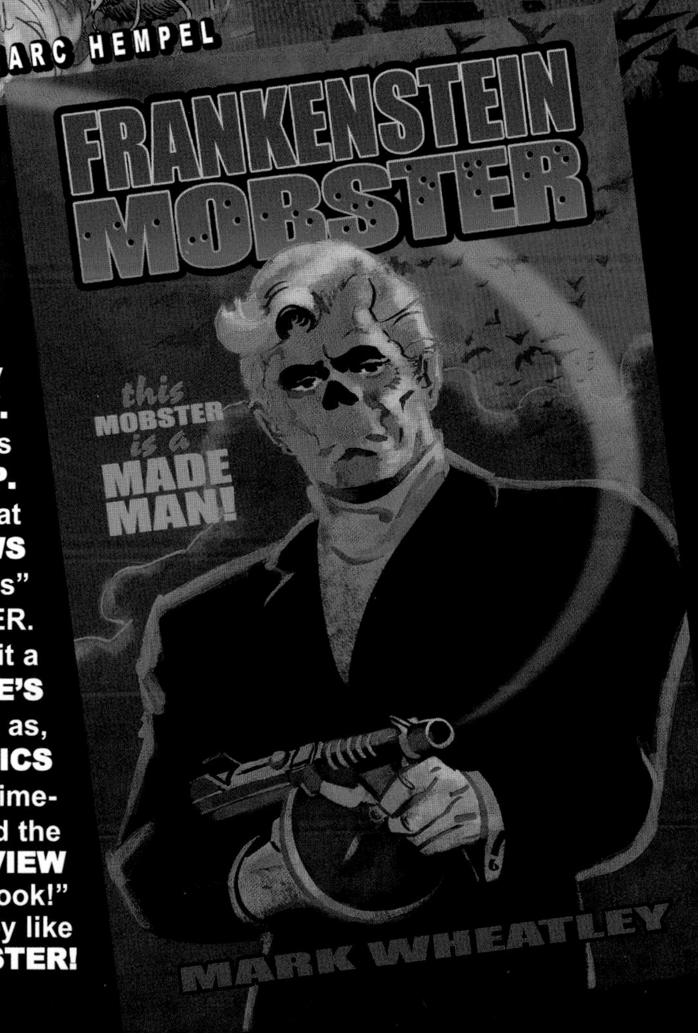
FRANKENSTEIN
MOBSTER
this
MOBSTER
is a
MADE
MAN!
MARK WHEATLEY

Recommended by **ENTERTAINMENT WEEKLY.** Placed in the top ten comics of the year by **SCOOP.** **Harry Knowles** at **AIN'T IT COOL NEWS** said he, "F#%king loves" FRANKENSTEIN MOBSTER. **OPTIC VERVE** judged it a "Quality read." **CREATURE'S CORNER** described it as, "Phenomenal." The **COMICS TREADMILL** named it, "crime-noir-monster fun." And the **HORROR COMICS REVIEW** insists that you, "Buy this book!" It's scary how much they like **FRANKENSTEIN MOBSTER!**